MW00579562

**Stilt houses, Kompong Pluk (p105)**

3

MICK2770/SHUTTERSTOCK ©

Cycling trail, Angkor Wat (p121)

# CAMBODIA
## THE JOURNEY BEGINS HERE

The magic of Cambodia cast a spell on me in 1995 and it has now been my home for more than 20 years. The temples of Angkor are the headline attraction, but Phnom Penh is a vibrant capital with a sociable spirit. Escape the cities to discover still-empty sands on tropical islands or wild, untamed mountains like the Cardamoms. Motorbiking is a ticket to freedom and adventure with the wind in your hair as you follow the mighty Mekong or cruise along the coast with a burnt-orange sunset painting the horizon.

Despite having the eighth wonder of the world in its back yard, Cambodia's real treasure is its people. Cambodians have been to hell and back, but thanks to an unbreakable spirit and infectious optimism, they have prevailed with their smiles intact. Nobody goes away without admiration and affection for the inhabitants of this enigmatic kingdom.

**My favourite experience** is cycling the hidden trails of Angkor (p121), a network of paths connecting the big hitters like Ta Prohm and Bayon.

**Nick Ray**
🐦 @lpnickray

# WHO GOES WHERE

Our writers and experts choose the places which, for them, define Cambodia

ANGKORVECTOR/SHUTTERSTOCK ©

I'm nostalgic for a Cambodia that no longer exists – where the pace of life was slower and *cyclos* (pedicabs) whirred quietly through jasmine-scented nights. **Kep** (p234), with its ramshackle modernist villas and enduring love of hammocks, has somehow held on to some of that languid magic. Bring a good book and avoid the weekend crowds and expats living their postcolonial fever dreams. Sunsets from Kimly's over-the-water terrace are unbeatable, as is its green-pepper crab.

### Madévi Dailly
ⓘ *@madevidailly*
*French-Cambodian Madévi is a food and travel writer, and custodian of her mother's legendary spring roll recipe.*

JM TRAVEL PHOTOGRAPHY/SHUTTERSTOCK ©

**Kampot** (p226) is Cambodia in microcosm: a river winding through town and a wildlife-packed national park on the doorstep, a laid-back, welcoming vibe that makes the days spent here pure pleasure, some choice architectural remnants of the colonial era, as well as a decent dining scene. And, just outside town, the revival of Kampot's famed pepper plantations is a symbol of Cambodia's resurgence in recent years.

### David Eimer
*David is a writer and journalist, and the author of books about China and Myanmar.*

**Angkor Wat**
Explore the famed archaeological site (p113)

**National Museum of Cambodia**
Browse the collection of Khmer treasures (p51)

**Psar Thmei**
Navigate Phnom Penh's 'new' market (p60)

**Phnom Penh**
Check the pulse of this hip capital (p42)

**Koh Rong Sanloem**
Laze on the crescent-shaped sands (p222)

**Kep**
Savour green-peppered crab at the Crab Market (p234)

THAILAND

O Smach
Choam
Sra Em
Anlong Veng
Choam Ksant
Samraong
Thmor Pouk
Preah Vihear City (Tbeng Meanchey)
*Phnom Kulen (487m)*
Poipet
Kralanh
Svay Leu
Sisophon
Mongkol Borei
Siem Reap
Dam Dek
Phnom Dek
Kouk Kduoch
Me Chrey
Battambang
Floating Village of Chong Kneas
Kampong Khleang
Kamrieng
*Kamping Poy*
Reang Kesei
Moung Russei
*Tonlé Sap*
Stoeng
Treng
Pailin
Kompong Luong (Floating Village)
Kompong Thom
*Phnom Krapang (1711m)*
Pursat
Krakor
*Phnom Sankos (1717m)*
*Phnom Knang Trapeang (1213m)*
*Phnom Aural (1813m)*
Romeas
Kompong Chhnang
Udong
Khlong Yai
Hat Lek
Krong Koh Kong
PHNOM PENH
*Koh Kong*
Chi Phat
Sre Ambel
Kompong Speu
*Koh Sdach*
*Gulf of Kompong Som*
Angk Tasaom
Takeo
*Koh Rong*
Veal Renh
Sihanoukville
Kampot
*Koh Thmri*
Kep
*Phu Quoc Island*

LAOS

Siem Pang

Voen Sai

*Tonlé San*

Preah Rumkel

Ban Lung
Bokheo

O Yadaw

Thala Boravit
Stung Treng
Lumphat

Rovieng

*Sen River*

*Mekong River*

Koh Nhek

Sambor

Sandan

Spoe
Tbong
Kratie

Sen
Monorom

Stung
Trang
Chhlong

Sre Kthum

Kompong Cham
Snuol

Trapeang
Sre

Suong
Memot

VIETNAM

Prey Veng

Neak
Luong
Ba Phnom

Kaam
Samnor
Svay Rieng
Bavet

Ho Chi Minh City

SOUTH

CHINA SEA

**Mekong
Discovery Trail**

Search for elusive
freshwater dolphins (p256)

**Mondulkiri Province**

Go wild among elephants
and gibbons (p263)

0   100 km
0   50 miles

# ANCIENT TEMPLES

The ancient Khmers packed the equivalent of all Europe's cathedrals into an area the size of Los Angeles, making the famed temples of Angkor a veritable Disney World for archaeology lovers. Temple-hoppers will find countless more ruins begging to be explored across Cambodia, particularly in the remote northern provinces of Preah Vihear and Banteay Meanchey. Channel your inner Lara Croft or Indiana Jones and dive into the fascinating history of one of the world's most illustrious empires.

**Chronological Order**

Visit the temples in chronological order, making stops at Sambor Prei Kuk (p184), Phnom Kulen (p146) and the Roluos Group (p122), and finishing with the key temples at Angkor.

**Another World Heritage Site**

The 10th-century temple complex of Koh Ker (p150) is on the tentative list to be Cambodia's next Unesco World Heritage Site.

## The Customs of Cambodia

Chinese emissary Chou Ta Kuan lived in Angkor in 1296; *The Customs of Cambodia* is a fascinating insight into life during the height of the empire.

## BEST TEMPLE EXPERIENCES

Marvel at the epic bas-reliefs and iconic *apsaras* (nymphs) of **Angkor Wat** ❶, the temple that puts all others in the shade. (p113)

Find the stuff of *Indiana Jones* fantasies, the tree roots of **Ta Prohm** ❷ locked in a muscular embrace with ancient stones. (p134)

Admire **Prasat Preah Vihear** ❸, the mountain temple perched on the cliff face of the Dangkrek Mountains. (p172)

Explore the great walled city of Angkor Thom to find the enigmatic faces of **Bayon** ❹ at its centre. (p126)

Visit the pre-Angkorian capital of **Sambor Prei Kuk** ❺, Cambodia's third Unesco World Heritage Site. (p184)

FROM LEFT: NHUT MINH HO/SHUTTERSTOCK ©, DAVDEKA/SHUTTERSTOCK ©, AYMAT30/SHUTTERSTOCK ©

Boeng Yeak Lom (p160)

# LIFE ON THE WATER

Cambodia truly bursts to life along its waterways. The mighty Mekong may get all the fame as it crashes over from Laos and pours out into Vietnam, but there are plenty of other rivers and lakes that define the nation. The regional towns that have sprung up alongside them are among the most charming in Cambodia.

### The Sangker River by Boat

The boat trip from Battambang to Siem Reap is the real deal – the Sangker River meanders past temples and villages before spilling into the Tonlé Sap lake.

### Kayaking in Kampot

After taking in the French architectural legacy in Kampot, explore the pretty Prek Tek Chhoun River by paddleboard or kayak (p227).

## BEST EXPERIENCES ON THE WATER

Follow the **Mekong Discovery Trail ❶** to spot dolphins, cycle remote islands or experience a family homestay. (p256)

Discover floating villages, bamboo skyscrapers and rare birds on the **Tonlé Sap ❷** lake. (p108)

Plunge into the crater lake of **Boeng Yeak Lom ❸**, Cambodia's most inviting natural swimming pool, located in Ratanakiri Province. (p260)

Trek to one of Cambodia's largest falls, the **Bou Sraa Waterfall ❹** in Mondulkiri Province. (p264)

Explore jungle scenery, shy wildlife, thundering waterfalls and dreamy ecolodges along the **Tatai River. ❺** (p203)

# MARKETS & SHOPPING

Be it fine silks, handwoven cotton, vibrant textiles, miniature statues, shiny lacquerware or intricate carvings, you can probably find it in one of Cambodia's regional markets or big-city boutiques. Cambodia is a hub for discount clothing made in garment factories – just be sure to bargain at markets as overcharging is common.

### Krama Chameleon

The colourful *krama* (checked scarf) is a potent symbol of Khmer identity and is still worn by many countryside folk. It's the definitive Cambodian keepsake.

### Shopping for a Cause

Phnom Penh and Siem Reap are home to shops that contribute to reviving traditional handicrafts, and support the disadvantaged or disabled.

### Market Dining

Almost every market in Cambodia has its own little food court; places to try include Psar Thmei in Phnom Penh and Psar Chaa in Siem Reap.

## BEST MARKET & SHOPPING EXPERIENCES

Visit Phnom Penh's **Psar Thmei ❶**, a striking art deco landmark and one of the best places to browse for souvenirs. (p60)

Shop for clothing, shoes, bags and local handicrafts among the jumble of stalls at the **Russian Market ❷** in Phnom Penh. (p70)

Snag crafts and souvenirs in **Psar Chaa** (Old Market) ❸, one of Siem Reap's major shopping destinations. (p97)

Discover an emerging art scene in the riverside town of **Battambang ❹**, with galleries selling local artists' work. (p161)

Buy fresh seafood at the popular **Crab Market ❺** in Kep, which doesn't disappoint day or night. (p234)

11

# SUN, SAND & SEA

Cambodia's up-and-coming southern islands offer your best chance to fulfill those paradise fantasies with hanging hammocks, swaying palms and plenty of sun-kissed solitude. Boom-to-bust Sihanoukville is the launchpad for most islands, with tranquil white-sand beaches just a quick ferry ride away. Sleepy Kep, Cambodia's original resort, is a more low-key alternative with a fine array of boutique hotels and seafood restaurants, as well as the backpacker beach of Koh Tonsay (Rabbit Island).

### Beach Season

The best time to visit Cambodia's beaches is the dry season (November to May). The wet season is not ideal due to choppy waters and frequent rain.

### Beachwear

Cambodians often bathe partially or fully clothed, so topless or nude bathing on a public beach is inappropriate; also, always cover up away from the beaches.

### Scuba Diving & Snorkelling

There are several dive companies on Koh Rong and Koh Rong Sanloem. Hotels and hostels can arrange snorkelling trips.

## BEST COASTAL EXPERIENCES

Laze on the powdery white sand of **Koh Rong** ❶, the island that's home to the backpacker strip of Koh Tuch and dreamy Long Beach. (p214)

Hop over to Koh Rong's smaller sibling, **Koh Rong Sanloem** ❷, to enjoy the crescent-shaped Saracen Bay and legendary Lazy Beach. (p222)

Visit Cambodia's original resort, **Kep** ❸, for boutique resorts, seafood specialities and Koh Tonsay with its sandy beaches. (p234)

Explore the castaway-cool archipelago of **Koh Sdach** ❹, with a handful of authentic restaurants and homestays plus some vibrant undersea life. (p220)

Wander the empty stretches of sand on practically uninhabited **Koh Kong Island** ❺ and find a hidden lagoon. (p200)

# WILD NIGHTS

Phnom Penh has incredibly vibrant nightlife, with everything from swanky cocktail lounges to Cambodian craft breweries and LGBTIQ-friendly clubs with lavish late-night drag shows. Elsewhere, Siem Reap boasts the infamous Pub St and the up-and-coming Boho district, while the southern islands have a permanent party vibe for those who worship the moon.

### Last Orders

Cambodia doesn't have any official closing time for bars, pubs and clubs, so they can stay open as long as they have customers.

### It's Happy Hour

Many bars and restaurants offer a generous happy hour, from the standard hour to all-day discounts; drinks are usually half-price or two for one.

### The National Beer

For a long time, Angkor Beer led the pack unchallenged, but in recent years many contenders have emerged, including the ubiquitous Cambodia Beer.

## BEST NIGHTLIFE EXPERIENCES

Warm up with a riverfront happy hour in **Phnom Penh ❶**, go on a bar crawl around the Bassac Lane area, and end up in a nightclub. (p71)

Explore the bars around the Old Market in **Siem Reap ❷**, where one strip has even earned the moniker of Pub St. (p99)

Join the infamous late-night parties on the backpacker strip of Saracen Bay on **Koh Rong Sanloem. ❸** (p222)

While away a night in the lively riverside town of **Kampot ❹**, which boasts some great restaurants and bars. (p226)

Enjoy the mellow nightlife scene of **Battambang ❺**, which has some atmospheric bars in the old quarter. (p158)

National Museum of Cambodia, Phnom Penh (p51)

# HISTORIC VISITS

When it comes to a stunning selection of palaces and museums, it's hard to beat Phnom Penh with its big-hitter combination of the Royal Palace and the National Museum of Cambodia. Siem Reap has an impressive museum of its own to showcase the best of Angkor, while Battambang offers the best of the provincial museums.

### A Right Royal Dress Code

It's important to wear appropriate clothing covering the upper arms and upper legs when visiting the Royal Palace in Phnom Penh.

### Angkor Conservation

One of the best collections of Khmer sculpture in Cambodia is housed at Angkor Conservation in Siem Reap; it can sometimes be visited for a small fee.

## BEST HISTORIC EXPERIENCES

Admire Phnom Penh's dominating **Royal Palace ❶**, which houses the spectacular Silver Pagoda. (p49)

Browse the world's finest collection of Khmer sculpture at the iconic **National Museum of Cambodia. ❷** (p51)

Get a crash course on the Khmer empire at Siem Reap's **Angkor National Museum. ❸** (p96)

Visit the **Sosoro Museum ❹**, showcasing the history of money in Cambodia with creative displays. (p62)

See the fine collection of lintels, pediments and sculpture at the **Battambang Museum. ❺** (p161)

15

# INTO THE JUNGLE

The endless ricefields and sugar palms that characterise the Cambodian landscape eventually yield to the rolling hills and verdant jungles of the 'wild east' in the little-visited provinces of Mondulkiri and Ratanakiri, both of which are home to some of the nation's top ecotourism projects. Out west, the Cardamom Mountains rise higher still, offering dense tropical rainforests where endangered wildlife thrives and some welcoming homestay options are found in Chi Phat and Stung Areng.

### Protected Areas

Cambodia has more than 50 protected areas comprising national parks, wildlife sanctuaries and biospheres which together protect 41% of the country.

### Wildlife Alliance

Wildlife Alliance (wildlifealliance.org) connects travellers with memorable ecotourism experiences including wildlife releases and homestays in the Cardamom Mountains.

### Rare Birdlife

Northern Cambodia is home to many rare water birds, including the sarus crane and the giant ibis.

## BEST JUNGLE EXPERIENCES

Head to **Mondulkiri Province ❶** to 'walk with the herd' at the Elephant Valley Project and spot gibbons in the Keo Seima Wildlife Sanctuary. (p263)

Explore the fabled **Cardamom Mountains ❷**, an area of astonishing biodiversity, and the jungle-flanked Tatai River. (p207)

Follow the red roads of **Ratanakiri Province ❸** to the vast Virachey National Park and the beautiful crater lake of Boeng Yeak Lom. (p258)

Visit the sacred mountain of **Phnom Kulen ❹**, home to the lost city of Mahendraparvata and some early Angkorian temples. (p146)

Walk the walls of **Angkor Thom ❺**, the last capital of the Khmer empire, through some of the oldest jungle in Cambodia. (p125)

# EPICUREAN ADVENTURES

Most of the Cambodian menu is based around rice, fish and soup, and delicious dishes are found everywhere, from humble markets to upmarket eateries. Siem Reap and Phnom Penh vie for the title of Cambodia's culinary capital, but you'll also have surprisingly rewarding food experiences in regional towns like Kep, Kampot and Battambang. Booking ahead is only occasionally necessary in Phnom Penh or Siem Reap during the peak of the peak season (December to February).

**Anyone for Cricket?**

In addition to eating the notorious tarantulas of Skuon, Cambodians also like to eat crickets, beetles, larvae and ants – a head start in the future of insect farming.

**Fish Sauce**

*Teuk trey* (fish sauce), one of the main condiments in Cambodian cooking, can't be taken on international flights due to regulations on strong-smelling substances.

**Cooking Courses**

Lovers of Cambodian cuisine can learn some tricks of the trade on a cooking course in Phnom Penh, Siem Reap, Battambang or Kampot.

Amok (p32)

## BEST EPICUREAN EXPERIENCES

Dine to help the disadvantaged get a hand in the hospitality industry in **Phnom Penh** ❶ with a meal at one of the many training restaurants. (p73)

Try one of the specialist foodie tours in **Siem Reap** ❷ or enjoy the lively new Khmer-cuisine scene in the up-and-coming Boho area. (p88)

Feast on the succulent fresh crab with Kampot pepper at the famous **Crab Market** ❸ in Kep. (p234)

Discover the delights of Cambodian cooking in **Battambang** ❹ with a cheap-and-cheerful cooking class in this relaxed riverside town. (p161)

Sample excellent seafood on Cambodia's **southern islands** ❺, including fresh fish, prawns and squid barbecued on the beach. (p194)

# REGIONS & CITIES

Find the places that tick all your boxes.

## Siem Reap & the Temples of Angkor

**THE GREATEST TEMPLES ON EARTH**

Siem Reap, gateway to the majestic Angkor, is starting to give the capital a run for its money with sophisticated restaurants, funky bars and chic boutiques. The World Heritage Site of Angkor is home to some of the most spectacular temples on earth.

p88

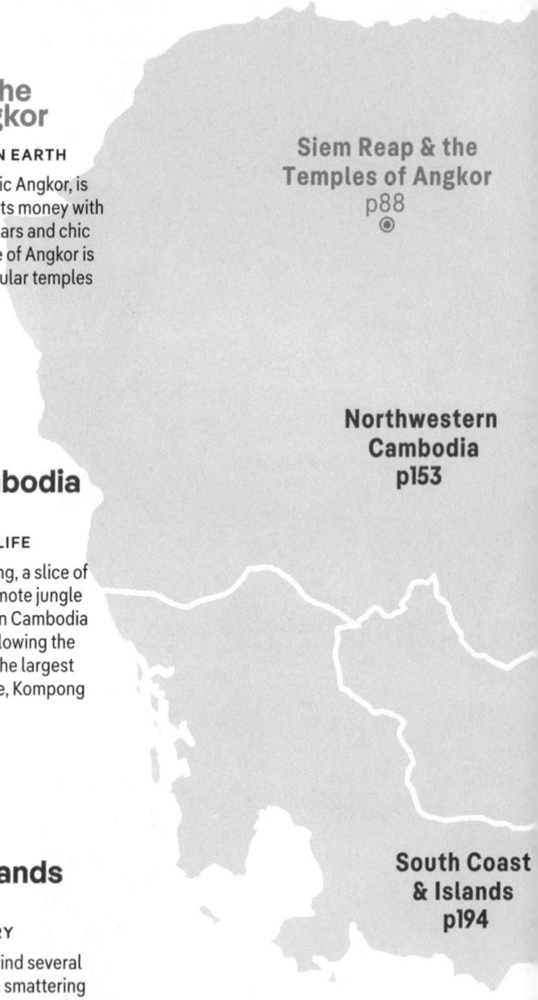

## Northwestern Cambodia

**RIVERSIDE TOWNS,
REMOTE TEMPLES, REAL LIFE**

The northwest is home to Battambang, a slice of more traditional life, and several remote jungle temples. One of the best boat rides in Cambodia links Battambang to Siem Reap following the Sangker River, or you can explore the largest floating village on the Tonlé Sap lake, Kompong Luong.

p153

## South Coast & Islands

**BEACHES, ISLANDS,
ECOTOURISM & HISTORY**

On Cambodia's South Coast you'll find several up-and-coming beach resorts and a smattering of tropical islands that are increasingly popular with travellers. National parks and protected areas dot the region, offering trekking, mountain biking, rock climbing, kayaking, snorkelling and scuba diving.

p194

**Siem Reap & the
Temples of Angkor**
p88

**Northwestern
Cambodia
p153**

**South Coast
& Islands
p194**

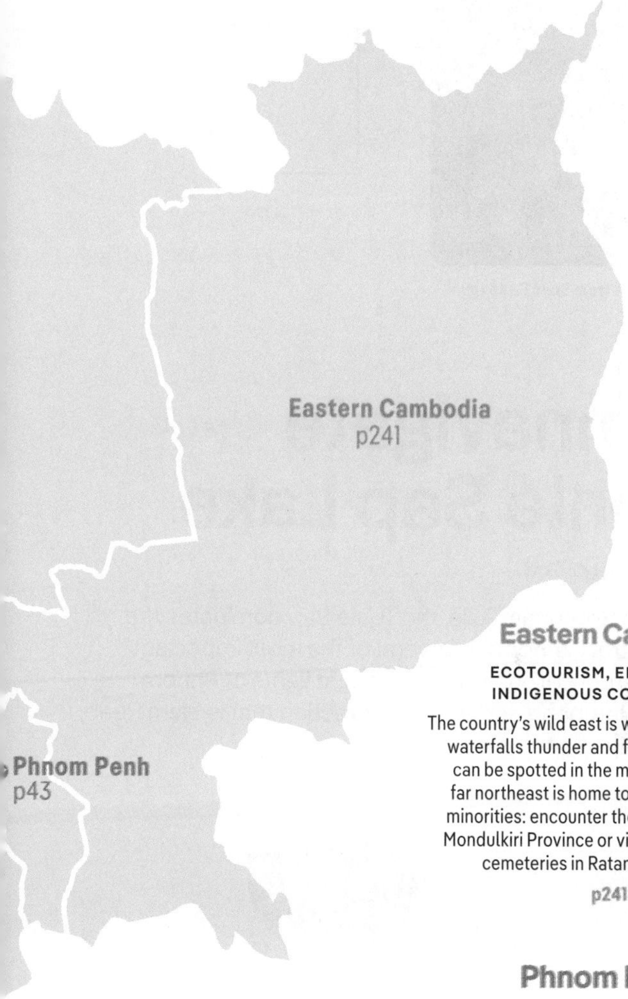

Eastern Cambodia
p241

Phnom Penh
p43

## Eastern Cambodia

### ECOTOURISM, ELEPHANTS & INDIGENOUS COMMUNITIES

The country's wild east is where elephants roam, waterfalls thunder and freshwater dolphins can be spotted in the mighty Mekong. The far northeast is home to a mosaic of ethnic minorities: encounter the Bunong people of Mondulkiri Province or visit the remote tribal cemeteries in Ratanakiri Province.

**p241**

## Phnom Penh

### PULSE OF CONTEMPORARY CAMBODIA

Cambodia's resurgent capital is the place to check the pulse of contemporary life in the kingdom. Beyond the headline sights, there's a diverse offering, from traditional markets to chic boutiques, street food to gourmet dining, and cheap happy hours to sophisticated sky-bar cocktails.

**p43**

NATUREPIXEL/SHUTTERSTOCK ©

View of Tonlé Sap lake from Siem Reap (p94)

## ITINERARIES

# Circumnavigate the Tonlé Sap Lake

**Allow:** 7 days   **Distance:** 850km

The largest lake in Southeast Asia, the Tonlé Sap dominates the landscape of central Cambodia. Several of the most important cities are dotted around it, including the bright lights of Phnom Penh, bucolic Battambang and the star attraction that is Siem Reap, gateway to the majestic temples of Angkor.

### ❶ PHNOM PENH ⏱ 2 DAYS

Start in **Phnom Penh** (p43), renowned for the remarkable Royal Palace and the impressive National Museum. The capital is also home to an eclectic dining scene, superb shopping at Russian Market, and a night shift that never sleeps.

🛶 *Detour: Follow the Tonlé Sap River to **Kompong Luong** (p189) on the Tonlé Sap lake. Everything floats on water here: houses, schools, clinics and even karaoke bars. ⏱ 3 hours*

### ❷ BATTAMBANG ⏱ 2 DAYS

Head northwest to **Battambang** (p158), one of Cambodia's best-preserved French-era towns and a base from which to discover the rhythms of rural life. Sights include the infamous bamboo train, the Cambodian circus of Phare Ponleu Selpak and the hilltop temples and shrines in the surrounding area. Then take the proverbial slow boat to Siem Reap along the snaking Sangker River.

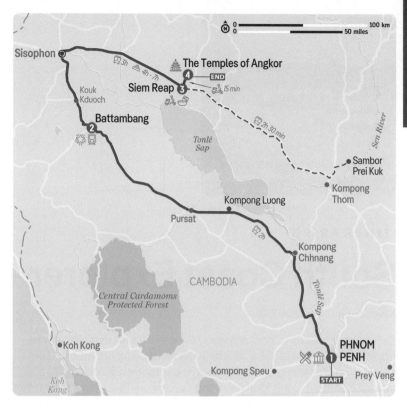

**③**
### SIEM REAP ⏱ 1 DAY

Spend some time soaking up **Siem Reap** (p94), one of the most diverse destinations in Cambodia with a host of activities on tap. Everything from cooking classes to Vespa tours is on offer, and some of these activities are a great way to punctuate the temple tours. Siem Reap even has a wake park and Angkor-themed mini-golf course.

**④**
### THE TEMPLES OF ANGKOR ⏱ 2 DAYS

The temples of Angkor are in a league of their own. See **Angkor Wat** (p113), perfection in stone; **Bayon** (p126), oddity in stone; and **Ta Prohm** (p134), nature triumphing over stone – before venturing further afield to **Kbal Spean** (p147) or jungle-clad **Beng Mealea** (p149).

🏍 *Detour:* The pre-Angkorian temples of **Sambor Prei Kuk** (p184) are less imposing than their world-famous counterparts but have a beautiful forest setting. ⏱ 3 hours

Fishing boats, Kep (p234)

## ITINERARIES

# South Coast Explorer

**Allow:** 10 days   **Distance:** 750km

Set out on this South Coast odyssey taking in a mix of riverside towns, tropical islands and blissful beaches. Consider using the train for some parts of the journey (Takeo to Kampot or Kampot to Sihanoukville) and make a diversion to the foothills of the Cardamom Mountains at Chi Phat.

### ① TAKEO ⏱1 DAY

Start in **Takeo** (p237), a small provincial capital south of Phnom Penh. Jump on a speedboat to explore the ancient pre-Angkorian capital of Angkor Borei and the hilltop temple of Phnom Da (pictured). If travelling by motorbike or car, consider stops at the Angkorian temples of Tonlé Bati and Phnom Chisor or the Phnom Tamao Wildlife Rescue Centre en route from the capital.

### ② KAMPOT ⏱2 DAYS

Continue south to the riverside town of **Kampot** (p226). From there, you can explore Bokor National Park, ancient cave pagodas and pepper plantations. Upriver are out-of-town resorts and hostels that are bases for kayaking, paddleboarding or floating water parks. Kampot is also emerging as a foodie destination with international flavours that complement the famous salt and pepper.

### ③ KEP ⏱1 DAY

Just down the road from Kampot lies the sleepy beach resort of **Kep** (p234), once known as Kep-sur-Mer and akin to the Cambodian Riviera. After years of abandonment and neglect, the town is once again waking up with numerous boutique hotels and resorts, a deserved reputation for fresh crab and seafood, and nearby islands like Koh Tonsay.

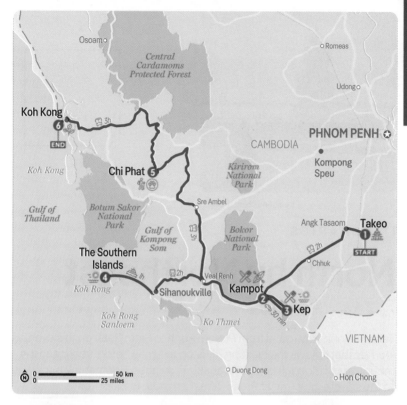

Central
Cardamoms
Protected Forest

Osoam

Romeas

Udong

Koh Kong
6
END
3h

CAMBODIA

PHNOM PENH ✪

Kompong
Speu

Chi Phat 5

Koh Kong

Kirirom
National
Park

Sre Ambel

Gulf of
Thailand

Botum Sakor
National
Park

Gulf of
Kompong
Som

Bokor
National
Park

Angk Tasaom

Takeo
1
START

Chhuk

The Southern
Islands
4

Koh Rong

1h

2h

Veal Renh

Kampot

2

Kep

3

Sihanoukville

Koh Rong
Sanloem

Ko Thmei

VIETNAM

Duong Dong

Hon Chong

N  0        50 km
   0     25 miles

### 4 THE SOUTHERN ISLANDS
⏱ 3 DAYS

Take the pretty train ride along
the coast from Kampot to
Sihanoukville, a gateway to
the idyllic twin islands of **Koh
Rong** (p214) and **Koh Rong
Sanloem** (p222). Both have
stunning beaches – choose from
Long Beach, Long Set Beach or
boutique Pagoda Beach on Koh
Rong, or the crescent-shaped
Saracen Bay on Koh Rong
Sanloem.

### 5 CHI PHAT ⏱ 2 DAYS

Venture into the foothills of
the Cardamom Mountains and
experience a local homestay in
**Chi Phat** (p205). This riverside
village is a hub for community-
based ecotourism experiences in
the surrounding jungle, including
trekking, biking, boat trips and
the excellent Wildlife Alliance
Release Station. If a homestay
sounds a bit rustic, consider
the Cardamom Tented Camp in
Botum Sakor National Park.

### 6 KOH KONG ⏱ 1 DAY

Continue west to **Koh Kong**
(p200), a border town with
Thailand that's fringed by
ecotourism attractions such
as the Peam Krasaop Wildlife
Sanctuary (pictured), the largest
mangrove forest in Cambodia,
and Koh Kong Island, the largest
offshore island in the country.
From Koh Kong, you can cross
the Cardamoms north to
Battambang or head across the
border to Thailand.

MAREK POPLAWSKI/SHUTTERSTOCK ©

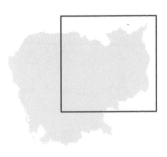

Kompong Cham (p246)

## ITINERARIES

# North by Northeast

**Allow:** 10 days   **Distance:** 1300km

Take the long way round from Phnom Penh to Siem Reap on this overland journey that follows the Mekong River up to Kratie before veering to the mountains of Mondulkiri and Ratanakiri Provinces. Boomerang back west to the spectacular Prasat Preah Vihear en route to Siem Reap.

**1**
### KOMPONG CHAM ⏱1 DAY

Follow the mighty Mekong up to the sleepy town of **Kompong Cham** (p246), a relaxed base to explore the pretty river island of Koh Paen and some temples old and new, including the Angkor-era fusion temple of Wat Nokor Bachey (pictured) and the 19th-century pagoda of Wat Maha Leap. If travelling by motorbike or car, follow the riverside roads to and from Kompong Cham for Mekong views.

**2**
### KRATIE ⏱2 DAYS

Continue north to **Kratie** (p250), the provincial capital boasting some of the best sunsets over the Mekong River. Spot the rare freshwater Irrawaddy dolphins near Kampi and rent a bicycle to explore the lanes and fruit farms of Koh Trong, a friendly island in the middle of the Mekong that also has places to stay.

**3**
### MONDULKIRI PROVINCE ⏱3 DAYS

Head for the hills of **Mondulkiri Province** (p263), Cambodia's wild east that's home to the Bunong people and majestic elephants. Walk with the herd at the Elephant Valley Project (pictured), track gibbons at the Keo Seima Wildlife Sanctuary or explore the thundering Bou Sraa Waterfall. The provincial capital of Sen Monorom is the best base for exploring this remote region.

THAILAND

LAOS

Prasat Preah
Vihear
**6** END

Preah Vihear City
(Tbeng Meanchey)

Virachey
National
Park

Ratanakiri
Province   Ban Lung
**4**

Stung Treng
**5**

Lumphat

Sen River

CAMBODIA

Kompong
Thom

Tonlé
Sap

Kompong
Chhnang

Kratie **2**

Sen Monorom

Mondulkiri
Province **3**

Kompong Cham **1** START

VIETNAM

0   100 km
0   50 miles

### 4 RATANAKIRI PROVINCE
⏱ 2 DAYS

Continue to the far northeastern
**Ratanakiri Province** (p258),
nestled against the borders of
Laos and Vietnam. This area is
famous for its many waterfalls
and the volcanic crater lake of
Boeng Yeak Lom (pictured),
just a few kilometres from Ban
Lung, the provincial capital.
Other attractions include gibbon
spotting and trekking in the
remote Virachey National Park.

### 5 STUNG TRENG ⏱ 1 DAY

Leaving the highlands behind,
descend back to the Mekong
River at **Stung Treng** (p254), an
important transit and trade hub
near the Laos border. Attractions
include the otherworldly flooded
forests bursting forth from the
river north to Laos and the Preh
Nimith Waterfall, part of a stretch
of the Mekong that forms a series
of waterfalls as the river drops
from Laos into Cambodia.

### 6 PRASAT PREAH VIHEAR
⏱ 1 DAY

Make a pilgrimage to the temple
of **Prasat Preah Vihear** (p172)
as part of a long overland trip
from Stung Treng to Siem Reap.
This most mountainous of
mountain temples has the most
spectacular location in all of the
former territories of the Khmer
empire, looming large at the
top of the Dangkrek Mountains.
There are guesthouses and
hotels in nearby Sra Em.

# WHEN **TO GO**

Cambodia is a year-round destination these days, but most visitors plump for the winter months to avoid the rains.

Some foreign residents quip that Cambodia has three seasons: hot, hotter and hottest. While it's true the temperature rarely dips below 30°C by day, it has been known to drop to 15°C in the chill of 'winter'. For Cambodians, there are three distinct seasons: the cool, windy season (November to February); the dry, hot season (March to May); and the wet season (June to October). A lot of visitors avoid the wet season, but in reality it only rains briefly each day and the landscape is lush and green with young rice. If there are months to avoid, it could be the intense heat of May or the severe rains of September.

## Bargaining for a Bed

It's sometimes possible to negotiate a discount for rooms during the low season (May to September), but it really varies from place to place. Popular centres will probably just promote their discounts online, but places off the grid may be open to a deal.

Khmer New Year celebrations, Angkor Wat (p114)

---

### ⊛ I LIVE HERE

#### RIVERS DEEP, MOUNTAINS HIGH

**Sovanda Horn is the owner of adventure travel company Solo Landscapes (sololandscapes.co).**

I love the wilds of Cambodia, the remote places in the Cardamoms or the northeast where you can really get away from it all in the lush, green landscapes during the transitional seasons. Trekking into the Cardamoms around Khnong Phsar or the Areng Valley is stunning thanks to the towering mountains and misty valleys. It's so peaceful among the pine trees and the air is cool and refreshing.

#### KNOW YOUR MONSOONS

The climate is dictated by the monsoon winds, creating two distinct seasons. From June to October, the winds of the southwest monsoon bring high humidity and heavy rains; from November to March, the light, dry winds of the northeast monsoon bring lower humidity and moderate temperatures.

## Weather Through the Year

| **JANUARY** | **FEBRUARY** | **MARCH** | **APRIL** | **MAY** | **JUNE** |
|---|---|---|---|---|---|
| Avg. daytime max: **31°C** | Avg. daytime max: **33°C** | Avg. daytime max: **34°C** | Avg. daytime max: **35°C** | Avg. daytime max: **35°C** | Avg. daytime max: **34°C** |
| Days of rainfall: 1 | Days of rainfall: 1 | Days of rainfall: 3 | Days of rainfall: 6 | Days of rainfall: 14 | Days of rainfall: 15 |

## LOW SEASON (MAY TO SEPTEMBER)

The rainy or 'green' season means emerald landscapes and awesome cloud formations. Accommodation discounts and protective cloud cover make this a great time to visit the temples. The South Coast can be busy with Europeans visiting over summer holidays.

# The Big Festivals

The Chinese inhabitants of Cambodia celebrate **Chinese New Year** – for the Vietnamese, this is Tet. There are dragon dances all over town.  **January/February**

The **Khmer New Year** is the big festival for Cambodians. It's a three-day celebration when people make offerings at wats, clean out their homes and exchange gifts. **April**

During **P'chum Ben** (Festival of the Dead), respects are paid to the dead through offerings made at wats. Local temples are a blaze of colour, ceremony and chanting. **September/October**

Celebrating the victory of Jayavarman VII over the Chams, **Bon Om Tuk (Water Festival)** also marks the reversal of the current of Tonlé Sap River with boat races in Phnom Penh and Siem Reap. **October/November**

**Bon Om Tuk boat race**

# Other Festivals & Events

Currently slated in January, the **Angkor Photography Festival** is a celebration of photography in Siem Reap. **January**

Led by the royal family, the **Royal Ploughing Ceremony** is a ritual agricultural festival held to mark the traditional beginning of the rice-growing season. **May**

**Pride Cambodia** is celebrated by the LGBTIQ+ community in Phnom Penh with events at the F3 Friends Futures Factory. **June**

The annual **Sea Festival** rotates between the four coastal provinces of Preah Sihanouk, Kampot, Kep and Koh Kong. **December**

## HIGH SEASON (NOVEMBER TO MARCH)

This is the most popular time of year to visit, when the weather is cooler and windy, with almost Mediterranean temperatures. Book accommodation in advance during the peak Christmas and New Year period.

|  **JULY** |  **AUGUST** |  **SEPTEMBER** |  **OCTOBER** |  **NOVEMBER** | **DECEMBER** |
|---|---|---|---|---|---|
| Avg. daytime max: **33°C** | Avg. daytime max: **33°C** | Avg. daytime max: **32°C** | Avg. daytime max: **32°C** | Avg. daytime max: **31°C** | Avg. daytime max: **31°C** |
| Days of rainfall: 16 | Days of rainfall: 16 | Days of rainfall: 19 | Days of rainfall: 17 | Days of rainfall: 9 | Days of rainfall: 4 |

LEFT: TWINSTERPHOTO/SHUTTERSTOCK © RIGHT: COLLECTION CHRISTOPHEL/ALAMY STOCK PHOTO ©

# GET PREPARED
# FOR CAMBODIA

Useful things to load in your bag, your ears and your brain

## Clothes

**Keep it casual:** Lightweight, loose-fitting clothes are the best all-round option in Cambodia, including cottons and linens to combat the humidity. Cambodia is not a very dressy place unless you're living the high life in Phnom Penh or Siem Reap, so smart clothes are not really a necessity.
**'Winter' warmers:** If heading to the upland northeastern provinces of Mondulkiri or Ratanakiri or the Cardamom Mountains in the 'winter months' of November to March, pack a jacket and/or sweater for the cool nights.
**Beachwear is for the beach:** On the South Coast, it's not considered appropriate to walk around in swimwear when not

on the beach; cover up with a sarong or something similar. Nude bathing on public beaches is a definite no.

## 📖 READ

**River of Time** (Jon Swain, 1995) A poetic account of his time caught up in the fall of Phnom Penh, as depicted in *The Killing Fields*.

**Hun Sen's Cambodia** (Sebastian Strangio, 2014) A no-holds-barred look at contemporary Cambodia and the rule of Prime Minister Hun Sen.

**The Gate** (François Bizot, 2003) The memoir's author was kidnapped by the Khmer Rouge, and later held by them in the French embassy.

**A Dragon Apparent** (Norman Lewis, 1951) Classic travelogue of exploring Cambodia and French Indochina on the cusp of independence.

## Words

English is widely spoken in Cambodia and many visitors are pleasantly surprised by the general level of English after travelling through neigbouring Thailand or Vietnam, where English speakers are often confined to the tourism industry.

It's worth learning a few basic words in Khmer as a matter of courtesy to the locals; they are usually very pleased if you can use phrases such as 'hello' and 'thank you'. The script is derived from the Indian alphabet of Sanskrit and is very difficult to learn during a short visit.

**Johm riab sua** The formal way to say 'hello' in Khmer.

**Arun suorsdey** 'Good morning'; just **suorsdey** can be a less formal way to say 'hello'.

**Sohk sabaay** 'How are you?' – as popular a greeting as 'hello'.

**Sohm** 'Please'; make it **sohm to** and you have 'excuse me' or 'sorry'.

**Aw kuhn** 'Thank you'; add **charan** for 'thank you very much'.

**Baat/jaa** 'Yes' – men should say **baat** and women should say **jaa**.

**Bong srei** 'Brother' or 'sister' for someone a similar age; **bong on** is for someone younger.

**Bai** 'Rice', the staple of any Cambodian meal; make it **bai char** for fried rice.

**Juay/chhouy pong** The key phrase for 'help' if you find yourself in trouble.

**T'lay pohnmann** 'How much is it?' – key phrase to use in the markets if planning to bargain for a buy.

## ▶️ WATCH

**The Killing Fields** (Roland Joffé, 1984; pictured) Definitive film on the Khmer Rouge, telling the story of an American journalist and a Cambodian photographer.

**First They Killed My Father** (Angelina Jolie, 2017) Adaptation of the bestseller by Luong Ung about childhood under the Khmer Rouge.

**The Missing Picture** (Rithy Panh, 2013) The first Cambodian film to be shortlisted for 'Best Foreign Language Film' at the 2014 Oscars.

**The Last Reel** (Kulikar Sotho, 2014) Award-winning film exploring the impact of Cambodia's dark past on the next generation.

## 🎧 LISTEN

**VannDa** Cambodia's biggest rap artist – check out his massive hit 'Time to Rise' with master *chapaye* (two-stringed wooden instrument) player Kong Nay.

**Yos Olarang** One of the greatest '70s legends to seek out; his most famous song, 'Jis Cyclo', is an absolute classic.

**Tiny Toones** (tinytoones.org) A hip-hop cooperative seeking to inspire Cambodian youth to adopt a drug-free lifestyle.

**Best Cambodia Podcasts** (player.fm/podcasts/cambodia) All things Cambodia from the history of Angkor via the Khmer Rouge to the influence of China.

KOHNGUI/GETTY IMAGES ©

**Grilled fish, Psar Thmei, Phnom Penh (p60)**

# THE FOOD SCENE

Khmer cuisine can be one of the standout discoveries of a visit to Cambodia, as it tends to fly under the radar internationally.

No matter what part of the world you come from, if you travel much in Cambodia you will encounter food that's unusual, strange, maybe even immoral, or just plain weird. The fiercely omnivorous Cambodians find nothing strange in eating insects, algae, offal or fish bladders. They will dine on a duck foetus, brew up some brains or snack on some spiders. They will peel live frogs to grill on a barbecue or down medicinal wine infused with scorpions to increase their virility.

To the Khmers there is nothing 'strange' about anything that will sustain the body. To them a food is either wholesome or it isn't; it's nutritious or it isn't; it tastes good or it doesn't. They'll try anything once, even a burger.

What really gives Khmer cuisine its kick are the secret roots, the welcome herbs and the aromatic tubers. Together they give the salads, snacks, soups and stews a special aroma and taste that smacks of Cambodia.

## Rice, Noodles & Soup

Rice from Cambodia's lush fields is the principal staple, enshrined in the Khmer word for 'eating', *nyam bai* (literally 'eat rice'). Many a Cambodian, particularly drivers, will run out of steam if they run out of rice. Battambang Province is Cambodia's rice bowl and produces the country's finest yield.

For the taste of Cambodia in a bowl, try the local *kyteow*, a rice-noodle soup that will keep you going all day. Not into

**Best Cambodian Dishes**

**AMOK**
Often deemed a national dish, this is an aromatic fish curry wrapped in banana leaf.

**NAM BEN CHOC**
Thin rice noodles served with a red chicken curry or a fish-based broth and fresh veggies.

**TUK KREUNG**
A pungent soup or dip that includes fermented fish and fresh veggies.

**KHOR CHROUK**
Stewed pork with sugar palm and an egg – sometimes mini quail eggs.

noodles? Try the *bobor* (rice porridge), a national institution that's best sampled with some fresh fish and a splash of ginger. A Cambodian meal almost always includes a *samlor* (traditional soup). *Samlor machou bunlay* (hot and sour fish soup with pineapple and spices) is popular.

## Fish

Cambodians have a proverb '*mien teuk, mien trey*' which translates as 'have water, have fish'. Cambodia's abundant waterways provide the fish that is fermented into *prahoc* (fermented fish paste), which forms the backbone of Khmer cuisine. Fish come in every shape and size, from the giant Mekong catfish to teeny-tiny whitebait, which are great beer snacks when deep-fried. *Trey ahng* (grilled fish) is a Cambodian speciality and can be eaten as pieces wrapped in lettuce or spinach leaves and then dipped into *teuk trey*, a potent fish sauce.

## Tropical Fruits

Cambodia is blessed with many tropical fruits and sampling these is an integral part of a visit to the country. Among the larger fruit, *khnau* (jackfruit) is very common and *tourain* (durian) needs no introduction, as you can smell it from a mile off.

Durian

Popular fruits include *mongkut* (mangosteen) and *sao mao* (rambutan). The small mangosteen has a purple skin and delicious white segments, while rambutan has a lychee-like interior and a red-and-green spiky exterior.

Best of all is *svay* (mango). The Cambodian mango season runs from March to May. Other varieties of mango are available year-round, but it's the hot-season ones that are a taste sensation.

### VEGETARIANS & VEGANS

Few Cambodians understand the concept of strict vegetarianism, and many will say something is vegetarian to please the customer when in fact it is not. If you're not a strict vegetarian and can deal with fish sauces and the like, you should have few problems ordering meals. Most international eateries feature a few vegetarian menu options, while in the major destinations there are now some fantastic vegetarian and vegan restaurants.

In Khmer and Chinese restaurants, stir-fried vegetable dishes are readily available, as are vegetarian fried-rice dishes. However, it's unlikely these 'vegetarian' dishes have been cooked in separate woks from other fish- and meat-based dishes. Indian restaurants in the popular tourist centres can cook up genuine vegetarian food.

Vegetable stall, Psar Chaa, Siem Reap (p99)

| BANH CHEV | LOK LAK | CUONG | SONGKHYA LAPEAU PAEM |
|---|---|---|---|
| Rice pancake stuffed with yummy herbs, bean sprouts and a meat, fish or seafood staple. | Diced beef in a homemade gravy, delicious when dipped in *ambel marit* (pepper, salt and lime sauce). | Fresh spring rolls; can be ordered vegan or with shrimp or meat. | Pumpkin custard that tastes similar to crème caramel, but is prepared inside a hollow pumpkin. |

# Local Specialities

One of the best ways to sample a range of Cambodian flavours is to hit the food court in a market or shopping mall.

## Cooking Styles

**Char** Stir-fried; a popular way to cook staple meat and fish with *kreung* (lemongrass, garlic, shallots, galangal, lime leaves and turmeric) or *kynay* (ginger).

**Ang** Grilled; the default way to prepare chicken, meat skewers, seafood or even veggies.

**Khor** Stewed; a delicious way to make clay-pot dishes such as caramelised pork with quail eggs.

**Chimhoy** Steamed; a common way to prepare fresh greens like morning glory or spinach and fresh sea fish.

## Street Snacks

**Bobor** Rice porridge, like congee in China, popular with dried fish and egg – or zip it up with chilli and black pepper.

**Chek chien** Deep-fried bananas; these are a popular street snack at any time of day.

**Loat** Small white noodles that almost look like bean sprouts; they taste delicious fried up with beef.

Chek chien

**Kralanh** Sticky rice with coconut milk and bean cooked in a bamboo tube over a charcoal grill.

**Teuk ampeau** Freshly squeezed sugar-cane juice with a dash of lime, pineapple or tangerine.

## Dare to Try

**Crickets** Anyone for cricket?

**Duck foetus** Unborn duck, feathers and all.

**Durian** Nasally obnoxious spiky fruit, banned on flights.

**Prahoc** Fermented fish paste, almost a biological weapon.

**Spiders** Just like it sounds, deep-fried tarantulas.

## MEALS OF A LIFETIME

**Sombok** (p50) Run by a female chef team, the Kimsan twins, this riverfront restaurant in Phnom Penh is taking Khmer fusion to another level.

**Cuisine Wat Damnak** (p99) One of the first gourmet Cambodian restaurants, based in Siem Reap. Try its eight-course seasonal tasting menus.

**Jaan Bai** (p163) Battambang's beloved restaurant, where minimalist decor offsets bold fusion food; also helps to train disadvantaged youth.

**Crab Market** (p235) A quintessential Kep experience for crab fried with local Kampot pepper, with small restaurants located over the sea.

**Twenty Three Bistro** (p229) Kampot's mod international bistro offers delicious flavours at affordable prices.

---

## THE YEAR IN FOOD

**FEBRUARY**

Up in the hills of Mondulkiri Province, it's avocado season and this delicious fruit is widely available around the country, used in shakes or smashed on toast.

**MARCH**

The Kampot pepper harvest starts in March and can run for two months before the wet season kicks in. Red pepper is the last to be picked and the most expensive.

**APRIL**

*Svay* (mango) season is upon us. The Cambodian mangoes that are ripened by the hot-season temperatures from March to May are legendary for their delicious and fulsome flavour.

**JUNE**

It's *kulen* (lychee) season in Cambodia and the fruit is widely available. The holy mountain of Phnom Kulen translates as Lychee Mountain thanks to the wild lychees.

HOW TO...

# Dine Like a Local

Enter the Cambodian kitchen and you will learn that fine food comes from simplicity. Essentials consist of a strong flame, clean water, basic cutting utensils, a mortar and pestle, and a well-blackened wok or two. Cambodians eat three meals a day, but they are also inveterate snackers and always have something sweet, savoury or sour to hand.

## Breakfast

Breakfast is most commonly *kyteow* (rice-noodle soup) or *bobor* (rice porridge). Baguettes are available at any time of day or night, and go down well with a cup of coffee. Cafes and bakeries are now very popular for students and office workers – a belated return of the French influence in the new century.

## Lunch

Lunch starts early for most Cambodians, around 11am, as they may have been up since 5am. Traditionally, lunch is taken with the family, but in towns and cities many workers now eat at local restaurants or markets. There are lots of cheap hole-in-the-wall Cambodian restaurants in every town across the country, but for business meetings, Khmers will choose a more sophisticated option with set menus or lunch deals.

## Dinner

Dinner is the time for family bonding. Dishes are arranged around the central rice bowl and each diner has a small eating bowl. The procedure is uncomplicated: spoon some rice into your bowl, and lay 'something else' on top of it. The same principle applies when dining out with Cambodian friends or colleagues, and it's a good idea to let the locals take care of the order, providing you let them know about dietary requirements or allergies.

## A Matter of Course

When ordering multiple courses from a restaurant menu, don't worry – don't even think – about the proper succession of courses. All dishes are placed in the centre of the table as soon as they are ready. Diners then help themselves to whatever appeals to them, regardless of who ordered what.

## Table Etiquette: Dos & Don'ts

When in Cambodia, do as the Cambodians do. Following is some basic dining diplomacy.

### Observe the Host

**Do** wait for your host to sit first to start proceedings.
**Don't** turn down food placed in your bowl by your host.

### Chopstick Diplomacy

**Do** learn to use chopsticks for noodle soups.
**Don't** leave chopsticks in a V-shape in the bowl – it's a symbol of death.

### Tips on Tipping

**Do** tip about 5% to 10% in restaurants, as wages are low and tips appreciated.
**Don't** tip if there is already a service charge on the bill.

### Learn to Toast

**Do** drink every time someone offers a toast.
**Don't** take a big gulp every time as the toasting may go on all night.

## COOKING CLASSES

Cooking classes are a popular activity in Cambodia and there are several places where you can learn the secrets of Khmer cuisine. This is a great way to share your Cambodian experience with friends – no one wants to sit through a photo slide show, but offer them a mouth-watering meal and they'll come running.

**Battambang** There are a couple of excellent cooking classes in the same street, Coconut Lyly and Nary Kitchen (p161), both offering great-value experiences.

**Kampot** Try a unique pepper-themed cooking class at La Plantation (p233) on its idyllic pepper farm in the foothills of Phnom Voar.

**Siem Reap** Sign up for a vegetarian cooking class at Peace Cafe (p103) if you're looking for a healthy option in temple town.

Kayaking, Kampot (p227)

# THE OUTDOORS

The mighty Mekong River cuts through the heart of Cambodia, dividing the mountainous northeast from the lowlands. National parks abound inland, and the country boasts a curvaceous coastline.

Cambodia is fast catching up with its neighbours: Phnom Penh and Siem Reap have plenty of activities, while the South Coast offers watersports and the northeast is the place for a walk on the wild side. Whether you're hiking, biking, ascending peaks or plumbing depths, Cambodia delivers the action. The kingdom has a huge number of protected areas and national parks, adding up to a total area of more than 7 million hectares or about 41% of the country.

## Trekking

Trekking is not the first activity most people would associate with Cambodia, due to the ongoing presence of landmines, but there are plenty of safe areas in the country where walking can be enjoyed. The northeastern provinces of Mondulkiri and Ratanakiri, with their wild scenery, abundant waterfalls and ethnic-minority populations, are emerging as Cambodia's leading trekking destinations.

Cambodia has an established network of national parks with visitor facilities. Bokor National Park, Kirirom National Park and Phnom Kulen National Park all offer day-trekking potential, while Virachey National Park in Ratanakiri has multiday treks. Take a walk on the wild side in Chi Phat, the Areng Valley, Khnong Phsar and the Cardamom Mountains; Angkor is good for peaceful walks between the temples.

| More Outdoor Pursuits | ROCK CLIMBING | ZIPLINING | QUAD BIKING |
| --- | --- | --- | --- |
| | **Climbodia** (p229) offers rock climbing down in Kampot Province, where the landscape is peppered with karst outcrops. | Ecotourism resorts and lodges offering zip lines include **Shinta Mani Wild** (p87), **Cardamom Tented Camp** (p207) and **BeTreed Adventures** (p175). | Quad bikes or ATVs are growing in popularity in Cambodia thanks to its dirt roads, with operators in **Siem Reap** (p106) and **Phnom Penh** (p64). |

## FAMILY ADVENTURES

Be a 'bear keeper' or go 'behind the scenes' for a day at the world-class **Phnom Tamao Wildlife Rescue Centre** (p81) near Phnom Penh.

**Walk with the herd** at the **Elephant Valley Project** (p266), a retirement home in the jungle-clad hills of Mondulkiri Province in northeastern Cambodia.

**Fly through ancient jungle** around the temples on the **Angkor Zipline** (p138) near Siem Reap and listen for the calls of the resident gibbons.

**Get up close with rare freshwater dolphins** that live in the **Mekong River at Kampi** (p252), just north of Kratie.

**Make a pilgrimage** to the sacred mountain of **Phnom Kulen** (p146), home to an iconic waterfall, a pretty riverbed and a giant reclining Buddha carved from a massive boulder.

## Cycling

Cambodia is a great place for adventurous cyclists to explore. Given the country's legendary potholes, a mountain bike is the best bet. Some roads remain in poor condition, but there's usually a flat unpaved trail along the side. Travelling at a gentle speed allows for more interaction with the locals. Rent bikes at guesthouses and hotels throughout Cambodia, and transport them on the roofs of minibuses.

Pedalling around Angkor is a rewarding experience, as it really helps to get a measure of the scale of the temple complex. Cycling along-side the mother river between Kratie and Stung Treng on the Mekong Discovery Trail offers glimpses of rural riverine lifestyles. Mountain biking is likely to take off in Mondulkiri and Ratanakiri provinces over the coming years, as there are some great trails.

### BEST SPOTS

For the best outdoor spots and routes, see map on p38.

## Watersports & Boat Trips

Snorkelling and diving are available off the islands of Koh Rong and Koh Rong Sanloem. While the underwater scenery may not be as spectacular as in Indonesia or the Philippines, there's still plenty out there in the deep blue yonder. It's best to venture to the more remote dive sites like Koh Tang and Koh Prins, staying overnight on a boat. There are many unexplored areas off the coast between Koh Kong and Sihanoukville that could one day put Cambodia on Asia's dive map. Other watersports available along the South Coast include kayaking, stand-up paddleboarding and sailing.

Boat trips are unsurprisingly popular with visitors. Some of these are functional, such as travelling along the Sangker River from Siem Reap to Battambang. During the wet season, when the Mekong River is in full flow and the Tonlé Sap at its maximum extent, do as the locals do and travel by boat.

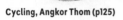

Cycling, Angkor Thom (p125)

| WILDLIFE-SPOTTING | BIRDWATCHING | WAKEBOARDING | KAYAKING & PADDLEBOARDING |
|---|---|---|---|
| Some curious critters call the Cambodian jungle their home; see gibbons and elephants at the **Keo Seima Wildlife Sanctuary** (p265). | Cambodia is home to many large waterbirds; the national bird, the rare giant ibis, can be spotted at **Tmat Boey** (p177) in Preah Vihear Province. | **ICF Wake Park** (p108) in Siem Reap offers wakeboarding, water-skiing, kneeboarding and a whole host of water-based activities. | Kampot is popular with stand-up paddleboarders and kayakers on the **Prek Tek Chhoun River** and **'Green Cathedral'** (p227). |

# ACTION AREAS

**Where to find Cambodia's
best outdoor activities.**

THAILAND

## Cycling
1. **Temples of Angkor** (p121)
2. **Battambang** (p161)
3. **Koh Dach** (p77)
4. **Kampot** (p229)
5. **Koh Trong** (p252)

## Snorkelling & Diving
1. **Koh Rong** (p214)
2. **Koh Rong Sanloem** (p223)
3. **Koh Tonsay** (p236)
4. **Koh Sdach Archipelago** (p221)
5. **Koh Thmei** (p213)

Anlong Veng

Sisophon

Siem Reap

Floating Village of Chong Kneas

Battambang

Pailin

Tonlé Sap

Moung Russei

Pursat

Ko Chang

Osoam

Cardamom Mountains

Romeas

Central Cardamoms Protected Forest

Tonlé Sap

Ko Kut

Koh Kong

Chi Phat

Kirirom National Park

Gulf of Thailand

Botum Sakor National Park

Gulf of Kompong Som

Bokor National Park

Takeo

Koh Sdach

Koh Rong

Sihanoukville

Veal Renh

Kampot

Koh Rong Sanloem

Ko Thmei

Prek Chak

Phu Quoc Island

Koh Tonsay

## National Parks

❶ **Phnom Kulen National Park** (p147)
❷ **Bokor National Park** (p232)
❸ **Kirirom National Park** (p84)
❹ **Southern Cardamom National Park** (p207)
❺ **Virachey National Park** (p261)

LAOS

*Virachey National Park*

○ Choam Ksant

○ Veun Sai

● Preah Vihear City (Tbeng Meanchey)

○ Trapeang Kriel

Preah Rumkel

● Ban Lung

❺ ● Stung Treng

*Mekong River*

*Sen River*

○ Koh Nhek

VIETNAM

Kompong Thom

❸ ❺ ● Kratie

● Baray

○ Chhlong

❸ ● Sre Kthum

○ Snuol

❸ ● PHNOM PENH

● Prey Veng

Kaam Samnor

## Kayaking, Paddleboarding & Wakeboarding

❶ **Southern Islands** (p194)
❷ **Kampot** (p226)
❸ **Kratie** (p253)
❹ **Tatai River** (p203)
❺ **Stung Treng** (p257)

## Trekking

❶ **Cardamom Mountains** (p86)
❷ **Temples of Angkor** (p132)
❸ **Keo Seima Wildlife Sanctuary** (p265)
❹ **Phnom Kulen National Park** (p146)
❺ **Virachey National Park** (p261)

*SOUTH CHINA SEA (EAST SEA)*

N  0 ————— 100 km
   0 ————— 50 miles

CAMBODIA

# THE GUIDE

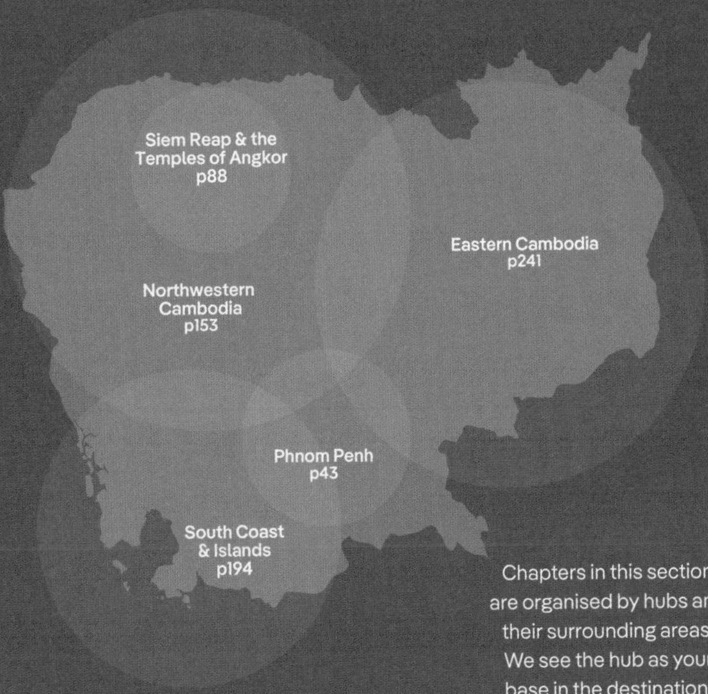
Siem Reap & the Temples of Angkor p88
Eastern Cambodia p241
Northwestern Cambodia p153
Phnom Penh p43
South Coast & Islands p194

Chapters in this section are organised by hubs and their surrounding areas. We see the hub as your base in the destination, where you'll find unique experiences, local insights, insider tips and expert recommendations. It's also your gateway to the surrounding area, where you'll see what and how much you can do from there.

**Angkor Wat (p114)**

GILLES VAN WINSEN/SHUTTERSTOCK ©

National Museum of Cambodia (p51)

# PHNOM PENH

## PULSE OF CONTEMPORARY CAMBODIA

Phnom Penh is the beating heart of political intrigue and entrepreneurialism, where glimpses of old Asia are revealed beneath the shadows of the ever-evolving new Cambodia.

For most, this region is all about the enigmatic Cambodian capital, Phnom Penh, a chaotic crossroads of Asia's past, present and future. If you can pull yourself away from the poolside or escape the lively bars, exploring the sights around the capital will reward. The glimmering spires of the Royal Palace, the fluttering saffron of monks' robes and the luscious location on the banks of the Mekong – this is the Asia many daydream about from afar.

Cambodia's fast-growing capital can be an assault on the senses. Motorbike riders whiz down lanes without a thought for pedestrians, markets exude pungent scents, and all the while the sounds of life, commerce, survival, reverberate through the streets. But this is all part of the mystery.

Once the 'Pearl of Asia', Phnom Penh's shine was tarnished by the impact of war and revolution. But the city has since risen from the ashes to take its place among the hip capitals of the region, with an alluring cafe culture, bustling bars, world-class dining and a glittery new skyline shooting ever upwards.

Beyond Phnom Penh, the beautiful Mekong island of Koh Dach is the easiest trip to undertake and is best done by mountain bike or local transport. Udong, once the stupa-studded capital of Cambodia, is a half-day trip and can be combined with a visit to Kompong Chhnang.

The Angkorian temple of Tonlé Bati and the hilltop pagoda of Phnom Chisor, located near National Highway (NH) 2 towards Takeo, can be combined with the excellent Phnom Tamao Wildlife Rescue Centre, where behind-the-scenes tours get visitors up close with endangered animals.

En route to the south coast, Kirirom National Park is the closest protected area to Phnom Penh, offering cool climes amid the pines. There are also many other up-and-coming trekking areas on the fringes of the Cardamom Mountains that are within day-tripping or overnight distance of the capital, featuring beautiful multilevel waterfalls and stunning mountaintop viewpoints offering vistas of cloud-covered valleys and unexplored peaks.

NALIOSA SUKPRASERT/GETTY IMAGES ©

## THE MAIN AREAS

**ROYAL PALACE & RIVERFRONT**
Shimmering spires and Mekong views. **p48**

**NORTH PHNOM PENH**
The old French quarter of town. **p58**

**SOUTH PHNOM PENH**
Bustling markets and buzzing bars. **p66**

**AROUND PHNOM PENH**
Rural rhythms and hilltop temples. **p75**

# Find Your Way

A relatively small capital by regional standards, Phnom Penh is quite easy to get around, although its traffic is getting worse. Traffic jams are common during the morning and evening rush hours, particularly around the two main north–south boulevards, Monivong and Norodom, as well as Russian Confederation Blvd to the airport.

### FROM THE AIRPORT

Phnom Penh International Airport is 7km west of the city centre. Facilities include free wi-fi and ATMs. There is an official taxi booth to arrange taxis/*tuk-tuk*s to town for US$15/10. Bus 3 passes the airport and stops at Psar Thmei (New Market; 1500r, 5am to 8.30pm).

### CAR & MOTORCYCLE

Car hire (from US$35 per day) is available through operators in Phnom Penh, but prices rise once you venture beyond the city. For motorbike hire, a 100cc scooter costs around US$5 per day and 250cc dirt bikes run from US$15 per day, but you'll have to deposit a passport.

### TUK-TUK

*Tuk-tuk*s come in two forms: *remorks* (homegrown motorbikes with carriages) and Indian-style auto-rickshaws. Fares are usually more expensive for the *remorks*, at around US$2 to US$3 for rides in the city centre. Either way, pay by the ride, not per person. PassApp and Grab are good apps for guaranteeing fixed fares.

### CYCLO & BICYCLE

*Cyclos* (bicycle rickshaws) are a more relaxing way to see sights in the centre of town, but don't work well for long distances. Short-distance fares are US$1 to US$3.

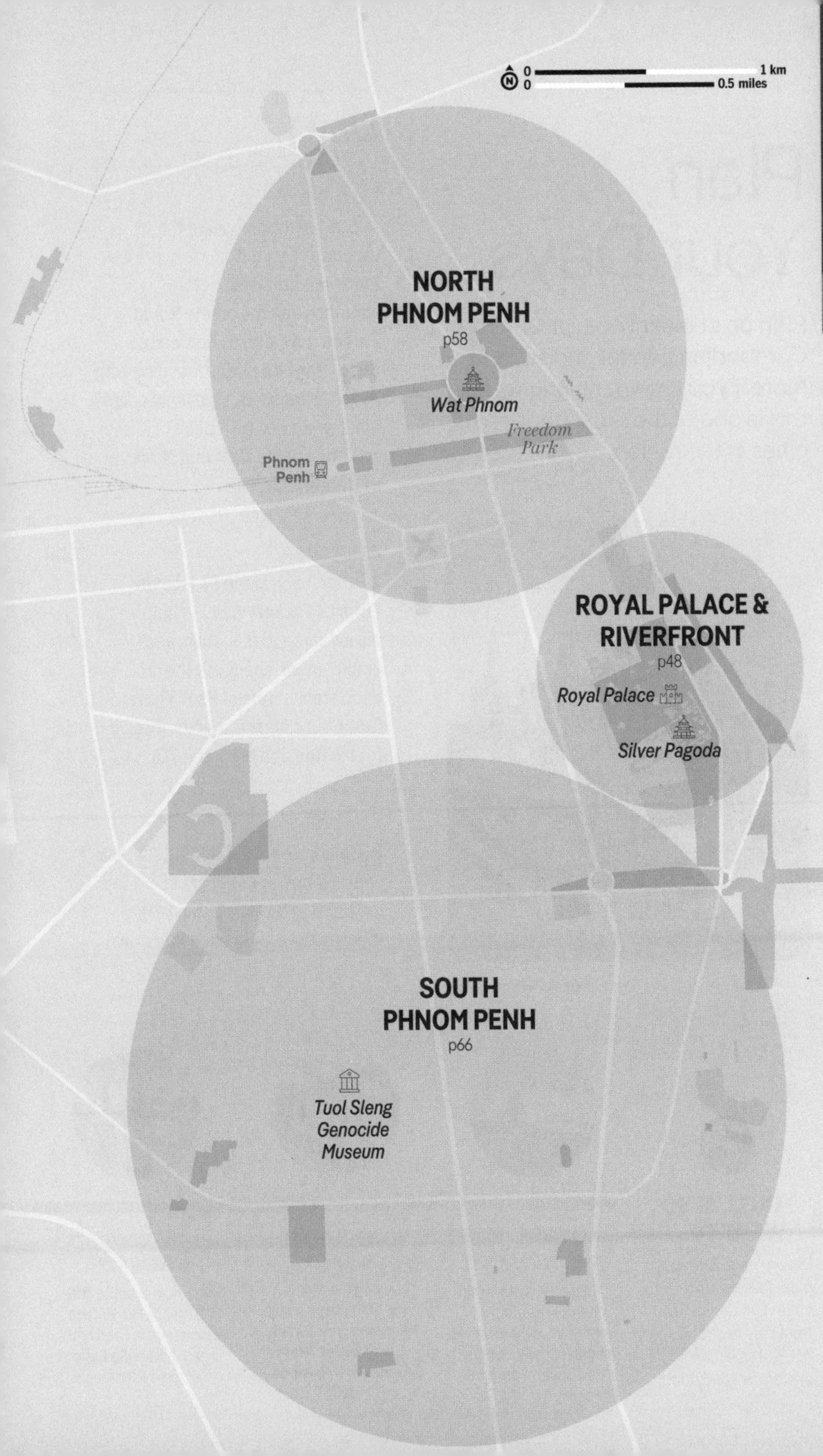

0 — 1 km
0 — 0.5 miles

**NORTH
PHNOM PENH**
p58

*Wat Phnom*

*Freedom
Park*

Phnom
Penh

**ROYAL PALACE &
RIVERFRONT**
p48

*Royal Palace*

*Silver Pagoda*

**SOUTH
PHNOM PENH**
p66

*Tuol Sleng
Genocide
Museum*

# Plan Your Days

Plan on at least two nights in the Cambodian capital and several more if you like your nightlife, as this is one of the most happening cities in the region.

Royal Palace (p49)

## Day 1

### Morning

● Start early to observe the aerobics sessions on the riverfront, then grab breakfast before venturing into the ornate **Royal Palace** (p49) and the incredible **Silver Pagoda** (p50), brimming with national treasures. Find the world's most wondrous collection of Khmer sculpture at the **National Museum of Cambodia** (p51).

### Afternoon

● After lunch at the **F3 Friends Futures Factory** (p56) to help disadvantaged teenagers into employment, check out the art-deco architecture of **Psar Thmei** (p60), but save the serious shopping for the **Russian Market** (p70).

### Evening

● Celebrate your shopping success with a happy-hour bar crawl around the buzzing **Bassac Lane** (p71), followed by a night out on the town.

## YOU'LL ALSO WANT TO...

Phnom Penh is a great place to soak up the street life, wandering from cafe to shop to bar. But save time to explore beyond, too.

### STROLL ON THE RIVERFRONT

Take a **sunset stroll** on the wide riverfront promenade where locals come for daily exercise and general grazing.

### DINE IN STYLE

Experiment with some Khmer gastronomy at one of the city's many fine-dining restaurants, like **Cuisine Wat Damnak** or **Sombok** (p50).

### EXPLORE LANEWAYS

Check out loveable little lanes (p73), like **Palace Lane** (street art and craft beer) or **Langka Lane** (diverse eateries).

# Day 2

### Morning

● Start your second day with a **KA Architecture Tours** (p63) walking tour of the old French quarter of town, or just wander around **Wat Phnom** (p59), where Khmers come to pray for luck.

### Afternoon

● Have lunch in the trendy BKK area, then visit the sobering **Tuol Sleng Genocide Museum** (p68), a factory of death during the Khmer Rouge, before continuing on to the **Killing Fields of Choeung Ek** (p69). While grim experiences, they are essential for understanding just how far Cambodia has come in the intervening years.

### Evening

● Wind up the day with a **sunset cruise** (p56) on the Mekong River, taking in the beautiful view over the Royal Palace.

# Day 3

### Morning

● It's time to escape the city for some countryside jaunts, ancient temples or wildlife encounters. Despite the rapidly expanding girth of the city limits, it doesn't take that long to get out to some of the lesser-visited temples around Phnom Penh, such as the stupa-studded former capital of **Udong** (p78).

### Afternoon

● On the way back to Phnom Penh, stop off at **Koh Dach** (p77) for a slice of Mekong island life on two wheels, where it is possible to see traditional silk weaving.

### Evening

● Experience some Khmer fine dining with some 'Cambodian living cuisine' at the highly regarded **Malis** (p50).

**DIVE INTO THE DISTILLING SCENE**

Visit the **Seekers** or **Samai distilleries** (p71) to lift the spirits, or a new microbrewery producing homegrown craft beers.

**SOAK UP THE ATMOSPHERE OF OLD PHNOM PENH**

Head to the **post-office square** (p61) to see some the city's best-preserved old French architecture.

**TAKE A CYCLO RIDE AROUND THE W PALACE QUARTER**

**Cyclos** (p64) are a relaxing, comfy way to explore the quiet streets near the Royal Palace.

**VENTURE INTO THE WILDERNESS**

Hit the foothills of the **Cardamom Mountains** (p86) and trek to multilevel waterfalls or misty viewpoints.

# ROYAL PALACE & RIVERFRONT

This is the most popular neighbourhood in Phnom Penh for international travellers, thanks to a cluster of the city's most important sights, including the beautiful Royal Palace, ornate Silver Pagoda and the impressive National Museum of Cambodia. However, it is the riverfront that is the real draw here, as Phnom Penh marks the confluence of the mighty Mekong River and the Tonlé Sap River, which reverses direction each year, acting as a natural flood barrier. The riverfront promenade is one of the most open in the region, with swaying palms and billowing flags – wandering up and down past sophisticated restaurants, corner bars and local shops is a great way to while away some time towards sunset. Locals also flock to this part of town thanks to the riverside breezes that take the edge off the heat, and many can be seen doing riverside aerobics or line dancing around dusk.

## TOP TIP

*Cyclos* are steadily losing ground to *tuk-tuks, motos* and taxis, but they're still a relaxing way to cover small distances in Phnom Penh. The Royal Palace and riverfront district is the best place to enjoy this experience, as the traffic can be lighter than on the big boulevards, particularly around the palace and museum.

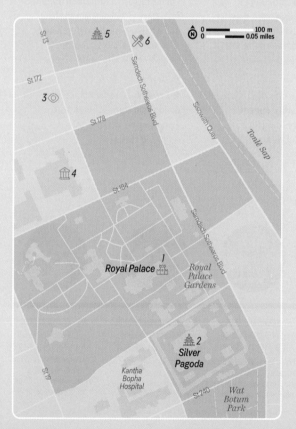

**HIGHLIGHTS**
1 Royal Palace
2 Silver Pagoda

**SIGHTS**
3 F3 Friends Futures Factory
4 National Museum of Cambodia
5 Wat Ounalom

**EATING**
6 The Waterside

**DRINKING & NIGHTLIFE**
(see 6) Rukkha Sky Bar & Tapas

# The Glittering Royal Palace

HOME TO CAMBODIA'S KINGS AND QUEENS

With its classic soaring Khmer roofs and ornate gilding, this **striking structure** once dominated the skyline of Phnom Penh. Located near the riverfront, it bears a remarkable likeness to its counterpart in Bangkok. Being the official residence of King Sihamoni, parts of the massive palace compound are closed to the public. Tourists are allowed to visit only the Throne Hall and a clutch of buildings surrounding it. The palace gets very busy on Sundays, when countryside Khmers come to pay their respects, but being among crowds of locals can be a fun way to experience the place.

Visitors enter into the eastern portion of the palace compound, not far from the stunning **Chan Chaya Pavilion**. Performances of classical Cambodian dance were once staged in this pavilion, which is still sometimes lit up at night to commemorate festivals or anniversaries.

The main attraction in the palace compound is the **Throne Hall**, topped by a 59m-high tower inspired by the Bayon at Angkor. The hall is used for coronations and ceremonies such as the presentation of credentials by diplomats. Many of the items once displayed here were destroyed by the Khmer Rouge.

South of the Throne Hall, check out the curious iron **Napoleon III Pavilion**. Given to King Norodom by Napoleon III of France, it was hardly designed with the Cambodian climate in mind. In fact, it was originally built for the inauguration of the Suez Canal in 1869, before being shipped to Cambodia in pieces.

## ROYAL PALACE 101

It costs US$10 to visit the palace, and tour guides are available to interpret the site for an additional US$10. Opening hours are 8am to 11am and 2pm to 5pm daily. All visitors need to wear shorts that reach to the knees, and a T-shirt or blouse that reaches to the elbows; otherwise you'll have to buy a sarong as a covering at the ticket booth. Due to COVID-19 you may still be asked to wear a face mask here.

**Napoleon III Pavilion**

ALTRENDO IMAGES/SHUTTERSTOCK ©

## THE SILVER PAGODA

The entry ticket to the Royal Palace compound includes admission to the **Silver Pagoda** (p50), a grand pagoda originally built for the private worship of the royal family.

## BEST KHMER FINE DINING IN PHNOM PENH

**Cuisine Wat Damnak $$$**
A Cambodian restaurant offering a superb-value set lunch menu plus an evening tasting menu based on seasonal ingredients.

**Sombok $$$**
This contemporary Khmer restaurant serves fusion flavours and intricate creations, with a stunning riverfront set-up.

**Kravanh $$**
A stylish restaurant set in a grand French villa, its menu includes traditional salads, scented soups and regional specialities.

**Malis $$**
A chic place to dine alfresco, with beef steamed in lotus leaf, and traditional soups and salads. Book ahead.

PACK-SHOT/SHUTTERSTOCK ©

**National Museum of Cambodia**

### MORE AROUND THE ROYAL PALACE & RIVERFRONT

# Home of the Emerald Buddha

A REPOSITORY OF ROYAL TREASURES

Located within the Royal Palace compound is this **extravagant temple**, also known as Wat Preah Keo or Temple of the Emerald Buddha thanks to the eponymous Buddha that occupies centre stage. The **Silver Pagoda** is so named for its floor, which is covered with 5 tonnes of gleaming silver. You can sneak a peek at some of the 5000 tiles near the entrance, but most are covered for protection. Inside is a series of lavish Buddha statues made of precious metals and containing priceless gemstones.

The pagoda was first constructed of wood in 1892 during the rule of King Norodom, who was apparently inspired by Wat Phra Kaew in Bangkok. It was rebuilt in 1962, and

### BEST BOUTIQUE HOTELS IN THE ROYAL PALACE AND RIVERFRONT AREA

**Palace Gate Hotel**
In a superb location opposite the Royal Palace, this place blends modern four-star rooms with an old French villa. **$$$**

**Pavilion**
Housed in an elegant French villa, this atmospheric place has four-poster beds and stunning furniture. No children. **$$**

**Penh House**
Urban hipster hotel with a lovely rooftop bar-restaurant and an infinity pool overlooking the palace gardens. **$$**

preserved by the Khmer Rouge to demonstrate to the outside world its concern for the conservation of Cambodia's cultural riches. However, more than half of the pagoda's contents were lost, stolen or destroyed in the turmoil that followed the Vietnamese invasion, including the sacred sword *(preah khan)* said to empower the Cambodian kings of old. Nonetheless, what remains is spectacular and this is one of the few places in Cambodia where bejewelled objects embodying some of the brilliance and richness of Khmer civilisation can still be viewed.

The staircase leading up to the Silver Pagoda is made of Italian marble. Rivalling the silver floor is the Emerald Buddha, an extraordinary Baccarat-crystal sculpture sitting atop an impressive gilded pedestal. Adding to the lavish mix is a life-sized solid-gold Buddha adorned with 2086 diamonds, the largest weighing in at 25 carats. Created in the palace workshops during 1906 and 1907, the gold Buddha itself weighs 90kg. Directly in front of it, in a Formica case, is a miniature silver-and-gold stupa containing a relic of Buddha brought from Sri Lanka. To the left is an 80kg bronze Buddha, and to the right a silver Buddha. On the far right, figurines of solid gold tell the story of the Buddha. Along the walls of the pagoda are examples of Khmer artisanship, including intricate masks used in classical dance and dozens of gold Buddhas. The many precious gifts given to Cambodia's monarchs by foreign heads of state appear rather spiritless when displayed next to such diverse and exuberant Khmer art. Note that photography is not permitted inside the Silver Pagoda.

The Silver Pagoda complex is enclosed by walls plastered with an extensive and, in parts, spectacular mural depicting the classic Indian epic of the *Ramayana* (known as the *Reamker* in Cambodia). The story begins just south of the east gate and includes vivid images of the Battle of Lanka. The mural was created in around 1900 and parts of it have recently undergone restoration.

# A Museum of Cambodian Treasures

THE WORLD'S FINEST KHMER SCULPTURES

The **National Museum of Cambodia** (cambodiamuseum.info) is home to the finest Khmer sculptures in the world: a millennium's worth and more of masterful Khmer design. It's housed in a graceful terracotta structure of traditional design (built from 1917 to 1920) with an inviting courtyard garden, just north of the Royal Palace. The museum

*continued on p53*

**WARNING: BAG & PHONE SNATCHING**

Bag snatching has become a real problem in Phnom Penh, with foreigners often targeted. Hot spots include the riverfront and busy areas around popular markets, but there is no real pattern: the speeding motorbike thieves, usually operating in pairs, can strike any time, any place. Countless expats and tourists have been injured falling off their bikes in the process of being robbed. Wear close-fitting bags (such as backpacks) that don't temptingly dangle from your body. Don't hang expensive cameras around your neck and keep mobile phones close to your body or out of sight. The thieves are real pros and only need one chance.

 **POPULAR CAMBODIAN RESTAURANTS IN PHNOM PENH**

**Sleuk Chhouk**
A stylish and authentic dining experience; dishes include fish-egg soup or zesty frogs' legs and quail eggs. **$$**

**Yi Sang Riverside**
Dine right by the riverside on Cambodian street flavours such as *naom banchok* (rice noodles with curry). **$**

**Bopha Phnom Penh**
Bopha (aka Titanic) is right on the river and designed to impress, with Angkorian-style carvings and exotic flavours. **$$**

With erratic traffic, overflow parking on the pavement and little deference for pedestrians, Phnom Penh may not seem like the best city for walking. Yet, if you can build up some confidence (and patience), you'll find it's the most rewarding way to explore the city's varied architecture. Start your walking tour in the very spot where the city began: **1 Wat Phnom** (p59). Heading south on Norodom Blvd, you'll pass several examples of French colonial architecture, including an old art-nouveau-inspired customs office. Then, let the looming art-deco market **2 Psar Thmei** (p60), its huge domed hall resembling a Babylonian ziggurat, lure you west on St 130.

Depart Psar Thmei onto St 63 and turn east on St 154 for more French-era architecture. Next, zigzag over to the **3 National Museum of Cambodia** (p51). French archi-

tect George Groslier is said to have been inspired by temple prototypes seen on ancient bas-reliefs when he built this striking scarlet-red marvel between 1917 and 1920. Nearby is the compound of the **4 Royal Palace** (p49), a treasure trove of traditional Khmer architecture with gilded halls, lavish pavilions and honorary shrines.

Continue south into the manicured **5 Wat Botum Park** before turning west at Sihanouk Blvd, where you'll encounter a 27m-high shrine holding a bronze **6 statue of King Father Norodom Sihanouk**, who died in 2012. Nearby is the **7 Independence Monument**, modelled on the central tower of Angkor Wat. If it's late afternoon and you've worked up a thirst, there are plenty of places for a drink just south of the Independence Monument, including popular **8 Bassac Lane** (p71).

**Wat Botum Park**

*continued from p51*

also contains displays of pottery and bronzes dating from the pre-Angkorian periods of Funan and Chenla (4th to 9th centuries), the Indravarman period (9th and 10th centuries) and the classical Angkorian period (10th to 14th centuries), as well as more recent works, such as a beautiful wooden royal barge.

Most visitors start left and continue in a clockwise, chronological direction. One of the first significant sculptures to greet visitors is a large fragment – including the relatively intact head, shoulders and two arms – of an immense bronze reclining Vishnu statue, which was recovered from the Western Mebon temple near Angkor Wat in 1936. Continue into the southern pavilion, where the pre-Angkorian collection begins, illustrating the journey from the human form of Indian sculpture to the more divine form of Khmer sculpture from the 5th to 8th centuries. Highlights include an imposing, eight-armed Vishnu statue from the 6th century, found at Phnom Da, and a staring

## BEST SKY BARS IN PHNOM PENH

**Sora**
This vertigo-inducing deck on the 37th floor of Vattanac Capital is part of Rosewood Hotel. No flip-flops or singlets.

**Celeste**
Another sky-high bar, Celeste is on the 32nd floor of Penthouse Residences and revolves slowly.

**Juniper**
A specialist gin bar on the 12th floor of the Point Hotel with wonderful views (happy hour 5pm to 7pm).

**Rukkha**
Occupying a riverfront location on the 4th floor, this outdoor bar has a vertical garden, creative cocktails, tapas and light bites.

## OTHER PHNOM PENH MARKETS WORTH SEEKING OUT

**Psar Reatrey**
More popular with Khmers than foreigners, this night market kicks off every evening. Bargain vigorously – prices are high.

**Psar O Russei**
The biggest market in town, selling food, imported toiletries, secondhand clothes and more from hundreds of stalls.

**Psar Olympic**
Items for sale include bicycle parts, clothes, electronics and assorted edibles. A modern market set in a covered location.

## WHEN TO VISIT PHNOM PENH

**Jan–Feb** The holiday crush is over and pleasant northeasterly breezes massage the riverfront. This time of year brings some of the coolest temperatures in the capital, although the mercury regularly hits 30°C.

**Sep–Oct** Heavy rains provide relief from the searing sun and many hotels offer steep discounts, but there can be some localised flooding in parts of the city.

**Oct–Nov** The Bon Om Tuk water festival is one giant street party on the riverbanks, while the rainy season comes to a close and the countryside around the capital is lush and green.

SERGEI MUGASHEV/SHUTTERSTOCK ©

**Wat Ounalom**

## OTHER LEADING MUSEUMS AROUND CAMBODIA

The National Museum of Cambodia is the flagship collection in the country, but there are some important cultural repositories elsewhere in Cambodia, including the excellent **Angkor National Museum** (p96) in Siem Reap and the **Battambang Museum** (p161).

Harihara, combining the attributes of Shiva and Vishnu, from Prasat Andet in Kompong Thom Province.

The Angkor collection includes several striking statues of Shiva from the 9th, 10th and 11th centuries; a giant pair of wrestling monkeys (Koh Ker, 10th century); a beautiful 12th-century stele (stone) from Oddar Meanchey Province inscribed with scenes from the life of Shiva; and the sublime statue of a seated Jayavarman VII (r 1181–1219), his head bowed slightly in a meditative pose (Angkor Thom, late 12th century). Looted statues that were housed in museum collections around the world have been making their way home over the past decade or so, including many masterful pieces from Koh Ker that were trafficked by British antiquities dealer Douglas Latchford and his nefarious network.

## BISTROS IN PHNOM PENH

**Pepe Bistro**
This French bistro oozes class, with an ever-changing menu of homemade pâté, foie gras and truffled everything. **$$**

**Bistro Langka**
Fine French dining in an intimate atmosphere; the tuna *tataki* and an original beef tartare are standouts. **$$**

**Penh 278**
A refined, deservedly popular bistro serving modern international flavours, with an air-con interior and inviting garden. **$$**

Note that visitors are not allowed to photograph the collection, only the central courtyard. English-, French-, Spanish- and Japanese-speaking guides are available for tours. A comprehensive booklet, *The New Guide to the National Museum*, is available to buy at the front desk, while the smaller *Khmer Art in Stone* covers some signature pieces. There are also audio guides available in eight languages. Allow at least one hour to visit, more like two hours if you like to browse slowly or want to have a drink at the Museum Cafe (p61) afterwards.

## Top Temple of Wat Ounalom

HOME OF THE BUDDHIST PATRIARCH

This **place of worship**, the headquarters of Cambodian Buddhism, was founded in 1443 and comprises 44 structures. The wat received a battering during the Pol Pot era, but today it has come back to life. The head of the country's Buddhist brotherhood lives here, along with a large number of monks.

On the 2nd floor of the main building, to the left of the dais, is a statue of Huot Tat, the fourth patriarch of Cambodian Buddhism, who was killed by Pol Pot. The statue, made in 1971 when the patriarch was 80 years old, was thrown in the Mekong River by the Khmer Rouge to show that Buddhism was no longer the driving force in Cambodia. It was retrieved after 1979. To the right of the dais is a statue of a former patriarch of the Thummayuth sect, to which the royal family belongs.

Seek out the stairway to the left behind the dais. It leads up to the 3rd floor, where a glass case houses a small marble Buddha of Burmese origin that was broken into pieces by the Khmer Rouge and later reassembled. There are some good views of the Mekong from up here, though the door at the top of the stairs is often locked.

Behind the main building is a stupa containing an eyebrow hair of Buddha, with an inscription in Pali (an ancient Indian language) over the entrance. Inside this golden stupa is a hidden Angkorian sandstone temple, which dates from the 12th century, but it is usually necessary to find a guardian to open the door.

### BEST INTERNATIONAL RESTAURANTS ON THE RIVERFRONT

**Metro Hassakan $$**
Metro has small sampling plates and large plates that include succulent steaks and honey-soy roasted chicken.

**The Waterside $$**
Boasting an epic location overlooking the Tonlé Sap River, with a menu including selected cuts, confit lamb and delicious platters. Open evenings only.

**La Croisette $$**
Stylish and popular, with homemade pasta and gnocchi, plus hearty steaks, lamb chops and Cambodian offerings, plus an impressively breezy upstairs balcony.

### THE FOUR FACES OF THE MEKONG RIVER

Taking a sunset **boat cruise** (p56) brings guests face to face with the 'Chaktomuk' or four faces of the Mekong, where the mother river splits into the Bassac and Tonlé Sap Rivers.

 **WHERE TO EAT ON A BUDGET**

**Aeon Mall Food Court**
Surprisingly cheap eats at the ground-floor food court of this swanky mall, with noodle soups, fried rice and sushi. **$**

**Russian Market**
The best food market, with a good range of local specialities. The large car park has seafood BBQs from around 4pm. **$**

**Flavours of Cambodia**
The 4th-floor food court at Sorya Shopping Centre is an air-cooled place for local fare, with stalls arranged by province. **$**

**BEST CLUBS IN PHNOM PENH**

**Pontoon**
Draws top local DJs and occasional big foreign acts. Adjacent Pontoon Pulse is more of a lounge club.

**Epic**
Superclub in a huge warehouse space, with decor that's anything but 'warehouse'. Primarily aimed at local rich young things.

**Heart of Darkness**
This institution has evolved into more of a nightclub than a bar, with drag shows Wednesday to Saturday nights.

**Vito**
Spinning older dance tunes; popular with an older crowd who want to have a conversation as well as a dance.

# Riveting River Cruises

SUNSET OVER PHNOM PENH

Boat trips on the **Tonlé Sap** and **Mekong Rivers** are deservedly popular with visitors. Sunset cruises are ideal, with the burning sun sinking slowly behind the glistening spires of the Royal Palace. A slew of cruising boats are available for hire on the riverfront about 500m north of the tourist-boat dock. Just rock up and arrange one on the spot. If you're in the mood for a tipple, you can either bring your own drinks or buy beer and soft drinks on the boat.

Public river cruises are another option. They leave every 30 minutes or so from 5pm to 7.30pm from the tourist-boat dock and last about 45 minutes.

**Memorable Cambodia** (memorablecambodia.com) operates half-day cruises to Koh Dach (Silk Island) and full-day excursions to Udong run by enthusiastic Cambodian students from a local hospitality school. It also operates popular sunset cruises at 5pm and 6.30pm. Public boat tours to Koh Dach depart at 9am and 11am from the tourist-boat dock (minimum three people).

# A Flourishing Cultural Epicentre

COMMUNITY SPACE FOR EATS AND ARTS

**F3 Friends Futures Factory** is a new community space aiming to become the cultural heart of central Phnom Penh, with a regular lineup of live music, family activities and gallery exhibitions, plus a market with indie shops, a bar and plenty of pallet furniture to lounge around in. The ever-popular Friends Restaurant was forced to close during the pandemic, but there are plans brewing to create a street-food dining experience in the courtyard here to resurrect some of the restaurant's most popular dishes.

Youth welfare organisation ChildSafe (think childsafe.org) runs a range of experiences from here that raise awareness about child protection and responsible travel. These entertaining and interactive activities include cooking classes at the vocational training restaurant, *tuk-tuk* tours of the city, cocktail-making and handicraft classes, all of which are linked to the social innovations by Friends International (friends-international. org), the organisation behind ChildSafe. These initiatives give tourists an alternative to harm-

**DON'T GET YOUR FACTORIES IN A TWIST**

There are two popular places called Factory in the capital. As well as F3 Friends Futures Factory in the centre, there is also the **Factory Phnom Penh** (p71), a huge creative shared working space in the south of the city.

**WHERE TO EAT NOODLES IN PHNOM PENH**

**Noodle House**
Set in a restored French-era building, it gives you a regional noodle tour, from Cambodian *kyteow* soup to pad thai. **$**

**Special Pho**
A great location near the riverfront for good pho, plus cheap fried noodles. **$**

**Sesame Noodle Bar**
One of the Russian Market's oldest little diners; cold noodles come heaped with caramelised pork or grilled tofu. **$**

**Sunset cruises, Mekong River**

ful school and institutional care facility visits, and offer them a chance to contribute to a social business while having fun and learning about Khmer culture.

The Nail Bar here also provides cheap manicures, pedicures and nail painting, plus haircuts and blow-drys, all to help the Mith Samlanh organisation train street children in a new vocation.

## WHERE TO BROWSE ART IN PHNOM PENH

**Chhan Dina** is a leading contemporary artist and owner of Chhan Dina Gallery. Here are some of her favourite galleries in town:

### The Gallerists
Located on gentrified St 240, The Gallerist showcases a continuously rolling collection of contemporary works by leading Cambodian artists.

### Java Creative Cafe
Both a cafe and a gallery, Java has been supporting Cambodian artists for more than two decades. It's also a great spot for excellent coffee.

### Meta House
This German-run cultural centre has a large art gallery with rotating exhibitions, while dance, theatre and music events round out the busy cultural calendar.

Also check out kumnooh.com, an online guide to the contemporary arts in Cambodia.

 **WHERE TO FIND LIVE MUSIC IN PHNOM PENH**

**Oscar's on the Corner**
Live bands play every night at this rockin' venue on the corner of St 104. Everything from blues to French punk.

**54 Langeach Sros**
Popular Cambodian BBQ beer-garden restaurant with live music most nights, it features on many foodie tours.

**Craft**
Located in the heart of Palace Lane, this bar has regular live music, including homegrown acts.

# NORTH PHNOM PENH

## THE OLD FRENCH QUARTER OF TOWN

This is where the French elite laid out the new-look city that is recognised as Phnom Penh today, with a focus on the main post office and a raft of grand civic buildings. Many of these remain standing and the post-office square is arguably the best-preserved corner of the city, with a host of French-accented restaurants and small cafes.

Wat Phnom is the defining feature of this neighbourhood: the oldest temple and a symbol of the capital. The park around Wat Phnom Penh is one of the leafiest in the city and popular with Cambodians seeking shade in the heat of the day.

Psar Thmei (Central Market) is another dominant feature of the landscape here, a cauldron of commerce in the heart of the city where many locals still come to bargain. A striking art-deco-style building, this is arguably the most interesting of the city's markets to browse in.

### TOP TIP

For an urban safari, head to the lush gardens of Wat Phnom, where birds and animals hang out. Most spectacular are the hornbills that forage here, and there are also lots of mischievous monkeys (keep a safe distance as they can bite). There are also fruit bats in the area that take flight at dusk.

Wat Phnom

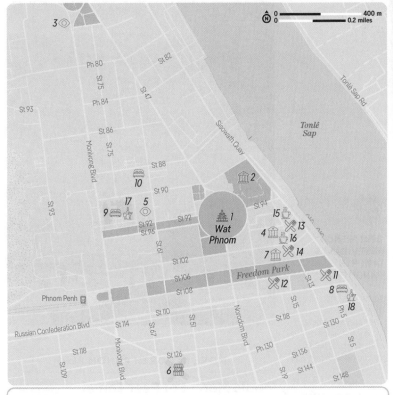

| HIGHLIGHTS | 4 Main Post Office | 9 Raffles Hotel Le Royal | 14 Palais de La Poste |
| --- | --- | --- | --- |
| 1 Wat Phnom | 5 National Library | 10 The Eighty8 | **DRINKING** |
| **SIGHTS** | 6 Psar Thmei | **EATING** | 15 Brown Coffee |
| 2 Council for the Devel- | 7 Sosoro Museum | 11 18 Rik Reay BBQ | 16 Cam Cup Café |
| opment of Cambodia | **SLEEPING** | 12 Armand's | 17 Elephant Bar |
| 3 French Embassy | 8 Onederz Hotel | 13 Le Manolis | 18 Oskar Bistro |

# Pray for Luck at Wat Phnom

FOUNDING TEMPLE OF THE CITY

This **temple** is on the only 'hill' in town, a 27m-high knoll. The main entrance is via the grand eastern staircase, guarded by lions and *naga* (mythical serpent-being) balustrades. Many come here to pray for good luck.

The *vihara* (temple sanctuary) was rebuilt in 1434, 1806, 1894 and 1926. To the west is a huge stupa containing the ashes of King Ponhea Yat (r 1405–67). In a pavilion on the south side of the passage between the *vihara* and the stupa is a statue of a smiling Lady Penh. Below the *vihara* is an eclectic shrine dedicated to the genie Preah Chau. Down the hill from the *vihara*, in the northwest corner of the complex, is an arts and crafts centre, where women and people with disabilities sell handicrafts.

**SAMBO THE ELEPHANT**

For many years, there was a resident elephant at Wat Phnom called Sambo, who was forced to give rides to locals for photo opportunities. In 2014 she retired to the **Elephant Valley Project** (p266) in Mondulkiri Province, where she now roams freely.

59

ANNAT30/SHUTTERSTOCK ©

**Psar Thmei**

## BEST FRENCH RESTAURANTS IN NORTH PHNOM PENH

**Armand's $$$**
The best steaks in town are served here in cognac flambe-style. Space is tight, so book ahead.

**Palais de la Poste $$$**
Dishes are presented with a decorative flourish; highlights include langoustine ravioli, beef carpaccio and grilled scallops with Kampot pepper.

**Khema $$**
The great-value French food here includes boeuf bourguignon, Toulouse sausages and lamb shank, along with pastas and delicious desserts.

### MORE IN NORTH PHNOM PENH

# Iconic Market of Psar Thmei

THE ORIGINAL PHNOM PENH SHOPPING MALL

A landmark building in the capital, the art-deco Psar Thmei (literally 'New Market') is often called the **Central Market**, a reference to its location and size. Constructed in 1937, the huge domed hall resembles a Babylonian ziggurat and, according to some, ranks as one of the 10 largest domes in the world.

The design allows for maximum ventilation, and even on a sweltering day the central hall is cool and airy. The market was recently renovated with French government assistance and is in good shape. It has four wings filled with stalls selling gold and silver jewellery, antique coins, dodgy watches, clothing and other such items. For photographers, the fresh-food section affords many opportunities. For a local lunch, there are a host of food stalls located on the western side,

### BEST LUXURY HOTELS IN NORTH PHNOM PENH

**Raffles Hotel Le Royal**
One of Asia's grand old dames, in the illustrious company of the Oriental in Bangkok and Raffles in Singapore. **$$$**

**Rosewood Phnom Penh**
An ultramodern luxury hotel in the iconic Vattanac Capital building; spacious rooms come with expansive views. **$$$**

**Hyatt Regency Phnom Penh**
Reception is in a restored heritage building. Views of the Royal Palace and National Museum from the rooms. **$$$**

which faces Monivong Blvd. The market is one of the best places to sample street food in the capital, with stalls selling everything from deep-fried insects to *bobor* (congee or rice porridge) and *kyteow* (noodle soup), all at bargain prices.

Psar Thmei is undoubtedly the best market for browsing. However, it has a reputation among Cambodians for overcharging on most products, known locally as 'shaving your head'.

# Exploring the Architecture of North Phnom Penh

ON THE TRAIL OF FRENCH INDOCHINE

Once known as the 'pearl of Asia', north Phnom Penh is where many of the best-preserved old buildings can be found. KA Architecture Tours (p63) offers walking and *cyclo* tours that include some of the most significant landmarks.

One of the most intact legacies of French Indochine, the post-office square is surrounded by grand old buildings a century or more old. The **main post office** itself dates from 1895 and is the place to send a postcard home. The excellent Cam Cup Cafe is located in a section of the building. Other notable structures include the restaurant Palais de la Poste, which was the former Banque Indochine and includes the heavy-duty safe doors that originally protected the savings; the former Manolis Hotel, used in the filming of *City of Ghosts* with Matt Dillon and Gérard Depardieu and is once again coming to life thanks to the **Le Manolis** wine bar and restaurant; and the former Hotel de la Poste, which is virtually in ruin, but rumours abound of a major restoration by the Royal Group.

Near Wat Phnom, the **National Library** is in a graceful old building constructed in 1924. During its rule, the Khmer Rouge turned the building into a stable and destroyed most of the books. Many were thrown out into the streets, where they were picked up by people, some of whom donated them back to the library after 1979; others used them as food wrappings. Today the library houses, among other things, a time-worn collection of English and French titles. Nearby, the **Raffles Hotel Le Royal** is a historic landmark as well as the best-known luxury hotel in the city. Between 1970 and 1975 many famous journalists working in Phnom Penh stayed here. More recent celebrated guests have included Joe Biden and Angelina Jolie.

## BEST CAFES IN PHNOM PENH

**Brown Coffee**
This flagship outlet of a homegrown coffee chain produces some of Phnom Penh's best coffee.

**Cam Cup Cafe**
This elegant little cafe serves fresh brews, herbal teas and some top-value Khmer dishes.

**Feel Good Cafe**
One of the only cafes in town to roast and grind its own coffee, with responsibly sourced blends.

**Museum Cafe**
Set in the spacious grounds of the National Museum, this is a cultured place for a cuppa.

### THE MAN WHO BUILT PHNOM PENH

Vann Molyvann is credited as the architect who shaped modern Phnom Penh, designing many of its 'New Khmer' architecture landmarks. These can be visited with **KA Architecture Tours** (p63). For more about him, check out the documentary *The Man Who Built Cambodia* (2014).

 **INTERNATIONAL EATERIES IN PHNOM PENH**

**Topaz**
The menu here includes delicate Burgundy snails drizzled in garlic, and steak tartare for those with rare tastes. **$$$**

**Mexicano**
In a swish new riverfront location, Mexicano offers delicious tacos, including pulled pork and succulent river fish. **$$**

**Hummus House**
A long-running Lebanese place offering a bite from Beirut, including the full range of kefta, falafels, grills and more. **$**

Located at the northern end of Monivong Blvd, the **French Embassy** played a significant role in the dramas that unfolded after the fall of Phnom Penh on 17 April 1975. About 800 foreigners and 600 Cambodians took refuge here. Within 48 hours, the Khmer Rouge informed the French vice-consul that they did not recognise diplomatic privileges – and if the Cambodians in the compound were not handed over, the lives of the foreigners inside would also be forfeited. Cambodian women married to foreigners could stay; Cambodian men married to foreign women could not. Foreigners wept as servants, colleagues, friends, lovers and husbands were escorted out of the embassy gates. At the end of the month, the foreigners were expelled from Cambodia by truck. Many of the Cambodians were never seen again. Today a high, white-washed wall surrounds the massive complex, and the French have returned to Cambodia in a big way, promoting French language and culture in their former colony.

Don't forget to include Wat Phnom (p59) in an architectural exploration of north Phnom Penh. If you end up here at dusk, you may see some giant fruit bats taking off from the trees in the gardens of the **Council for the Development of Cambodia (CDC)** to the east of the temple. This grand French building was home to the governor-general of Cambodia during the colonial era and was used as a main office by Pol Pot during his time as leader of Democratic Kampuchea from 1975 to 1979.

# It's All About the Money

MUSEUM OF ECONOMY AND MONEY

The name may not immediately conjure up excitement, but the **Sosoro Museum** is one of the best-presented contemporary museums in Cambodia, telling the story of money and Cambodia's economy, from the early days of barter trade at Angkor during the Khmer Empire, to the abolition of money by the Khmer Rouge and the destruction of the Central Bank, right through to the modern era of relative stability. Located in a grand civic building dating from 1908, the museum is full of interactive exhibits and brings the story of money (and absence of money) alive. Check out the website sosoro.nbc.org.kh for more details.

## BEST COCKTAIL BARS IN PHNOM PENH

**Elephant Bar**
The Raffles Hotel Le Royal bar has been drawing journalists, politicos and the rich and famous for almost a century. Happy hour is from 4pm to 9pm.

**Oskars**
This upscale gastropub blends bar and restaurant to perfection. Choose from creative cocktails, a huge wine list or a late-night feed.

**Batbong**
An always-packed speakeasy; look out for the Coca-Cola machine at the end of Langka Lane and locate the hidden button. Inside you'll find signature craft cocktails.

 **WHERE TO GO FOR GAY NIGHTLIFE**

**Blue Chilli**
Popular drag shows from Wednesday to Saturday nights at 11pm draw a mixed crowd of gay and straight visitors.

**Space Hair Salon**
This hair and beauty salon by day morphs into a lively gay bar by night thanks to the friendly owner and retro tunes.

**Prumsodun Ok & Natyarasa**
Cambodia's first gay dance company blends Khmer classics with a contemporary spirit at its evocative performances.

GODONGPHOTO/SHUTTERSTOCK ©

Elephant Bar

## BEST HOSTELS IN PHNOM PENH

**Mad Monkey $**
This vibrant hostel is justifiably popular and recently relocated to a former boutique hotel.

**The Eighty8 $**
A variety of private rooms, clean dorms and Japanese-style pods, plus a courtyard bar with a pool table and swimming pool.

**Big Easy $**
Located on the backpacker strip of St 172, this popular hostel has cheap dorms, private rooms and a lively bar.

**Onederz $**
This crashpad has a great location just off the riverfront, plus a rooftop pool and bar.

# Specialist Tours in Phnom Penh

ARCHITECTURE, ADVENTURE AND A MYSTERY

Those interested in exploring the French-era legacy of central Phnom Penh, diving into Cambodia's four main religions at local holy sites, or walking a circuit of new-wave Khmer architecture from the Sangkum era (1953–70) should look no further than **KA Architecture Tours**. One of these three signature tours runs each Sunday. Check its website (ka-tours.org) for dates and times. You can arrange private or custom tours any day of the week. While this is more expensive, rates drop the bigger your group.

City tour meets treasure hunt in an interactive adventure with **Urban Tales**, where you'll follow in the footsteps of a mysterious French explorer in search of a lost Khmer antique. Tours

## A POPULAR MOVIE LOCATION

The **post-office square** (61) has been repeatedly used as film location, having starred as a 1920s market in the movie *Two Brothers*, directed by Jean-Jacques Annaud, and in *City of Ghosts* by Matt Dillon, also starring Gérard Depardieu as a grumpy hotelier in Le Manolis.

**WHERE TO BUY SELF-CATERING SUPPLIES**

**Super Duper**
This rare 24-hour supermarket is handy for midnight munchies. Containers arrive direct from the US and Australia.

**Thai Huot**
A chain store stocking many French products, including the city's best cheese and cold-cuts selection.

**Lucky Market**
This original homegrown supermarket chain in Cambodia is still going strong, with branches all over the city.

## BEST-VALUE CAMBODIAN CUISINE IN PHNOM PENH

**18 Rik Reay BBQ $**
One of the best local barbecue restaurants near the riverfront, it's packed with locals thanks to its succulent grilled meat and seafood.

**Sovanna II BBQ $**
Always jumping with locals and a smattering of expats, due to the huge menu and cheap local beer.

**Nesat Seafood House $**
Incredibly cheap and fresh seafood cooked to perfection and served in trendy, sea-inspired surrounds.

**Boat Noodle Restaurant $**
Long-running Thai-Khmer restaurant, with delicious noodle soups and spicy curries.

MARK ANDREWS/ALAMY STOCK PHOTO ©

**Fried fish and mango salad, Boat Noodle Restaurant**

depart from the National Library and traverse about 3km of the historic centre. Bookings (urbantales-phnompenh.com) must be made at least 48 hours in advance.

Dedicated to supporting *cyclo* drivers in Phnom Penh, who often live on the streets while trying to pedal their way to a living wage, **Cyclo Tours** are a great way to see the sights. Themed trips such as pub crawls or cultural tours are also available.

**Village Quad Bike Trails** offers quad biking in the countryside around Phnom Penh. The quads are automatic – easy to handle for beginners (maximum two passengers per bike). Full-day tours take in Tonlé Bati and Phnom Tamao; despite the area's proximity to the capital, this is rural Cambodia and very beautiful. Longer trips are also available. Follow signs to the Killing Fields of Choeung Ek; it's about 300m before the entrance. Call ahead as numbers are limited.

 **BEST BARS WITH SPORTS SCREENS**

**Score**
With its cinema-sized screen and TV banks on every wall, this bar is the best place to watch big games.

**Hops Brewery**
An upscale beer garden that brews on-site, this place also shows plenty of football action.

**Duplex**
A self-styled Belgian tavern with an extensive beer selection, Duplex is also a wide-open space that shows big games.

# Good-Cause Shopping

HANDICRAFTS TO HELP CAMBODIA

There are lots of tasteful shops selling handicrafts and textiles to raise money for projects that assist disadvantaged Cambodians, including amputee landmine victims and trafficked and other vulnerable women. These are worthwhile places to spend some money, as it'll help to put a little bit back into the country.

The **Cambodian Handicraft Association** sells fine handmade silk clothing, scarves, toys and bags produced by victims of landmines.

**Daughters of Cambodia** is an NGO that runs a range of programmes to train and assist former sex workers and victims of human trafficking. The fashionable clothes, bags and accessories here are made with ecofriendly cotton and natural dyes.

One of the best all-round handicraft stores, **Rajana** aims to promote fair wages and training. It has some quirky metalware products, jewellery, bamboo crafts, lovely shirts, gorgeous wall hangings and candles: you name it, Rajana probably has it.

Established by Princess Marie, **Sobbhana** is a not-for-profit organisation training women in traditional weaving. Its stylish boutique has beautiful silks.

At the entrance to Wat Than is **Watthan Artisans**, selling silk and other products, including contemporary handbags, made by a cooperative of landmine victims and polio sufferers. It also has on-site woodworking and weaving workshops.

## WHERE TO EAT & DRINK IN PHNOM PENH

**Keo 'Thida' Chenda** is the owner of Back Street Bar.

What made you open a bar? It's not common for a woman to run a bar in Cambodia. Even my family doesn't really understand, but I love it, as it allows me to be an independent woman, and I found my community here.

Do you have a favourite eatery in the area? There's a huge variety, from Cambodian street food to fine French food. Nobody goes hungry on Bassac Lane.

What's the best bar in Bassac Lane? We work hard to make Back Street Bar the best spot on the lane, but there are lots of great bars nearby. But sure, for me, it is Back Street or bust.

## WHERE TO GET A BURGER IN PHNOM PENH

**Burgershack**
One of the city's best burger places, offering originals like the Quarter-Flounder (fishburger). $

**The Vine**
Much loved for its tasty burgers, this place also doubles as a cocktail bar and hair salon! $

**Garage Sale**
Another bar-and-burger joint in the Langka Lane area, specialising in pounded 'smashburgers'. $

# SOUTH PHNOM PENH

## BUSTLING MARKETS AND BUZZING BARS

Head south to hit the hipster districts of town and play in the local lanes. St 240½ was the original dive alley and has been rebranded as Palace Lane, complete with lively bars and graffiti. Bassac Lane is the don among the laneways and offers a huge number of wining and dining options in a small space.

The Russian Market is one of the biggest draws here: a chaotic and cramped shopping area piled high with clothing and souvenirs. It's also the epicentre of the happening Tuol Tom Pong district, which has seen an explosion of restaurants, cafes and bars.

However, for most visitors, the most moving experiences are associated with the Khmer Rouge genocide – the Tuol Sleng Genocide Museum and the Killing Fields of Choeung Ek. While Cambodia has completely reinvented itself in the past couple of decades, these poignant sites demonstrate how far the country has come.

**TOP TIP**

Spend an afternoon and evening in the, as there's plenty on offer, including retail therapy, street-food grazing and busy bars. Wander around the labyrinthine market before decamping to the car-park food court for some street eats. Then check out the market from a different angle at Sundown Social Club on St 440.

JEFF CAGLE/SHUTTERSTOCK ©

**Russian Market (p70)**

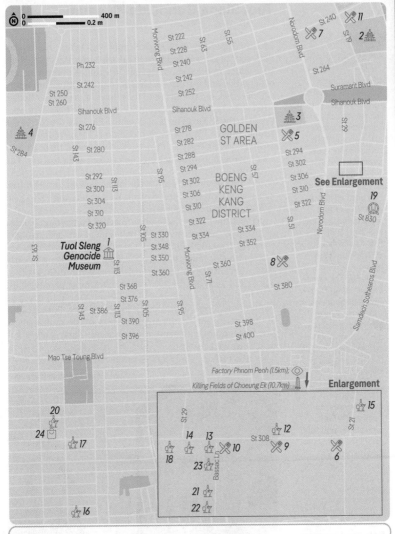

## HIGHLIGHTS
1 Tuol Sleng
Genocide Museum

## SIGHTS
2 Wat Botum
3 Wat Langka
4 Wat Moha Montrei

## EATING
5 Burgershack
6 Elia Greek Kitchen
7 Enso Cafe
8 Farm To Table
(see 5) Garage Sale
(see 5) Langka Bistro
9 Mama Wong's
10 Piccola Italia Da Luigi
11 Planta

## DRINKING
## & NIGHTLIFE
12 Back Street Bar
(see 11) Bong
Bong Bong
13 Casa Diego
14 Harry's Bar
15 Hub Street Cocktails
16 La Petanque
17 Long After Dark

(see 14) Phnom Penh
Yacht Club
18 Red Bar
19 Samai Distillery
20 Sundown Social Club
21 The Library
22 Welsh Embassy
23 White Rabbit

## SHOPPING
24 Russian Market

# Tuol Sleng Genocide Museum

KHMER ROUGE FACTORY OF DEATH

In 1975 Tuol Svay Prey High School was taken over by Pol Pot's security forces and turned into Security Prison 21 (S-21; tuolsleng.gov.kh); it soon became the country's largest centre of detention and torture. S-21 has been turned into a **museum**, which serves as a testament to the crimes of the Khmer Rouge.

Between 1975 and 1978, some 20,000 people held here were taken to the Killing Fields of Choeung Ek. Like the Nazis, the Khmer Rouge leaders were meticulous in keeping records of their barbarism. Each prisoner who passed through S-21 was photographed, sometimes before and after torture. The museum displays include room after room of harrowing B&W photographs; virtually all of the men, women and children pictured were later killed. Several Westerners were also held at S-21 before being murdered.

As the Khmer Rouge 'revolution' reached ever greater heights of insanity, the torturers and executioners who worked here were in turn killed by those who took their places.

When the Vietnamese army liberated Phnom Penh in early 1979, there were only seven prisoners alive at S-21, all of whom had used their skills, such as painting or photography, to stay alive. Fourteen others had been tortured to death as Vietnamese forces were closing in on the city. Photographs of their gruesome deaths are on display in the rooms where their decomposing corpses were found. Their graves are nearby in the courtyard.

Needless to say, Tuol Sleng is not for the squeamish.

**Tuol Sleng Genocide Museum**

THANACHET MAYIANG/SHUTTERSTOCK ©

# The Killing Fields of Choeung Ek

A MEMORIAL FOR VICTIMS OF GENOCIDE

Between 1975 and 1978, about 20,000 men, women, children and infants who had been detained and tortured at S-21 prison were transported to the extermination camp of Choeung Ek. It is a peaceful **memorial site** today, where visitors can learn of the horrors that unfolded here decades ago. Admission includes an excellent audio tour, available in several languages.

The remains of 8985 people, many of whom were bound and blindfolded, were exhumed in 1980 from mass graves in this one-time longan orchard; 43 of the 129 communal graves here have been left untouched. Fragments of human bone and bits of cloth are scattered around the disinterred pits. More than 8000 skulls, arranged by gender and age, are visible behind the clear glass panels of the Memorial Stupa, which was erected in 1988.

The audio tour includes stories by those who survived the Khmer Rouge, plus a chilling account by Him Huy, a Choeung Ek guard and executioner, about some of the techniques they used to kill innocent and defenceless prisoners, including women and children. There's also a museum here with some interesting information on the Khmer Rouge leadership and the ongoing trial. A memorial ceremony is held annually at Choeung Ek on 20 May.

The site, a half-day visit by *tuk-tuk* about 7.5km south of the city limits, is well signposted in English.

## THE KHMER ROUGE REGIME IN NUMBERS

It is still not known exactly how many Cambodians died at the hands of the Khmer Rouge during the three years, eight months and 20 days of its rule. The Vietnamese claimed three million deaths, while foreign experts long considered the number closer to one million. Yale University researchers undertaking ongoing investigations estimated that the figure was close to two million. Hundreds of thousands of people were executed by the Khmer Rouge leadership, while hundreds of thousands more died of famine and disease.

**Memorial Stupa, Killing Fields of Choeung Ek**

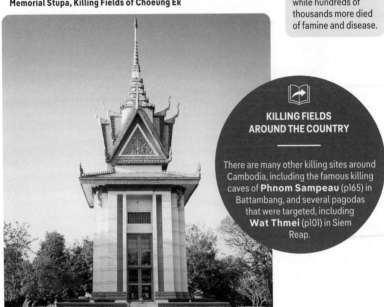

TELNYAWKA/GETTY IMAGE ©

### KILLING FIELDS AROUND THE COUNTRY

There are many other killing sites around Cambodia, including the famous killing caves of **Phnom Sampeau** (p165) in Battambang, and several pagodas that were targeted, including **Wat Thmei** (p101) in Siem Reap.

IFOODJOURNEY/SHUTTERSTOCK ©

**Textiles, Russian Market**

**BEST BRUNCH
MENUS IN
PHNOM PENH**

**Enso Cafe $$**
A mod Australian cafe
with tasty brunch
treats and a hangover-
tastic *chakchouka*
(poached eggs in
tomato, pepper and
onion sauce).

**The Shop $**
Sandwiches and
salads with creative
ingredients such as
wild lentils and forest
mushrooms, plus
delectable pastries,
cakes and chocolates.

**Farm to Table $**
Aiming to promote
organic farming, Farm
to Table offers all-day
breakfasts, salads,
sandwiches and
shakes. It has a lush
garden setting.

MORE IN SOUTH PHNOM PENH

# Bargain in the Russian Market

SHOP TILL YOU DROP

This sweltering **bazaar** is the one market all visitors should
come to at least once during a trip to Phnom Penh. The Russian
Market, so named because the predominantly Russian expat
population shopped here in the 1980s, is the place to buy sou-
venirs and discounted name-brand clothing. We can't vouch
for the authenticity of everything, but, along with plenty of
knockoffs, you'll find genuine articles stitched in local factories.

Brands you're likely to see include Banana Republic, Billa-
bong, Calvin Klein, Colombia Sportswear, Gap and Next. There's
also a large range of handicrafts and antiquities (many fake),
including miniature Buddhas, woodcarvings, betel-nut boxes,
silks, silver jewellery, musical instruments and so on. Bargain
hard, as hundreds of tourists pass through here every day.

 **GUESTHOUSES IN SOUTH PHNOM PENH**

**Mini Banana Guesthouse**
Decent dorms with sturdy
bunks, comfortable rooms and
a lively little bar-restaurant in
Langka Lane. **$**

**Smiley's Hotel**
Smiley's is a huge seven-storey
hotel with 40 spacious rooms
that border on chic. And yes,
there's a lift. **$**

**Tat Guesthouse**
A superfriendly spot with a
breezy rooftop hang-out for
chilling. Functional fan and
air-con rooms. **$**

There are some good food stalls here if you are feeling peckish, and the wider Russian Market area has become very hip, with lots of cafes, restaurants and bars. To view the Russian Market from a different angle, head to rooftop bar **Sundown Social Club** on St 440, and choose from sundowners, including Club Tropicana–inspired cocktails and craft beers, and the menu of innovative pub grub and bar snacks. **Long After Dark** is a cool and cosy bar that will keep you hanging around the market area long after dark, with its combination of rare single-malt whiskies, Cambodian craft beers and a vinyl collection that spins on weekends. Or check out bar-restaurant **La Petanque**, for some petanque (boules) action day or night. It's tucked away in a little alley off St 155, where a wide range of drinks, live-music events and a lively French expat crowd round things off.

## Discover Art at Factory Phnom Penh

A PRODUCTION LINE OF CREATIVITY

Factory Phnom Penh, a 3.4-hectare Levi's garment factory 2km south of the city centre, was completely transformed in 2018 into a **graffiti-covered hub** for entrepreneurs, artists and creative thinkers. On a ride through the sprawling campus (there are 50 free-to-use bikes) you'll encounter several art galleries, most of them run by Kbach Arts, as well as a skate park, trampoline park, craft brewery, stage, cinema, market and the Workspace 1 coworking space. It's virtually impossible to visit this aspirational complex and leave uninspired.

Kbach covers three galleries over 400 sq metres. Its mission is to provide a platform for young Khmer artists to showcase their work, while also utilising resident artists from abroad to serve as mentors. Dazzling murals cover the exterior, and the interior houses urban and mixed-medium art.

## Bar-Hopping in Bassac Lane

PHNOM PENH PUB CRAWL

Bassac Lane has cemented its reputation as the new **bohemian district** of Phnom Penh and is now one of the most happening nightspots in the city. The name refers to a small alley that leads south off St 308 and is packed with hole-in-the-wall bars. This is an ideal area to embark upon a pub crawl or bar hop, as there

---

### PHNOM PENH DISTILLERIES

**Seekers** produces an excellent range of gins, like the purple-coloured Jason Kong Gin made with butterfly pea flowers. Visit its distillery in the far south of town for a guided tasting tour (Thursday to Sunday) or head down at the weekend when there are tasty meals, free-flow gin deals and regular live music.

**Samai Distillery** makes zesty rum with local sugar cane and opens its doors on Thursday nights for lavish parties, typically with guest bartenders and live music. The artisan rums, including one with Kampot pepper, taste far superior to mass-market spirits. Across the street, the shop sells bottled rum in all shapes and sizes.

---

### THE ORIGIN OF BOPHANA

Award-winning French-Cambodian director Rithy Panh's 1996 film *Bophana* tells the true story of Hout Bophana, a young woman, and Ly Sitha, a regional Khmer Rouge leader, who fall in love and are executed at **S-21 Prison** (p68) for their 'crime'.

---

 **INTERNATIONAL RESTAURANTS IN THE RUSSIAN MARKET AREA**

**Brooklyn Bistro**
Stylish American diner popular with expats in the know. Proper pizzas, a menu of wings and delicious deli sandwiches. **$$**

**Buffalo Sister**
Famous for its Sunday roast, plus a roast pork and apple sauce sandwich and grilled veggie and falafel wraps. **$**

**Trattoria Bello**
Hidden away near the Russian Market, serving some of the most delicious pizzas in town at low prices, as well as pastas. **$**

are so many places crowded into this small area, which includes St 308 and is now even spilling onto St 21.

Start out at the strategic vantage point of **Phnom Penh Yacht Club**, occupying the entrance to Bassac Lane on St 308. Happy hour is from 5pm to 7pm and they mix some potent cocktails. If you're feeling peckish, directly opposite is **Casa Diego**, a homely little kitchen cantina with authentic tapas and a spacious upstairs. Continuing down the lane, there are lots of potential diversions, including **Harry's Bar**, with an L-shaped rooftop terrace that heaves with the city's youngsters; **White Rabbit**, an *Alice in Wonderland*-themed bar with magnifying glasses to select the original cocktails in the low light; and **The Library**, where the shelves are stocked with classic reads (happy hour from 5pm to 7pm). Further down towards the end of the lane is the **Welsh Embassy**, though it most definitely does not issue UK visas. It does have some Welsh beer, however.

Beyond Bassac Lane in St 308, the crawl continues in no particular order. **Red Bar** is a friendly little local bar with cheap pours, ensuring drinkers find themselves lingering long into the night. Further east lies **Back Street Bar**, one of the most rockin' places in town, with a lively crowd, occasional live music and quiz nights. There are also some great places to eat (and drink) along this stretch if you're hungry. **Piccola Italia Da Luigi** is a bustling kerbside eatery and has a claim to some of the best pizza in town. **Mama Wong's** brings a contemporary touch to the city's Chinese dining scene, serving up inventive dumplings, noodle bowls and Asian tapas such as duck pancakes or chilli and garlic prawns. Or get the Greek with a fix at **Elia Greek Kitchen**, an inviting taverna serving up multiples mezes, delicious gyros and huge sharing platters.

There are lots of bars to continue on to, but one of the best is **Hub Street Cocktails**, beloved by expats and Cambodians alike. Cheap craft cocktails and killer street cuisine collide to great effect at this buzzing bamboo bar, where it feels like you've stumbled upon a familiar yet exotic block party.

## Wats in South Phnom Penh

ON THE TRAIL OF OLD TEMPLES

Phnom Penh has a wealth of old wats (also known as pagodas or temples) and some of the most interesting are located in the south of the city.

**Wat Moha Montrei** was named in honour of one of King Monivong's ministers, Chakrue Ponn, who initiated the founding of the pagoda (*moha montrei* means 'the great

**CREATIVE CAFES IN PHNOM PENH**

**Integrite**
This cafe/restaurant/ bar is a bite-sized slice of sophistication, with fair-trade coffee and detox juice. **$**

**Java Creative Cafe**
Its creative menu includes crisp salads, homemade sandwiches, burgers and excellent coffee from several continents. **$**

**Lot 369**
Healthy bowls, all-day breakfasts and heat-beating smoothies in a breezy open-air setting. **$**

**Red Bar, Bassac Lane**

Phnom Penh is criss-crossed by little lanes and several of these are now emerging to give Bassac Lane a run for its money.

**Palace Lane** is the new name for the old St 240½. Popular spots include **Craft**, a bar-restaurant with beer, cocktails, comfort food and a great-value weekend brunch, and sister restaurant **Planta**. Nearby is **Bong Bong Bong**, a cocktail bar with Franco-Khmer owners who ensure that strangers become friends.

**Langka Lane** runs off St 51 in the BKK district, and is home to lots of cool little bars and restaurants, including the excellent **Langka Bistro** and some top burger joints such as **Burgershack** and **Garage Sale**.

minister'). The cement *vihara*, topped with a 35m-high tower, was completed in 1970. Between 1975 and 1979 it was used by the Khmer Rouge to store rice and corn. Check out the assorted Cambodian touches incorporated into the wall murals of the *vihara*, which tell the story of Buddha. The angels accompanying Buddha to heaven are dressed as classical Khmer dancers, while the assembled officials wear the white military uniforms of the Sihanouk period. The wat is close to the Olympic Stadium.

One of the oldest temples in Phnom Penh, **Wat Langka** was originally constructed in 1422. It is a colourful Buddhist temple in the heart of the city (near the Independence Monument) that was established as a sanctuary for holy writings of the Trinity.

Another historic wat, originally built by King Ponhea Yat (1405–67) in the 15th century, **Wat Botum** is officially known as Wat Botum Watey

**BRANCHING OUT FROM BASSAC LANE**

Several of the businesses in the Bassac Lane area have other branches in the area around the **Russian Market** (p70), including the excellent Elia Greek Kitchen and the Welsh Embassy (also known as the Welsh Consulate).

### WHERE TO DINE FOR A CAUSE IN SOUTH PHNOM PENH

**Daughters Cafe**
The Daughters of Cambodia visitor centre's cafe features soups, smoothies, cupcakes and Western mains. **$**

**Eleven One Kitchen**
A training restaurant serving healthy Cambodian cuisine, with pesticide-free vegetables and affordable set-lunch deals. **$**

**Jars of Clay**
More than a bakery, with authentic Khmer mains, plus drinks and welcome air-con; 10% of profits go to those in need. **$**

## WHY I LOVE PHNOM PENH

**Nick Ray,** writer

I have lived in Phnom Penh for more than 20 years now and have witnessed huge changes as it moved from a post-conflict zone to a contemporary capital that can compete with the best in the region. The real attraction of Phnom Penh is the way it blends Asia old and new together so seamlessly, so you can wander through a traditional market for a local lunch, then enjoy a world-class meal in a sophisticated brasserie at night. The city's nightlife is legendary and places like Bassac Lane have helped to put it on the map. Ultimately though, it's all about the people, and Phnom Penh is one of the friendliest capitals you're likely to find anywhere in the world.

AUTUMN SKY PHOTOGRAPHY/SHUTTERSTOCK ©

**Wat Botum**

Reacheveraram, or the 'Temple of Lotus built by the King'. This Buddhist temple with its saffron coloured robes flapping in the wind is particularly photogenic and is located opposite Wat Botum Park.

### WATCH OUT FOR HOMEMADE HOOCH

As well as sophisticated spirits produced for a discerning market by new **distilleries** (p71), there is also the more traditional *sraa sor* (rice wine), popular in the countryside around Phnom Penh. It is best avoided as it is often laced with methanol.

## MALLS IN PHNOM PENH

**Aeon Mall**
This Japanese-run mall has international boutiques, dining outlets, a multiplex cinema and a bowling alley.

**Chip Mong Noro Mall**
This semi-alfresco mall is popular with a younger crowd thanks to international cafes and sports-brand retailers.

**Sorya Mall**
The first major mall in town, with shops aplenty, a food court, a central location and superb views over Psar Thmei.

# AROUND PHNOM PENH

## RURAL RHYTHMS AND HILLTOP TEMPLES

While Phnom Penh is the area's main attraction for visitors, there are lots of interesting places within day-tripping distance that offer a stark contrast to the bustling urban environment.

Koh Dach (Silk Island), just 5km north of Phnom Penh, is a step back to a soporific, slower-paced way of life. Further afield lie several old temples, including the shimmering stupas of Udong and the Angkorian temples of Tonlé Bati and Phnom Chisor.

The impressive Phnom Tamao Wildlife Rescue Centre offers immersive tours to meet elephants, tigers and other rare mammals, while Kirirom National Park and its expansive pine forests have even more expansive views over the Cardamom Mountains.

The Cardamoms offer a near-wild escape from Phnom Penh. There are several emerging destinations within a few hours of the capital, including spectacular waterfalls like Chreav and Anlong Svay, and the rolling mountains and infinite vistas of Khnong Phsar.

### TOP TIP

For experienced riders, a motorbike is a good way to explore some of the sights around Phnom Penh, including the hilltop stupas of Udong and the temples of Tonlé Bati and Phnom Chisor. A bicycle is the best way to get around Koh Dach, a tranquil slice of rural life near Phnom Penh.

CAMNET/SHUTTERSTOCK ©

Udong (p78)

# AROUND PHNOM PENH

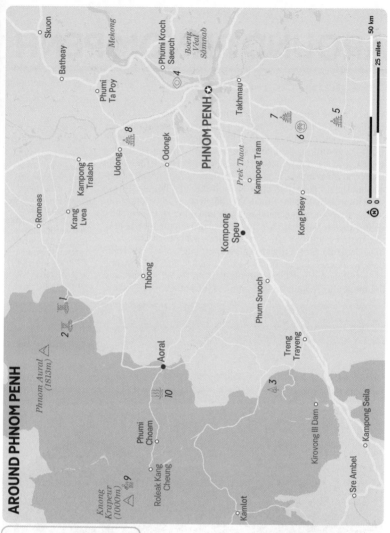

**SIGHTS**
1 Anlong
Svay Waterfall
2 Chreav Waterfall
3 Kirirom
National Park
4 Koh Dach
5 Phnom Chisor
6 Phnom Tamao
Wildlife Rescue
Centre

7 Tonlé Bati
8 Udong

**ACTIVITIES,
COURSES &
TOURS**
9 Khnong Phsar
10 Te Tuk
Pus Hot Springs

Udong (p78)

# A Rural Escape to Silk Island

EXPERIENCE A KOH DACH MOMENT

Known as 'Silk Island' by foreigners, **Koh Dach** is actually a pair of islands lying in the Mekong River about 5km northeast of the Japanese Friendship Bridge. It's an easy, half-day excursion for those who want to experience the 'real Cambodia', with the hustle-bustle of Phnom Penh light years away.

The name derives from the preponderance of silk weavers who inhabit the islands. When you arrive by ferry, you may be approached by one or more smiling women who speak a bit of English and will invite you to their house to observe weavers in action and – they hope – buy a *krama* (checked scarf), sarong or other silk items. If you're in the market for silk, you might follow them and have a look. Otherwise, feel free to smile back and politely decline their offer. You'll see plenty of weavers as you journey around the islands.

Most visitors to Koh Dach stay overnight in Phnom Penh. However, there's now a handful of homestays and guesthouses on Koh Dach, where you can experience life with a local family. Most of them are within walking distance of each other in the northern part of the island.

There are some food stalls and local restaurants on Koh Dach, but they are fairly rustic. The best restaurants are located at the guesthouses and homestays. Fresh fruit is available, including coconut and sugar-cane juice. The best options are the dry-season picnic stalls on the northern tip of the island.

**GETTING TO KOH DACH**

*Tuk-tuk* drivers offer half-day tours to Koh Dach, while boat tours from the tourist-boat dock run daily – operators include **Memorable Cambodia** (memorablecambodia. com).

Otherwise, hire a mountain bike or motorbike and go it alone. Ferries cross the Mekong in three places – the southernmost ferry crossing is the most convenient. To get here, cross the Japanese Friendship Bridge and follow NH6 for 4km, then turn right just after the Medical Supply Pharmaceutical Enterprise. Then turn left and follow a small dirt road north for about 500m until you see the ferry crossing.

**Silk weaver, Koh Dach**

RIGHT: JOERG-DRESCHER/SHUTTERSTOCK ©. LEFT: IGOR_SINUS/SHUTTERSTOCK ©

NEWEY/SHUTTERSTOCK ©

**Damrei Sam Poan, Udong**

**FOOD TOURS IN PHNOM PENH**

There are several good street-food tours on offer in the Cambodian capital. **Urban Forage** (urbanforage.co) has long-running street-food tours of the city, with stops for succulent ribs (veggie options available), traditional Cambodian dishes, local desserts and tropical fruits. There are even some bugs on offer for the brave, all washed down with draught beer.

Explore the history of Cambodia through its food on excellent culinary tours with **Lost Plate** (lostplate. com), which take in four off-the-beaten-path restaurants and a craft-beer and cocktail bar. The evening *tuk-tuk* tour kicks off at 5.30pm and tells the history of Cambodia through its iconic dishes.

MORE AROUND PHNOM PENH

# The Old Royal Capital of Udong

STUPA-STUDDED HILLS NEAR PHNOM PENH

This **town**, whose name means 'victorious' in Khmer, served as the capital of Cambodia between 1618 and 1866, during which time 'victorious' was an optimistic epithet, as Cambodia was in terminal decline. A number of kings, including King Norodom, were crowned here. The main attractions today are the twin humps of Phnom Udong, which have several stupas on them. Both ends of the ridge have good views of the Cambodian countryside. Phnom Udong fills up with locals at weekends, but is quiet during the week.

The larger main ridge – the one you'll hit first if approaching from NH5 – is known as **Phnom Preah Reach Throap** (Hill of the Royal Fortune), so named because a 16th-century Khmer king is said to have hidden the national treasury here during a war with the Thais.

 **MORE PLACES TO STAY IN PHNOM PENH**

**SLA Boutique Hostel**
This shoes-off 'poshpacker' is the city's cleanest hostel, with dorms and sleek privates, all with crisp white linens. **$**

**You Khin Art House**
Tucked away down St 830, it's considerably bigger on the inside and has the feel of a large private home. **$$**

**Plantation**
Ticks all the boxes, with high ceilings, stylish fixtures, open-plan bathrooms and balconies, plus two swimming pools. **$$$**

Ascend the 509 steps of the main, monkey-lined north stairway from the parking area and the first structure you come to at the top of the ridge is a modern temple containing 5334 small Buddhas. There's also a relic of the Buddha, brazenly stolen in 2013 (though later recovered). Follow the path behind this stupa along the ridge and you'll come to three large stupas. The first (northwesternmost) is **Damrei Sam Poan**, built by King Chey Chetha II (r 1618–26). The second stupa, **Ang Doung**, is decorated with coloured tiles; it was built in 1891 by King Norodom. The last stupa is **Mak Proum**. Decorated with *garudas* (mythical half-man, half-bird creatures), floral designs and elephants, it has four faces on top.

Continuing along the path beyond Mak Proum, you'll pass a stone *vihara* with a cement roof and a revered five-star general seated inside, then arrive at a clearing dotted by structures, including three small *vihara* and a stupa. The first *vihara* is **Vihear Prak Neak**. Inside is a seated Buddha, guarded by a mythical naga serpent-being ('prak neak' means 'protected by a naga'). The second structure also has a seated Buddha inside. The third structure is **Vihear Preah Keo**, containing a statue of Preah Ko, the sacred bull; the original statue was taken by the Thais long ago. Beyond this, near the stupa, red and black mountain lions guard the entrance to a modern brick-walled *vihara*.

Continue southeast along a lotus-flower-lined concrete path to the most impressive structure on Phnom Preah Reach Throap, **Vihear Preah Ath Roes**. The *vihara* and an enormous Buddha, dedicated in 1911 by King Sisowath, were blown up by the Khmer Rouge in 1977. The *vihara*, supported by eight enormous columns, has since been rebuilt, as was the 20m-high Buddha.

At the base of the main (northern) staircase leading up to Phnom Preah Reach Throap, near the restaurants, is a **memorial** to the victims of Pol Pot. It contains the bones of some of the people who were buried in approximately 100 mass graves, each containing about a dozen bodies. Instruments of torture were unearthed along with the bones when some of the pits were disinterred in 1981 and 1982.

Southeast of Phnom Preah Reach Throap, the smaller ridge has two structures and several stupas. **Ta San Mosque** faces westward towards Mecca. Across the plains to the south of the mosque, you can see **Phnom Vihear Leu**, a small hill on which a *vihara* stands between two white poles. To the right of the *vihara* is a building that was used as a prison under Pol Pot's rule. To the left of the *vihara* and below it is the **Arey Ka Sap** pagoda.

## BEST FASHION BOUTIQUES IN PHNOM PENH

**Ambre**
The perfect showcase for Cambodian fashion designer Romyda Keth's stunning silk collection, plus stylish homewares.

**Artisans Angkor**
Classy Phnom Penh branch of the venerable Siem Reap sculpture and silk specialist, supporting craftspeople across the country.

**Muoy Chorm**
This outlet in the F3 Friends Futures Factory has expressive evening wear and creative casual clothing.

**Scarlet Fiber**
Lovingly handmade clothes, from casual cotton and linen daywear to tailor-made evening couture and wedding dresses.

 **PLACES TO STAY ON KOH DACH (SILK ISLAND)**

**Bonnivoit Homestay**
Set in a traditional old wooden house, and run by a tour guide who really understands what guests need. **$**

**Le Kroma Villa**
Boutique accommodation at this attractive French-run establishment with its own swimming pool. **$**

**The Balé**
Not exactly on Koh Dach, but this luxury retreat has unblemished views across the Mekong to Silk Island. **$$$**

A guide can offer more context on everything. If you don't bring one from Phnom Penh, ask for Oy at the small booth where you pay your entrance fee. He has no phone or email, but was born in Udong, speaks pretty good English and knows a lot about the history of the place.

Most day-trippers to Udong base themselves in Phnom Penh or stop en route from the capital to Battambang. The renowned **Cambodia Vipassana Dhura Buddhist Meditation Center** is at Udong if you want to work on a deeper sleep. There are scores of food stalls around the bustling main parking area at the base of the northern staircase.

Udong is around 37km from the capital. Take a Kompong Chhnang bus (one hour to Udong). It will drop you off at the access road to Phnom Udong; from there it's 3km. To return to Phnom Penh, flag down a bus on NH5. Taxis and *tuk-tuks* from Phnom Penh can take you to Udong for the day. Several hostels promote half-day tours here, which typically include a stop in the silversmith village of Kompong Luong to see craftspeople at work. If you're going it alone by motorbike, head north out of Phnom Penh on NH5 and turn left (south) at a prominent archway between the 36km and 37km markers.

## Old Temples of Tonlé Bati

TOUCH OF ANGKOR NEAR THE CAPITAL

Tonlé Bati is the collective name for a pair of old **Angkorian-era temples**, Ta Prohm and Yeay Peau, and a popular lakeside picnic area. It's worth a detour if you are on the way from the capital to Phnom Tamao and Phnom Chisor.

You can eat at one of many picnic restaurants set on stilts over the water (enjoying the local delicacy – frogs' legs) and hire an inner tube to float around the lake. Just avoid Tonlé Bati at weekends, when it's mobbed with locals. Renting a motorbike or car from Phnom Penh is the easiest way to get here.

The laterite temple of **Ta Prohm** was built by King Jayavarman VII (r 1181–1219) on the site of a 6th-century Khmer shrine. The main sanctuary consists of five chambers, each containing a modern Buddha. The facades of the chambers feature intricate and well-preserved bas-reliefs. In the central chamber is a *linga* (phallic symbol) that shows signs of the destruction wrought by the Khmer Rouge.

What little remains of the temple **Yeay Peau**, named after King Prohm's mother, can be found 150m north of Ta Prohm on the grounds of a modern pagoda. Legend has it that Peau gave birth to a son, Prohm. When Prohm discovered his father was King Preah Ket Mealea, he set off to live with the

**PHNOM PENH
TO HO CHI MINH
CITY BY BUS**

The original Bavet–Moc Bai land crossing between Vietnam and Cambodia (open 8am to 8pm) has seen steady traffic for more than two decades. The easiest way to get to Ho Chi Minh City (HCMC; Saigon) is to catch a six-hour international bus from Phnom Penh. There are several companies making this trip. At the border long lines entering either country are not uncommon, but otherwise it's a straightforward process provided you purchase a Vietnamese visa in advance (should you require one). If you are not on the international bus, it's not hard to find onward transport to HCMC or elsewhere.

 **CHINESE AND VIETNAMESE RESTAURANTS IN PHNOM PENH**

**Sam Too Restaurant**
Chinese Khmers swear this eatery has the best food, including its Sam Doo fried rice and fresh dim sum. **$**

**Magnolia**
The affordable menu features wafer-thin *banh xeo* (Vietnamese savoury pancakes) and other classics. **$**

**Ngon**
This place brings Vietnamese and Cambodian street food to a sophisticated setting. **$**

**Iguana, Phnom Tamao Wildlife Rescue Centre**

**BEST VEGAN RESTAURANTS IN PHNOM PENH**

**Backyard Cafe $**
A cool and contemporary superfoods cafe; come for raw smoothies, gluten-free protein bowls and vegan burgers.

**Vibe Cafe $**
The capital's first 100%-vegan restaurant creates original homemade superfood recipes, including the signature Ritual Bowl and innovative cleansing juices (10% of profits go to the Good Vibe Foundation).

**Mercy House $**
This outdoor vegetarian eatery serves Japanese dishes with a Cambodian twist. Try the teppan-yaki hot plates with mock meat or the sweet-and-sour 'pork ribs'.

king. After a few years he returned to his mother but did not recognise her; taken by her beauty, he asked her to become his wife. He refused to believe Peau's protests that she was his mother. To put off his advances and avoid the impending marriage, Peau suggested a temple-building contest whereby the winner would get their wish. When Yeay Peau was completed first, Prohm was forced to acknowledge Peau as his mother.

## The Wild Things of Phnom Tamao

THE FRONT LINE IN ANIMAL PROTECTION

The wonderful **Phnom Tamao Wildlife Rescue Centre** (phnomtamaozoologicalpark.com) is home to gibbons, sun bears, elephants, tigers, lions, deer, enormous pythons and a massive bird enclosure. The animals were all taken from poachers or abusive owners and receive care and shelter here as part of a sustainable breeding programme. Wherever possible, they're released back into the wild once they have recovered.

### ORIGINAL STORES IN PHNOM PENH

**Smateria**
Smateria's speciality is bags, including quirky kids' backpacks made from fishing net and other recycled materials.

**Space Four Zero**
This pop-art gallery pays tribute to the lost artists of Cambodia's golden years with its 'sticky fingers' art prints.

**Tuol Sleng Shoes**
Scary name, but there's nothing scary about the price of these custom-fit, handmade shoes.

## BEST FAMILY ACTIVITIES IN PHNOM PENH

**Coconut Park**
Fountains for kids to cool off, an adventure playground, an indoor rollerdome, a Lego laboratory and ceramics painting, plus an inviting cafe for parents.

**The Factory**
A good spot for fading parents thanks to a range of activities including trampoline and skateboard parks. There's also a playground, a cafe and a weekend market.

**Urban Space**
A contemporary adventure playground with an inviting swimming pool in the central courtyard. The restaurant here has live music at weekends.

**Phnom Chisor**

Occupying a vast site south of the capital, the centre feels like a sustainable zoo crossed with a safari park. Many of the animals have plenty of room to roam in enclosures that have been improved and expanded over the years with help from Wildlife Alliance, Free the Bears and other international wildlife NGOs. However, some animals have rather basic enclosures due to a lack of funding, which may be distressing to some visitors.

The centre operates breeding and release programmes for a number of globally threatened species, including pileated gibbons, smooth-coated otters and Siamese crocodiles, and provides a safe home to other iconic species, such as tigers and the gentle giants – Asian elephants. The centre is also home to the world's largest captive collection of Malayan sun bears, and you'll find a walk-through area with macaques, deer and a huge aviary.

### VISIT THE WILDLIFE ALLIANCE

As well as operating the immersive behind-the-scenes tour at Phnom Tamao Wildlife Rescue Centre, the Wildlife Alliance team also operates the **Wildlife Alliance Release Station** (p206) near Chi Phat in the heart of the Cardamom Mountains, with a flagship release programme.

### WHERE TO GET AN ITALIAN-FOOD FIX IN PHNOM PENH

**4Ps Pizza**
This Japanese-run newcomer is incredibly popular thanks to split-topping pizzas and creative fusion flavours. **$**

**Limoncello**
Simply outstanding pizza (among the city's best), great desserts, plus limoncello shots to wash it all down. **$$**

**Terrazza**
Bulging antipasto platters, ambitious pastas and Neapolitan pizza available by the metre. *Saluti!* **$$**

Cambodia's wildlife is usually very difficult to spot, as larger mammals inhabit remote areas of the country, so Phnom Tamao is the perfect place to discover more about the country's incredible variety of animals. This is not a typical zoo: remember that these animals have been rescued from traffickers and poachers and need a home. Visitors who come here will be doing their own small bit to help in the protection and survival of Cambodia's varied wildlife.

**Wildlife Alliance** (wildlifealliance.org) offers a behind-the-scenes tour that includes access to feeding areas and the nursery area. **Free the Bears** (freethebears.org) has a 'Bear Care Tour', which allows guests to help out the on-site team for the day. These tours include transport from Phnom Penh. Otherwise, the easiest option is a rental motorbike or car from Phnom Penh in combination with a visit to Tonlé Bati or Phnom Chisor.

In 2022 Phnom Tamao was threatened with closure due to the development of a satellite housing estate, but Wildlife Alliance vigorously campaigned against this and was able to get the decision reversed. The deforestation that had begun for the development was rectified with mass tree planting, and it looks like the future of Phnom Tamao is safe for now.

## The Hilltop Temple of Phnom Chisor

SPECTACULAR VIEWS OVER THE CAMBODIAN COUNTRYSIDE

A **temple** from the Angkorian era, Phnom Chisor is set upon a solitary hill in Takeo Province, offering superb views of the countryside. Try to get here early in the morning or late in the afternoon, as it is an uncomfortable climb in the heat of the midday sun. Phnom Chisor lies about 55km south of Phnom Penh.

The main temple stands on the eastern side of the hilltop. The complex is surrounded by the partially ruined walls of a 2.5m-wide gallery with windows. Inscriptions found here date from the 11th century, when this site was known as Suryagiri. On the plain to the west of Phnom Chisor are the sanctuaries of **Sen Thmol** (just below Phnom Chisor), **Sen Ravang** and the former sacred pond of **Tonlé Om**. All three form a straight line from Phnom Chisor in the direction of Angkor. During rituals held here 900 years ago, the king, his Brahmans and their entourage would climb 400 steps to Suryagiri from this direction.

If you haven't got the stamina for an overland adventure to Preah Vihear or Phnom Bayong (near Takeo), this is the next best thing for a temple with a view. Near the main temple is a modern Buddhist *vihara*, used by resident monks.

### PHNOM PENH DURING THE KHMER ROUGE REGIME

As the Vietnam War spread into Cambodian territory, Phnom Penh's population swelled to nearly three million by early 1975. The Khmer Rouge took the city on 17 April that year, and as part of its radical revolution immediately forced the entire population into the countryside. Whole families were split up on those first fateful days of 'liberation'.

During the time of Democratic Kampuchea, many tens of thousands of former Phnom Penhois – including the vast majority of the capital's educated residents – were killed. The population of Phnom Penh during the Khmer Rouge regime was never more than about 50,000, a figure made up of senior party members, factory workers and trusted military leaders.

**FITNESS AND WELLNESS IN PHNOM PENH**

**The Place**
This place is absolutely state of the art, with myriad machines, a big pool and a range of cardio classes.

**FitnessOne Himawari**
The Himawari has one of the best hotel pools in town. Admission includes use of the FitnessOne gym.

**Azahar Cambodia**
Offers daily yoga sessions, plus classes in reiki healing, meditation and bokator (a Khmer martial art).

Renting a motorbike in Phnom Penh is one of the most enjoyable ways to get here, combined with Tonlé Bati or the Phnom Tamao Wildlife Rescue Centre. A share taxi is a comfortable option in the wet or hot seasons, or you can take a Takeo-bound bus to the access road, about 49km south of Phnom Penh, and arrange a *moto* from there.

# Exploring Kirirom National Park

PINE FOREST IN THE CLOUDS

You can really get away from it all at this lush, elevated **national park**, a three-hour drive southwest of Phnom Penh. Winding trails lead through pine forests to cascading wet-season waterfalls and cliffs with amazing views of the Cardamom Mountains, and there's some great mountain biking to be done if you're feeling adventurous.

From NH4, it's 10km on a sealed road to a small village near the park entrance. From the village you have two choices: the left fork takes you 50m to the park entrance and then 17km up a fairly steep sealed road to the unstaffed Kirirom Information Centre inside the national park; the right fork takes you 10km along the perimeter of the park on a dirt road to Chambok commune, the site of the established **Chambok-community-based ecotourism programme**. These are two vastly different experiences, and they are nowhere near each other, so it's recommended to devote a day to each.

Up in the actual national park, you'll find myriad walking trails and dirt roads (apt for mountain biking) that lead to small wet-season waterfalls, lakes, wats and abandoned 1960s-era mansions, including one built for former King Norodom Sihanouk. You'll need a map or a guide to navigate them. **Kirirom Pine Resort** can provide both at its excellent activities centre, which also offers kayaking, ziplines, mountain bikes and cooking classes, among an array of tours, courses and rentals.

One of the best hikes is the 14km trail up to **Phnom Dat Chivit** (End of Life Mountain), where an abrupt cliff face offers an unbroken view of the Elephant Mountains and Cardamom Mountains to the west. vKirirom calls this trek the 'Kirirom Heaven Climb' and provides a guide and transport to the trailhead.

The main attraction at the Chambok community-based ecotourism site is a 4km hike to a series of five waterfalls (no guide required). The second waterfall has a swimming hole; the third one is an impressive 40m high. Bikes are available for hire, but won't get you very far as the trail deteriorates fairly quickly after the first kilometre. Other activities include traditional ox-cart rides, basic cooking or handicraft classes and guided nature walks to a bat cave. To reach the ecotour-

## PHNOM PENH TO HO CHI MINH CITY BY BOAT

The most scenic way to end your travels in Cambodia is to sail the Mekong to Kaam Samnor (about 100km south-southeast of Phnom Penh), cross the border to Vinh Xuong in Vietnam, and proceed to Chau Doc overland or on the Tonlé Bassac River via a small channel. All boats depart from Phnom Penh's tourist-boat dock. Both Capitol Tour and Hang Chau have services departing at 12.30pm. The entire journey is by boat and lasts about five hours. The more upmarket and slightly faster Blue Cruiser departs at 1pm; Victoria Chau Doc Hotel also has a boat making several runs a week between Phnom Penh and its Chau Doc hotel.

## PLACES TO STAY IN KIRIROM

### Kirirom Resort
Accommodation here includes circular-pipe rooms, open-plan Khmer cottages and luxurious bungalows. **$$**

### Chambok Homestays
Many homestays are available in Chambok commune as part of the well-run community-based ecotourism programme. **$**

### Shinta Mani Wild
An exclusive tented camp that helps to protect the forest and its wildllife near Kirirom National Park. **$$$**

**Chambok Waterfall**

## FESTIVALS & EVENTS

As the Cambodian capital and largest city in the country, Phnom Penh can be an interesting place to join in some local festivities. The city tends to empty out on big holidays such as **Khmer New Year** (April) and **P'chum Ben** (September/October), when residents return to their home provinces to visit family. However, the **Water Festival** (Bon Om Tuk; October/November) sees the opposite phenomenon, as hundreds of thousands of rural residents flood the city to watch the boat races on the Tonlé Sap. The festival doesn't always go ahead though, and has been cancelled several times in the past decade.

ism office, turn left at Wat Chambok and drive 1km. Ask for Mr Morn or Mr Cham, who both speak English.

There are two hotels within the boundaries of Kirirom National Park, as well as cheaper homestays located near Chambok as part of the long-running community tourism initiative. There are not many independent restaurants around Kirirom, only those attached to hotels and resorts in and around the national park. There are a handful of food stalls in the park, some located near local beauty spots, that can cook up grilled chicken or fish for a picnic. Chambok has two basic eateries with Khmer food.

Kirirom National Park is accessed from the village of Treng Trayern, which straddles NH4, 87km southwest of Phnom Penh. Take a taxi from either city, or have a bus drop you at the turn-off in Treng Trayern, where a *moto* can get you to the entrance (or to Chambok commune or into the national park itself). Travelling under your own steam is highly recommended.

### CONTINUING SOUTH ON NATIONAL HIGHWAY 2

It's possible to visit some of the sights on NH2, such as Tonlé Bati, the Phnom Tamao Wildlife Rescue Centre and Phnom Chisor, as part of a longer journey south to **Phnom Da** (p238) or the beachside retreat of **Kep** (p234).

### ✐ JAPANESE RESTAURANTS IN PHNOM PENH

**Iza**
On the Rosewood Hotel's 37th floor, offering beautiful Japanese classics and high-end *omakase* (set meals). **$$$**

**Nigiri Lab**
This 'lab' in the Russian Market area prepares fresh sushi and sashimi as part of its tasting menus. **$$$**

**Chidori**
Serving everything from ramen to yakitori, sushi to succulent sliced steak, this place also has unlimited draught-beer deals. **$**

PICH MAKTHORA/SHUTTERSTOCK ©

**Khnong Phsar**

# The Foothills of the Cardamom Mountains

ESCAPE TO THE NEAR WILD

Cambodia has some serious potential for ecotourism in its protected areas, and some of these lie surprisingly close to the Cambodian capital in the foothills of the Cardamom Mountains.

The seven-tier **Chreav Waterfall** drops out of the Cardamoms in Kompong Speu Province and is about 2½ hours (112km) from Phnom Penh via Udong. It is very popular with locals at weekends and holidays so is best visited during a quieter weekday. Set aside a full day to journey here and hike to several levels of the falls, which include swimming holes. Take care during wet-season months, as the trails will be slippery and the waterfalls thundering. Lining the approach to the first set of falls are several local picnic stalls serving local barbecued chicken and fish.

 **INDIAN RESTAURANTS IN PHNOM PENH**

**Namaste**
One of the city's best Indian restaurants, offering a slice of the subcontinent in two locations (Sts 308 and 63). **$**

**Sher-e-Punjab**
The top spot for curry, according to many in Phnom Penh's Indian community; the tandoori dishes are particularly good. **$**

**Taste Budz**
The speciality here is Kerala cuisine, including spicy, divine kedai dishes. Order *porotta* (flatbread) on the side. **$**

Located very close to Chreav Waterfall, although across the border in neighbouring Kompong Chhnang Province, nine-tier **Anlong Svay Waterfall** is another beautiful spot for trekking and taking a plunge in one of the many natural pools. Facilities are still quite basic here, although with the two sets of waterfalls just a few kilometres apart, there are plans to establish connecting hiking trails and a community campground for overnight stays.

One of the only hot springs in Cambodia, **Te Tuk Pus Hot Springs** is located 112km from Phnom Penh in Aural District, on the way out towards trekking country and the Rolerk Kang Chheung community gateway to Khnong Phsar. While it is no Japanese *onsen* or Icelandic Blue Lagoon, the sulphuric waters are believed by locals to have some healing powers. It is a very basic set-up, with bamboo benches for dipping the feet and a few ponds.

Known in English as the 'Back of the Mountain', **Khnong Phsar** is one of the most popular overnight trekking areas in touching distance of Phnom Penh. Trekkers access the trails via the community-based ecotourism community of and hike up into the peaks of Khnong Phsar (1160m) via rolling grasslands and clumps of pine forests. The main draw is the sunrise from the summit, which offers infinite views of mist-filled valleys and mysterious peaks on a clear day. There are several informal **campgrounds** around the summit area, but plans are afoot to develop improved trails, community campgrounds and even some lodges up here. There is also the tantalising prospect of a trans-Cardamom trek to Stung Areng in Koh Kong Province, as there are also connections to both Khnong Phsar and Khnong Krapeau from the west. This offers the potential for one-way treks from Rolerk Kang Chheung to Stung Areng, bridging the 'missing link' in the Cardamoms in the near future.

Check out some of the leading local adventure operators and wildlife NGOs for more information on developments with these potential trans-Cardamom linkages, including **Solo Landscapes** (sololandscapes.co) and **Stung Areng Community-Based Ecotourism** (areng-valley.org).

The **Cambodia Sustainable Landscape & Ecotourism (CSLE) Project** is a flagship initiative between the Ministry of Environment and the World Bank to promote sustainable ecotourism in the Cardamom Mountains' Tonlé Sap Basin, a vast watershed in southwest Cambodia that covers eight provinces and provides much of the country's fresh water.

## BEST WINE BARS IN PHNOM PENH

**Bouchon Wine Bar**
Bouchon is as much a classy restaurant as an elegant wine bar. Potent cocktails plus a great selection of French wines by the glass.

**Le Manolis**
A sophisticated wine bar (with a huge selection), tapas restaurant and French bistro set in a beautifully restored section of the old Manolis Hotel.

**Little Wine Bistro**
A hole-in-the-wall wine bar in bustling Bassac Lane, this is a friendly spot with many wines by the glass.

## STAY AT THE FARMHOUSE RESORT & SPA

If you want to get away from it all and experience the charms of the Cambodian countryside around Udong, check out the **Farmhouse Resort & Spa** (p193), which supports disadvantaged Cambodians by offering young staff training and employment in the hospitality business.

 **ALTERNATIVE CAFES IN PHNOM PENH**

**Happy Damrei**
The epicentre of board games in Phnom Penh, with everything from Risk and Cluedo to Cards Against Humanity.

**Treehouse**
Recover from the Tuol Sleng Genocide Museum over a cold brew, bubbly kombucha or an earthy matcha latte.

**La Chronique**
An impressive French-influenced cafe in the Russian Market area paying homage to Cambodia in the 1960s.

# SIEM REAP & THE TEMPLES OF ANGKOR

## THE GREATEST TEMPLES ON EARTH

Most visitors come for the mother of all temples, Angkor Wat, but Siem Reap is fast catching up as a destination in itself.

Welcome to heaven on earth. The temples of Angkor are the perfect fusion of creative ambition and spiritual devotion. The Cambodian 'god-kings' of old each strove to better their ancestors in size, scale and symmetry, culminating in the world's largest religious building, Angkor Wat. The temples of Angkor are one of the world's foremost ancient sites, a source of national pride and a place of pilgrimage for all Khmers, and no traveller to the region should miss their extravagant beauty.

The life-support system and gateway for the temples, Siem Reap was always destined for great things. Siem Reap has reinvented itself as the epicentre of chic Cambodia, with everything from backpacker party pads to hip hotels, world-class wining and dining across a range of cuisines, sumptuous spas, great shopping, local tours to suit both foodies and adventurers, and a creative cultural scene that includes Cambodia's leading contemporary circus. It has also genuinely 'built back better' since the COVID-19

pandemic began, with new cycle paths running throughout town and also connecting up the major temples of Angkor.

The region is home to a number of other impressive attractions, including the otherworldly floating and stilted villages of the Tonlé Sap, some high-profile bird sanctuaries that are home to rare large waterbirds, and new wildlife attractions like Kulen Elephant Forest. The province is also emerging as an accessible place to experience a homestay and a slice of local life in a traditional village. Throw in some remote jungle temples and sacred mountains, and you'll want to extend your stay by a few days.

Siem Reap and the temples of Angkor were devastated by the complete collapse of the tourism industry during the early years of the pandemic, but Cambodia and its people have been to hell and back before and shown their resilience in the face of greater adversity. What is two years, when the temples were once wiped off the travel map for two decades? Angkor is eternal and Siem Reap is back.

URF/GETTY IMAGES ©

### THE MAIN AREAS

**CENTRAL SIEM REAP**
Cool and contemporary face of Angkor. p94

**AROUND SIEM REAP**
Floating villages and wildlife encounters. p104

**ANGKOR WAT & AROUND**
Potent symbol of a nation. p113

**Angkor Wat (p114)**

**ANGKOR THOM**
The great walled city of Angkor.
p125

**BANTEAY SREI**
Much more than a temple. p142

**KOH KER**
Lost and looted jungle capital.
p150

# Find Your Way

Siem Reap is still a small town at heart and it's easy enough to navigate the central districts on foot or with pedal power or local *tuk-tuks*. When planning adventures further afield, to Angkor and beyond, consider a car or a motorbike, as *tuk-tuks* can be slow going.

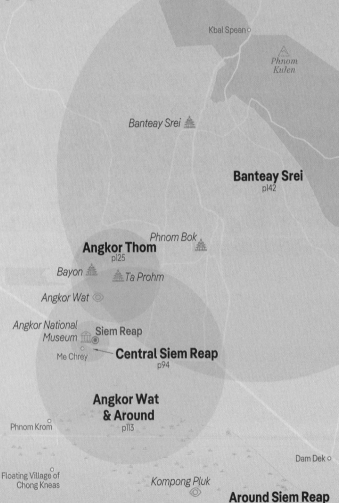

Kbal Spean

*Phnom Kulen*

*Banteay Srei*

**Banteay Srei**
p142

*Phnom Bok*

**Angkor Thom**
p125

*Bayon*

*Ta Prohm*

*Angkor Wat*

*Angkor National Museum*

Siem Reap

Me Chrey

**Central Siem Reap**
p94

**Angkor Wat & Around**
p113

Phnom Krom

Floating Village of Chong Kneas

*Kompong Pluk*

Dam Dek

Soutr Nikom

**Around Siem Reap**
p104

🛕
*Prasat Thom*

**Koh Ker**
p150

○ Srayong

○ Svay Leu

○ Beng Mealea

### FROM THE AIRPORT

Many hotels and guesthouses in Siem Reap offer a free airport pickup service with advance bookings. Official taxis/*tuk-tuks* are available next to the terminal for US$10/8. Book using a taxi app like Grab or PassApp and the price drops to US$6/4.

### CAR & MOTORCYCLE

Most hotels and guesthouses can organise car hire, with a going rate of US$35 and up per day. Foreigners were long forbidden to rent motorcycles in and around Angkor, but the rules seem to have relaxed and motorbike hire is now widely available for about US$10 per day.

### TUK-TUK

The Cambodian *tuk-tuks* – motorcycles with hooded carriages towed behind – are a popular way to get around Siem Reap and Angkor, as fellow travellers can talk to each other as they explore. Prices run from US$15 to US$25 per day, but it is necessary to negotiate.

### BICYCLE

Some guesthouses and shops hire out bicycles, usually for US$2 a day. Imported mountain bikes are available from cycling tour operators for around US$8 to US$10 per day, and some also have e-mountain bikes. Green e-bike (greene-bike.com) provides standard e-bikes at US$11 per day.

N 0 ━━━━━━ 20 km
0 ━━━━━ 10 miles

# Plan Your Days

The ideal amount of time in Siem Reap is three to five days to see the temples of Angkor, explore the lively town and visit some other attractions in the countryside.

Ta Prohm (p134)

SUTTIRAT WIRIYANON/SHUTTERSTOCK ©

## Day 1

### Morning
● Beat the crowds with an early morning jaunt to **Banteay Srei** (p143) – the art gallery of Angkor thanks to its beautiful carvings. Continue to **Kbal Spean** (p167) to undertake a jungle trek to the River of a Thousand Lingas, but drop into the **Angkor Centre for Conservation of Biodiversity** (p107) and the 9am wildlife tour first.

### Afternoon
● Enjoy a local lunch at **Borey Sovann Restaurant** (p145) and then visit the inspirational **Cambodia Landmine Museum** (p144).

### Evening
● Back in Siem Reap, browse the shops of Kandal Village, book a massage or spa, sample some local flavours and explore the lively bars of **St 26** (p100).

## You'll Also Want to...

Choose from a cultural kick at museums and temples, a shopping fix at a market, a shot in a local bar or a brush with resident wildlife.

**SEE THE ANGKOR NATIONAL MUSEUM**

The **museum** (p96) is a showcase for Angkorian art and an essential stop before visiting the temples of Angkor.

**EXPLORE THE HOLY MOUNTAIN OF PHNOM KULEN**

**Phnom Kulen** (p146) is a mysterious plateau of temples, waterfalls and clifftop views.

**GO ON A PUB STREET CRAWL**

Raucous and infamous **Pub St** (p99) has been a staple of Siem Reap's nightlife for more than two decades.

FROM LEFT: RAINYCLUB/SHUTTERSTOCK ©, F9PHOTOS/SHUTTERSTOCK ©, MIKEINLONDON/GETTY IMAGES ©

# Day 2

### Morning
● Make for the north gate of jungle temple **Ta Prohm** (p134) by around 7.15am to beat the crowds. Look at the jungle canopy from a different angle at the **Angkor Zipline** (p138).

### Afternoon
● Try a local lunch at one of the eateries at **Sra Srang** (p135), then head to **Angkor Thom** (p125) and tackle the walking tour to take in the best of the temples.

### Evening
● Go on an after-dark **Vespa tour** (p106) or a food tour with **Taste Siem Reap** (p102). Celebrate the day's sights with some Khmer fine dining at **Cuisine Wat Damnak** or **Embassy** (p99).

# Day 3

### Morning
● Patience is a virtue – it's time to be rewarded with the mother of all sunrises at **Angkor Wat** (p114). Make for the back door on the eastern side, avoiding the crowds on the western causeway. Continue to the vast, mysterious jungle giant of a temple that is **Beng Mealea** (p149).

### Afternoon
● Boomerang yourself south and visit the floating community of **Kompong Khleang** (p108), one of the largest villages on the Great Lake, with ornate pagodas and houses built on stilts.

### Evening
● Experience a dazzling performance by **Phare the Cambodian Circus** (p102) in their signature big top on the edge of town.

**SEE THE TEMPLES OF ROLUOS & KOMPONG PLUK**

Pair the temples of the **Roluos group** (p122) with a boat trip through the stilted village of **Kompong Pluk** (p105).

**VISIT THE KULEN ELEPHANT FOREST**

Learn about these noble creatures at a 'retirement home' for **elephants** (p107), deep in the forest of Siem Reap Province.

**BROWSE PSAR CHAA**

The **Old Market** (Psar Chaa, p97) is Siem Reap's original shopping mall, operating long before the glitzy air-con imposters came to town.

**SPOT LARGE RARE WATERBIRDS**

Spot pelicans, storks, cranes and more at **Prek Toal** (p110) and **Ang Trapaeng Thmor** (p111) bird sanctuaries.

93

# CENTRAL SIEM REAP

## COOL AND CONTEMPORARY FACE OF ANGKOR

The Siem Reap River is the dominant feature of the town centre, winding its way from Phnom Kulen via the moats of Angkor Thom and Angkor Wat, then through the heart of town before spilling into the Tonlé Sap lake. The river is lined with hotels, restaurants and a few grand old buildings from the time of French rule.

Pub St is an infamous landmark of the river's West Bank, where many of the popular bars, restaurants, cafes and shops are located. On the quieter East Bank, the back streets around Wat Bo are emerging as the up-and-coming Boho area for wining and dining.

Siem Reap was given a major facelift during the enforced tourism shutdown of the pandemic, with new roads, public gardens and an impressive new cycle path linking the downtown with the temples of Angkor.

**TOP TIP**

Negotiate local transport prices on arrival in Siem Reap, because if you like your driver, then you may find yourself using them to explore the temples of Angkor. It's also possible to use local apps like PassApp or Grab to book *tuktuks* around town for very reasonable fixed prices.

**Pub St (p99)**

STEFANO EMBER/SHUTTERSTOCK ©

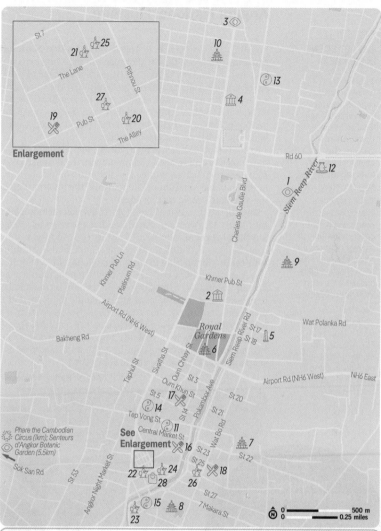

SIEM REAP & THE TEMPLES OF ANGKOR

**SIGHTS**
**1** Angkor Conservation
**2** Angkor
National Museum
**3** Apopo Visitor Centre
**4** Bayon
Information Centre
**5** Miniature Replicas
of Angkor's Temples
**6** Preah Ang
Chek Preah Ang
Chorm Shrine

**7** Wat Bo
**8** Wat Dam Nak
**9** Wat Preah Inkosei
**10** Wat Thmei

**ACTIVITIES,
COURSES & TOURS**
**11** Frangipani Spa
**12** Khmer
Ceramics Centre
**13** Krousar Thmey
**14** Lemongrass Garden

**15** Seeing
Hands Massage

**EATING**
**16** Chanrey Tree
**17** Embassy
**18** Pou Restaurant
**19** Red Piano

**DRINKING
& NIGHTLIFE**
**20** Angkor What?

**21** Asana
Wooden House
**22** Beatnik Speakeasy
**23** Embargo
**24** Laundry
**25** Miss Wong
**26** SO 26
**27** Temple Club

**SHOPPING**
**28** Psar Chaa

## THE ART SCENE IN SIEM REAP

**Siem Reap Art Tours** (siemreaparttours. com) showcases the ever-evolving local art scene. Tours include four leading galleries and boutiques around town and usually last about four hours.

**Theam's House** (theamshouse. com) is a stunning gallery and studio of lacquer creations and artwork by renowned artist Theam. Highly original and a must for serious collectors.

**Develter Gallery** (christiandevelter. com) is located in FCC Angkor, with stunning modernist portraits inspired by Chin tribal tattoos from Myanmar.

# Angkor National Museum

A SHOWCASE OF ANGKORIAN ART

Looming large on the road to Angkor is the **Angkor National Museum**, a state-of-the-art showpiece on the Khmer civilisation and the majesty of Angkor. Displays are themed by era, religion and royalty as visitors move through the impressive galleries. After a short presentation, enter the Zen-like Gallery of a Thousand Buddhas. Other exhibits include the pre-Angkorian periods of Funan and Chenla; the great Khmer kings; Angkor Wat; Angkor Thom; and the inscriptions.

Exhibits include touch-screen videos, epic commentary and the chance to experience a panoramic sunrise at Angkor Wat. Although there appears to be less sculpture on display than in the National Museum in Phnom Penh, the presentation of the artefacts here is cutting edge.

Some of the standout pieces in the collection include a late-12th-/early-13th-century seated Buddha sheltered by a *naga* (mythical serpent-being), a 7th-century standing Vishnu from Sambor Prei Kuk in Kompong Thom, and a stunning 10th-century lintel from the beautiful temple of Banteay Srei.

As the museum is entirely air conditioned, plan a visit during the middle of the day to avoid the sweltering midday temperatures at the temples of Angkor. Audio tours are useful for those who want a more comprehensive understanding of the exhibits on display. Wheelchairs are available free of charge for visitors with mobility impairment. Allow about two hours to visit the museum in depth and to stop by the shop and small cafe at the end of your visit.

**Angkor National Museum**

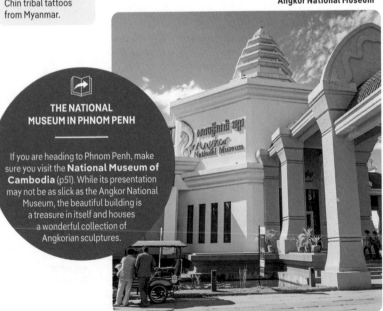

BOYLOSO/SHUTTERSTOCK ©

### THE NATIONAL MUSEUM IN PHNOM PENH

If you are heading to Phnom Penh, make sure you visit the **National Museum of Cambodia** (p51). While its presentation may not be as slick as the Angkor National Museum, the beautiful building is a treasure in itself and houses a wonderful collection of Angkorian sculptures.

Psar Chaa (Old Market), the commercial heart of old Siem Reap, attracts local shoppers and international browsers in equal numbers. The market is a game of two halves – one filled with fresh produce, exotic fruits and homewares, the other with handicrafts, fake antiques, textiles and clothing.

Start on the northwestern side of the market at the **1 Scales of Justice**, placed here to settle any disputes between vendors and customers over the weight of an item. If you smell something fishy about this, that would be the nearby stalls of dried fish, a traditional way to preserve the daily catch.

Head deeper into the market and you will discover the **2 fresh produce section**, where colourful heaps of fruit and vegetables, both familiar and foreign, are piled high. You may want to buy something for a pick-me-up when exploring the temples.

Emerging on the other side of the food area, you will come across **3 cheap accessories** such as shoes and backpacks, some fake, some the real deal. Explore the aisles of trinkets, souvenirs and statues, keeping in mind that much of it may be imported from neighbouring countries.

Pass through the 'jewellery quarter', a separate shop within the market, before entering the other side into a **4 clothing section**, where lots of seconds from the garment factories turn up. 'Tin Tin au Cambodge', 'Danger!! Mines!!' and Angkor Wat T-shirts are widely available.

Swerve south at the western side of the market, passing recycled bags and creative *kramas* (checked scarves), and head to the southern side where there is a good-cause store, **5 Susu**, selling handicrafts to help support women's development in Cambodia.

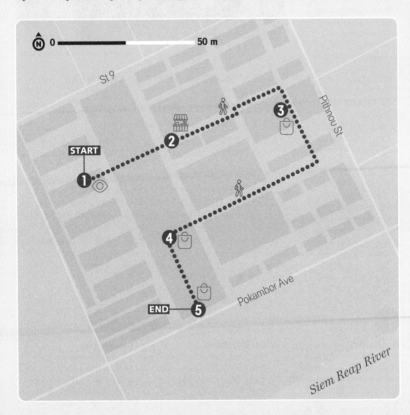

## A BEGINNER'S GUIDE TO KHMER CUISINE

**Kethana Dunnet** is the owner of Sugar Palm restaurant.

**What makes Khmer cuisine distinct from its neighbours?** It's less spicy than Thai cuisine, but we share many common herbs with the Vietnamese. And soups are integral.
**What are the key ingredients?** Our *kreung* paste, made with lemongrass and turmeric. And infamous *prahoc*, a pungent fermented-fish paste.
**Which Sugar Palm dish best captures Cambodia's essence?**
I recommend fish *amok* (mild fish curry), steamed in a coconut shell with the texture of a soufflé.
**You taught Gordon Ramsay how to cook Khmer cuisine. How was that experience?** It was a real thrill. He was really interested in discovering Khmer food. I can honestly say he did not swear once in my kitchen!

Hero rat, Apopo Visitor Centre

MORE IN CENTRAL SIEM REAP

## Meet the Hero Rats of Apopo

INNOVATIVE DE-MINING IN CAMBODIA

This is the place to meet the incredible rats that are helping to clear landmines in Cambodia. Apopo has trained the highly sensitive, almost-blind Gambian pouched rat to sniff explosives, which dramatically speeds up the detection of mines in the countryside. The **Apopo Visitor Centre** gives background on the work of Apopo, with a short video and the chance to meet the rats themselves. In 2020 one of their Cambodia-based rats, Magawa, won the PDSA Gold Medal for 'life-saving devotion to duty', the animal equivalent of the George Cross or a Purple Heart. Some excellent merch is for sale, including some great T-shirts, which are a cut above the average souvenir tee.

### HOSTELS IN SIEM REAP

**Mad Monkey**
One of Siem Reap's many super-hostels, with private rooms and dorms that include free access to the pool. **$**

**Onederz Hostel**
Winner of several 'Hoscars' (Hostelworld's Oscars), this is one of the smartest hostels in town. **$**

**Funky Village**
A popular backpacker party address, with a whole courtyard taken up with a swimming pool for regular water polo. **$**

# The Sacred Shrine of Siem Reap

PRAY FOR LUCK WITH LOCALS

Located just west of the Royal Residence is the **Preah Ang Chek Preah Ang Chorm Shrine**. Said to represent two Angkorian princesses, these sacred statues were originally housed at the Preah Poan gallery in Angkor Wat, but were moved all over Siem Reap to protect them from invaders, eventually settling on this location in 1990. Locals, especially newlyweds, throng here to pray for luck, and it is an atmospheric place to visit around dusk, as the incense smoke swirls around.

Next to the shrine are the tall trees of the Royal Gardens, home to a resident colony of fruit bats (also known as flying foxes), which take off to feed on insects around sunset.

# Pub Street Bar Crawl

DISCOVER SIEM REAP AFTER DARK

Pub St and the Angkor What? Bar have become almost as renowned as the temples of Angkor for a generation of backpackers. While Pub St draws the headlines and the revellers, there is a whole series of lanes and alleys criss-crossing the old French quarter in this part of town that makes for a great location to embark on a bar crawl.

Kick off your night at **Asana Wooden House**, an impressive traditional country residence in the backstreets. Infused rice wine is used to give the creative cocktails a kick and it even has cocktail classes as an alternative to cooking classes.

Continue to **Beatnik Speakeasy**, with a great location on the corner, and discover that hipsters existed back in the 1950s, only without the beards. Drop into **Psar Chaa (Old Market)** for a local dinner at one of its many Cambodian food stalls to ensure you are lined for the libations ahead.

Head into Pub St proper, but prepare for the volume to be cranked up. Check out **Red Piano**, one of the first bar-restaurants to open in Pub St, and where Angelina Jolie helped create the 'Tomb Raider' cocktail. Further along the road is another stalwart in **Temple Club**, although the Temple empire is so large now that many of the bars in this area are owned by the same group.

Finish up at the one and only **Angkor What?**, a bar that claims to have been promoting irresponsible drinking since 1998. If you manage to stay here until 5am, you could combine Angkor What? with an Angkor Wat sunrise, but you may not remember much about the experience.

## BEST KHMER FINE DINING

**Cuisine Wat Damnak $$$**
Chef Joannès Rivière's iconic restaurant delivers the ultimate contemporary Khmer gastronomic experience. Seasonal set menus focus on market-fresh ingredients and change weekly.

**Embassy $$$**
It's all about Khmer gastronomy here, with an evolving menu that changes with the seasons. Under the supervision of the Kimsan twins, this is Khmer cuisine at its most creative.

**Chanrey Tree $$**
Chanrey Tree combines a stylish setting with expressive presentation of contemporary Khmer cuisine while retaining the essentials of traditional Cambodian cooking.

 **BOUTIQUE HOTELS IN SIEM REAP**

**Baby Elephant Boutique Hotel**
Run by a friendly Australian clan, this has great beds and bathrooms, a fine pool area and a lovely rooftop. **$$**

**Rambutan Resort**
An atmospheric, gay-friendly resort spread over two stunning villas, each with spacious and stylish rooms and a pool. **$$**

**Shinta Mani Angkor**
With a contemporary chic design, Shinta Mani features two pools, a spa and supports responsible tourism. **$$$**

## BEST CRAFT-BEER BARS

**Pomme Brewhouse & Kitchen**
One of Siem Reap's most inviting bar-restaurants, with an on-site microbrewery producing the best beer in temple town. The food is also great, plus they have quiz nights and live music weekly.

**Embargo**
A new outpost of a Phnom Penh institution located on Siem Reap River's southeast bank, this small place has a big selection of beers from Cambodia, Vietnam and the region beyond. Food is available via delivery from leading local eateries.

### CRAFT BREWING IN PHNOM PENH

Phnom Penh is home to a thriving craft-brewing scene, including **Noisy Chilli** (p86), from the Riel Brewery; **Botanico** (p86), the home of Cerevisia Brewery; and **Hops Brewery** (p64), the popular German microbrewery.

# A Night on St 26

WHERE SIEM REAP BECOMES BOHO

St 26 has emerged as the hip hangout in Siem Reap after the dark days of the early years of the pandemic and is now known as Boho, thanks to its proximity to Wat Bo.

**Miss Wong** carries you back to chic 1920s Shanghai. The cocktails are a draw here and there's a menu offering dim sum. It's gay-friendly and popular with the well-heeled expat crowd.

One of the most chilled, chic bars in town, **Laundry** is the place to come for electronica and ambient sounds, though it's heaving on weekends.

**SO 26** is a happening spot for light bites and a rocket-fuel-strength espresso martini to lengthen your night. Regular DJ events on weekends draw a crowd.

# Conserving Angkor

HIDDEN COLLECTIONS AND A RESTORATION DISPLAY

Aptly located on Angkor Conservation St, **Angkor Conservation** is a Ministry of Culture compound that houses more than 5000 statues, *lingas* (phallic symbols) and inscribed stelae, stored here to protect them from the wanton looting that has blighted hundreds of sites around Angkor. The finest statuary is hidden away inside Angkor Conservation's warehouses, meticulously numbered and catalogued. While it's not officially open to the public, it is sometimes possible to get a peek at the collection for a fee.

In nearby northern Siem Reap, the **Bayon Information Centre** introduces visitors to the history of the Khmer empire and the restoration projects around Angkor through a series of short films and displays. Set in the beautiful Japanese Team for Safeguarding Angkor (JSA) compound, it's considerably cheaper than the Angkor National Museum, although there is no statuary on display.

# Old Wats of Siem Reap

BUDDHIST SOUL OF TEMPLE TOWN

As befitting the gateway to the sacred temples of Angkor, Siem Reap is home to some beautiful old wats (Buddhist temples) dating back to the 19th century.

One of the town's oldest temples, **Wat Bo** has a collection of well-preserved wall paintings from the late 19th century depicting the *Reamker*, Cambodia's interpretation of the *Ramayana*. The monks here regularly chant sometime between 4.30pm and 6pm, and this can be an enthralling and spiritual moment if you happen to be visiting.

 **LUXURY HOTELS IN SIEM REAP** ─────────

**Amansara**
Set in the former guest villa of King Sihanouk, this ultimate luxury hotel has a price tag to match. **$$$**

**Phum Baitang**
This beautiful resort's rooms are set in spacious, elegantly furnished wooden villas, some with private pools. **$$$**

**Maison Polanka**
A luxurious home catering to your every whim, Maison Polanka is a lush private estate offering a handful of rooms. **$$$**

**Wat Bo**

## BEST MODERN KHMER CUISINE

**Pou Restaurant $$**
Pou, in Maison 557 in Boho, has an innovative menu, with grilled beehive salad or chicken with red ant as starters, and Phnom Kulen pork-belly sausage or spicy vegetable-cake curry.

**Jomno Street Food $**
Earning rave reviews for its original flavours, with dishes from the Cambodian street such as *naom banchok* noodles and Battambang sausage.

**Tavern Restaurant $$**
This beautiful spot in a stunning house in the Chreav countryside offers fish cooked in Kampot rock salt and stuffed frog with Khmer spices.

**Wat Dam Nak** was formerly a royal palace during the reign of King Sisowath, hence the name *dam nak* (palace). Today it's home to the Center for Khmer Studies (khmerstudies.org), an independent institution promoting a greater understanding of Khmer culture with a drop-in research library on-site.

**Wat Preah Inkosei** is located in the far north of town and is built on the site of an early Angkorian brick temple, which still stands today at the rear of the compound.

South of the city centre, **Wat Athvear** is an attractive pagoda on the site of an ancient temple. The old temple is still in very good condition and sees far fewer visitors than the main Angkor temples, making it a peaceful spot in the late afternoon. It requires an Angkor pass to enter.

**Wat Thmei** has a small memorial stupa containing the skulls and bones of victims of the Khmer Rouge. It also has plenty of young monks eager to practise their English.

## TRAVELS WITH MY FATHER

British comedian and actor Jack Whitehall travelled to Cambodia with his father Michael to make this popular show for Netflix. He witnessed a spellbinding shadow-puppet performance at Wat Preah Inkosei and and went out de-mining for the day with the 'hero rats' of **Apopo** (p98).

## WHERE TO EAT ON A BUDGET IN SIEM REAP

**Road 60 Night Market**
Sample local Cambodian snacks, including deep-fried insects and barbecue dishes. Plenty of cheap beer too. **$**

**Pot & Pan Restaurant**
Specialises in affordable, well-presented, authentic dishes – the local rice is beautifully served in lotus leaf. **$**

**Tevy's Place**
This delightful little family-run restaurant on St 26 has reasonably priced Cambodian classics. Recommended. **$**

## BEST FOODIE EXPERIENCES

**Taste Siem Reap**
Offering private evening dine-arounds in leading restaurants and bars – a great way to discover the town's vibrant developing culinary scene.

**Siem Reap Food Tours**
Choose from a morning tour that takes in local markets and the *naom banchok* stalls of Preah Dak, or an evening tour of street stalls and local barbecue restaurants.

**Vegetarian Cooking Class**
A vegetarian cooking class with tofu *amok*, papaya salad and veggie spring rolls on the menu, held daily at 1pm.

RAQUEL MOGADO/ALAMY STOCK PHOTO ©

**Phare the Cambodian Circus**

## Miniature Replicas of Angkor's Temples
BIRD'S-EYE VIEW OF ANGKOR

One of the more quirky places in town is the garden of local master-sculptor Dy Proeung, which houses **miniature replicas of Angkor's temples**, such as Angkor Wat, the Bayon and Banteay Srei. It is the bluffer's way to get an aerial shot of Angkor without chartering a helicopter, although the astute might question the presence of oversized insects in the shot. There is also a display of scale miniatures at Preah Ko temple.

## A Contemporary Botanic Garden
WILLY WONKA'S FOR THE SENSES

At **Senteurs d'Angkor Botanic Garden** you can sample infused teas and speciality coffees in the on-site cafe. More a laboratory than a garden, here the operators also make soaps, oils and perfumes, all using homegrown organic materials. It is located in a stunning purpose-built centre near the Angkor Golf Resort and free tours are available daily that showcase the production process, from the extraction of essential oils to the distillation of original beauty products.

### PHARE CIRCUS IN BATTAMBANG

If you're heading to Battambang on your journey through Cambodia, check out the **Phare Circus** (p164) there, which is where the story of Phare Ponleu Selpak ('the brightness of the arts') began.

## Roll Up, Roll Up...
THE CIRCUS IS IN TOWN

Cambodia's answer to Cirque du Soleil, **Phare the Cambodian Circus** (pharecircus.org) is so much more than a conventional circus, with an emphasis on

### WHERE TO EAT COMFORT FOOD IN SIEM REAP

**Jungle Burger**
There are more than 10 types of burger on offer here, plus pizzas, foot-long subs and homemade pies. **$**

**Viva**
Spice up your life with Mexican food and margaritas at this long-running place, strategically situated opposite Psar Chaa. **$**

**Wat Beast**
A great little menu of customised burgers, creative sliders and fusion mac and cheese, plus craft beers. **$**

performance art and a subtle yet striking social message behind each production. Cambodia's leading circus, theatre and performing-arts organisation, Phare Ponleu Selpak opened its big top for nightly shows in 2013, and the results are a unique, must-see form of entertainment.

Several generations of performers have graduated through Phare's original Battambang campus and have gone on to perform in international shows around the world. Many of the performers have deeply moving personal stories of abuse and hardship, making their talents a triumph against the odds. An inspiring night out for adults and children alike, with all proceeds reinvested into Phare Ponleu Selpak activities. Animal lovers will be pleased to note that no animals are used in any performance.

# Creative Clay at Khmer Ceramics Centre

LEARN TO THROW SOME POTS

Located on the banks of the Siem Reap River in the north of town, the **Khmer Ceramics Centre** (khmerceramics.com) is dedicated to reviving the Khmer tradition of pottery, which was an intricate art during the time of Angkor. It's possible to visit and try your hand at the potter's wheel, and courses in traditional techniques, including pottery and ceramic painting, are available. The activities are particularly popular with younger children, as it offers something creative to try beyond sightseeing at the temples. Even if not signing up for a course, there are some beautiful keepsakes available here in the on-site shop.

If you are really potty about pots, there is also the **Tani Museum of Ceramics** in Banteay Srei District. The tiny 'museum' showcases a collection of Angkorian pottery from the days of the Khmer empire. Only pottery enthusiasts are likely to get fired up by the limited displays. A good guide can show you some Angkor-era kilns in the area where fragments of ancient pottery are scattered about the landscape. It is not far from the hilltop temple of Chau Srei Vibol and can be combined with a visit there.

**BEST MASSAGE & SPAS IN SIEM REAP**

**Lemongrass Garden**
Smart spa in a central location offering a range of affordable treatments, including family massages.

**Frangipani Spa**
This delightful hideaway offers massages and a whole range of spa treatments.

**Seeing Hands Massage 4**
Seeing Hands trains blind people in the art of massage. Watch out for copycats, as some of them are exploiting blind people.

**Krousar Thmey**
Massages performed by blind masseurs. In the same location is a 'Seeing in the Dark' interactive exhibition exploring what it's like to be blind.

 **VEGETARIAN DINING IN SIEM REAP**

**Banllé Vegetarian Restaurant**
With its own organic vegetable garden, this is a great place for veggie *amok* and fruit and vegetable shakes. **$**

**Peace Cafe**
This popular garden cafe serves affordable vegetarian meals and a tempting selection of vegetable juices. **$**

**Vitking House**
In the East Bank area of the riverfront, with affordable vegetarian food that includes the creative use of mock meat. **$**

# AROUND SIEM REAP

## FLOATING VILLAGES AND WILDLIFE ENCOUNTERS

Venture beyond Siem Reap and the landscape quickly yields to the rural idyll of verdant ricefields, lotus ponds and traditional stilt houses. Many of the most popular villages to visit are floating or stilted villages on the Tonlé Sap lake. These communities have enjoyed the bounty of the Great Lake for generations, but now find their livelihoods under threat from the challenges of climate change and overfishing. '*Mien tuk, mien trey*' is an old Cambodian proverb meaning 'have water, have fish', but this is no longer a truism and tourism is an increasing contributor to the communities' survival.

There are many new wildlife attractions in Siem Reap Province offering a more rounded experience to travellers with kids who might tire of the temples. Kulen Elephant Forest gives you a chance to interact with a herd of retired pachyderms and the new Angkor Wildlife & Aquarium is home to rare giant freshwater fish.

### TOP TIP

Many of these places are a fair distance from Siem Reap and can be combined with popular temples, such as Chong Kneas and Phnom Krom (p124), Kompong Pluk and the Roluos temples (p122), or Kompong Khleang and Beng Mealea (p149). It is best to use a *tuk-tuk* or car for these long journeys.

**Stilt houses, Kompong Pluk**

PIER GIORGIO CARLONI/SHUTTERSTOCK ©

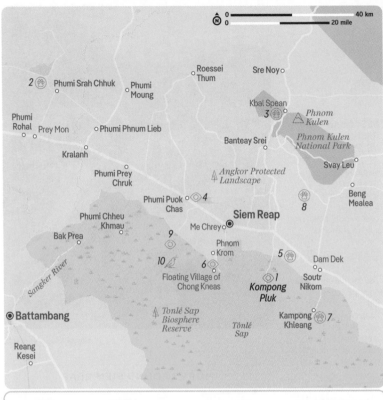

**HIGHLIGHTS**
1 Kompong Pluk

**SIGHTS**
2 Ang Trapaeng
Thmor Reserve

3 Angkor Centre for
Conservation
of Biodiversity
4 Angkor Silk Farm

5 Angkor Wildlife
& Aquarium
6 Floating Village
of Chong Kneas
7 Kompong Khleang

8 Kulen Elephant Forest
9 Me Chrey
10 Prek Toal
Bird Sanctuary

# Kompong Pluk

LAKE-DWELLING VILLAGE OF 'BAMBOO SKYSCRAPERS'

The village of Kompong Pluk is a friendly, otherworldly place where houses are built on soaring stilts. Nearby is a flooded forest, best visited from July to December when there is high water in the lake and exploring by wooden dugout is very atmospheric. It's a different scene from January to June, though it is still rewarding to explore the dry flooded forest on foot

Fixed prices to visit are high, so it may be cheaper to sign up to a budget tour out of Siem Reap. There are a couple of basic homestays in Kompong Pluk and lots of good floating restaurants for lunch or a snack.

The most popular access route is via the town of Roluos by a combination of road (by *moto*, *tuk-tuk* or taxi) and then boat, a journey that takes up to two hours depending on the season.

**CHONG KNEAS TO KOMPONG PLUK**

It is possible to approach Kompong Pluk via the floating village of **Chong Kneas** (p106) to the west, where a boat (1¼ hours) can be arranged, but note that large waves can form on the shallow open lake during the windy and rainy seasons.

LEONARD ZHUKOVSKY/SHUTTERSTOCK ©

**Vespa Adventures tour**

## BEST QUAD-BIKING & VESPA TOURS

**Cambodia Quad Bike**
Quad-bike tours around the countryside, including sunrise and sunset options.

**Quad Adventure Cambodia**
The original quad-bike operator in town. Rides around Siem Reap involve rice fields at sunset, pretty temples and back roads through traditional villages.

**Siem Reap Quad Bike Adventure**
A locally owned ATV company with fully automatic quad bikes.

**Vespa Adventures**
The Vespa tour operator from Vietnam offers a popular combination of countryside experiences and temple tours, plus Siem Reap by night.

### MORE AROUND SIEM REAP

# The Water World of Chong Kneas

BUSY BUT SCENIC FLOATING VILLAGE

The famous **Floating Village of Chong Kneas** has become somewhat of a circus in recent years. Tour groups have taken over and there are countless scams to separate tourists from their money. In-the-know travellers opt for harder-to-reach but more memorable spots such as Kompong Khleang or Prek Toal. But for all its flaws, Chong Kneas is very scenic in the warm light of late afternoon, and can be combined with a sunset from the nearby hilltop temple of Phnom Krom.

There's an entrance fee and boat prices are fixed. Avoid the crowds by asking your boat driver to take you down some back channels. Your boat driver will invariably try to take you to an overpriced floating restaurant and souvenir shop, but there is no obligation to buy anything.

 **WHERE TO DINE FOR A CAUSE IN SIEM REAP**

**Haven**
The best of East-West dining. Proceeds help young adult orphans make the step from institution to employment. **$**

**Marum**
Marum serves up Cambodian street food from pop-up stalls. Part of the Tree Alliance group of training restaurants. **$**

**Spoons Cafe**
This excellent contemporary Cambodian restaurant supports education and employment opportunities in hospitality. **$$**

One of the best ways to visit Chong Kneas is to hook up with the Tara Boat (taraboat.com), which offers all-inclusive trips with a meal aboard its converted cargo boat. Prices include transfers, entry fees, local boats, a tour guide and a two-course meal.

You can get to Chong Kneas from Siem Reap by *moto* or taxi. The round trip, including the village visit, takes two to three hours. Alternatively, rent a bicycle in town and just pedal out here, as it is a leisurely 11km through pretty villages and rice fields.

Visitors arriving by boat from Phnom Penh or Battambang get a sneak preview, as the floating village is near Phnom Krom, where the boat docks.

# Wildlife Encounters

WHERE THE WILD THINGS ARE

Providing a retirement home for the former working elephants of Angkor that used to give rides to temple visitors, **Kulen Elephant Forest** is a peaceful place to walk with the herd and learn about the lives of elephants at leisure. It's set in the Bos Thom Community Forest, where the 12 resident elephants have more than 1000 hectares to roam. Limited numbers of visitors are welcome to spend the morning or afternoon with these majestic creatures, observing their relationships and behaviour. Lunch is included in the experience at a beautiful wooden house that doubles as a visitor reception.

Newly opened at the end of 2022, **Angkor Wildlife & Aquarium** is designed to showcase the best of Cambodia's invisible freshwater giants lurking in the muddy waters of the Mekong. Notable residents include the giant Mekong catfish and the giant Mekong stingray (the latter believed to be the largest freshwater fish in the world), as well as the much smaller 'river monster', the freshwater puffer fish that famously featured as a star on the popular *National Geographic* show. There are also seawater fish such as reef sharks and eagle rays.

Other animals are housed here too, such as tigers, bears and crocodiles. The vision for this place is to act as both a conservation and education centre for local people. If you don't like zoos, this may not be your cup of tea, but it is a great opportunity to see these 'river monsters' in clear water. It is located about 30km southeast of Siem Reap on NH6.

**ANGKOR CENTRE FOR CONSERVATION OF BIODIVERSITY**

Conveniently located at the base of the trail to Kbal Spean (p147) is the **Angkor Centre for Conservation of Biodiversity (ACCB)**, which is committed to rescuing, rehabilitating and releasing threatened wildlife into Cambodian forests. It also operates conservation breeding programmes for selected threatened species in an attempt to save them from extinction. Daily 1½-hour tours in English are available at 9am and 1pm (except Sunday). Tours outside core hours and special private tours are available upon request.

The centre takes care of about 45 species, totalling more than 550 animals. It is possible to see pileated gibbons, Indochinese silvered langurs, several turtle and tortoise species, green peafowls, small carnivores and a variety of birds of prey.

| **Sala Bai** | **New Leaf Book Cafe** | **Common Grounds** |
|---|---|---|
| Excellent international and Khmer set lunches at a hotel training school that supports disadvantaged youth. **$$** | The menu includes western favourites and Cambodian specials. Profits support NGOs working in Siem Reap. **$** | A sophisticated cafe supporting good causes, with great coffee, homemade cakes, light bites, a kids menu and free wi-fi. **$** |

# A Traditional Floating Village

FLOATING HOUSES AND AN ISLAND PAGODA

One of the more recently 'discovered' floating villages, **Me Chrey** lies midway between Siem Reap and Prek Toal. It is one of the smaller villages in the area and sees far fewer tourists than busy Chong Kneas. Arrange transport by road with a *moto, tuk-tuk* or taxi before switching to a boat to explore the area.

Me Chrey moves with the water level and is prettier during the wet season, when houses are anchored around an island pagoda. It is located to the south of Puok District, about 25km from Siem Reap, on a dirt road through lush rice fields if you're travelling between July and November. This is one of the Cambodian floating communities under threat, as the dwindling fish, eel and snake catches are forcing the village elders to consider relocating to dry land.

# Take a Spin to the Silk Farm

WEAVE TEXTILES INTO YOUR TRIP

Les Chantiers Écoles maintains the **Angkor Silk Farm**, which produces some of the best work in the country, including clothing, interior-design products and accessories. All stages of the production process can be seen here, from the cultivation of mulberry trees to the nurturing of silkworms to the dyeing and weaving of silk. Prior to the COVID-19 pandemic, free tours were available daily, and there are plans to restart them. Previously a free shuttle bus departed from Les Chantiers Écoles in Siem Reap at 9.30am and 1.30pm. The farm is about 16km west of Siem Reap, just off the road to Sisophon in the village of Puok. It also operates shops at the Phnom Penh and Siem Reap airports for those in need of some retail therapy before flying home.

**FLOATING VILLAGE OF KOMPONG LUONG**

Siem Reap is not the only province to have iconic floating villages. **Kompong Luong** (p189) in Pursat Province is the largest floating village on the Tonlé Sap lake and lies midway between Phnom Penh and Battambang.

# Stilted Houses of Kompong Khleang

LARGEST LAKE COMMUNITY IN SIEM REAP

One of the largest communities on the Tonlé Sap, **Kompong Khleang** is more of a town than the other villages, and comes complete with several ornate pagodas. Most of the houses here are built on towering stilts to allow for a dramatic change in water level. There is only a small floating community on the lake, but the stilted town is an interesting place to

**POPULAR CAMBODIAN RESTAURANTS IN SIEM REAP**

**Sugar Palm**
A lovely space to try traditional flavours infused with herbs and spices, like *char kreung* (curried lemongrass) dishes. **$$**

**Khmer Kitchen**
Can't get no (culinary) satisfaction? Follow Mick Jagger's lead and try this spot offering Khmer favourites. **$**

**Kanell**
This is one of the few sophisticated Cambodian restaurants with a regular classical dance show. **$**

**Kampong Khleang**

## BEST CAFES IN SIEM REAP

**Little Red Fox $**
Popular with long-term residents, who swear that the Feel Good Coffee is the best in town. Designer breakfasts, bagels, salads, creative juices and air-con.

**Sister Srey Cafe $**
Near Psar Chaa, with a breakfast menu including 'eggs bene-delicious' – perfect after a temple sunrise. Profits support the 'hero rats' of Apopo (p98).

**Footprints Cafe $**
This popular not-for-profit cafe on lively St 26 supports good causes in Siem Reap. All-day breakfasts, Cambodian favourites and western flavours.

browse for an hour or two. You can take a boat trip around town and to the lake, which also includes a glimpse of the unique flooded forest that fringes the Tonlé Sap in this part of the lake. Fewer tourists visit here compared with the floating villages closer to Siem Reap, so this is a good reason to visit in itself. There are a handful of homestays in Kompong Khleang for those who want to stay the night. All are set in imposing stilted houses and there's even a 'boutique' homestay available. Several food stalls cook up fresh fish and other dishes and most homestays also provide meals for guests.

Kompong Khleang is about 50km from Siem Reap and not difficult to reach thanks to an all-weather road via the junction town of Dam Dek. The trip takes around an hour by taxi (it's a longer ride by *tuk-tuk*). Some visitors like to combine Kompong Khleang with a visit to the jungle temple of Beng Mealea, about 45km to the north via Dam Dek, but it could also be combined with the Roluos group of temples or Angkor Wildlife & Aquarium.

 **SHOPS WORTH SEEKING OUT IN SIEM REAP**

**Satcha**
This beautiful new handicrafts incubation centre (picking up where Artisans Angkor left off) supports independent artisans.

**AHA Fair Trade Village**
For locally produced souvenirs, drop by the stalls at this handicraft market, which sell a range of traditional items.

**SATU Concept Store**
This impressive store showcases a curated selection of Cambodia's best homegrown products in one handy location.

## SIEM REAP SHOPPING

**Kandal Village**, a popular shopping strip located on Hup Guan St, is packed with galleries, boutiques, cafes and restaurants. Places to check out include fair-trade silk designers **Soieries du Mekong** and **Sra May**, lifestyle store **Louise Labatieres** and jewellery emporium **Garden of Desire**.

A new shopping destination next to the Aviary Hotel, **Aviary Square** is a micro mall bringing together some of the country's leading fashion designers and homegrown brands, including the evening-wear collection of **Ambre** from Cambodian designer Romyda Keth, the stunning haute couture of **Eric Raisina**, the versatile linens and cottons of **Sirivan**, and the recycled bags and accessories from **Smateria**.

Pelicans, Prek Toal Bird Sanctuary

# Birder's Paradise of Prek Toal

A UNESCO BIOSPHERE RESERVE

Prek Toal is one of three biospheres on the Tonlé Sap lake, and this stunning **bird sanctuary** makes it the most worthwhile and straightforward of the three to visit. It's an ornithologist's fantasy, with a significant number of rare breeds gathered in one small area, including huge lesser and greater adjutant storks, milky storks, painted storks, spot-billed pelicans and grey-headed fish eagle. Even the uninitiated will be impressed, as these birds have huge wingspans and build enormous nests.

During the peak season (December to early February), visitors will find the concentration of birds like something out of a Hitchcock film. As water starts to dry up elsewhere, the birds congregate here. They remain beyond February but the sanctuary becomes virtually inaccessible due to low water levels. It is also possible to visit from September, but bird numbers may be lower. Serious twitchers know that the best

 **WHERE TO EAT ASIAN FOOD IN SIEM REAP**

**Curry Walla**
Visit for good-value Indian food, including bargain *thalis* (set meals). Owner Ranjit knows his spicy subcontinental specials. **$**

**Hashi**
A big, bright and boisterous sushi parlour, with spicy tuna rolls, chirashi sushi bowls and even wagyu beef tenderloin. **$$**

**Lelawadee Restaurant**
A reliable Thai restaurant, where Thai expats head when they need a spicy fix, including *tom yum kung* (hot and sour soup). **$**

time to see birds is early morning or late afternoon and this means an early start or an overnight at a local homestay or at Prek Toal's environment office.

Several ecotourism companies in Siem Reap arrange trips out to Prek Toal, including **Sam Veasna Conservation Tours** (SVC; samveasna.com), **Cambodia Bird Guide Association** (birdguideasso.org), **Osmose** (osmosetonlesap. net) and **Prek Toal Tours & Travel** (prektoal-tours.com), which is run by Prek Toal villagers. The cost of each tour includes transport, entrance fees, guides, breakfast, lunch and water. Binoculars are available on request, plus SVC has spotting scopes that they set up at observation towers within the park. All outfits can arrange overnight trips for serious enthusiasts. Day trips include a hotel pickup at around 6am and a return by 5pm.

Getting to the sanctuary under your own steam requires you to take a 20-minute *moto* or taxi ride to the floating village of Chong Kneas (depending on the time of day additional fees may have to be paid at the new port), and then a boat to the environment office (one hour each way). From here, a small boat (the fee includes a park guide) will take you into the sanctuary, which is about one hour beyond. The park guides are equipped with booklets with the bird names in English, but they speak little English themselves, hence the advantage of visiting with a tour company that provides English-speaking guides.

Trips to the sanctuary also bring you up close and personal with the fascinating floating village of Prek Toal, a much more rewarding destination than over-touristed, scam-ridden Chong Kneas closer to Siem Reap. Part of your entrance to the sanctuary goes towards educating children and villagers about the importance of the birds and the unique flooded-forest environment.

Always bring sunscreen and head protection to Prek Toal, as it's a long day riding in boats and the sun can be relentless.

# Bird-Spotting at Ang Trapaeng Thmor

SEE THE MAJESTIC SARUS CRANE

**Ang Trapaeng Thmor Reserve** (ATT) is one of only a handful of places in the world where it is possible to see the extremely rare sarus crane, as depicted on the bas-reliefs at Bayon. Reputedly the tallest bird in the world, these grey-feathered creatures have immensely long legs and striking red heads.

**Sam Veasna Conservation Tours** (SVC; samveasna.com) arranges birdwatching excursions out here, which is probably the easiest way to undertake a trip. A conservation contribution is included in the cost of all SVC tours, which supports

## INTERNATIONAL LAND-BORDER CROSSINGS NEAR SIEM REAP

There are several border crossings shared with Thailand that are within target distance of Siem Reap. Visa-on-arrival is available at all the borders, but the only border where a Cambodian e-visa is accepted is Poipet.

Following is a list of the most popular or commonly used border crossings:
**Poipet/Aranya Prathet** (p169) The most popular border crossing, 148km west of Siem Reap.
**Psar Pruhm/Ban Pakard** (p168) A border crossing near Battambang and Pailin, 270km southwest of Siem Reap.
**O Smach/Chong Chom** (p182) A quiet border near Samraong, 164km northwest of Siem Reap.
**Choam/Chong Sa-Ngam** (p180) A remote border near Anlong Veng, 139km north of Siem Reap.

## WHERE TO ORDER COCKTAILS IN SIEM REAP

**The Keys by Tomoka**
On the grounds of a beautiful villa, this is the Siem Reap home of leading cocktail mixology company Tomoka.

**Barcode**
A super-stylish gay bar. Cocktails here are worth a visit, as is the regular drag 9.30pm show.

**Picasso**
A hole-in-the-wall tunnel bar where everyone sits at the semi-circular bar for strong cocktails, including absinthe.

**Angkor Golf Resort**

## SWINGING A CLUB IN SIEM REAP

The world-class course at **Angkor Golf Resort** was designed by British golfer Nick Faldo, while the **Phokeethra Country Club** hosts an annual golf tournament on the Asian tour, and includes an ancient Angkor bridge amid its manicured fairways and greens.

The **Angkor Wat Putt** minigolf (or 'crazy golf') course contrasts with the big golf courses out of town. Navigate minitemples and creative obstacles for 14 holes and win a beer for a hole-in-one. Now located in Chreav District, it is well worth seeking out.

projects that benefit the communities in the conservation areas. At ATT, this has been used to fund a rice bank, which lends rice to families and also repairs roads.

The best time of year to spot the sarus crane is from January to May or at the height of the dry season when water levels are low. More than 200 species of other birds have also been recorded here, including black-necked stork, greater spotted eagle and the oriental plover. It is also possible to see the rare Eld's deer here.

The sanctuary is based around a reservoir created by forced labour during the Khmer Rouge regime, and facilities are very basic, but it is an incredibly beautiful place. SVC also has Swarovski Optik binoculars available to rent if required.

The bird sanctuary is just across the border in the Phnom Srok region of Banteay Meanchey Province, about 100km from Siem Reap. To get here, follow the road to Sisophon for about 72km before turning north at Prey Mon. It's then 22km to the site, passing through some famous silk-weaving villages.

 **SELF-CATERING SUPPLIES IN SIEM REAP**

**Angkor Market**
The best all-round supermarket in town, this huge place on Airport Rd has a huge range of international treats.

**Lucky Market**
A branch of the homegrown national chain, this supermarket is part of the Lucky Mall on Sivatha St.

**Makro**
Makro is a giant wholesale hypermarket located about 5km southeast of town.

# ANGKOR WAT & AROUND

## POTENT SYMBOL OF A NATION

The traveller's first glimpse of Angkor Wat is matched by only a few select spots on earth. Built by Suryavarman II (r 1112–52) and surrounded by a vast moat, the temple is one of the most inspired monuments ever conceived. Stretching around the central temple complex is an 800m-long series of bas-reliefs, and rising 55m above the ground is the central tower in the shape of a lotus, which gives the whole ensemble its sublime unity.

Relish the very first approach, as that spine-tingling moment when you emerge on the inner causeway will rarely be felt again. You are in the presence of the gods, crossing the naga bridge to an earthly representation of Mt Meru, home of the Hindu pantheon. Angkor Wat is the best-preserved temple in Cambodia and repeat visits are rewarded with previously unnoticed details.

### TOP TIP

Allow at least two hours for a visit to Angkor Wat and plan a half-day if you want to decipher the bas-reliefs with a tour guide and ascend to Bakan, the upper level. It's also possible to enter via the eastern causeway – a good way to avoid the crowds if planning a sunrise visit.

### SIGHTS

1 Angkor Wat
2 Bakong
3 Phnom Krom
4 Preah Ko

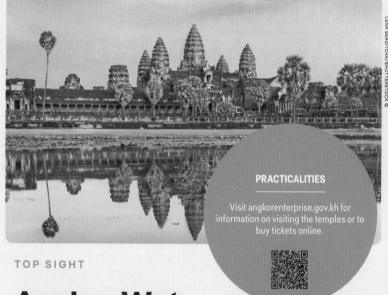

LENA SERDITOVA/SHUTTERSTOCK ©

**PRACTICALITIES**

Visit angkorenterprise.gov.kh for information on visiting the temples or to buy tickets online.

TOP SIGHT

# Angkor Wat

Angkor Wat is the heart and soul of Cambodia: it is the national symbol, the epicentre of Khmer civilisation and a point of fierce national pride. Soaring skyward and surrounded by a moat that would make European castles blush, Angkor Wat was never abandoned to the elements and has been in virtually continuous use since it was built in the 12th century.

**DON'T MISS**

Western Causeway

Statue of Vishnu

Sunrise Ponds

Churning of the Ocean of Milk Bas-Relief

Army of Suryavarman II Bas-Relief

Gallery of a Thousand Buddhas

Bakan Sanctuary

## Western Causeway

From the west, a sandstone causeway crosses the moat. The sandstone blocks from which Angkor Wat was built were quarried more than 50km away (from the holy mountain of Phnom Kulen) and floated down the Siem Reap River on rafts. The logistics of such an operation are mind-blowing, consuming the labour of thousands. According to inscriptions, the construction of Angkor Wat involved 300,000 workers and 6000 elephants, yet it was still not fully completed.

## Statue of Vishnu

The rectangular outer wall, which measures 1025m by 800m, has a gate on each side, but the main entrance, a 235m-wide portico richly decorated with carvings and sculptures, is on the western side. There is a statue of Vishnu, 3.25m in height and hewn from a single block of sandstone, located in the southeast tower (it was originally housed in the central tower of the temple). You may also see locks of hair lying about. These are offerings both from young people preparing to get married and from pilgrims giving thanks for their good fortune.

## Sunrise Ponds

There are two royal bathing ponds on the west side of Angkor Wat and these are the most popular place to witness sunrise over this iconic temple. Traditionally the northern pond was the most popular, but due to ongoing archaeological work there, most visitors now choose the southern pond. Sunrise is usually around 5.45am, but most people try to arrive at the temple by 5.30am to find a good spot. If you are lucky enough to be at Angkor Wat for the spring or autumn equinox, you will see the sun rise directly over the central tower.

## Bas-Reliefs

Stretching around the outside of the central temple complex is an 800m-long series of intricate and astonishing bas-reliefs. The majority were completed in the 12th century, but in the 16th century several notably inferior new reliefs were added to unfinished panels. Highlights include the Churning of the Ocean of Milk and the Army of Suryavarman II.

## Gallery of a Thousand Buddhas

The Gallery of a Thousand Buddhas (Preah Poan) used to house hundreds of Buddha images before the war, but many of these were removed or stolen, leaving just the handful we see today. Many Cambodians make a pilgrimage here to be blessed in front of the standing Buddha.

## Bakan Sanctuary

Also known as Bakan, the upper level of Angkor Wat is open (8am to 5pm daily, except religious holidays; 12 years and over) to a limited number of visitors per day with a timed queuing system. Ascend to the 55m summit, savour the cooling breeze, take in the extensive views and then find a quiet corner in which to contemplate the sheer scale of this Everest of temples. Clothing that covers to the elbows and knees is required to visit this upper level.

**TOP TIPS**

- Enter via the eastern causeway to avoid the larger tour groups entering via the western causeway.
- Remember that a three- or seven-day pass doesn't have to be used on consecutive days, so you can mix up your days with some non-temple activities.
- Save Angkor Wat until later in a temple itinerary, as it makes sense to build anticipation in terms of size and scale.

**SUNRISE**

When planning an iconic sunrise visit to Angkor Wat, set the alarm for earlier than 5am and head out to arrive at the temple by around 5.15am. The sun usually comes up at about 5.30am to 5.45am, depending on the time of year. Bring a torch – it will be dark and the sandstone causeway is uneven. Stick around after sunrise, as most tour groups head back to their hotels, leaving Angkor Wat mercifully empty by around 7am.

# Temples of Angkor

## Three-Day Exploration

The temple complex at Angkor is simply enormous and the superlatives don't do it justice. This is the site of the world's largest religious building, a multitude of temples and a vast, long-abandoned walled city that was arguably Southeast Asia's first metropolis, long before Bangkok and Singapore got in on the action.

Starting at the Roluos group of temples, one of the earliest capitals of Angkor, move on to the big circuit, which includes the Buddhist-Hindu fusion temple of **1 Preah Khan** and the ornate water temple of **2 Preah Neak Poan**.

On the second day downsize to the small circuit, starting with an early visit to **3 Ta Prohm**, before continuing to the temple pyramid of Ta Keo, the Buddhist monastery of Banteay Kdei and the immense royal bathing pond of **4 Sra Srang**.

Next venture further afield to Banteay Srei temple, the jewel in the crown of Angkorian art, and Beng Mealea, a remote jungle temple.

Saving the biggest and best until last, experience sunrise at **5 Angkor Wat** and stick around for breakfast in the temple to discover its amazing architecture without the crowds. In the afternoon, explore **6 Angkor Thom**, an immense complex that is home to the enigmatic **7 Bayon**.

Three days around Angkor? That's just for starters.

## TOP TIPS

- To avoid the crowds, try dawn at Sra Srang, post-sunrise at Angkor Wat and lunchtime at Banteay Srei.
- Three-day passes can be used on non-consecutive days over the course of a week, but be sure to request this.

**Bayon**
The surreal state temple of legendary king Jayavarman VII, where 216 faces stare down on pilgrims, asserting religious and regal authority.

Terrace of the Leper King
Preah Palilay
Phimeanakas Temple
Tep Pranam
West Gate Angkor Thom
Baphuon Temple
Terrace of the Elephants
**7**
South Gate Angkor Thom
Phnom Bakheng
Baksei Chamrong
**5**

**Angkor Wat**
The world's largest religious building. Experience sunrise at the holiest of holies, then explore the beautiful bas-reliefs – devotion etched in stone.

### Angkor Thom
The last great capital of the Khmer empire conceals a wealth of temples and its epic proportions would have inspired and terrified in equal measure.

### Preah Khan
A fusion temple dedicated to Buddha, Brahma, Shiva and Vishnu; the immense corridors are like an unending hall of mirrors.

### Preah Neak Poan
If Vegas ever adopts the Angkor theme, this will be the swimming pool; a petite tower set in a lake, surrounded by four smaller ponds.

North Gate, Angkor Thom

Preah Pithu

Thommanon Temple

Prasat Suor Prat

Victory Gate Angkor Thom

East Gate Angkor Thom

Chau Say Tevoda

Ta Keo Temple

Ta Nei Temple

Banteay Srei

Banteay Kdei Temple

Roluos, Beng Mealea

Prasat Kravan

Bat Chum Temple

### Ta Prohm
Nicknamed the *Tomb Raider* temple; *Indiana Jones* would be equally apt. Nature has run riot, leaving iconic tree roots strangling the surviving stones.

### Sra Srang
Once the royal bathing pond, this is the ablutions pool to beat all ablutions pools and makes a good stop for sunrise or sunset.

117

BOB KRIST/GETTY IMAGES ©

**Vishnu statue, Angkor Wat**

## THE DECLINE OF ANGKOR

Angkor was the epicentre of an incredible empire that held sway over much of the Mekong region, but like all empires, the sun was to eventually set. There are indications that the irrigation network was overworked and slowly started to silt up due to the massive deforestation that had taken place around Angkor. This was also exacerbated by prolonged periods of drought in the 14th century.

Another challenge for the later kings was religious conflict and internecine rivalries. The state religion changed back and forth several times during the twilight years of the empire, and kings spent more time engaged in iconoclasm, defacing the temples of their predecessors, than building monuments to their own achievements.

---

MORE IN & AROUND ANGKOR WAT

---

# The One & Only Angkor Wat

EIGHTH WONDER OF THE WORLD

**Angkor Wat** is, figuratively, heaven on earth. It is the earthly representation of Mt Meru, the Mt Olympus of the Hindu faith and the abode of ancient gods. The 'temple that is a city', Angkor Wat is simply unique, a stunning blend of spirituality and symmetry, an enduring example of humanity's devotion to its gods. Angkor Wat is surrounded by a 190m-wide moat, which forms a giant rectangle measuring 1.5km by 1.3km. An avenue, 475m long, 9.5m wide and lined with naga balustrades, leads from the main entrance to the central temple, passing between two graceful libraries and then two pools, both popular spots from which to watch the sun rise.

The central temple complex consists of three storeys, each made of laterite, which enclose a square surrounded by

---

 **WHERE TO GET A POST-ANGKOR ICE-CREAM FIX** —————

**Gelato Lab**
State-of-the-art equipment, natural ingredients and plenty of passion from the owner add up to great ice cream. **$**

**Swenson's**
One of America's favourites has become one of Siem Reap's favourites, at the Angkor Trade Centre. **$**

**Glasshouse**
Velvety ice creams, including white chocolate and tangy sorbets, located in the Park Hyatt Hotel. **$**

intricately interlinked galleries. The corners of the second and third storeys are marked by towers, each topped with symbolic lotus-bud towers. The stairs to the upper level are immensely steep, because reaching the kingdom of the gods was no easy task.

Eleanor Mannikka explains in her book *Angkor Wat: Time, Space and Kingship* that the spatial dimensions of Angkor Wat parallel the lengths of the four ages (Yuga) of classical Hindu thought. Thus the visitor to Angkor Wat who walks the causeway to the main entrance and through the courtyards to the final main tower, which once contained a statue of Vishnu, is metaphorically travelling back to the first age of the creation of the universe.

There is much about Angkor Wat that is unique among the temples of Angkor. The most significant fact is that the temple is oriented towards the west. Symbolically, west is the direction of death, which once led many scholars to conclude that Angkor Wat must have existed primarily as a tomb. This idea was supported by the fact that the magnificent bas-reliefs of the temple were designed to be viewed in an anticlockwise direction, a practice that has precedents in ancient Hindu funerary rites. Vishnu, however, is also frequently associated with the west, and it is now commonly accepted that Angkor Wat most likely served both as a temple and as a mausoleum for Suryavarman II.

Like the other temple-mountains of Angkor, Angkor Wat also replicates the spatial universe in miniature. The central tower is Mt Meru, with its surrounding smaller peaks, bounded in turn by continents (the lower courtyards) and the oceans (the moat). The seven-headed naga becomes a symbolic rainbow bridge for humanity to reach the abode of the gods.

While Suryavarman II may have planned Angkor Wat as his funerary temple or mausoleum, he was never buried here, as he died in battle during a failed expedition to subdue the Dai Viet (Vietnamese).

The southern section of the east gallery is decorated by the most famous of the bas-relief scenes at Angkor Wat, the **Churning of the Ocean of Milk**. This brilliantly executed carving depicts 88 *asuras* on the left, and 92 *devas*, with crested helmets, churning up the sea to extract from it the elixir of immortality.The demons hold the head of the serpent Vasuki and the gods hold its tail. At the centre of the sea, Vasuki is coiled around Mt Mandala, which turns and churns up the water in the tug of

## GUIDED TOURS AROUND ANGKOR

Visitors who have only a day or two at this incredible site may prefer something organised locally. It is possible to link up with an official tour guide in Siem Reap, where a number of operators run tours ranging from simple day trips to cycling tours to excursions to more remote temple sites.

The Khmer Angkor Tour Guide Association represents some of Angkor's authorised guides. English- or French-speaking guides are available; guides speaking other languages, such as Italian, German, Spanish, Japanese and Chinese, are available at higher rates as there are fewer of them.

## THE SACRED BUDDHAS OF PREAH POAN

Many of the 16th-century polychrome or wooden Buddha statues from Preah Poan or the Gallery of a Thousand Buddhas at Angkor Wat are now on display in a permanent collection in the **National Museum of Cambodia** (p51) in Phnom Penh.

## BOUTIQUE HOTELS CLOSE TO ANGKOR WAT

**Montra Nivesha**
A beautiful boutique hotel, with rooms set around lush gardens and two pools. **$$**

**Templation**
An impressive resort offering spacious pool suites in its extensive gardens, as well as its unique 'jungloo' cabins. **$$$**

**Pavillon Indochine**
Offers charming colonial-chic rooms decorated with Asian antiquities, set around a small swimming pool. **$$**

war between the demons and the gods. Vishnu, incarnated as a huge turtle, lends his shell to serve as the base and pivot of Mt Mandala. Brahma, Shiva, Hanuman (the monkey god) and Lakshmi (the goddess of wealth and prosperity) all make appearances, while overhead a host of heavenly female spirits sing and dance in encouragement.

The remarkable western section of the south gallery depicts a triumphal battle march of **Suryavarman II's army**. In the southwestern corner about 2m from the floor is Suryavarman II on an elephant, wearing the royal tiara and armed with a battleaxe; he is shaded by 15 parasols and fanned by legions of servants.

Compare this image of the king with the image of Rama in the northern gallery and you'll notice an uncanny likeness that helped reinforce the aura of the god-king.

Further on is a procession of well-armed soldiers and officers on horseback; among them are bold and warlike chiefs on elephants. Just before the end of this panel is the rather disorderly Siamese mercenary army, with their long headdresses and ragged marching, at that time allied with the Khmers in their conflict with the Chams. The Khmer troops have square breastplates and are armed with spears; the Thais wear skirts and carry tridents.

The southern portion of the west gallery depicts the **Battle of Kurukshetra**, from the Hindu *Mahabharata* epic, in which the Kauravas (coming from the north) and the Pandavas (coming from the south) advance upon each other, meeting in furious battle. Infantry are shown on the lowest tier, with officers on elephants, and chiefs on the second and third tiers.

Over the centuries, some sections have been polished (by the millions of hands that have fallen upon them) to look like black marble. The portico at the southwestern corner is decorated with sculptures representing characters from the *Ramayana*.

The punishments and rewards of the **37 heavens and 32 hells** are depicted in the eastern half of the south gallery. On the left, the upper and middle tiers show fine gentlemen and ladies proceeding towards 18-armed Yama (the judge of the dead) seated on a bull; below him are his assistants, Dharma and Sitragupta. On the lower tier, devils drag the wicked along the road to hell.

To Yama's right, the tableau is divided into two parts by a horizontal line of *garudas* (mythical half-man, half-bird creatures): above, the elect dwell in beautiful mansions, served by women and attendants; below, the condemned suffer horri-

## VISITOR CODE OF CONDUCT

While Angkor is not a million miles away from the beaches of the South Coast, it is important to remember that the temples represent a sacred religious site to the Khmer people, and the authorities have begun cracking down on inappropriate dress at the temples. Expect to be sent back to your guesthouse to change if you are wearing sleeveless tops, hot pants or short skirts.

Local authorities have recently released visitor 'code of conduct' guidelines and a video to encourage dressing appropriately, and to remind tourists not to touch or sit on the ancient structures, to pay attention to restricted areas, and to be respectful of monks.

 **RESTAURANTS CLOSE TO ANGKOR WAT**

**Angkor Parvis**
The western approach to the complex has been remodelled as a parvis with restaurants, cafes and souvenir shops. **$**

**Mahob**
The *mahob* (the Khmer word for 'food') here is delicious, with dishes like wok-fried beef with red ants. **$$**

**Amok Khmer**
An open-air poolside restaurant serving traditional Khmer cuisine, including the one and only *amok* (baked fish dish). **$$**

Bas-relief of the Battle of Kurukshetra, Angkor Wat

## THE APSARAS OF ANGKOR WAT

Angkor Wat is famous for its beguiling *apsaras* (heavenly nymphs). Almost 2000 *apsaras* are carved into the walls of Angkor Wat, each of them unique, and there are 37 different hairstyles for budding stylists to check out. Many of these exquisite *apsaras* have been damaged by centuries of bat droppings and urine, but they are now being restored by the **German Apsara Conservation Project** (GACP; gacp-angkor. de). The organisation operates a small information booth in the northwestern corner of Angkor Wat, near the modern wat, where beautiful postcards and images of Angkor are available.

ble tortures that might have inspired the Khmer Rouge. The ceiling in this section was restored by the French in the 1930s.

The northern half of the west gallery shows scenes from the *Ramayana*. In the **Battle of Lanka**, Rama (on the shoulders of Hanuman), along with his army of monkeys, battles 10-headed, 20-armed Ravana, captor of Rama's beautiful wife Sita. Ravana rides a chariot drawn by monsters and commands an army of giants.

The western section of the north gallery depicts a **Battle of Gods and Demons**, between the 21 gods of the Brahmanic pantheon and various demons. The gods are featured with their traditional attributes and mounts. Vishnu has four arms and is seated on a *garuda,* while Shiva rides a sacred goose.

The eastern section of the north gallery shows Vishnu incarnated as **Krishna** riding a *garuda.* He confronts a burning walled city, the residence of

## OTHER SURYAVARMAN II TEMPLES

Suryavarman II built several other impressive temples in the Angkor area, including the vast jungle ruin of **Beng Mealea** (p149) and the smaller temple of **Banteay Samré** (p145). He also expanded the iconic mountain temple of **Prasat Preah Vihear** (p172).

 **CYCLING TOURS AROUND ANGKOR**

**Angkor Village Cycling Tour**
A nice range of countryside cycling tours, plus well-priced bike rentals, with child-seat options available.

**Camouflage**
Specialist operator with tours taking in temples, remote sites and the beautiful countryside around Phnom Kulen.

**Off Track Tours**
Trips around Angkor and the countryside beyond the Western Baray. Proceeds go towards education and training.

Bakong

## BEST WEBSITES ON ANGKOR

**Angkor – Unesco World Heritage Site** (whc.unesco.org/en/list/668) Information, images and videos on the world's top temples.

**Lonely Planet** (lonelyplanet.com/cambodia/angkor-wat) Destination information, inspiration and more.

**National Geographic** (nationalgeographic.com/magazine/article/divining-angkor) An in-depth feature on the rise and fall of Angkor.

**Bana, the demon king**. The *garuda* puts out the fire and Bana is captured. In the final scene Krishna kneels before Shiva and asks that Bana's life be spared.

The northern section of the east gallery shows a furious and desperate encounter between **Vishnu**, riding on a *garuda,* and innumerable **devils**. Needless to say, he slays all comers. This gallery was most likely completed in the 16th century, and the later carving is notably inferior to the original work from the 12th century.

### WAR & PEACE IN SIEM REAP

There are more sights related to war (or peace) for a modern history fix. Meet the 'hero rats' at **Apopo Visitor Centre** (p98) or explore the **Cambodia Landmine Museum** (p144) near Banteay Srei.

# Classical Khmer Temples of Roluos

THE ANCIENT CAPITAL OF HARIHARALAYA

The monuments of Roluos. which served as Indravarman I's capital, Hariharalaya, are among the earliest large, permanent temples built by the Khmers and mark the dawn of Khmer classical art. Before the construction of Bakong temple, generally only

 **MOTORBIKE TOURS AROUND ANGKOR**

**Hidden Cambodia**
Siem Reap–based company specialising in motorcycle trips to the remote temples of northern Cambodia and beyond.

**Khmer Ways**
Live the dream…or at least ride a Honda Dream. Choose from a countryside tour or a Phnom Kulen adventure.

**Siem Reap Vespa Adventures**
The modern Vespa is a great way to explore temples, learn about local life or find street food after dark.

lighter (and less durable) construction materials such as brick were employed. As well as the imposing pyramid temple of Bakong, the Roluos group also includes the brick temple of Preah Ko and Lolei, originally an island temple.

Allow three hours or so to explore the three temples of Roluos and nearby handicraft projects. It is also possible to visit the nearby small country town of Roluos, complete with a very traditional local market. Plan a half-day visit to the temples together with the stilted village of Kompong Pluk on the Tonlé Sap lake.

**Bakong** is the largest and most interesting of the Roluos group of temples. Built and dedicated to Shiva by Indravarman I, it's a representation of Mt Meru, and it served as the city's central temple. The east-facing complex consists of a five-tier central pyramid of sandstone, 60m square at the base, flanked by eight towers of brick and sandstone, and by other minor sanctuaries. A number of the lower towers are still partly covered by their original plasterwork.

The complex is enclosed by three concentric walls and a moat. There are well-preserved statues of stone elephants on each corner of the first three levels of the central temple. There are 12 stupas – three to each side – on the third tier. The sanctuary on the fifth level of Bakong temple was a later addition during the reign of Suryavarman II, in the style of Angkor Wat's central tower. There is an active Buddhist monastery here, dating back a century or more, which has recently been restored.

**Preah Ko** was erected by Indravarman I in the late 9th century and dedicated to Shiva. In 880 CE the temple was also dedicated to his deified ancestors: the front towers relate to male ancestors or gods, the rear towers to female ancestors or goddesses. Lions guard the steps up to the temple. Preah Ko (Sacred Ox) features three *nandis* (sacred oxen), all of whom look like a few steaks have been sliced off over the years.

The six *prasat* (stone halls), aligned in two rows and decorated with carved sandstone and plaster reliefs, face east; the central tower of the front row is a great deal larger than the other towers. Some of the best surviving examples of plasterwork in Angkor can be seen here, restored by the German Apsara Conservation Project (p121). There are elaborate inscriptions in the ancient Hindu language of Sanskrit on the doorposts of each tower.

## THE ISLAND TEMPLE OF LOLEI

The four brick towers of **Lolei** here are almost an exact replica of the towers of Preah Ko, although they are in a much worse shape of preservation. They were originally built on an island in the centre of a large reservoir known as Indratataka or the Northern Baray – now rice fields – by Yasovarman I, the founder of the first city at Angkor.

The sandstone carvings in the niches of the temples are worth a closer inspection, and there are Sanskrit inscriptions on the doorposts. According to one of the inscriptions, the four towers were dedicated by Yasovarman I to his mother, his father and his maternal grandparents on 12 July 893.

## PLACES TO STAY & EAT NEAR ROLUOS

| **Lom Lam Homestay** | **Angkor Rural Boutique Hotel** | **Stung Trorcheak Restaurant** |
|---|---|---|
| Set in a large Cambodian house, with furnishing and bedding that are more like that of an upscale guesthouse. **$** | This charming place offers a slice of countryside comfort. Rooms are set around a garden and pool. **$** | Choose from Cambodian classics, Chinese favourites and Thai tasters at this restaurant in a shady riverside garden. **$** |

## SIGHTS & SHOPPING AROUND ROLUOS

The CMAC (Cambodian Mine Action Centre) **Peace Museum of Mine Action** gets very few visitors due to its out-of-the-way location, but it is an educational and sobering experience to learn about the legacy of landmines in Cambodia. Exhibits include decommissioned bombs and landmines. A local guide will show you around.

Several good-cause initiatives have sprung up around the Roluos area. Right opposite Preah Ko is the **Khmer Group Art of Weaving**, turning out silk and cotton scarves on traditional looms. Also here is **Dy Proeung Master Sculptor**, who has created scale replicas of Preah Ko, Bakong, Lolei, Angkor Wat, Preah Vihear and Banteay Srei. Not far from here on NH66 is the **Lo-Yuyu Ceramics** workshop, producing traditional Angkorian-style pottery.

ALES MARYAN/SHUTTERSTOCK ©

**Phnom Krom**

## Hilltop Temple of Phnom Krom

SUNSET VIEWS OVER TONLÉ SAP

The temple of Phnom Krom, 12km south of Siem Reap on a hill overlooking Tonlé Sap lake, dates from the reign of Yasovarman I in the late 9th or early 10th century. The name means 'Lower Hill' and is a reference to its geographic location in relation to its sister temples of Phnom Bakheng and Phnom Bok. Phnom Krom remains one of the more tranquil spots from which to view the sunset, complete with an active wat. The sunsets can be spectacular, with vast cloud formations in the wet season and vivid streaks of orange and purple cirrus clouds in the dry season, and the floating village of Chong Kneas visible below on the shimmering water.

The three towers, dedicated (from north to south) to Vishnu, Shiva and Brahma, are in a ruined state. It is necessary to have an Angkor pass to visit the temple at the summit of Phnom Krom, so don't come all the way out here without one, as the guards won't allow you access to the summit of the hill. If visiting here by *moto* or car, try to get the driver to take you to the summit, as it is a long, hot climb otherwise, taking about 30 minutes. Consider a half-day visit in tandem with exploring the village of Chong Kneas. There are also some very photogenic lotus farms on the way out to Phnom Krom from Siem Reap, as the vast area around the hill is completely flooded in the wet season.

 **LESSER-KNOWN GODS AROUND ANGKOR**

**Garuda**
Vehicle of Vishnu; this half-man, half-bird was combined with the naga to promote religious unity under Jayavarman VII.

**Kala**
This temple guardian (aka Rehu) was so hungry he devoured his own body, appearing only as a giant head above doorways.

**Makara**
A giant sea serpent featuring on the corner of pediments, spewing forth a naga or some other creature.

# ANGKOR THOM

## THE GREAT WALLED CITY OF ANGKOR

It's hard to imagine any building bigger or more beautiful than Angkor Wat, but in Angkor Thom (Great City) the sum of the parts add up to a greater whole. Centred on Bayon, the surreal state temple of Jayavarman VII, Angkor Thom is enclosed by a formidable wall, 8m high and 13km in length, and encircled by a 100m-wide moat that would have stopped all but the hardiest invaders in their tracks.

In the centre of the walled enclosure are the city's most important monuments, including Bayon, Baphuon, the Royal Enclosure, Phimeanakas and the Terrace of Elephants. Set aside a half-day to explore Angkor Thom in depth. Beyond Angkor Thom, you can make for the atmospheric jungle temple of Ta Prohm, where nature continues its timeless march. Other important sites include the sister temple of Preah Khan, the giant pyramid of Ta Keo and the petite ornamental fountain complex of Preah Neak Poan.

## TOP TIP

If coming from Angkor Wat, you'll enter Angkor Thom through the south gate. From Ta Prohm, you'll enter through the Victory Gate on the eastern side. The immense north gate of Angkor Thom connects the walled city with Preah Khan and the temples of the Grand Circuit. The west gate leads to the Western Baray.

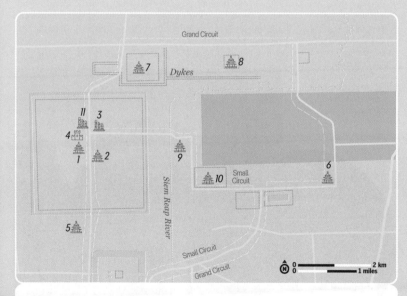

**SIGHTS**
1 Baphuon
2 Bayon
3 Kleangs
4 Phimeanakas
5 Phnom Bakheng
6 Pre Rup
7 Preah Khan
8 Preah Neak Poan
9 Ta Keo
10 Ta Prohm
11 Terrace of the Leper King

# Face to Face with the Bayon

THE SMILING AVALOKITESHVARA

**KING JAYAVARMAN VII**

A devout follower of Mahayana Buddhism, Jayavarman VII (r 1181–1219) built the city of Angkor Thom and many of the temples around Angkor. However, he is a figure of contradiction. Bayon's bas-reliefs depict him presiding over ferocious battles, while statues of him show a meditative, otherworldly aspect. His programme of temple construction was done in great haste, no doubt bringing enormous hardship to the labourers. But in many ways he was also Cambodia's first progressive leader, proclaiming the population equal, abolishing castes and embarking on school, hospital and road building.

At the heart of Angkor Thom is the 12th-century **Bayon**, the mesmerising, if slightly mind-bending, state temple of Jayavarman VII. It epitomises the creative genius and inflated ego of Cambodia's most celebrated king. Its 54 Gothic towers are decorated with 216 gargantuan smiling faces of Avalokiteshvara, and it is adorned with 1.2km of extraordinary bas-reliefs incorporating more than 11,000 figures.

Unique, even among its cherished contemporaries, the architectural audacity of Bayon was a definitive political statement about the shift from Hinduism to Mahayana Buddhism. Known as the 'face temple' thanks to its iconic visages, these huge heads glare down from every angle, exuding power and control with a hint of humanity. This was precisely the blend required to hold sway over such a vast empire, ensuring the disparate and far-flung population yielded to Jayavarman VII's magnanimous will. As you walk around, a dozen or more of the heads are visible at any one time, full face or in profile, sometimes level with your eyes, sometimes staring down from on high.

Though Bayon is now known to have been built by Jayavarman VII, for many years its origins were unknown. Shrouded in dense jungle, it also took researchers some time to realise that it stands in the exact centre of the city of Angkor Thom. There is still much mystery associated with Bayon – such as its exact function and symbolism – and this seems only appropriate for a monument whose signature is an enigmatic smiling face.

**Bayon**

**BUSTS OF KING JAYAVARMAN VII**

The meditative bust of King Jayavarman VII is an iconic symbol of Cambodia and is a popular purchase for tourists. There are some beautiful original examples in the **Angkor National Museum** (p96) and in Phnom Penh's **National Museum of Cambodia** (p51).

DMITRY RUKHLENKO/SHUTTERSTOCK ©

**South gate of Angkor Thom**

MORE IN ANGKOR THOM

## The Bas-Reliefs of the Bayon

LIFE IN 12TH-CENTURY CAMBODIA

The basic structure of the **Bayon** comprises a simple three levels, which correspond more or less to three distinct phases of building. This is because Jayavarman VII began construction of this temple at an advanced age, so he was never confident it would be completed. Each time one phase was completed, he moved on to the next. The first two levels are square and adorned with bas-reliefs. They lead up to a third, circular level, with the towers and their faces.

The temple's eastward orientation leads most people to visit it in the morning, though Bayon looks equally good in the late afternoon. The upper level of Bayon was closed for restoration when we visited and is scheduled to reopen in 2024. However, the lower levels, including the epic bas-reliefs, remain open throughout the restoration.

### A LOCAL ARCHAEOLOGIST ON ANGKOR

**Professor Ang Choulean** is a leading anthropologist, archaeologist and Cambodian scholar.

**What is the most important Khmer temple?** Angkor Thom is the most striking and challenging for archaeologists, as it was a living city with humans and gods co-inhabiting there.

**Who is the most important king in Cambodian history?** Suryavarman I, who had a real political vision, which can be measured by the monuments he built, such as Preah Vihear and Wat Phu in southern Laos.

**What is your position on the debate between romance and restoration at jungle temples like Ta Prohm and Beng Mealea?** It is a matter of balance. The trees are most impressive, but maintaining the monuments is our duty to future generations.

### ◎ THE GATES OF ANGKOR THOM

**South Gate**
The best preserved of Angkor Thom's gates; epic depiction of the Churning of the Ocean of Milk.

**East Gate**
Also known as the Gate of the Dead, where the kings of Angkor departed the walled city for cremation.

**Victory Gate**
This eastern-wall gate was for the return of victorious kings after vanquishing enemies in battle.

## THE GARGANTUAN GATES OF ANGKOR THOM

It's the gates that grab you first, flanked by a representation of the Churning of the Ocean of Milk, 54 demons and 54 gods engaged in an epic tug of war. Each gate towers above the visitor, the magnanimous faces of the Bodhisattva Avalokiteshvara surveying the kingdom.

The south gate is most popular with visitors, as it has been fully restored and many of the heads (mostly copies) remain in place. The gate gets very busy; more peaceful are the east and west gates.

STEVE ESTVANIK/SHUTTERSTOCK ©

**Bas-relief of the Naval Battle**

Some say that the Khmer empire was divided into 54 provinces at the time of Bayon's construction, hence the 54 pairs of all-seeing eyes keeping watch on the kingdom's outlying subjects.

### THE BAS-RELIEFS OF BANTEAY CHHMAR

There are only two temples in the country that display scenes of daily life from 12th-century Cambodia, both constructed by King Jayavarman VII. Along with the Bayon, the other place to see similar bas-reliefs is **Banteay Chhmar** (p169) in northwest Cambodia.

The famous carvings on the outer wall of the first level depict vivid scenes of everyday life in 12th-century Cambodia. The bas-reliefs on the second level do not have the epic proportions of those on the first level and tend to be fragmented. The reliefs described are those on the first level. The sequence assumes that you enter the Bayon from the east and view the reliefs in a clockwise direction.

Moving in a clockwise direction from just south of the east gate you'll encounter your first bas-relief, **Chams on the Run**, a three-level panorama. On the first tier, Khmer soldiers march off to battle – check out the elephants and the oxcarts, which are almost exactly like those still used in Cambodia today. The second tier depicts coffins being carried back

 **TOP TIPS FOR ANGKOR THOM**

**Monkey Business**
Watch out for the macaques around Angkor Thom's south gate and along the main avenue to Bayon: they can bite.

**Bird-Spotting**
When walking Angkor Thom's walls, keep an eye out for forest birds in the trees and wetland birds at the moat.

**Food Stalls**
Angkor Thom has no restaurants, but food stalls are behind the Terrace of the Leper King and in front of Preah Pithu.

from the battlefield. In the centre of the third tier, Jayavarman VII, shaded by parasols, is shown on horseback followed by legions of concubines (to the left).

Moving on, the first panel north of the southeastern corner shows **Hindus praying to a linga** (phallic symbol). This image was probably originally a Buddha, later modified by a Hindu king.

The **Naval Battle** panel has some of the best-carved reliefs. The scenes depict a naval battle between the Khmers and the Chams (the latter with head coverings), and everyday life around the Tonlé Sap lake, where the battle was fought. Look for images of people picking lice from each other's hair, of hunters and, towards the western end of the panel, a woman giving birth.

In the **Chams Vanquished**, scenes from daily life are featured while the battle between the Khmers and the Chams takes place on the shore of Tonlé Sap lake, where the Chams are soundly thrashed. Scenes include two people playing chess, a cockfight and women selling fish in the market. The scenes of meals being prepared and served are in celebration of the Khmer victory.

The most western relief of the south gallery, depicting a **Military Procession**, is unfinished, as is the panel showing elephants being led down from the mountains. Brahmans have been chased up two trees by tigers.

The next panel depicts scenes that some scholars maintain is a **Civil War**. Groups of people, some armed, confront each other, and the violence escalates until elephants and warriors join the melee.

Just north of the Civil War panel, the fighting continues on a smaller scale in the **All-Seeing King**. An antelope is being swallowed by a gargantuan fish; among the smaller fish is a prawn, under which an inscription proclaims that the king will seek out those in hiding.

At the western corner of the northern wall is a **Khmer circus**. A strongman holds three dwarfs, and a man on his back is spinning a wheel with his feet; above is a group of tightrope walkers.

The **Sacking of Angkor** shows the war of 1177, when the Khmers were defeated by the Chams, and Angkor was pillaged. The wounded Khmer king is being lowered from the back of an elephant and a wounded Khmer general is being carried on a hammock suspended from a pole. Directly above, despairing Khmers are getting drunk. The Chams (on the right) are in hot pursuit of their vanquished enemy.

The next panel, the **Chams Enter Angkor**, depicts a meeting of the Khmer and Cham armies. Notice the flag bearers

## THE TERRACE OF ELEPHANTS

The 350m-long Terrace of Elephants was used as a giant viewing stand for public ceremonies and served as a base for the king's grand audience hall. Try to imagine the pomp and grandeur of the Khmer empire at its height, with infantry, cavalry, horse-drawn chariots and elephants parading across the Central Square. Looking on is the god-king, shaded by parasols and attended by mandarins and handmaidens.

The Terrace of Elephants has five piers extending towards the Central Square – three in the centre and one at each end. The middle section of the retaining wall is decorated with life-size *garudas* and lions; towards either end are the two parts of the famous parade of elephants, complete with their Khmer mahouts.

 **LESSER-KNOWN MUSEUMS AROUND ANGKOR**

**MGC Asian Traditional Textiles Museum**
Showcases the best in Asian textiles in the region, including from Cambodia, Laos and India.

**Preah Norodom Sihanouk Angkor Museum**
A Cambodian-Japanese museum housing rare Buddhas found at Banteay Kdei.

**Wat Bo Museum**
Exhibits the private collection of Chief Monk Preah Moha Vimal Dhamma Serey Sovanno Pin Sem. Located in Wat Bo Pagoda.

among the Cham troops (on the right). The Chams were defeated in the war, which ended in 1181, as depicted on the first panel in the sequence.

# Buddhism Meets Hinduism at Baphuon

THE WORLD'S LARGEST JIGSAW PUZZLE

Before Cambodia's civil war the **Baphuon** was painstakingly taken apart piece by piece by a team of archaeologists, but their meticulous records were destroyed during the Khmer Rouge regime in the 1970s. This left Khmer and French experts with 300,000 stones to put back into place when they returned to restoration work in the early 1990s.

After years of painstaking research, this temple has been partially restored, with the construction of a vast concrete base to shore up its foundations, as the sheer weight of the immense structure was threatening to collapse in on itself as had happened at Borobudur in Indonesia in the early 20th century.

In its heyday, Baphuon would have been one of the most spectacular of Angkor's temples. Located 200m northwest of Bayon, it's a pyramidal representation of mythical Mt Meru. Construction probably began under Suryavarman I and was later completed by Udayadityavarman II. It marked the centre of the capital that existed before the construction of Angkor Thom.

The site is approached by a 200m elevated walkway made of sandstone, and the central structure is 43m high. Clamber under the elevated causeway for an incredible view of the hundreds of pillars supporting it. In the 16th century the retaining wall on the western side of the second level was fashioned into a 60m reclining Buddha and you can make out the face and part of the body.

It takes around one hour to explore Baphuon in its entirety, although it is possible to have a faster visit if you skip the upper levels.

# Resting Place of the Leper King

ENTER THE ROYAL CREMATORIUM

The **Terrace of the Leper King** is just north of the Terrace of Elephants. Dating from the late 12th century, it is a 7m-high platform, on top of which stands a replica of a nude, though sexless, statue. The front retaining walls of the terrace are decorated with at least five tiers of meticulously executed carvings.

## THE BUDDHIST TEMPLES OF ANGKOR THOM

**Preah Palilay** is located about 200m north of the Royal Enclosure's northern wall. It was erected during the rule of Jayavarman VII and originally housed a Buddha, which has long since vanished. There are several huge tree roots looming large over the central tower, making for a memorable photo opportunity of a classic 'jungle temple'.

**Preah Pithu**, located across Northern Ave from Tep Pranam, is a group of 12th-century Hindu and Buddhist temples enclosed by a wall. It includes some beautifully decorated terraces and guardian animals in the form of elephants and lions. It sees few tourists, and so is a good place to explore at a leisurely pace, taking in the impressive jungle backdrop.

## SILK WEAVING AROUND ANGKOR

**Angkor Silk Farm**
Run by Les Chantiers Écoles and producing some of the country's best clothing, interior-design products and accessories.

**Samatoa**
Samatoa experiments in organic fibres, blending silk and cotton with lotus.

**Golden Silk**
Golden silk is produced by the yellow silkworm; visitors are welcome at this Banteay Srei weaving centre.

**Statue of the Leper King**

## TOP 5 KINGS OF ANGKOR

A mind-numbing array of kings ruled the Khmer empire from the 9th to 14th centuries. All of their names include the word 'varman', which means 'armour' or 'protector'.

**Jayavarman II**
(r 802–50) Founder of the Khmer empire in 802 CE.

**Yasovarman I**
(r 889–910) Moved the capital to Angkor and built Phnom Bakheng.

**Jayavarman IV**
(r 924–42) Usurper king who moved the capital to Koh Ker.

**Suryavarman II**
(r 1112–52) Legendary builder of Angkor Wat.

**Jayavarman VII**
(r 1181–1219) The king of god-kings, who built Angkor Thom and Ta Prohm.

The aforementioned statue is yet another of Angkor's mysteries and various theories have been advanced to explain its meaning. Legend has it that at least two of the Angkor kings had leprosy, and the statue may represent one of them. Another theory – a more likely explanation – is that the statue is of Yama, the god of death, and that the Terrace of the Leper King housed the royal crematorium.

The carved walls include seated *apsaras* and kings wearing pointed diadems, armed with short double-edged swords and accompanied by the court and princesses.

On the southern side of the Terrace of the Leper King (facing the Terrace of Elephants), there is access to the front wall of a hidden terrace that was covered up when the outer structure was built, a sort of terrace within a terrace. The

### THE STATUE OF THE LEPER KING

The original of the statue is housed at the **National Museum of Cambodia** (p51) in Phnom Penh, in one of the main galleries that surrounds a beautiful courtyard garden complete with four ornamental ponds.

*continued on p133*

 **SIEM REAP HOTELS PAYING HOMAGE TO ANGKOR**

**Shadow of Angkor Residence**
In a French-era building overlooking the river, this place offers stylish air-conditioned rooms close to Psar Chaa. **$**

**Memoire d'Angkor Boutique Hotel**
Located on Sivatha St, this hotel has some impressive local lacquerwork on display. **$$**

**Raffles Grand Hotel d'Angkor**
This historic hotel has been welcoming guests such as Charlie Chaplin and Jackie Kennedy since 1932. **$$$**

Angkor Thom is a top trekking spot thanks to its manageable size and rewarding temples. Start at the spectacular **1 south gate**, admiring the immense representation of the Churning of the Ocean of Milk before ascending the wall and heading west. Reaching the southwestern corner, admire **2 Prasat Chrung**, one of four identical temples marking the corners of the city.

Back on the gargantuan wall, continue to the **3 west gate**, looking out for a view to the immense Western Baray on your left. Descend at the west gate and wander east along the path into the heart of Angkor Thom, but don't be diverted by the beauty of Bayon, as this is best saved until last. If you are with a tour guide, you will have to travel this first and follow the designated running order, but independent travellers can plot their own course.

Veer north into **4 Baphuon** and wander to the back of this temple. Then pass the small temple of **5 Phimeanakas** and the former royal palace compound, an area of towering trees, tumbling walls and atmospheric foliage. Continue further north to petite but pretty **6 Preah Palilay**, overshadowed by an impressive cluster of kapok trees.

It's time to make for the mainstream with a walk through the **7 Terrace of the Leper King** and along the front of the royal viewing gallery, the **8 Terrace of the Elephants**. If there's time, you may want to zigzag east to visit the laterite towers of Prasat Suor Prat and the atmospheric Buddhist temple of Preah Pithu. Otherwise, continue to the top billing of **9 Bayon**: weird yet wonderful, this is one of the most enigmatic of the temples at Angkor.

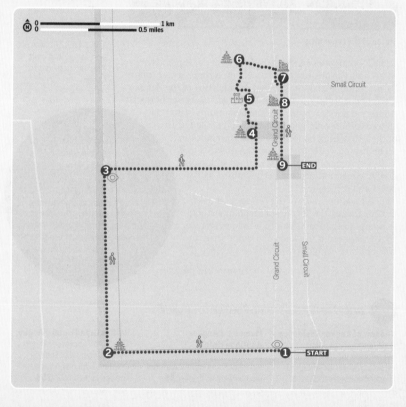

*continued from p131*

four tiers of *apsaras* and other figures, including nagas, look as fresh as if they had been carved yesterday, thanks to being covered up for centuries. As you follow the inner wall of the Terrace of the Leper King, notice the increasingly rough chisel marks on the figures, an indication that this wall was never completed, like many of the temples at Angkor.

# Phimeanakas & the Royal Palace

HOME TO KINGS AND QUEENS

**Phimeanakas** stands close to the centre of a walled area that once housed the royal palace. There's very little left of the palace today except for two sandstone pools near the northern wall. These pools are lined with beautiful carvings of deities and each is a peaceful place to escape the crowds at Bayon.

Phimeanakas means 'Celestial Palace', and some scholars say that it was once topped by a golden spire. Construction of the palace began under Rajendravarman II, although it was used by Jayavarman V and Udayadityavarman I. It was later added to and embellished by Jayavarman VII and his successors. The Royal Enclosure is fronted to the east by the Terrace of Elephants. The northwestern wall of the Royal Enclosure is very atmospheric, with immense trees and jungle vines cloaking the outer side, easily visible on a forest walk from Preah Palilay to Phimeanakas.

The temple is another pyramidal representation of Mt Meru, with three levels. Most of the decorative features are broken or have disappeared, including some guardian lions with very amateurish concrete pillars as replacement forelegs.

A Khmer myth tells of a naga or snake god paying a visit to the king each night in the form of a beautiful woman. The kings would have to sleep with this apparition or risk the stability of the kingdom. The naga is a potent symbol of Khmer power and adorns all the major temples at Angkor. Not only were the god-kings of Angkor earthly incarnations of Hindu deities, but through this myth their very existence rested on the power of the naga.

# Kleangs & Prasat Suor Prat

TEMPLE OF THE TIGHTROPE DANCERS

Along the eastern side of the Central Square are two groups of buildings, called **Kleangs**. The North Kleang (dating from the period of Jayavarman V) and the South Kleang may at one time have

**SIGNIFICANT SYMBOLS AROUND ANGKOR**

**Flame**
The flame motif, found flanking steps and doorways, is intended to purify pilgrims as they enter the temple.

**Linga**
A phallic symbol of fertility, lingam would have originally been located within the towers of most Hindu temples.

**Lotus**
A symbol of purity, the lotus features extensively in decoration and in the shapes of towers and entrance steps.

## A BRIEF HISTORY OF ANGKOR

The Angkorian period spans more than 600 years (802 to 1432 CE). This incredible age saw the construction of the temples of Angkor and the consolidation of the Khmer empire's position as one of the great powers in Southeast Asia. The hundreds of temples surviving today are but the sacred skeleton of the vast political, religious and social centre of the Khmer empire, a city that, at its zenith, boasted a population of one million when London was a small town of 50,000. The buildings of Angkor were constructed of wood – now long decayed – because the right to dwell in structures of brick or stone was reserved for the gods.

**ANGKOR WAT FROM THE AIR**

Options to see **Angkor Wat** (p114) from the air include the fixed-line Angkor Balloon, located about 1.3km away from the world's largest religious building, or a helicopter ride over the temples with Helistar.

## WESTERN BARAY & WESTERN MEBON

The **Western Baray**, measuring an incredible 8km by 2.3km, was constructed by hand to provide water for the intensive cultivation of lands around Angkor. These enormous *barays* weren't dug out, but had huge dykes built up around the edges. The Western Baray is the main local swimming pool around Siem Reap. There is a small beach of sorts at the western extreme, complete with picnic huts and inner tubes for rent, which attracts plenty of Khmers at weekends. The **Western Mebon** is a small temple on an island in the centre of this vast *baray* and is only accessible by boat.

### THE RECLINING VISHNU OF WESTERN MEBON

In the ruins of the Western Mebon temple, the giant bronze statue of Vishnu, now in the **National Museum of Cambodia** (p51) in Phnom Penh, was found.

been palaces. Along the Central Square in front of the two Kleangs are 12 laterite towers – 10 in a row and two more at right angles facing the Ave of Victory – known as the Prasat Suor Prat ('Temple of the Tightrope Dancers').

Archaeologists believe the towers, which form an honour guard, were constructed by Jayavarman VII. It is likely that each one originally contained either a *linga* or a statue. It is said artists performed for the king on tightropes or rope bridges strung between these towers, hence the name.

According to 13th-century Chinese emissary Chou Ta-Kuan, the towers of Prasat Suor Prat were also used for public trials of sorts. During a dispute the two parties would be made to sit inside two towers, one party eventually succumbing to illness and proven guilty.

Today the area is used for major events and celebrations, including the annual Angkor Sangkran, which was held for several years before the COVID-19 pandemic and relaunched in 2022. The festivities include concerts, activities, historic recreations and more, and often draw up to one million Cambodian visitors to Siem Reap and the temples of Angkor, making for legendary traffic jams. It can be an interesting time to see the locals enjoying the temples, but it is very hard to move between temples at this time unless you are on two wheels.

# The Jungle Temple of Ta Prohm

THE TOMB RAIDER TEMPLE

The so-called 'Tomb Raider Temple', **Ta Prohm** is cloaked in dappled shadow, its crumbling towers and walls locked in the slow muscular embrace of vast root systems. Undoubtedly the most atmospheric ruin at Angkor, Ta Prohm should be high on the hit list of every visitor. Its appeal lies in the fact that, unlike the other monuments of Angkor, it has been swallowed by the jungle, and looks very much the way most of the monuments of Angkor appeared when European explorers stumbled upon them.

Well, that's the theory, but in fact the jungle is pegged back and only the largest trees are left in place, making it manicured rather than raw like Beng Mealea. Still, a visit to Ta Prohm is a unique, otherworldly experience. There is a poetic cycle to this venerable ruin, with humanity first conquering nature to rapidly create, and nature once again conquering humanity to slowly destroy. If Angkor Wat is testimony to the genius of the ancient Khmers,

## SIGNIFICANT SYMBOLS AROUND ANGKOR

**Moat**
One of the largest symbols at Angkor are the moats around the major temples, representing the oceans around Mt Meru.

**Vine**
Another purity symbol, gracing doorways and lintels and meant to help cleanse visitors on their journey to this heaven on earth.

**Yoni**
Female fertility symbol that is combined with the lingam to produce holy water infused with the essence of life.

**Monk, Ta Prohm**

Ta Prohm reminds us equally of the awesome fecundity and power of the jungle.

This is a maze-like temple of towers, closed courtyards and narrow corridors. Many of the corridors are impassable, clogged with jumbled piles of delicately carved stone blocks dislodged by the roots of long-decayed trees. Bas-reliefs on bulging walls are carpeted with lichen, moss and creeping plants, and shrubs sprout from the roofs of monumental porches. Trees, hundreds of years old, tower overhead, their leaves filtering the sunlight and casting a greenish pall over the whole scene.

Built from 1186 and originally known as Rajavihara (Monastery of the King), Ta Prohm was a Buddhist temple dedicated to the mother of Jayavarman VII. It is one of the few temples in the Angkor region where an inscription provides information about the temple's dependents and inhabitants. Almost 80,000 people were required to maintain or attend

**BANTEAY KDEI & SRA SRANG**

**Banteay Kdei**, a massive Buddhist monastery from the latter part of the 12th century, is surrounded by four concentric walls. Each of its four entrances is decorated with *garudas*, which hold aloft one of Jayavarman VII's favourite themes: the four faces of Avalokiteshvara. The outer wall of Banteay Kdei measures 500m by 700m. It is considerably less busy than nearby Ta Prohm and this alone can justify a visit. East of Banteay Kdei is a vast pool of water, **Sra Srang**, measuring 800m by 400m, reserved as a bathing pool for the king and his consorts. This is a beautiful body of water from which to take in a quiet sunrise.

**TOP TIPS FOR TA PROHM**

**The North Gate**
If exploring Angkor on two wheels, consider entering via the north gate, as the guards will let you ride into the temple.

**Where Dinosaurs Roamed**
Look out for a carving of a stegosaurus on the inner wall of the western courtyard of Ta Prohm.

**The Art of Restoration**
Check out the southeast corner of the temple for an excellent before-and-after montage of a restored gallery.

JIXIN YU/SHUTTERSTOCK ©

'Tomb Raider' tree, Ta Prohm

## ON LOCATION WITH TOMB RAIDER

Several sequences for the film *Lara Croft: Tomb Raider* (2001), starring Angelina Jolie as Lara Croft, were shot around the temples of Angkor. The Cambodia shoot opened at Phnom Bakheng, with Lara looking through binoculars for the mysterious temple. The baddies were already trying to break in through the east gate of Angkor Thom by pulling down a giant (polystyrene!) *apsara*. Lara made a few laps around Bayon in her Land Rover before discovering a back way into the temple from Ta Prohm. After diving off the waterfall at Phnom Kulen, she emerged in a floating market in front of Angkor Wat, later venturing into the Gallery of a Thousand Buddhas where she was healed by the abbot.

at the temple, among them more than 2700 officials and 615 dancers.

The most popular of the many strangulating root formations is the one on the inside of the easternmost *gopura* (entrance pavilion) of the central enclosure, nicknamed the **Crocodile Tree**. One of the most famous spots in Ta Prohm is the so-called **'Tomb Raider' tree**, where Angelina Jolie's Lara Croft picked a jasmine flower before falling through the earth into...Pinewood Studios. It used to be possible to climb onto the damaged galleries, but this is now prohibited, to protect both the temple and its visitors. Many of these precariously balanced stones weigh a tonne or more and would do some serious damage if they came down. Ta Prohm is currently under stabilisation and restoration by an Indian team of archaeologists working with their Cambodian counterparts.

The temple is at its most impressive early in the day. Allow as much as two hours to visit, especially if you want to explore the maze-like corridors and iconic tree roots.

### TOUR OPERATORS PROMOTING RESPONSIBLE TOURISM

**Terre Cambodge**
Francophone operator offering tours to remote sites around Angkor, bicycle tours and Great Lake boat trips.

**Indochine Ex**
Me Chrey kayaking, trekking adventures, remote temple tours and more.

**Sam Veasna Conservation Tours**
Leading local ecotourism operator with birding tours to some of the remote temples.

# The Mountain Temple of Phnom Bakheng

SEE ANGKOR WAT FROM ABOVE

Located around 400m south of Angkor Thom, the main attraction at **Phnom Bakheng** is the sunset view over Angkor Wat. For many years the whole affair turned into a circus, with crowds of tourists ascending the slopes of the hill and jockeying for space. Numbers are now restricted to just 300 visitors at any one time, so get here early (4pm) to guarantee a sunset spot. The temple, built by Yasovarman I (r 889–910), has five tiers, with seven levels.

Phnom Bakheng lays claim to being home to the first of the temple-mountains built in the vicinity of Angkor. Yasovarman I chose Phnom Bakheng over the Roluos area, where the earlier capital (and temple-mountains) had been located.

At the base are – or were – 44 towers. Each of the five tiers had 12 towers. The summit of the temple has four towers at the cardinal points of the compass as well as a central sanctuary. All of these numbers are of symbolic significance. The seven levels represent the seven Hindu heavens, while the total number of towers, excluding the central sanctuary, is 108, a particularly auspicious number and one that correlates to the lunar calendar.

Some prefer to visit in the early morning, when it's cool (and crowds are light), to climb the hill. That said, the sunset over the Western Baray is very impressive from here. Allow about two hours for the sunset experience.

To get a decent photo of Angkor Wat in the warm glow of the late-afternoon sun from the summit of Phnom Bakheng you will need a serious zoom lens, as the temple is 1.3km away.

## The Fusion Temple of Preah Khan

TEMPLE OF THE SACRED SWORD

The temple of **Preah Khan** is one of the largest complexes at Angkor, a maze of vaulted corridors, fine carvings and lichen-clad stonework. It is a good counterpoint to Ta Prohm and generally sees slightly fewer visitors. Like Ta Prohm it is a place of towered enclosures and shoulder-hugging corridors. Unlike Ta Prohm, however, the temple of Preah Khan is in a good state of preservation thanks to the ongoing restoration efforts of the World Monuments Fund (WMF).

Preah Khan was built by Jayavarman VII and probably served as his temporary residence while

### PRASAT KRAVAN & THE LONG STRIDER

Just off the road between Angkor Wat and Banteay Kdei, **Prasat Kravan** is best known for its interior brick carvings concealed within its towers. The five towers, arranged in a north–south line and oriented to the east, were built in 921 CE.

One of Vishnu's best-loved incarnations is the dwarf Vamana, who reclaimed the world from the evil demon king Bali. Vamana asked Bali for space to meditate, saying he only needed enough land to walk across in three paces. Bali agreed, only to see the dwarf swell into a giant who strode across the universe in three enormous steps. From this legend, depicted at Prasat Kravan, Vishnu is known as the 'long strider'.

### THE OTHER PREAH KHAN

There are two Preah Khan temples in Cambodia – the other one is located in the jungles of Preah Vihear Province. **Preah Khan of Kompong Svay** (p175) is one of the most remote temples in Cambodia and is the ultimate overland adventure.

**TOP TIPS FOR PREAH KHAN**

**Sponsor a Garuda**
Look out for the incredible *garudas* mounted on Preah Khan's outer walls, available to sponsor for restoration.

**Headless Guardians**
Explore the quieter southern corridors of Preah Khan to find a pair of headless divinities guarding the entrance.

**Nature Runs Riot**
Look out for a giant pair of trees with monstrous, embracing roots on the outer retaining wall of the east entrance.

## ANGKOR ZIPLINE

Angkor provides the ultimate backdrop for this zipline experience, although you won't actually see the temples while navigating the course, despite it being located inside the Angkor protected area. **Angkor Zipline** (angkorzipline.com) includes 10 ziplines, 21 treetop platforms, four skybridges and an abseil finish. There's a panoramic rest stop halfway, and highlights include a tandem line for couples.

Safety is a priority and high-flyers are permanently clipped to lines via karabiners, with clear English instruction throughout. There is also a conservation element to the project, with a resident gibbon family living in the forest here. The price includes a minivan transfer to/from town, and you do not require a temple pass to enjoy the zipline experience.

Angkor Thom was being built. The central sanctuary of the temple was dedicated in 1191. A large stone stela tells us much about Preah Khan's role as a centre for worship and learning. Originally located within the first eastern enclosure, this stela is now housed safely at Angkor Conservation in Siem Reap. The temple was dedicated to 515 divinities, and during the course of a year 18 major festivals took place here, requiring a team of thousands just to maintain the place.

Preah Khan covers a very large area, but the temple itself is within a rectangular enclosing wall of around 700m by 800m. Four processional walkways approach the gates of the temple, and these are bordered by another stunning depiction of the Churning of the Ocean of Milk, as in the approach to Angkor Thom, although most of the heads have disappeared. From the central sanctuary, vaulted galleries extend in the cardinal directions. Many of the interior walls were once coated with plaster that was held in place by holes in the stone. Today many delicate reliefs remain, including *rishi* and *apsara* carvings.

It's a genuine fusion temple, with the eastern entrance dedicated to Mahayana Buddhism with equal-sized doors, and the other cardinal directions dedicated to Shiva, Vishnu and Brahma with successively smaller doors, emphasising the unequal nature of Hinduism.

The main entrance to Preah Khan is in the east, but most tourists enter at the west gate near the main road, walk the length of the temple to the east gate before doubling back to the central sanctuary and exiting at the north gate. (Another option is to enter from the north and exit from the east.) Approaching from the west, there is little clue to nature's genius, but on the outer retaining wall of the east gate is a **pair of trees** with monstrous roots embracing, one still reaching for the sky. There is also a curious **Grecian-style two-storey structure** in the temple grounds, the purpose of which is unknown, but it looks like an exile from Athens. Nearby is the **Hall of Dancers**, a former performance space that has some impressive *apsara* carvings.

Given its vast size, it is sensible to set aside at least 1½ to two hours to explore this temple.

## Petite Temple of Preah Neak Poan

HEALTH RETREAT OF JAYAVARMAN VII

The Buddhist temple of **Preah Neak Poan** is a small yet perfect temple constructed by Jayavarman VII in the late 12th century. It has a large square pool surrounded by four small-

**WHERE TO EAT INTERNATIONAL FOOD IN SIEM REAP** ————

**Mamma Shop**
Delicious homemade pasta is the signature of this Italian bistro in the bohemian Kandal Village district. **$**

**Cul-de-Sac**
This elegant French restaurant serves choice cuts and Gallic favourites in the garden of a restored wooden house. **$$**

**Wild**
In a garden setting, Wild offers a creative menu of fusion spring rolls, including Italian and Indian. **$**

**Chau Say Tevoda**

## TWIN TEMPLES OF CHAU SAY TEVODA & THOMMANON

Just east of Angkor Thom's Victory Gate is **Chau Say Tevoda**. It was probably built during the second quarter of the 12th century, under the reign of Suryavarman II, and dedicated to Shiva and Vishnu. It has been renovated by the Chinese to bring it up to the condition of its twin temple, Thommanon.

Just north of Chau Say Tevoda, **Thommanon** borrows many features from Angkor Wat and was dedicated to Shiva and Vishnu. The small temple is in good condition thanks to extensive work undertaken in the 1960s. It is regularly used for high-end gala dinners for VIP visitors.

er square pools. In the middle of the central pool is a circular 'island' encircled by the two nagas whose intertwined tails give the temple its name.

It's a safe bet that if an 'Encore Angkor' casino is eventually developed in Las Vegas or Macau, Preah Neak Poan will provide the blueprint for the ultimate swimming complex.

In the pool around the central island there were once four statues, but only one remains, reconstructed from the debris by the French archaeologists who cleared the site. The curious figure has the body of a horse supported by a tangle of human legs. It relates to a legend that Avalokiteshvara once saved a group of shipwrecked followers from an island of ghouls by transforming into a flying horse. A beautiful replica of this statue decorates the main roundabout at Siem Reap International Airport.

### TROVE OF HIDDEN BUDDHAS

Archaeologists working at the Buddhist temple of **Banteay Kdei** (p135) found a buried trove of Buddhist statues, which had been hidden there centuries ago to protect them from desecration by Hindu militants in the 14th century.

---

**Elia Greek Kitchen**
This little taverna near Psar Chaa looks like it comes straight out of the Med, and the food tastes pretty authentic too. **$**

**FCC Angkor**
This landmark building draws people in thanks to a reflective pool, and serves a range of international and Asian food. **$$**

**Il Forno**
Aficionados of fine Italian cuisine will love this little place's fresh antipasti, authentic pizzas and home-cooked dishes. **$$**

### TA SOM & EASTERN MEBON

Standing to the east of Preah Neak Poan, **Ta Som** is one of the late-12th-century Buddhist temples of prolific builder Jayavarman VII. The most impressive feature at Ta Som is the huge tree completely overwhelming the eastern *gopura*, which provides one of the most popular photo opportunities in the Angkor area.

The Hindu temple **Eastern Mebon**, erected by Rajendravarman II, would once have been situated on an islet in the centre of the Eastern Baray. Its temple-mountain form is topped off by a quintet of towers. The elaborate brick shrines are dotted with neatly arranged holes, which attached the original plasterwork. The base of the temple is guarded at its corners by perfectly carved stone figures of elephants.

ARKADY ZAKHAROV/SHUTTERSTOCK ©

**Ta Keo**

Water once flowed from the central pool into the four peripheral pools via ornamental spouts, which can still be seen in the pavilions at each axis of the pool. The spouts are in the form of an elephant head, a horse head, a lion head and a human head. The pool was used for ritual purification rites.

Preah Neak Poan was once in the centre of a huge 3km-by-900m *baray* serving Preah Khan, known as Jayatataka, once again partially filled with water. Access is restricted to the edge of the complex via a causeway, so a visit takes only 30 minutes.

## The Pyramid Temple of Ta Keo

AN UNSOLVED MYSTERY OF ANGKOR

Ta Keo is a stark, undecorated temple that undoubtedly would have been one of the finest of Angkor's structures, had it been finished. Built by Jayavarman V, it was dedicated to Shiva and was the first Angkorian monument built entirely of sandstone. The summit of the central tower, which is surrounded

 **WHERE TO ENJOY A LATE-NIGHT DRINK IN SIEM REAP**

**Harbour**
This self-styled 'pirate tavern' is a lovable bar housed in an atmospheric wooden house in Stung Thmei.

**Silk Garden**
A popular dive bar in the alley near Pub St with a pool table, loud tunes and rockin' late hours.

**Long's Bar**
A great little bolt-hole hidden away among the lanes; creative cocktails include ginger and lemongrass mojitos.

by four lower towers, is almost 50m high. The four towers at the corners of a square and a fifth tower in the centre is typical of many Angkorian temple-mountains.

No one is certain why work was never completed, but a likely cause may have been the death of Jayavarman V. Others contend that the hard sandstone was impossible to carve, and that explains the lack of decoration. According to inscriptions, Ta Keo was struck by lightning during construction, which may have been seen as a bad omen and led to its abandonment. Allow about 30 minutes to visit Ta Keo.

# The Royal Crematorium of Pre Rup

SUNSET VIEWS OVER THE COUNTRYSIDE

Pre Rup, built by Rajendravarman II, is about 1km south of the Eastern Mebon. The temple consists of a pyramid-shaped temple-mountain with the uppermost of the three tiers carrying five lotus towers. Pre Rup means 'Turning the Body' and refers to a traditional method of cremation in which a corpse's outline is traced in the cinders: this suggests that the temple may have served as an early royal crematorium.

The brick sanctuaries here were once decorated with a plaster coating, fragments of which remain on the southwestern tower; there are some amazingly detailed lintel carvings here.

Pre Rup is a popular, crowded sunset spot, as the view over the surrounding rice fields is beautiful, although some lofty trees have rather obscured it these days.

## TA NEI TEMPLE & SPEAN THMOR

**Ta Nei**, 800m north of Ta Keo, was built by Jayavarman VII. There is something of the spirit of Ta Prohm here, albeit on a lesser scale, with moss and tentacle-like roots covering many outer areas of this small temple. The number of visitors is also on a lesser scale, making it very atmospheric.

**Spean Thmor**, of which an arch and several piers remain, is 200m east of Thommanon. Jayavarman VII constructed many roads, with these immense stone bridges spanning watercourses. This is the only large bridge remaining in the immediate vicinity of Angkor. It vividly highlights how the water level has changed over the centuries and may offer another clue about the collapse of Angkor's extensive irrigation system.

## WHERE TO EAT BAKERY TREATS IN SIEM REAP

**Bayon Pastry School Coffee Shop**
Sample fluffy croissants and cakes for a good cause: training disadvantaged youths. **$**

**Paris Bakery**
One of the best bakeries in town, with fresh pastries, elaborate cakes and lots of affordable sandwiches. **$**

**Brown Coffee**
Cambodia's leading cafe and bakery chain, with two stylish Siem Reap locations, including on the riverfront. **$**

# BANTEAY SREI

## MUCH MORE THAN A TEMPLE

There is more to Banteay Srei than its iconic Angkor sites, such as the 12th-century temple of Banteay Samré. New destinations and experiences, including homestays, village walks, oxcart rides, fruit farms and handicraft workshops, are under development to encourage visitors to stay longer and explore further.

Venture beyond Banteay Srei and you'll enter the backwaters of Siem Reap Province, home to rugged mountain plateaus and some of the most rewarding remnants of the Khmer empire. The holy mountain of Phnom Kulen was the birthplace of the Khmer empire at the start of the 9th century, and the remains of the 'lost city' of Mahendraparvata are best explored by motorbike, although it is possible to visit the main sights by car. Further afield lies another River of a Thousand Lingas at Kbal Spean and the epic jungle ruin of Beng Mealea, slowly being suffocated by vines and creepers.

### TOP TIP

Banteay Srei temple is best combined with other far-flung temple sites to make the most of the longer 32km journey out here. Combine this temple with a day trip to the sacred mountain of Phnom Kulen (p146) or a trek to the River of a Thousand Lingas at Kbal Spean (p147).

**Phnom Bok**

WILLIAM J WARREN/SHUTTERSTOCK ©

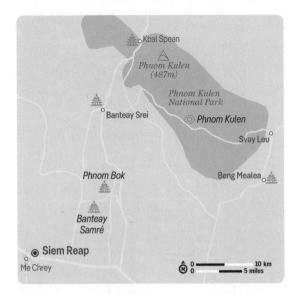

Kbal Spean

Phnom Kulen
(487m)

Phnom Kulen
National Park

Banteay Srei

Phnom Kulen

Svay Leu

Phnom Bok

Beng Mealea

Banteay
Samré

Siem Reap

Me Chrey

0 — 10 km
0 — 5 miles

# The Hilltop Temple of Phnom Bok

LINGA-TOPPED SACRED MOUNTAIN

One of three temple-mountains built by Yasovarman I in the late 9th or early 10th century, this peaceful but remote location (about 25km from Siem Reap) sees few visitors. The small temple of Phnom Bok is in reasonable shape, but it is the views of Phnom Kulen to the north and the plains of Angkor to the south from this 212m hill that make it worth the trip. The remains of a 5m *linga* are visible at the opposite end of the hill, and it's believed there were similar *lingas* at Phnom Bakheng and Phnom Krom.

There is a long, winding trail snaking up the hill at Phnom Bok, which takes about 20 minutes to climb, plus a faster cement staircase, but the latter is fairly exposed. Avoid the heat in the middle of the day and carry plenty of water, which can be purchased locally.

Phnom Bok is clearly visible from the road to Banteay Srei. It is accessed by continuing east on the road to Banteay Samré for another 6km. It is possible to loop back to Siem Reap via the temples of Roluos by heading south instead of west on the return journey, and gain some rewarding glimpses of the countryside. Unfortunately it is not a sensible place for sunrise or sunset, as this would require a long journey in the dark.

## THE ANASTYLOSIS METHOD OF RESTORATION

Initial attempts to clear Angkor under the aegis of the École Française d'Extrême-Orient (EFEO) were fraught with difficulties and disputes. The jungle grew back as soon as it was cleared, and scholars debated the extent to which temples should be restored. In the 1920s a solution was found, known as anastylosis. This was the method the Dutch had used to restore Borobudur in Indonesia; a way of reconstructing monuments using original materials, in keeping with a structure's original form. New materials, discreetly used, were permitted only when originals weren't available.

### OTHER EXAMPLES OF ANASTYLOSIS AT ANGKOR

Beyond Banteay Srei, another good example of anastylosis can be seen on the causeway leading to the entrance of **Angkor Wat** (p114), where the right-hand side was originally restored by the French. More recently they've been restoring the left-hand side, which was beginning to subside.

OLEG ZNAMENSKIY/SHUTTERSTOCK ©

Banteay Srei

### INTERESTING SITES BEYOND BANTEAY SREI

The **Cambodia Landmine Museum** has eye-opening displays on the curse of landmines in Cambodia. Its collection includes mines, mortars, guns and weaponry, and there is a mock minefield where visitors can attempt to locate the deactivated mines. The museum is about 25km from Siem Reap, near Banteay Srei.

One of the largest fully enclosed butterfly centres in Southeast Asia, the **Banteay Srei Butterfly Centre** has more than 30 species of Cambodian butterflies fluttering about. It is a good experience for children, as they can see the whole life cycle from egg to caterpillar to cocoon to butterfly. It's about 7km before Banteay Srei temple.

## MORE IN BANTEAY SREI

# The Beguiling Beauty of Banteay Srei

THE ART GALLERY OF ANGKOR

Considered by many to be the jewel in the crown of Angkorian art, **Banteay Srei** is cut from stone of a pinkish hue and includes some of the finest stone carving anywhere on earth. Begun in 967 CE, it is one of the smallest sites at Angkor, but what it lacks in size it makes up for in stature. This Hindu temple dedicated to Shiva is wonderfully well preserved, and many of its carvings are three-dimensional.

Classic carvings include delicate women with lotus flowers in hand and traditional skirts clearly visible, as well as breathtaking recreations of scenes from the epic *Ramayana* adorning the library pediments. However, the sum of the parts is no greater than the whole – almost every inch of these interior buildings is covered in decoration. Standing watch over such perfect creations are mythical guardians, all of which are copies of originals stored in the National Museum

 **HOMESTAYS NEAR BANTEAY SREI**

**Bayon Smile Homestay**
This group of spacious and attractive village homes is just north of Banteay Srei temple. **$**

**Bong Thom Homestay**
This boutique rural homestay has beautiful wooden houses complete with four-poster beds and tasteful decor. **$**

**Tbeng Village Homestays**
Tbeng, a pretty little village east of Banteay Srei, has a homestay project with around a dozen houses. **$**

of Cambodia in Phnom Penh. Banteay Srei means 'Citadel of the Women', and it is said that it must have been built by a woman, as the elaborate carvings are supposedly too fine for the hand of a man.

Banteay Srei is one of the few temples around Angkor to be commissioned not by a king but by a Brahman, who may have been a tutor to Jayavarman V. The temple is square and has entrances at the east and west, with the east approached by a causeway. Of interest are the lavishly decorated libraries and the three central towers, which display male and female divinities and beautiful filigree relief work.

Banteay Srei was the first major temple restoration undertaken by the EFEO in 1930 using the anastylosis method (p143). The project, as evidenced today, was a major success and soon led to other larger projects such as the restoration of Bayon. Banteay Srei is also the first to have been given a full makeover in terms of facilities, with a large car park, a designated dining and shopping area, clear visitor information and a state-of-the-art exhibition on the history of the temple and its restoration. There is also a small *baray* behind the temple where local boat trips are possible through the lotus pond.

When Banteay Srei was first rediscovered it was assumed to be from the 13th or 14th centuries, as it was thought that the refined carving must have come at the end of the Angkor period. It was later dated to 967, from inscriptions found at the site.

It takes 45 minutes to explore Banteay Srei temple, but allow 1½ hours to visit the information centre and explore the area.

## The Temple of Banteay Samré

A CONTEMPORARY OF ANGKOR WAT

Banteay Samré dates from the same period as Angkor Wat and was built by Suryavarman II. The temple is in a fairly healthy state of preservation due to some extensive renovation work, although its isolation has resulted in some looting during the past few decades. The area consists of a central temple with four wings, preceded by a hall and also accompanied by two libraries, the southern one remarkably well preserved.

The whole ensemble is enclosed by two large concentric walls around what would have been the unique feature of an inner moat, now dry.

Banteay Samré is 400m east of the Eastern Baray. A visit here can be combined with a trip to Banteay Srei and/or Phnom Bok.

### THE FORGOTTEN TEMPLE OF CHAU SREI VIBOL

Petite hilltop temple **Chau Srei Vibol** is actually part of a larger complex that spanned the entire hill. It's under-visited compared with other temples, making it an atmospheric option for sunset. The central sanctuary is in ruins but is nicely complemented by an early-20th-century wat nearby. Surrounding the base of the hill are laterite walls outlining the dimensions of what was once a significant temple.

To get here turn east off the Bakong–Anlong Veng highway about 8km north of NH6, or 5km south of Phnom Bok – there's a small, easy-to-miss sign that marks the turn. Locals are friendly and helpful should you find yourself lost.

### BANTEAY SREI: BEYOND ITS NAMESAKE TEMPLE

Combine Banteay Srei and the River of a Thousand Lingas at **Kbal Spean** (p147) on a long day trip, or include the **Cambodia Landmine Museum** (p144) and **Banteay Samré** (p145) on a half-day itinerary.

### WHERE TO EAT NEAR BANTEAY SREI

**Naom Ben Chok Noodles**
Preah Dak village is renowned for its *naom banchok* (thick rice noodles) stalls, which hug the main road to Banteay Srei. **$**

**Parvis Banteay Srei**
Parvis is the most sophisticated of the many local restaurants in the well-organised Banteay Srei visitor area. **$**

**Borey Sovann Restaurant**
The inviting place is great for winding down before or after an ascent to the River of a Thousand Lingas. **$**

# The Sacred Mountain of Phnom Kulen

BIRTHPLACE OF THE KHMER EMPIRE

Considered by Khmers to be the most sacred mountain in Cambodia, **Phnom Kulen** is a popular place of pilgrimage on weekends and during festivals. It played a significant role in the history of the Khmer empire, as it was from here in 802 CE that Jayavarman II proclaimed himself a *devaraja* (god-king), giving birth to the Cambodian kingdom. Plan on spending an entire day at Phnom Kulen, as there are many spectacular sights up here, including a giant reclining Buddha, hundreds of *lingas* carved in the riverbed, an impressive waterfall, remote temples, the stone guardian animals of Sra Damrei and the hermit retreat of Poeung Tbal.

From the entrance, a sealed road winds its way through some great jungle scenery, emerging on the plateau after a 12km ascent. The road eventually splits: the left fork leads to the picnic spot, waterfall and ruins of a 9th-century temple; the right fork continues over a bridge (you'll find the riverbed carvings around here) to the base of **Wat Preah Ang Thom**, which sits at the summit of the mountain and houses the large **reclining Buddha** carved into the sandstone boulder upon which it is built. This is the focal point of a pilgrimage for Khmer people, so it is important to take off your shoes and any head covering before climbing the stairs to the sanctuary. These days the views from the 487m peak are partially obstructed by foliage run amok.

The **waterfall** was featured in the movie *Lara Croft: Tomb Raider*. It's a popular spot for families picnicking on the weekends, so it can be busy. Near the top of the waterfall is a jungle-clad temple known as **Prasat Krau Romeas**, dating from the 9th century.

There are plenty of other Angkorian sites on Phnom Kulen, including as many as 20 minor temples around the plateau, the most important of which is **Prasat Rong Chen**, the first pyramid or temple-mountain to be constructed in the Angkor area. Most impressive of all are the giant stone animals or guardians of the mountain, known as **Sra Damrei** (Elephant Pond). These are quite difficult to reach, particularly during the wet season. The few people who do make it, however, are rewarded with a life-size replica of a stone elephant and smaller statues of lions, a frog and a cow. These were constructed on the southern face of the mountain and from here there are spectacular views across the plains below. Getting to Sra Damrei requires taking a *moto* from Wat Preah Ang Thom for about 12km on very rough trails. Don't try to find it on your own; it's a two-hour trip to explore this area and you should carry plenty of water.

 **TOP TIPS FOR PHNOM KULEN**

**The Cliffs of Peung Ta Kho**
Make a short stop at this incredible clifftop viewpoint overlooking the forests around Phnom Kulen.

**Explore Waterfalls in Popel**
There are lots of small waterfalls upstream from the big waterfall, many of which flow through Popel Commune.

**Enter the Bat Cave**
Located below the giant stone animals of Sra Damrei is the Bat Cave, a holy place of shrines and spirits.

**Waterfall, Phnom Kulen**

Other worthwhile sites that could be included in an adventurous day trip around Phnom Kulen include the ancient rock carvings of **Poeung Tbal**, an atmospheric site of enormous boulders, and the partially restored temple of **Prasat Damrei Krap**. There are big plans for Phnom Kulen moving forward with a new **Orchid Centre** at the national park entrance and two community-based tourism centres in Anlong Thom and Popel districts offering guided treks to follow waterfall trails and heritage trails.

Phnom Kulen is a huge plateau around 50km from Siem Reap and about 15km from Banteay Srei. It is only possible to go up Phnom Kulen before 11am and only possible to come down after noon, to avoid vehicles meeting on the narrow road. There is a new road under construction that links Phnom Kulen to Svay Leu to the east, so a one-way system may be introduced: ascending by the old road and descending via the new road.

It's a long journey here (take a *moto* or rented car, not a *tuk-tuk* as the hill climb is too tough), so it's best to plan on spending the best part of a day exploring, although it can be combined with either Banteay Srei or Beng Mealea.

## The Carvings of Kbal Spean

RIVER OF A THOUSAND LINGAS

A spectacularly carved riverbed, **Kbal Spean** is set deep in the jungle to the northeast of Angkor. More commonly referred to in English as the 'River of a Thousand Lingas', the name actually means 'bridgehead', a reference to the natural rock bridge here. *Lingas* have

---

**THE LOST CITY**

Phnom Kulen hit headlines in 2013 thanks to the 'discovery' of a lost city once known as Mahendraparvata. Using jungle-piercing LIDAR radar technology, the structures of a more extensive archaeological site were unveiled beneath the jungle canopy. The research confirmed the size and scale of the ancient city, complete with canals and *barays*. Some new temples and features were found beneath the jungle, but they remain remote and inaccessible due to terrain and the possibility of landmines. An additional LIDAR survey of the entire Kulen plateau was conducted in 2015.

---

**CAPITALISING ON ROYAL POWER**

Phnom Kulen was the first capital of the Khmer empire from 802, but the capital moved during the following centuries, including to **Roluos** (p122) in the late 9th century and **Angkor Thom** (p125) and, briefly, **Koh Ker** (p150) in the early 10th century.

---

 **PLACES TO SLEEP & EAT ON PHNOM KULEN**

| **Pich Seu Guesthouse** | **Homestays** | **A Cambodian Picnic** |
|---|---|---|
| This small family-run guesthouse is managed by the knowledgeable Pich Seu, who has lived here for a decade. **$** | There are several inexpensive homestays in the main village of Anlong Thom. **$** | Buy grilled fish and meats at stalls and picnic in the riverside huts above the waterfall, like Cambodian visitors do. **$** |

## WHY I LOVE PHNOM KULEN

**Nick Ray,** writer

I first visited Phnom Kulen in 1998, soon after it had been liberated from the Khmer Rouge. Visitors had to trek up the mountain to the River of a Thousand Lingas, taking about three hours. I took film director Jean-Jacques Annaud on a scout to the guardian animals of Sra Damrei in 2001, zipping between 'Danger!! Mines!!' signs on a motorbike.

I was fortunate to know many of the lead archaeologists on the LIDAR mission that revealed the lost city of Mahendraparvata in 2012 and they have been generous in sharing the secrets of the sacred mountain with me in the past decade. There is a magic about this mountain that is hard to put into words.

MEUNIERD/SHUTTERSTOCK ©

**Reclining Buddha, Wat Preah Ang Thom (p146)**

been elaborately carved into the riverbed, and images of Hindu deities are dotted about the area. It was 'discovered' in 1969, when ethnologist Jean Boulbet was shown the area by a hermit.

It is a 2km uphill walk to the carvings, along a pretty path that winds its way up into the jungle, passing some interesting boulder formations. Make sure you pack plenty of water for your journey up the hill, as there is none available beyond the parking area. The path eventually splits to the waterfall or the river carvings. There is an impressive carving of Vishnu on the upper section of the river, followed by a series of carvings at the bridgehead itself, some of which were hacked off in recent years, but have since been replaced by excellent replicas.

Following the river down, there are several more impressive carvings of Vishnu, and Shiva with his consort Uma, and further downstream hundreds of *lingas* appear on the riverbed. At the top of the waterfall are many animal images, including a cow and a frog, and a path winds around the boulders to a wooden staircase leading down to the base of the falls. Visitors between January and June will be disappointed to see very little water here. The best time to visit is between July and December. When exploring Kbal Spean, it's best to start with the river carvings and work back down to the waterfall to cool off.

 **WHERE TO SLEEP AROUND KOH KER**

**Koh Ker Jungle Lodge**
This striking old wooden house in Koh Ker has two private bedrooms and can host groups. $

**Mom Morokod Koh Ker Guesthouse**
This quiet guesthouse has 11 clean, spacious rooms with bathrooms. $

**Koh Ker Temple Gardens Hotel**
This boutique retreat has individual air-con bungalows set around a swimming pool. $$

From the car park, the visit takes about two hours including the walk, nearer three hours with a natural shower or a picnic. A day trip here can be combined with Angkor Centre for Conservation of Biodiversity (p107), Banteay Srei temple (p144) and the Cambodia Landmine Museum (p144).

Kbal Spean is about 50km northeast of Siem Reap and about 18km beyond the temple of Banteay Srei. The road is in great shape, as it forms part of the main road north to the Thai border, so it takes only an hour or so from town. There are food stalls at the bottom of the hill that can cook up fried rice or a noodle soup, otherwise the fancier, excellent Borey Sovann Restaurant is located near the entrance. Admission to Kbal Spean is included in the general Angkor pass and last entry to the site is at 3.30pm.

## Slumbering Giant of Beng Mealea

AN AUTHENTIC JUNGLE RUIN

A spectacular sight to behold, **Beng Mealea** is one of the most mysterious temples at Angkor, as nature has well and truly run riot here. Exploring this Titanic of temples, built to the same floor plan as Angkor Wat, is the ultimate Indiana Jones experience. If Ta Prohm is a film set with perfectly placed ancient trees, Beng Mealea is the real-deal location. Built in the 12th century under Suryavarman II, Beng Mealea is enclosed by a moat measuring 1.2km by 900m.

One of Angkor's most spectacular jungle ruins, this temple used to be utterly consumed by vines and creepers, but some of the dense foliage has been cut back and cleaned up in recent years. Entering from the south, make your way over piles of finely chiselled sandstone blocks, through long, dark chambers and between hanging vines. The **central tower** has completely collapsed, but hidden away among the rubble and foliage are several impressive carvings, including a small but striking rendition of the **Churning of the Ocean of Milk** and a well-preserved **library** in the northeastern quadrant.

Beng Mealea is located 68km northeast of Siem Reap and 6.5km southeast of Phnom Kulen. It's about an hour by car (longer by *moto* or *tuk-tuk*) from Siem Reap. The shortest route is via the junction town of Dam Dek, located on NH6 about 37km southeast of Siem Reap. Turn north immediately after the market and continue on this road for 31km. The entrance to the temple lies just beyond the left-hand turn to Koh Ker. Allow a half-day to visit, including the journey time from Siem Reap, or combine it with Koh Ker in a long day trip (best undertaken by car or motorbike).

**SLEEPS AND EATS NEAR BENG MEALEA**

**Srey Mom Beng Mealea Homestay**
Just a short walk from Beng Mealea. Overnight rates include all home-cooked meals. **$**

**Beng Mealea Kitchen**
One of the larger restaurants in the area, with an air-con interior, breezy balcony and a chill pavilion with hammocks. **$**

**Romduol Angkor II Restaurant**
This local spot turns out authentic Khmer dishes at affordable prices. **$**

# KOH KER

## LOST AND LOOTED JUNGLE CAPITAL

Abandoned to the forests of the north, Koh Ker (pronounced 'ko-kay-er'), capital of the Angkorian empire from 928 to 944, is one of the most remote temple complexes around Angkor. Most visitors start at Prasat Krahom, where impressive stone carvings grace lintels, doorposts and slender window columns. The principal monument is Mayan-looking Prasat Thom, a 55m-wide, 40m-high sandstone-faced pyramid whose seven tiers offer spectacular views across the forest.

Several of the most impressive pieces in the National Museum of Cambodia in Phnom Penh come from Koh Ker, including the huge *garuda* that greets visitors in the entrance hall and a unique carving depicting a pair of wrestling monkey-kings.

The toll road from Dam Dek has placed Koh Ker within day-trip distance of Siem Reap. To really appreciate the temples – the ensemble has 42 major structures – some visitors spend a night here.

**TOP TIP**

Approaching Koh Ker from the south, there is a circular route that takes in all the major temples in this former royal capital, including Prasat Bram in the southeast, Prasat Krahom and Prasat Thom in the north and Prasat Leung in the northeast, winding its way around the *baray*.

**Prasat Thom (Prasat Prang)**

LONG LYSONG/SHUTTERSTOCK ©

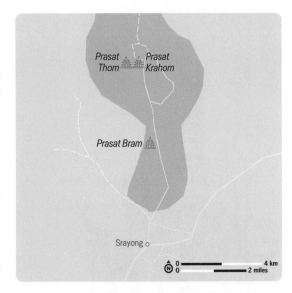

Prasat Thom

Prasat Krahom

Prasat Bram

Srayong

0  4 km
0  2 miles

## The Forgotten Temples of Koh Ker

PYRAMIDS AND PRASATS IN THE JUNGLE

**Prasat Thom** dominates the landscape around Koh Ker, looming large above the surrounding ricefields and sugar palms. The complex is huge and includes several smaller temples and an inner moat with a depth of up to 7m. **Prasat Krahom**, the second-largest structure at Koh Ker, is so named for the red bricks from which it is constructed. Sadly, none of the carved lions that this temple was once known for remain, though there's still plenty to see, with stone archways and galleries leaning haphazardly. A naga-flanked causeway and a series of sanctuaries, libraries and gates lead past trees and vegetation-covered ponds. Just west of Prasat Krahom, at the far western end of a half-fallen colonnade, are the remains (most of the head) of a statue of Nandin.

Once at the pyramid itself, known as Prasat Prang (or 'pyramid temple') to locals, the staircase to the top is open to a limited number of visitors and the views are spectacular. Some 40 inscriptions, dating from 932 to 1010, have been found here. The shaft of the pyramid is filled with debris from centuries of neglect and may include some ancient buried carvings.

Among the many smaller temples found around Koh Ker, **Prasat Bram** is a real highlight. It consists of a collection of brick towers, at least two of which have been completely smothered by voracious triffid-like strangler figs; the probing roots have cut through the brickwork like liquid mercury.

### THE LINGAS OF KOH KER

Fertility symbols are prominent around the temples of Angkor. The *linga* is a phallic symbol and would've originally been located within the towers of most Hindu temples. It sits inside a *yoni*, the female fertility symbol, combining to produce holy water, charged with the sexual energy of creation. Some of Cambodia's largest *lingas* can still be seen in a cluster of four temples about 1km northeast of Prasat Thom, collectively known as the *linga* temples. The largest is found in **Prasat Thneng**, while **Prasat Leung** is similarly well endowed.

### RETURNING LOOTED SCULPTURES

Many of Koh Ker's beautiful statues and sculptures were pillaged by organised looting networks between the 1970s and 1990s, ending up in museums all over the world. Many are now being repatriated and some are on display in Phnom Penh's **National Museum of Cambodia** (p51).

BTWIMAGES/SHUTTERSTOCK ©

**Phnom Sampeau (p165)**

## THE MAIN AREAS

### BATTAMBANG
Architecture, art and
atmosphere. **p158**

### PREAH VIHEAR PROVINCE
Mother of all mountain temples.
**p171**

### KOMPONG THOM PROVINCE
Early capital of Sambor Prei
Kuk. **p183**

# NORTH-WESTERN CAMBODIA

## RIVERSIDE TOWNS, REMOTE TEMPLES, REAL LIFE

Too often in the shadow of Siem Reap, the northwest is the place to detour off the trail and tap into the rural rhythm of Cambodia.

A vast and remote region that encircles the northern shores of the Tonlé Sap lake, this is the place for spectacular temples without the tourist legions. The remote temples of northwestern Cambodia have a different personality from their nearby siblings at Angkor. While mountaintop Prasat Preah Vihear is the big hitter, the other temple complexes like Preah Khan of Kompong Svay (Prasat Bakan) and Sambor Prei Kuk, wrapped in vines and half-swallowed by jungle, are fabulous to explore.

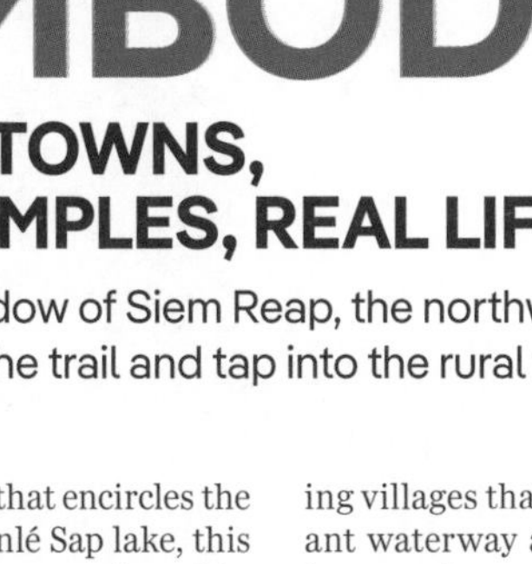

At the region's heart is the great lake, teeming with fish and a birder's paradise. Boat trips from Kompong Chhnang and Krakor (near Pursat) to the rickety float-ing villages that cluster along this important waterway allow you to dip your toes into an alternative lifestyle on the water.

When forays into the northwest's far-flung corners are complete, this region has one more surprise up its sleeve. Laid-back Battambang, with its French-era architecture and burgeoning arts scene, is the gateway city here. A wealth of rewarding sights are found within day-tripping distance of town, making it an excellent base before or after some upcountry adventures. Once you have ridden the 'bamboo train', explored hilltop temples and spotted bats at sunset, there are some lovely little restaurants and bars to slake the thirst.

AHMAT30/SHUTTERSTOCK ©

---

**PURSAT PROVINCE**
Looming mountains and floating villages. **p186**

**KOMPONG CHHNANG PROVINCE**
Sugar-palm-dotted river hamlets. **p190**

# Find Your Way

Northwest Cambodia sprawls over eight provinces. Navigate your way around the Tonlé Sap lake to bucolic Battambang and the lakeside rice bowls of Pursat, Kompong Chhnang and Kompong Thom. In the remote north are the temples of Preah Vihear.

O Smach

Banteay Chhmar
Protected
Landscape

Samraong

THAILAND

Thmor
Pouk

Ang Trapeng Thmor
Protected Forest

Poipet

Prey Mon

Sisophon

Mongkol
Borei

Kralanh

Siem Reap

Kouk Kduoch

Floating Village of
Chong Kneas

Kompe

## Battambang, p158

Located on the soporific Sangker River, this charmer of a heritage town blends modernity and tradition and is the gateway to verdant countryside and hilltop temples.

Kamrieng

Battambang

Sneng

Reang
Kesei

Tônlé
Sap

Psar Pruhm

Pailin

Treng

Sangker River

Moung
Russei

Samlaut

Pursa

Cardamom Mountains
(Chuor Phnom Kravanh)

## Pursat Province, p186

It's all about the watery thoroughfares in the floating village of Kompong Luong, where it is possible to experience a very different homestay.

THAILAND

Chhrok
Preal
Forest

Pramoay

Stung Pou Ihisat

Thma Da

Ko
Chang

## BUS, CAR & MOTORBIKE

Roads are much improved in northwestern Cambodia. There are reliable bus services to Battambang from Phnom Penh, Siem Reap and Poipet. When it comes to remote temples or upcountry jaunts, it is necessary to charter a private car or rent a motorbike.

Gulf of
Thailand

Ko Kut

Koh Kong

Ⓝ 0        100 km
       0     50 miles

INGEHOGENBIJL/SHUTTERSTOCK ©

THAILAND

○ Choam
Angkrong ○● ○ Anh Seh
*Prasat Preah Vihear*
○ Choam
blong ○ Sra Em ○ Choam
eng Ksant

## Preah Vihear Province, p171
The most mountainous of all mountain temples is perched on a dramatic clifftop in the Dangrek Mountains near the Thai border, with spectacular views.

○ Prey Veng
hnom *Preah Vihear Protected Forest*
ulen
387m)
○ Kulen ○ Preah Vihear City (Tbeng Meanchey)
Srayong ○
△ *Phnom Tbeng*
*Phnom Kulen National Park* ○ Svay Leu
Sangkom Thmei ○
○ Svay Pak
○ Khvau ○ Ta Seng
○ Rovieng
○ Dam Dek
Phnom Deko ○
○ Rumchek

## Kompong Thom Province, 183
Before Angkor, there was Chenla and its 7th-century capital of Sambor Prei Kuk, a collection of vine-entwined, brick temples and a Unesco World Heritage Site.

○ Kompng Kdei
○ Spean Praptos
○ Stoeng
*Sambor Prei Kuk*
● **Kompong Thom**
Trapeang ○ Veng

○ Chheu Tom
○ Barayo
**Kompong Chhnang**
*Chhuk Laeng Cascades*
Ondong Rossey ○◉

## Kompong Chhnang Province, p190
Swaying sugar palms, clay-fired pottery and remote floating villages combine to make this an accessible rural escape from the capital.

nom Aural (1813m) △
○ Romeas
○ Udong
**PHNOM PENH** ✪

### 🚤 BOAT
The fast boat service between Battambang and Siem Reap is one of the most beautiful river journeys in Cambodia, passing along the sleepy Sangker River and on to the Tonlé Sap lake. However, it can take up to eight hours in low-water dry season.

### 🚆 TRAIN
There's a daily train service connecting Phnom Penh with Battambang, although it is pretty slow. There's also the infamous 'bamboo train' near Battambang, but this is more a tourist experience.

# Plan Your Days

Enjoy life in the slow lane in northwestern Cambodia, safe in the knowledge that you have ventured off the tourist trail to discover a timeless landscape with top-class temples.

**Battambang (p158)**

## If You Only Do One Thing

**Battambang** (p158) is calling to the banks of the Sangker River. Check out the French architectural legacy on a walking tour of the city or let a *cyclo* take the strain. Enjoy lunch in one of the many eateries in the old quarter before heading into the countryside for some adventures. Ride the **bamboo train** (p162), visit the hilltop temple of **Prasat Banan** (p165) and explore the stupa-studded mountain of **Phnom Sampeau** (p165) where millions of bats fly into the sunset each night. Finish by running away to the circus of **Phare Ponleu Selpak** (p164) if you're in town on show night.

## Seasonal Highlights

The ideal time to visit is November to February. June to October offers a lush landscape but challenging road conditions.

**FEBRUARY**

**Chinese New Year** usually falls in this month and Battambang's Chinese-Khmer community comes out to play.

**APRIL**

Usually the hottest month in the calendar, a good time to head for the cooler heights of the **Cardamom Mountains** (p187).

**JUNE**

Battambang's Phare Circus (p164) hosts the **Tini Tinou International Circus Festival** every two years, including a puppet parade.

156

## Three Days to Travel Around

After a thorough two-day immersion in the delights of **Battambang** (p158), make for the vast Angkor-era temple of **Banteay Chhmar** (p169), which is an easy side trip when travelling to or from Siem Reap. There's an excellent homestay network in this pretty rural village as well as a community-based tourism programme with friendly English-speaking guides. It is possible to arrange a special dinner at the temple if you book ahead, or you can enjoy an oxcart ride in the village and see traditional silk weaving in action at **Soieries du Mékong** (p170).

## If You Have More Time

Spend a week in northwestern Cambodia and you can hit all the big-ticket attractions. Take a road trip through the far north to see the remote temples of Preah Vihear Province, including the epic mountaintop temple of **Prasat Preah Vihear** (p172) and the 'Indiana Jones' lost temple of **Preah Khan of Kompong Svay** (p175). If you really can't get enough of ancient temples, there are also the seldom-visited brick sanctuaries of **Prasat Neak Buos** (p179). Beyond the temples lie some remote protected areas, including **Tmat Boey** (p177) where it's possible to spot the giant ibis, the critically endangered national bird of Cambodia.

### SEPTEMBER

The impressive wats of Battambang (p158) are thronging with the faithful during **P'chum Ben** or the Festival of the Dead.

### OCTOBER

**Bon Om Tuk** or the Water Festival features boat races in Battambang (p158) and on the moat at Banteay Chhmar (p169).

### NOVEMBER

The **Chamnor Arts Festival** is held on St 2½ and promotes the up-and-coming art scene in Battambang (p158).

### DECEMBER

One of the best months for exploring the northwest, as the **landscape is lush** but the roads have dried out.

# BATTAMBANG

● Battambang

✪ Phnom Penh

A subtle charmer that was traditionally the second city of Cambodia, Battambang works its magic on many visitors. While there may not be a huge amount to do in the city proper, its riverside setting, timeless temples, old French architecture and chilled-out cafes and bars all make up for it. It's the perfect blend of relatively urban modernity and small-town friendliness. Battambang has an enduring tradition of producing many of Cambodia's best-loved singers, actors and artists, and Cambodia's best-known circus, the magnificent Phare Ponleu Selpak, is here.

Outside the city's confines, timeless hilltop temples and bucolic villages await – plus the most scenic river trip in the country, which links Battambang with Siem Reap. Battambang Province is said by proud locals to produce Cambodia's finest rice and tastiest oranges (don't bring this up in Pursat). It has a long border with Thailand and a short stretch of the Tonlé Sap shoreline.

## TOP TIP

Battambang is spread out across the banks of the. The heart of the old town is on the west bank between Sts 1 and 3, including the uniquely named Sts 1½ and 2½.

CANNET/SHUTTERSTOCK ©

**Sangker River**

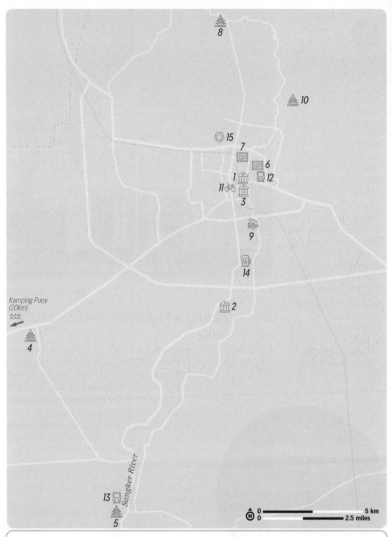

**SIGHTS**
1 Battambang Museum
2 Cambodia
Peace Gallery
3 Governor's Residence
**(see 9)** Khor
Sang House
**(see 9)** Mrs Bun
Roeung's Ancient House
4 Phnom Sampeau
5 Prasat Banan

**(see 7)** Psar Nath
6 Romcheik 5 Artspace
7 Tep Kao Sol
8 Wat Ek Phnom
9 Wat Kor
10 Wat Somrong Knong

**ACTIVITIES,
COURSES & TOURS**
11 Audio Tour by Cyclo
12 Bamboo Train
13 Banan Bamboo Train

**(see 7)** Coconut Lyly
**(see 2)** Green
Orange Kayaks
**(see 7)** Nary Kitchen
**(see 7)** Soksabike

**EATING**
**(see 7)** Chinese Noodle
Dumpling
**(see 7)** Jaan Bai
**(see 7)** Lonely Tree Café
**(see 7)** Riceholic

**DRINKING
& NIGHTLIFE**
14 Gecko
**(see 7)** K'Trey-K'Trok
**(see 7)** Miss Wong
**(see 7)** Pomme
**(see 7)** Vintage
Wine Bar

**ENTERTAINMENT**
15 Phare Ponleu Selpak

STEFANO EMBER/SHUTTERSTOCK ©

## BEST TOURS IN BATTAMBANG

**Soksabike**
Social enterprise aiming to connect visitors with the Cambodian countryside and its people. Half- and full-day trips cover 25km and 40km respectively.

**Green Orange Kayaks**
Kayaks can be rented from Green Orange Kayaks, 8km south of Battambang. Paddle back to the city along the Sangker River.

**Audio Tour by Cyclo**
Explore the heritage architecture of Battambang with this tour available from Au Cabaret Vert boutique hotel.

**Governor's Residence**

# Battambang's Heritage Architecture

GEMS OF THE OLD TOWN

Much of Battambang's charm lies in its early-20th-century architecture, a mix of vernacular shophouses and French-era construction that makes up the historic core of the city. Phnom Penh–based **Khmer Architecture Tours** is highly regarded for its specialist tours in and around the capital and has collaborated with Battambang Municipality to create heritage walks in Battambang's historic centre. The walks concentrate both on the French period and on the modernist architecture of the 1960s. Check out urbandatabase. khmerstudies.org/get-datas/243 for two downloadable PDFs including a colour map and numbered highlights.

Some of the finest French-era buildings are dotted along the waterfront (St 1), especially just south of **Psar Nath** or Meeting Market, itself a monument to modernist architecture. One of the best examples from the early 20th century is the two-storey **Governor's Residence**, with its sweeping balconies and louvered wooden shutters, a

### BUCOLIC BATTAMBANG

Many of the most popular Battambang experiences lie in the lush countryside beyond the city, including the caves of **Phnom Sampeau** (p165), the hilltop temple of **Prasat Banan** (p165) and the legendary **bamboo train** (p162).

## WHERE TO SHOP IN BATTAMBANG

**Lonely Tree Shop**
Fine silk bags, chunky jewellery, fashionable shirts – this is definitely not a regular charity gift shop.

**Phare Ponleu Selpak**
The big-top campus here has an excellent store selling all sorts of quirky merch, including T-shirts.

**Psar Nath Market**
For a traditional shopping experience, Psar Nath has a small food court and fresh produce.

THE GUIDE

NORTHWESTERN CAMBODIA

handsome legacy of the early 1900s. The interior is now open to the public and has a collection of grand old furnishings, old photographs and traditional costumes. It was designed by an Italian architect for the last Thai governor, who departed in 1907. Entrance is via a small gate on St 139 on the southern side of the extensive gardens.

This is a great way to spend half a day exploring the city. Those with less time can rent a bicycle and run the combined routes in just an hour or so.

# Museums & Galleries of Battambang

ANCIENT AND MODERN CULTURE COLLIDE

Before the Khmer Rouge era, Battambang had a long history as the nation's hub for art and culture. Today, a new generation of artists is building on this heritage and Battambang is regaining its reputation as Cambodia's cultural capital. A clutch of galleries has set up in recent years creating an informal arts district right in the heart of town.

**Romchiek 5 Artspace** has a permanent collection displaying the edgy, contemporary works of its four founders, who in their youth were expelled from Thailand and forced to work as child labourers, before being rescued by an NGO and encouraged to express themselves through art. **Tep Kao Sol** is the gallery space of local artist Loeum Lorn, who's known for creating works out of melting coloured ice and then photographing them. It's open sporadically.

There are also a couple of small yet interesting museums in Battambang to explore at your leisure. Located on the riverfront, **Battambang Museum** has been given a full makeover thanks to the generous support of Friends of Khmer Culture and now has state-of-the-art lighting and detailed signage. There are some beautiful Angkorian lintels and elegant statuary from all over Battambang Province, including pieces from Prasat Banan and Sneng.

Further out of town, the small **Cambodia Peace Gallery** tells the big story of Cambodia's long journey from war to peace. Exhibits are well presented in a series of buildings in the spacious compound, including original stained-glass windows showing different aspects of Cambodia's recent history. To get here, follow the road south to Prasat Banan for about 7km.

## COOKING CLASSES IN BATTAMBANG

Chef Lyly, a graduate from Siem Reap's Paul Dubrule Cooking School, runs the **Coconut Lyly** cooking class. Three-hour classes (start times 9am and 3.30pm) include a visit to Psar Nath market, preparing four typical Khmer dishes (recipe book included) and then eating your handiwork. The excellent restaurant here is open from 9am to 10pm.

Another popular cooking class, **Nary Kitchen**, includes a visit to the market, a four-course menu and a keepsake recipe book. Courses start at 9am and 3.30pm, lasting about three hours plus time to eat your creations. Nary's restaurant is open from 8am to 10pm.

## CRAFT BREWS IN BATTAMBANG

Craft beer is growing in popularity across Cambodia and a couple of places in Battambang serve home-grown tipples, including **Pomme** (p166) with its sister Brewhouse in Siem Reap, and **Gecko** (p166) in a romantic riverside setting out of town.

 **BUDGET BEDS IN BATTAMBANG**

**Pomme**
The leading backpacker pad in town to sleep, eat and drink. Accommodation is in small pod-style units. $

**The Place**
Battambang's first flashpacker hostel, The Place is a welcoming retreat with a rooftop bar. $

**Seng Hout Hotel**
Friendly staff are switched on to traveller needs, and this pad has an open-air rooftop and 3rd-floor pool. $

**Thang Vuthyra**,
HR coordinator
at Phare Ponleu
Selpak (phareps.
org), shares her
favourite Battambang
experiences.

Battambang is a city
to soak up slowly.
The many pagodas
along the river reflect
its wealthier past.
A favourite is **Wat
Somrong Knong**
(p165), and the nearby
**Wat P'Nouv** with its
amusing sculptures.

A stroll through the
old town, stopping
in little galleries
and cafes, is a must.
**K'Trey-K'Trok** (p165)
cafe is in a beautifully
restored shophouse
on St 1½. **Tep Kao
Sol** and **Romcheik 5
Art Space** (p161) are
well worth a visit for
browsing art.

Walking through St
2½, you'll see many
murals, results of the
art festivals brought
to the city by **Phare
Ponleu Selpak**
(p164). Watch one
of the circus shows
showcasing their
energy and creativity.

# Wat Kor Village Wander

THE SPIRIT OF OLD BATTAMBANG

About 2km south of central Battambang, the village of **Wat Kor** is centred around the temple of the same name. It's a great place to wander, especially late in the afternoon when the opposite (east) bank of the Sangker River is bathed in amber tones by the sinking sun. Picturesque bridges span the river, the spires of Wat Kor glow bright platinum and Khmer village life is on full display.

About 1.5km beyond Wat Kor, you'll encounter the cluster of Khmer heritage houses that the village is known for. Built of now-rare hardwoods over a century ago and surrounded by orchard gardens, they have wide verandas and exude the ambience of another era. Two of the approximately 20 heritage houses in the Wat Kor area are open to visitors: **Mrs Bun Roeung's Ancient House** and neighbouring **Khor Sang House**. The owner of each offers a short tour in French or English. They have floors worn lustrous by a century of bare feet and are decorated with old furniture and family photos.

Mrs Bun Roeung's Ancient House was built in 1920 by a local lawyer. The owners have turned the rear section of the house into homestay accommodation, a unique option for architecture and history fans. Khor Sang House was built in 1907 by the French-speaking owner's grandfather, who served as a secretary to the province's last Thai governor. The rear section dates from 1890.

# All Aboard the Bamboo Train

RIDE CAMBODIA'S UNIQUE HOMEMADE RAILWAY

One of the world's unique rail journeys, Battambang's **bamboo train** has had many an obituary written about it over the years but somehow it's still on the rails, despite the launch of proper passenger services linking Battambang with Phnom Penh and Poipet.

The original bamboo train used to trundle from O Dambong, a few kilometres east of Battambang's Wat Kor Bridge, to O Sra Lav along warped, misaligned rails and vertiginous bridges left by the French. Each bamboo train – known in Khmer as a *norry* – consists of a 3m-long wooden frame, covered lengthwise with slats made of ultralight bamboo, resting on two barbell-like bogies, connected by belts to a 6HP gasoline engine. With a pile of 10 or 15 people, or up to 3 tonnes of rice, it could cruise along at about 15km/h.

This genius system offers a solution to the inescapable problem faced on any single-track line: what to do when two trains

**BOUTIQUE BEDS IN BATTAMBANG**

**Bambu Hotel**
Delightful rooms with a
Franco-Khmer motif are set
around an inviting pool and
popular bar-restaurant. **$$**

**Maisons Wat Kor**
Secluded sanctuary of elegant
rooms in traditional-style
Khmer houses that once
hosted Brangelina. **$$$**

**Battambang Resort**
Surroundings include tropical
gardens and rice fields,
while the interior features
Cambodian artefacts. **$$**

**Bamboo train**

### BEST RESTAURANTS IN BATTAMBANG

**Jaan Bai $$**
Meaning 'rice bowl' in Khmer, this is foodie heaven, with delectable dishes like slow-cooked coconut-infused beef rib.

**Lonely Tree Cafe $**
This homely cafe serves Spanish tapas-style dishes and Khmer options. Proceeds support people with disabilities.

**Riceholic $**
Run by a Japanese couple; specialising in making a traditional *koji* (fermented sauce) from Battambang rice.

**Chinese Noodle Dumpling $**
The Chinese chef at this Battambang institution does bargain dumplings and serves fresh noodles a dozen or more ways.

going in opposite directions meet. With bamboo trains, the answer is simple: one car is quickly disassembled and set on the ground beside the tracks so that the other can pass.

The original stretch of line is up and running again, albeit with new bridges and straight tracks. Encroaching foliage has been cut back along the track, but this sanitised version of the old bamboo train is still a fun experience. However, due to mainline passenger and cargo services now operating on the line, the bamboo train doesn't run between about 1pm and 3.30pm, mercifully corresponding to the hottest part of the day.

A local investor has also created the new **Banan bamboo train**, about 20km away near Prasat Banan, to reconstruct the experience. However, it's more like a kiddies' roller-coaster ride than the original bamboo train, but it does pass through some scenic rock formations around the base of Phnom Banan. There's no need to decamp from the bamboo train on this line, as the track has passing points.

If you're weighing up which of the bamboo trains is the best experience, most independent travellers prefer the original version while families with young children might prefer the scenic ride on the new bamboo train.

### CROSSING THE CARDAMOM MOUNTAINS

It's possible to travel from Battambang to **Koh Kong** (p200) during the dry season via Samlaut and Pramaoy, small towns with guesthouses and hotels. As highways are upgraded, this should become an all-weather route.

 **WHERE TO GET A MASSAGE OR A WORKOUT**

**Lemongrass Spa**
The city's most sophisticated spa is set in a restored heritage building and offers professional rubs and scrubs.

**Hope of Blind Seeing Hand Massage**
Trained blind masseurs offer soothing workovers in an air-conditioned space in town.

**Aerobics Classes**
Head to Battambang's east bank to join the locals burning off the rice carbs doing aerobics.

TEPIKINA NASTYA/SHUTTERSTOCK ©

**Prasat Banan**

## THE KILLING DAM

**Kamping Puoy** was one of the many Khmer Rouge projects intended to recreate the irrigation networks that helped Cambodia flourish under the kings of Angkor. Around 10,000 Cambodians are thought to have perished during its construction, worked to death under the shadow of executions, malnutrition and disease.

Today, the lake is a scenic spot where locals come to picnic and take row boats on the water. Thanks to the dam, this is one of the few parts of Cambodia to produce two rice crops a year. It's 27km west of Battambang (go via NH5 and follow the irrigation canal).

## Watch a Phare Circus Performance

ACCLAIMED CIRCUS AND ARTS CENTRE

Battambang's signature attraction is the internationally acclaimed circus of **Phare Ponleu Selpak**, a superb arts centre for Cambodian youngsters. Although it also runs shows in Siem Reap, it's worth timing your visit to Battambang to watch this amazing spectacle where it began. Shows are held two to four nights per week, depending on the season (check the website), and kick off at 7pm.

Phare, as it's known to locals, is not just a circus – it is involved in lots of other projects. It trains musicians, visual artists and performing artists as well. Many of the artists you'll bump into around town lived and studied at Phare. Guests are welcome to take a guided tour of the Phare complex during the day and observe circus, dance, music, drawing and graphic-arts classes.

Tickets are sold at the door from 6pm and at many retailers around town. It's quite a way from the city centre, so plan on taking a *tuk-tuk*.

### DON'T MISS THE BIG TOP

If you're unlucky enough to be in Battambang on the nights when there's no circus show taking place, there is also a **Phare big top** (p102) in Siem Reap where they have nightly shows.

 **INTERNATIONAL FLAVOURS IN BATTAMBANG**

**La Pizza**
Pizzas come in every shape and size here, including by the slice to extra large. **$**

**Flavors of India**
This Battambang outpost opened after some curry-craving expats ordered takeaway from Phnom Penh. **$**

**Garage Sandwich Bar**
A curious combination of bike-repair shop and bakery, but it works thanks to fresh bread and tasty sandwiches. **$**

# Hilltop Temples & Stunning Views

TEMPLES, SHRINES AND CAVES

The countryside around Battambang is dotted with old temples and other worthwhile sights. Heading south, two temples can be combined for a rewarding half-day trip by *moto* or *tuk-tuk*.

It's a 358-stone-step climb up Phnom Banan to reach **Prasat Banan**, but the incredible views across surrounding countryside from the top are worth it. Udayadityavarman II, son of Suryavarman I, built Prasat Banan in the 11th century; some locals claim the five-tower layout here was the inspiration for Angkor Wat, although this seems optimistic. There are impressive carved lintels above the doorways to each of the towers and bas-reliefs on the upper parts of the central tower.

From the temple, a narrow stone staircase leads south down the hill to three caves, which can be visited with a local guide. Prasat Banan is 23km from Battambang.

The fabled limestone outcrop of **Phnom Sampeau**, 12km from Battambang, is known for its gorgeous views and mesmerising display of bats, which pour out of a massive cave in its cliff face. Access to the summit is via a cement road or – if you're in need of a workout – a steep staircase. *Moto* drivers hang out near the base of the hill and can whisk you up and back.

About halfway up to the summit, a road leads under a gate and 250m up to the Killing Caves of Phnom Sampeau, now a place of pilgrimage. A staircase, flanked by greenery, leads into a cavern, where a golden reclining Buddha lies peacefully next to a glass-walled memorial filled with bones and skulls – the remains of some of the people bludgeoned to death by Khmer Rouge cadres and thrown through the skylight above. Next to the base of the stairway is the old memorial, a rusty cage made of chicken wire and cyclone fencing and partly filled with human bones.

On the summit, several viewpoints can be discovered amid a complex of temples. As you descend from the summit's golden stupa, dating from 1964, turn left under the gate decorated with a bas-relief of Eiy Sei (an elderly Buddha). A deep canyon, its vertical sides cloaked in greenery, descends 144 steps through a natural arch to a 'lost world' of stalactites, creeping vines and bats; two Angkorian warriors stand guard.

Near the westernmost of the two antennae at the summit, two government artillery pieces, one with markings in Russian, the other in German, are still deployed. Near the base of the western antenna, jockey for position with other

## TEMPLE-HOPPING

Hidden behind a colourful modern pagoda and a gargantuan Buddha statue, **Wat Ek Phnom** is a partly collapsed 11th-century temple, surrounded by the remains of a laterite wall and an ancient reservoir. A lintel showing the Churning of the Ocean of Milk is above the eastern entrance to the central temple. It's about 10km north of Battambang.

Built in the 19th century on the site of a pre-Angkorian temple complex, **Wat Somrong Knong** was used by the Khmer Rouge as a prison – it's believed that around 10,000 people were executed here. The complex houses the gorgeous main pagoda and a mishmash of ancient ruins, modern structures and memorials to those who perished here. It's about 4km north of Battambang.

**WHERE TO GET A CAFFEINE HIT**

**Kinyei**
Besides having the best coffee in town, teensy-weensy Kinyei offers an eclectic menu. **$**

**Cafe HOC**
This social enterprise is best known for its all-you-can-eat breakfast for just US$3. **$**

**K'Trey-K'Trok**
Distressed walls and funky artwork are the signature at this hole-in-the-wall coffee shop with bargain brews. **$**

## BEST BARS IN BATTAMBANG

**Pomme**
The bar-restaurant in this popular hostel appeals to travellers and locals alike thanks to a diverse menu and cheap draft beer towers.

**Miss Wong**
This characterful old shophouse looks like a slice of old Shanghai. Creative cocktails and dim sum are available.

**Vintage Wine Bar**
Inviting little French bar that offers a menu of tapas-style light bites, plus some tasting boards.

**Gecko**
Set in a stylish riverside villa with a rooftop terrace, Gecko serves craft beers and some excellent Japanese food.

ANNAT30/SHUTTERSTOCK ©

**Stupas, Phnom Sampeau (p165)**

tourists on the sunset lookout pavilion. Looking west you'll spy Phnom Krapeu (Crocodile Mountain), a one-time Khmer Rouge stronghold.

If visiting alone, a local guide may try to escort you around the sites and give you some history. Back down at the hill base, people gather at dusk (around 5.30pm) to witness the spectacle of a thick column of bats pouring from a cave high up on the north side of the cliff face. The display lasts a good 30 minutes as millions of bats head out in a looping line to their feeding grounds near Tonlé Sap. There are lots of monkeys at this site, so you should not be flashy with your food as they can become aggressive.

### GETTING THERE & AROUND

Battambang is 293km northwest of Phnom Penh along NH5, 67km south of Sisophon along NH5 and 83km northeast of Pailin along NH57. You can reach it by bus, minivan or taxi, a boat connection with Siem Reap or the slow train to Phnom Penh. Most travellers go by road, as it's good value and pretty quick (four to five hours) thanks to NH5 now being part of the Asian Highway 1 (AH1). The train is cheap, but takes seven to eight hours. For Siem Reap, the boat is an iconic option along the Sangker River and across the Tonlé Sap lake, but it can take seven to eight hours when the water levels are low.

English-speaking *tuk-tuk* drivers are commonplace in Battambang. A half-day trip out of town to a single sight such as Phnom Sampeau might cost US$12 to US$15, while a full-day trip taking in three sights costs US$20 to US$25, depending on negotiations. *Tuk-tuk* rides around town start from US$1.50.

Small motorbikes are available at hostels and guesthouses around town from US$6 to US$10 per day. Mountain bikes can be rented at Soksabike for US$5 per day; guesthouses offer local bicycles for about US$2.

# Beyond Battambang

Choose from the Angkorian temple of Banteay Chhmar and Pailin, a gem-mining centre in the foothills of the Cardamoms.

Banteay Chhmar

Battambang

Pailin

The area beyond Battambang is vast and geographically disparate so it pays to focus on one attraction or the other, either Pailin to the southwest or Banteay Chhmar to the northwest. Pailin was once a hideout for geriatric Khmer Rouge commanders, but is also famous for gem mining and offers a glimpse of the rolling hills and mountains of the Cardamoms. Banteay Chhmar is one of the largest Angkor-era temples in northwest Cambodia and sees refreshingly few tourists compared with iconic Angkor Wat. Connecting this temple with Battambang are the strategic towns of Sisophon, with links east to Siem Reap, and Poipet, gateway to eastern Thailand. Both have lots of hotels, guesthouses and eateries.

## TOP TIP

This region is too spread out to explore by *tuk-tuk,* so consider hiring a taxi or renting a motorbike.

**Banteay Chhmar (p169)**

CHATNARONG RAKCHART/SHUTTERSTOCK ©

167

## CROSSING TO THAILAND AT PSAR PRUHM

The laid-back **Psar Pruhm/Ban Pakard** border crossing (7am to 7pm) is 102km southwest of Battambang and 18km northwest of Pailin via good sealed roads. From Pailin, patient travellers might get a share taxi (US$2) to the border, or you can take a *moto* (US$7.50) or private taxi (US$15). Formalities are straightforward and quick on both sides of the border. Immigration officials usually quote US$35 for Cambodia tourist visas here. Ignore offers from touts on the Thai side to help with visas. From nearby Chanthaburi's bus station there are frequent buses to Bangkok (200B, four hours).

TANES NGAMSOM/SHUTTERSTOCK ©

**Wat Phnom Yat**

### WHAT A RELIEF

Many segments of the bas-reliefs looted from Banteay Chhmar and intercepted by the Thai police are now on display in Phnom Penh's **National Museum of Cambodia** (p51), home to the world's finest collection of Khmer sculpture.

## Temples & Waterfalls Around Pailin

WELCOME TO CAMBODIA'S WILD WEST

Pailin is a former Khmer Rouge stronghold that was once famous for its precious gemstones, particularly the striking sapphires. It can be visited as a day trip from Battambang, taking about 1½ hours to cover the 83km each way. Apart from shopping for gemstones and a colourful hilltop temple, the remote town itself has little to recommend it. However, the forested Cardamom foothills surrounding the city are beautiful. Just don't wander into them by yourself or you may, quite literally, be walking into a minefield.

**Wat Phnom Yat** is a psychedelic temple centred on an ancient *po* (sacred fig) tree. A 27m Buddha looms over the top of the staircase, while a path leads up to the colourful temple and the large golden stupas at the top of the hill. Along the path a life-sized cement tableau shows naked sinners and their punishments. The sunsets from the summit are usually nice enough to take your mind off the fire and brimstone.

### WHERE TO SLEEP AND EAT IN PAILIN

**Pailin Ruby Guesthouse**
A good-value place, with 63 clean, spacious rooms. The air-con options have natural light. $

**Memoria Palace**
This resort has spacious bungalows with boutique touches, great views and a 20m swimming pool. $$

**Bamboo Restaurant**
Bamboo serves excellent Khmer and Thai food in outdoor pavilions, but is about 2km west of town. $

At the base of Phnom Yat hill, an impressive gate dating to 1968 leads to **Wat Khaong Kang**, an important centre for Buddhist teaching before the Khmer Rouge insanity. The exterior wall is decorated with a long bas-relief of the Churning of the Ocean of Milk.

**Phnom Khieu** is the most accessible of the numerous waterfalls in the area, dropping out of the Cardamoms south of Pailin, and has water year-round.

# The Narrow Fortress of Banteay Chhmar

MAGNIFICENT TEMPLE WITHOUT THE CROWDS

Beautiful, peaceful and covered in astonishingly intricate bas-reliefs, **Banteay Chhmar** is one of the most impressive remote temple complexes beyond the Angkor area. It was constructed by Cambodia's most prolific builder, Jayavarman VII (r 1181–1219), on the site of a 9th-century temple. The Global Heritage Fund is assisting with conservation efforts here, and it is now a serious candidate for Unesco World Heritage Site status.

Next to the ruins, Banteay Chhmar village is part of a worthwhile community-based tourism (CBT) scheme offering homestays, activities and guides for temple tours to assist with community development in the area. If you're looking for an opportunity to delve into Cambodian rural life and spend some quality time amid a temple complex far from the crowds, this is a great option. All activities can be booked through the **CBT office** (visitbanteaychhmar.org).

The recently restored main temple housed one of the largest and most impressive Buddhist monasteries of the Angkorian period, and was originally enclosed by a 9km-long wall. Now atmospherically encroached on by forest, it features several towers bearing enigmatic, Bayon-style four-faced Avalokiteshvara (a Buddhist deity), with its mysterious and iconic smile. The temple is also renowned for its 2000 sq metres of intricate carvings, which depict victorious battles and scenes from daily life.

The artistic highlights are the bas-reliefs of multi-armed images of Avalokiteshvara, unique to Banteay Chhmar, on the exterior of the southern section of the temple's western ramparts. Unfortunately, several of these were dismantled and trucked into Thailand in a brazen act of looting in 1998; only two figures – one with 22 arms, the other with 32 – remain in situ out of an original eight, but they still evoke the dazzling, intricate artistry involved in creating these carvings.

**CROSSING TO THAILAND AT POIPET**

Long the armpit of Cambodia, notorious for its squalor, scams and sleaze, Poipet has splurged on a facelift. Thanks mainly to the patronage of neighbouring Thais, whose own country bans gambling, its casino resorts are turning this border town into Cambodia's little Las Vegas. The most popular border crossing with Thailand, the **Poipet/Aranya Prathet** crossing is notorious for its scams on visas by overcharging in Thai baht and there are often long queues to cross the border. Buses, minivans and taxis connect Poipet with Sisophon (48km) and Battambang and Siem Reap beyond. Heading in to Thailand, there are frequent minivans to Bangkok, as well as slow trains from Aranya Prathet twice a day.

 **WHERE TO STAY AROUND BANTEAY CHHMAR**

**CBT Homestay**
Rooms in private homes come with mosquito nets and fans, plus a shared bathroom. $

**Pyramid Hotel**
Solid for Sisophon, the Pyramid has 44 spick-and-span rooms in a central location. $$

**City Poipet Hotel**
If you find yourself stuck in Poipet, this place has a touch of style, plus decent wi-fi. $

NORTHWESTERN CAMBODIA

## MEKONG SILK MILL

It's possible to see silk being woven and to purchase top-quality silk products destined for the French market at **Soieries du Mékong**, 150m south of where NH56 from Sisophon meets the moat. It's affiliated with the French NGO Enfants du Mékong, which has been working in Cambodia since 1993 and has opened four education centres to avoid the school dropouts that are particularly common in the border areas near Thailand. For those who can't make the overland trip to Banteay Chhmar, they also have a shop in Kandal Village (p170) in Siem Reap where they sell beautiful silk scarves and other delicate items.

SAHABHAP/SHUTTERSTOCK ©

**Stone carving of Brahma, Banteay Chhmar**

On the temple's east side, a huge bas-relief on a partly top-pled wall dramatically depicts naval warfare between the Khmers (on the left) and the Chams (on the right), with the dead (some being devoured by crocodiles) at the bottom. Further south (to the left) are scenes of land battles with infantry and elephants. There are more martial bas-reliefs along the exterior of the temple's south walls.

The once-grand entry gallery is now a jumble of fallen sandstone blocks, though elsewhere a few intersecting galleries have withstood the ravages of time, as have some almost hidden 12th-century inscriptions. Sadly, all the *apsaras* (nymphs) have been decapitated by looters.

The **satellite temples**, many hidden deep in the jungle and with Bayon-style faces of their own, are all in a ruinous state, and some are accessible only if you chop through the undergrowth. They include **Prasat Chen Chiem Trey**, which vaguely translates as 'Fish Farm Temple'; it's about 1km north of the main temple and has been all but consumed by trees.

**Banteay Top** (Fortress of the Army) may be small, but its impressively tall, damaged towers are highly photogenic. Constructed around the same time as Banteay Chhmar, it may be a tribute to the army of Jayavarman VII, which confirmed Khmer dominance over the region by comprehensively defeating the Chams. To get here from Banteay Chhmar, head towards Sisophon along NH56 for 7km, take the left-hand turn through the red ornamental gate and head east down the track for 5km.

## GETTING AROUND

Minivans and taxis link Battambang with Pailin (83km), Sisophon (67km) and Poipet (112km), but to get to Banteay Chhmar (110km), it's necessary to change vehicle in Sisophon. Renting a motorbike to visit Pailin is easy

enough in Battambang and makes it easier to do side trips to local waterfalls, but this option doesn't work so well for Banteay Chhmar as you are likely to be continuing to Siem Reap.

# PREAH VIHEAR PROVINCE

Preah Vihear
Province

⊙ Phnom Penh

Vast and hardly touched by tourism, Preah Vihear Province is home to three of Cambodia's most impressive Angkorian legacies. Stunningly perched on a promontory high in the Dangrek Mountains, Prasat Preah Vihear became Cambodia's second Unesco World Heritage Site in 2008, sparking an armed stand-off with Thailand. Further south are the lonely, jungle-clad temples of Preah Khan, totally isolated and imbued with secret-world atmosphere.

The province remains desperately poor, partly because many areas were under Khmer Rouge control until 1998, and partly because until recently its transport infrastructure was in a disastrous state. The needs of the Cambodian army in its confrontation with Thailand have expedited dramatic road upgrades here, although public transport is still sparse on some routes.

## TOP TIP

Preah Vihear City, formerly know as Tbeng Meanchey, is the provincial capital and a useful transport hub for this remote province. There are minivans and taxis running to Kompong Thom, Sra Em (for Prasat Preah Vihear), Siem Reap and Stung Treng.

STEVE BARZE/SHUTTERSTOCK ©

**Prasat Preah Vihear (p171)**

# PREAH VIHEAR CITY PROVINCE

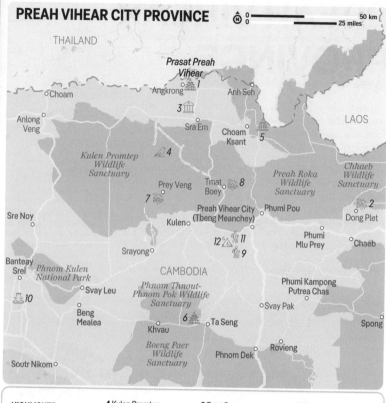

| | THAILAND | | | | LAOS |

**HIGHLIGHTS**
1 Prasat Preah Vihear

**SIGHTS**
2 Dong Plet
3 Eco Global Museum

4 Kulen Promtep
Wildlife Sanctuary
5 Prasat Neak Buos
6 Preah Khan of
Kompong Svay
7 Prey Veng

8 Tmat Boey

**ACTIVITIES,
COURSES & TOURS**
9 Phnom Tbeng Natural
Heritage Park

10 Rumchek
11 Tang You
Ecotourism Site

**SLEEPING**
12 Tang You Pagoda

## Ascend to Prasat Preah Vihear

MOTHER OF ALL MOUNTAIN TEMPLES

Cambodia's most dramatically situated Angkorian monument, this 800m-long temple is perched atop an escarpment in the Dangrek Mountains, with breathtaking views of lowland Cambodia stretching as far as the eye can see. In

**WHERE TO STAY IN SRA EM, GATEWAY TO PRASAT PREAH VIHEAR**

**Chhouk Tep Guesthouse**
A great-value spot with clean rooms and an excellent coffee shop with iced macchiatos. **$**

**Preah Vihear Jaya Hotel**
Spacious rooms include a contemporary theme and large bathrooms, plus there's a pool. **$$**

**Preah Vihear Boutique Hotel**
PVBH is looking for Siem Reap exiles with its lush bedding and 20m outdoor pool. **$$**

AMNAT30/SHUTTERSTOCK ©

**Prasat Preah Vihear**

2008, **Prasat Preah Vihear** was declared Cambodia's second Unesco World Heritage Site (after the Angkor Archaeological Park in Siem Reap).

Cambodia and Thailand have been sparring over ownership of Prasat Preah Vihear (called Khao Phra Wiharn by the Thais) for centuries, with tensions flaring up most recently from 2008 to 2011. There's still a large military presence in and around the temple, ostensibly for security, though it might make some visitors uncomfortable, and money or cigarettes are occasionally requested by soldiers. Always check the latest security situation when in Siem Reap or Phnom Penh, before making the long overland journey here.

An important place of pilgrimage for millennia, the temple was built by a succession of seven Khmer monarchs, beginning with Yasovarman I (r 889–910) and ending with Suryavarman II (r 1112–52). Like other temple-mountains from this period, it was designed to represent Mt Meru, the sacred mountain of Buddhism and Hinduism, and was dedicated to the Hindu deity Shiva.

The area was ruled by Thailand for several centuries, but returned to Cambodia during the French protectorate, under the treaty of 1907. In 1959 the

### PREAH VIHEAR'S ECO GLOBAL MUSEUM

Don't be put off by the overlong name, **Eco Global Museum Samdech Techo Hun Sen Preah Vihear**, as this is actually a very informative little museum put together with the support of Unesco. Sections include an archaeology gallery, an arts gallery, an ethnographic gallery and an environment gallery. Information is well presented in English and Khmer and there's an excellent short video detailing Prasat Preah Vihear's history. It's located about 5km beyond Sra Em on the road to Prasat Preah Vihear, and plans are afoot to turn the entire area into a visitors centre for the mountaintop temple.

### CROSS-BORDER PATROL

Note that there is no international border crossing at Prasat Preah Vihear at this time, as the border remains firmly closed. The nearest border crossing is at **Choam** (p181) near Anlong Veng.

### WHERE TO STAY IN PREAH VIHEAR CITY

**Home Vattanak Guesthouse**
The best-value digs in town; rooms include comfortable beds and smart bathrooms. $

**Ly Hout Guesthouse**
Popular with NGOs, the smart rooms here have white bedspreads and woven bed runners. $

**Heng Heng Guesthouse**
Rooms at this pink concrete monstrosity are time-worn but a good deal at under 10 bucks with a fan. $

## WHY I LOVE PRASAT PREAH VIHEAR

**Nick Ray,** writer

There is no more dramatic setting for an ancient temple than perched on the edge of the Dangrek Mountains. My first visit in 2000 was a real eye-opener due to the sheer number of 'Danger! Mines!' signs everywhere. I spent various nights camping up top, including a particularly memorable overnight with Cambodian soldiers during one of the stand-offs with Thailand. I also descended via the ancient stairway, more than 2000 steps, and my legs felt like jelly. A recent trip saw some filming at the temple for a USAID video and we were privileged to witness sunrise. It requires a monumental effort to visit Prasat Preah Vihear, but this monument is well worth it.

Churning of the Ocean Milk, Prasat Preah Vihear

Thai military seized the temple from Cambodia; then–Prime Minister Sihanouk took the dispute to the International Court of Justice in the Hague, gaining worldwide recognition of Cambodian sovereignty in a 1962 ruling.

The next time Prasat Preah Vihear made international news was in 1979, when the Thai military pushed more than 40,000 Cambodian refugees across the border in one of the worst cases of forced repatriation in UN history. The area was mined and many refugees died from injuries, starvation and disease before the occupying Vietnamese army could cut a safe passage and escort them on the long walk south to Kompong Thom.

Prasat Preah Vihear hit the headlines again in May 1998, when the Khmer Rouge regrouped here after the fall of Anlong Veng and staged a last stand that soon turned into a final surrender. The temple was heavily landmined during these final battles and de-mining was ongoing up until the outbreak of the conflict with Thailand in 2008.

In July 2011, the International Court of Justice ruled that both sides should withdraw troops from the area to establish a demilitarised zone. Then in November 2013, the ICJ confirmed its 1962 ruling that the temple belongs to Cambodia, although it declined to define the official borderline, leaving sovereignty of some lands around the temple open to dis-

 **WHERE TO EAT IN PREAH VIHEAR CITY**

**Ly Hout Coffee**
This coffee shop is straight out of Phnom Penh with aircon, wi-fi and a swish coffee machine. **$**

**Phnom Tbaeng Restaurant**
One of the few places in town with an English menu and adventurous entrees like fried eel and pig's intestines. **$**

**Psar Kompong Pranak**
Home to plenty of food stalls hawking local baguettes, grilled chicken and rice and noodle dishes. **$**

pute. The border dispute has died down in recent years and all has been peaceful during the last few research trips we have made, but tensions could reignite any time.

The temple is laid out along a north–south processional axis with five cruciform *gopura* (pavilions), decorated with exquisite carvings, separated by esplanades up to 275m long. Start at **Gopura V** at the base of the temple and gradually ascend to Gopura I at the edge of the cliff.

From the parking area, walk up the hill to toppled and crumbling Gopura V at the north end of the temple complex. From here, the grey-sandstone **Monumental Stairway** leads down to the Thai border. Back when the temple was open from the Thai side, this stairway was how most tourists entered the temple complex. Thailand claims that this part of the temple is theirs. That Gopura V appears on both the 50,000r and 2000r banknotes is an emphatic statement that Cambodia disagrees.

East of Gopura V, a set of stairs drops off into the abyss. This is the 1800m **Eastern Stairway**. Used for centuries by pilgrims climbing up from Cambodia's northern plains, it was recently de-mined, rebuilt as a 2242-step wooden staircase and reopened.

Walking south up the slope from Gopura V, the next pavilion is **Gopura IV**. On the pediment above the southern door, look for an early rendition of the Churning of the Ocean of Milk, a theme later depicted awesomely at Angkor Wat.

Keep climbing through Gopura III and II to **Gopura I**, where the galleries, with their inward-looking windows, are in a remarkably good state of repair, but the Central Sanctuary is just a pile of rubble. Outside, the cliff affords a stupendous viewpoint over Cambodia's northern plains, with the holy mountain of Phnom Kulen (487m) looming in the distance. This is a fantastic spot for a picnic.

The best guidebook to Prasat Preah Vihear's architecture and carvings is *Preah Vihear* by Vittorio Roveda (published 2010). These days it may be hard to find in Cambodia, as it was published in Thailand and the text is in English and Thai.

### THE IRON KUY OF CAMBODIA

The Kuy (also Kouy) are an ethnic minority found in northern Cambodia, southern Laos and northeastern Thailand. It's thought that the Kuy may have produced iron – used for weaponry, tools and construction support – since the Angkorian period.

The Kuy stopped smelting iron in the 1950s, but high-quality smithing continues to be practised in some communities. When travelling along NH62 between Kompong Thom and Preah Vihear City, it's possible to stop at **Rumchek**, about 2km south of the iron mines of Phnom Dek. Kuy smith Mr Ma Thean can produce a traditional Kuy jungle knife in just one hour.

# Expedition to Preah Khan of Kompong Svay

THE ULTIMATE JUNGLE TEMPLE

For tantalising lost-world ambience, this remote temple complex about 90km south of Preah Vihear City can't be beaten. Covering almost 5 sq km, and smothered by vines and trees, **Preah Khan of Kompong Svay** (not to be confused with the similarly gargantuan Preah Khan temple at Angkor) is the largest temple enclosure constructed during the Angkorian

### GET YOUR KICKS ON ROUTE 66

An alternative route to Preah Khan of Kompong Svay is from **Beng Mealea** (p149) along NH66 to Khvau, crossing splendid Angkorian naga (mythical serpent-being) bridges. The road deteriorates after Khvau and is impassable in the rainy season.

 **WHERE TO SLEEP NEAR PREAH KHAN OF KOMPONG SVAY**

**Preah Khan Homestays**
Homestays in nearby Ta Seng village offer basic beds with an intermittent fan and a shared bathroom. **$**

**BeTreed Adventures**
A jungle hideaway with two traditional wooden houses on stilts and a treehouse built from reclaimed hardwood. **$$**

**Temple Safari**
For the ultimate glamping experience, book a 'temple safari' with a pop-up campsite through Hanuman Travel. **$$$**

### LANDMINES IN PREAH VIHEAR PROVINCE

Until 1998, landmines were used by the Khmer Rouge to defend Prasat Preah Vihear against government forces. During the past decade, de-mining organisations made real headway in clearing the site. However, the advent of a border conflict with Thailand led to this area being heavily militarised once again. Both sides denied laying new landmines during the armed stand-off between Cambodia and Thailand from 2008 to 2011, but rumours persist, so do not, under any circumstances, stray from marked paths around Prasat Preah Vihear. The rest of the province is heavily landmined, too, especially around Choam Ksant. Those with their own transport should travel only on roads or trails regularly used by locals.

period – quite a feat when you consider the competition. Thanks to its back-of-beyond location, the site is astonishingly peaceful and you'll very likely be the only visitor.

Preah Khan's history is shrouded in mystery, but it was long an important religious site, and some structures here date back to the 9th century. Both Suryavarman II, builder of Angkor Wat, and Jayavarman VII lived here at various times during their lives, suggesting Preah Khan was something of a second city in the Angkorian empire. Originally dedicated to Hindu deities, Preah Khan was reconsecrated to Mahayana Buddhist worship during a monumental reconstruction in the late 12th and early 13th centuries.

As recently as the mid-1990s, the main temple was thought to be in reasonable shape, but at some point in the second half of the decade, looters arrived seeking buried statues under each *prang* (temple tower). Assaulted with pneumatic drills and mechanical diggers, the ancient temple never stood a chance, and many of the towers simply collapsed in on themselves, leaving the mess we see today. Once again, a temple that had survived so much couldn't stand the onslaught of the 20th century and its all-consuming appetite.

Among the many carvings found at Preah Khan – or recovered from looters – was the bust of Jayavarman, now in Phnom Penh's National Museum of Cambodia (p51) and widely copied as a souvenir for tourists. The body of the statue was discovered in the 1990s by locals who alerted authorities, making it possible for a joyous reunion of head and body in 2000.

Most locals refer to Preah Khan of Kompong Svay as Prasat Bakan; scholars officially refer to it as Bakan Svay Rolay, combining the local name for the temple and the district name.

The **main temple** is surrounded by a now dry moat similar to the one around Angkor Thom. Once through the grand gateway, the trail meanders past a *dharmasala* (pilgrim's rest house) and through another crumbling pavilion to the central temple area of half-toppled towers, entangled with trees and overgrown by forest. Despite all the damage by looters in the 1990s and more recent problems with theft, this crumbling temple, half lost to the jungle, is a remarkable site with some well-preserved bas-reliefs.

The US$5 entry fee to the complex gains you admission to the **satellite temples** as well.

There's no public transport to the temple so it's necessary to get to nearby Ta Seng village, 4km east. Transport options include approaching from Preah Vihear City via Sangkum Thmey District or from the Stoeung District in Kompong Thom Province. Roads are much better than the bad old days and the temple can be reached by chartered taxi, minivan or motorbike.

 ### SATELLITE TEMPLES AT PREAH KHAN OF KOMPONG SVAY

**Prasat Preah Stung**
Known to locals as Prasat Muk Buon (Temple of the Four Faces), it has four enigmatic, Bayon-style faces.

**Prasat Damrei**
The 'Elephant Temple' lies at the eastern end of a 3km-long *baray* (reservoir).

**Prasat Preah Thkol**
An island temple located on the western shore of Preah Khan's *baray*.

BEE-EATER/SHUTTERSTOCK ©

Sarus crane

# Birdwatching in Preah Vihear Province

SPOT GIANT IBIS AND VULTURES

Cambodia's remote northern plains, the largest remaining block of deciduous dipterocarp forest, seasonal wetlands and grasslands in Southeast Asia, have been described as Southeast Asia's answer to Africa's savannas. Covering much of northwestern Preah Vihear Province, they are one of the last places on the planet where you can see Cambodia's national bird, the critically endangered giant ibis.

Other rare species that can be spotted here include the woolly-necked stork, white-rumped falcon, green peafowl, Alexandrine parakeet, grey-headed fish eagle and no fewer than 16 species of woodpecker, as well as owls and other raptors like vultures. Birds are easiest to see from January to April.

In a last-ditch effort to ensure the survival of the giant ibis, protect the only confirmed breeding sites of the white-shouldered ibis and save the habitat of other globally endangered species, including the sarus crane and the greater adjutant, the Wildlife Conservation Society (WCS) set up a pioneering community-ecotourism project here.

## RARE BIRDS TO SPOT IN PREAH VIHEAR PROVINCE

**Giant ibis**
Cambodia's national bird is on the critically endangered IUCN Red List – only about 300 remain worldwide.

**Sarus crane**
The tallest bird in the world at more than 1.5m. There are around 25,000 remaining worldwide and up to 300 resident in Cambodia.

**Red-headed vulture**
Also on the critically endangered IUCN Red List – only around 20 or so of these vultures are thought to be in Cambodia.

**White-winged duck**
For twitchers this is a holy-grail bird, with just 1000 remaining worldwide and 100 in Cambodia. On the critically endangered IUCN Red List.

### SPOTTING THE SARUS CRANE

There are significant populations of the sarus crane in other parts of Cambodia, including the **Ang Trapaeng Thmor Bird Sanctuary** (p111) near Siem Reap.

 **WHERE TO SLEEP IN THE BIRD SANCTUARIES**

**Tmat Boey**
Visitors to this remote village sleep in wooden bungalows with bathrooms and solar-powered hot water. **$$**

**Prey Veng**
Similar to Tmat Boey, the accommodation here is in wooden bungalows with basic bathrooms and solar power. **$$**

**Boeng Toal**
Sleep in the dry forest in pop-up camps using comfortable safari-style tents with cotton bedding. **$$$**

## REDD+ PROJECTS IN PREAH VIHEAR PROVINCE

REDD stands for 'Reducing Emissions from Deforestation and Forest Degradation', while the plus sign indicates the role of conservation, sustainable management of forests and enhancement of forest carbon stocks. In Cambodia, REDD+ pays the Cambodian government to protect the forests and to support sustainable development of local communities. International companies have already purchased Cambodian forest carbon credits worth tens of millions of dollars, which helps fund the management of protected areas, tourism infrastructure and development projects for local communities.

In Preah Vihear there are several REDD+ projects under development. Northern Plains is the most advanced and links to several CBETs including Tmat Boey, Prey Veng and Boeng Toal (178), the region's major birding sites.

Situated in the isolated village of Tmat Boey inside the **Kulen Promtep Wildlife Sanctuary**, the initiative provides local villagers with education, income and a concrete incentive to do everything possible to protect the ibis. All visitors make a donation to the village conservation fund to help with maintenance and improvements to the project.

**Tmat Boey** village lies about 5km off the smooth highway that links Preah Vihear City and Sra Em. The turn-off is 46km southeast of Sra Em and 39km northwest of Preah Vihear. The village is accessible year-round. To arrange a four-day, three-night visit, contact the Siem Reap–based **Sam Veasna Conservation Tours** (SVC).

For those wanting to explore an even more remote corner of Cambodia, the Kulen Promtep Wildlife Sanctuary's latest birding site is based at the tiny outpost village of **Prey Veng**, about 60km from Tmat Boey (as the giant ibis flies). Here the WCS and SVC aim to replicate the success of Tmat Boey to ensure conservation of this habitat. More than 150 bird species have been spotted here, including the giant ibis, greater adjutant and white-winged duck.

As well as birding, Prey Veng offers great opportunities for hiking through the open dry forest to a hilltop Angkorian temple. Prey Veng's community-managed guesthouses provide simple accommodation.

Trips to both Tmat Boey and Prey Veng can include visits to Beng Mealea, Koh Ker and Prasat Preah Vihear en route and are often combined with visits to the vulture feeding station. These location can be visited through SVC's five-day Critical Cambodia tour.

In order to save three critically endangered species – the white-rumped, slender-billed and red-headed vultures – the Wildlife Conservation Society set up the **Boeng Toal Vulture Restaurant** in the village of **Dong Plet**, northeast of Chaeb on the edge of the Preah Vihear Protected Forest. A cow carcass is placed in a field, and visitors waiting in a nearby bird hide watch as these incredibly rare vultures move in to devour the carrion. Visits are offered by SVC and involve an overnight at a WCS forest safari camp. Access to the site is year-round, but give SVC at least a week's notice to assure your spot.

# The Pristine Plateau of Phnom Tbeng
UNEXPLORED MOUNTAIN FOR ADVENTUROUS TREKKERS

Looming large over Preah Vihear City lies **Phnom Tbeng Natural Heritage Park**. Accessible only via a steep climb, Phnom Tbeng is a spiritual and natural refuge which was recently nominated for Unesco World Heritage Site status.

 **COMMUNITY-BASED ECOTOURISM SITES ON PHNOM TBENG**

**Tang You Ecotourism Site**
The most organised CBET project for Phnom Tbeng (facebook.com/tangyou.cbt).

**Chak Angre**
A stunning waterfall atop Phnom Tbeng is the highlight of this CBET site.

**Datavek**
Dynamic women manage this CBET which is the closest to Preah Vihear City.

There are two principal trails up the mountain. Near the southern edge of the mountain, signposted off NH62 heading towards Kompong Thom, are two sets of concrete stairs which lead to a large pagoda and meditation complex. Trekkers who follow this route can also visit a large waterfall about 500m past the pagoda.

Explorers looking for more adventure should take NH62 in the direction of Siem Reap and stop at the **Tang You Ecotourism Site**, located about 10km from Preah Vihear City. Tang You is one of three ecotourism sites which offer trekking and camping on Phnom Tbeng. From here, trekkers and their community guides use a combination of ropes, stairs and wooden ladders to ascend almost 1000m. The trekking is quite challenging in places, but numerous rest points offer spectacular views.

After reaching the summit, it's another 6km to the community visitors centre located at the base of the **Tang You Pagoda**, balanced atop a boulder. The route to the visitors centre passes through groves of ancient trees, waterfalls and water holes frequented by some of the 50 species of wildlife resident here. Camping equipment and meals can be provided by the community, but must be arranged in advance. Clean latrines are available, and the mountain stream and waterfall are used for swimming and bathing.

**PHNOM KULEN WITHOUT THE TOURISTS**

Phnom Tbeng is similar in size and scale to the holy mountain of **Phnom Kulen** (p146) near Siem Reap, but unlike Phnom Kulen, it has no road access and no villages, making for a pristine environment.

**VISITING THE NEAK BUOS TEMPLE**

The remote brick sanctuaries of **Prasat Neak Buos** are only for the dedicated temple enthusiast, thanks to their remote location in the foothills of the Dangrek Mountains. However, they boast a beautiful, peaceful setting with an ancient *baray* (reservoir) teeming with birdlife and the stunning backdrop of the Dangrek peaks. Built under King Jayavarman I at the end of the 8th century, this pre-Angkorian brick temple may have formed a key staging post on the ancient highways linking Sambor Prei Kuk in Kompong Thom Province with Wat Phu Champasak in southern Laos. The temple was venerated by later kings, and other structures date from the 10th and 11th centuries. It's about 7km northeast of Choam Ksant town.

**GETTING AROUND**

Preah Vihear City has a mix of minivan and share-taxi services to Kompong Thom (157km) in the south, Sra Em (86km) and Prasat Preah Vihear (116km) in the north, Siem Reap (162km) to the west and Stung Treng (140km) to the east. Sra Em also has a range of transport options to Anlong Veng and Siem Reap.

There are *tuk-tuks* and *motos* in Preah Vihear City that can take visitors on short hops around town. For access to Prasat Preah Vihear, take a *moto* to Kor Muy (about US$15 return)

from Sra Em's central roundabout. From Kor Muy, an official park-supplied *moto* will take you up to the temple (US$5 return). There is no public transport from Sra Em to Kor Muy.

Preah Vihear Province remains one of the best provinces to explore on two wheels for experienced dirt bikers, with some rutted old oxcart tracks weaving their way through the jungle to remote temples. However, arrange a dirt bike in Phnom Penh or Siem Reap, as there are none available to rent in Preah Vihear City.

# Beyond Preah Vihear Province

Choam
• Anlong Veng

• Preah Vihear City

Famous for the final resting place of Pol Pot, the notorious Khmer Rouge leader of Democratic Kampuchea, Anlong Veng is dark tourism.

For almost a decade Anlong Veng was the ultimate Khmer Rouge stronghold, home to notorious former leaders of Democratic Kampuchea, including Pol Pot, Nuon Chea, Khieu Samphan and Ta Mok. The town fell to government forces in April 1998 and about the same time Pol Pot died mysteriously nearby. Soon after, Prime Minister Hun Sen ordered that the NH67 road be bulldozed through the jungle, to ensure the population didn't have second thoughts about ending the war.

Today, Anlong Veng is an outpost town with little going for it beyond an association with former genocidal leaders. However, a nearby border crossing connects Cambodia with an isolated part of Thailand, and for those interested in contemporary Cambodian history, the area's Khmer Rouge sites will intrigue.

## TOP TIP

Consider renting a motorbike or car in Siem Reap and looping through Anlong Veng, Prasat Preah Vihear (p172) and Koh Ker (p150).

**View of Ta Mok's Lake (p182) from Ta Mok's House**

AMNAT30/SHUTTERSTOCK ©

ANNA730/SHUTTERSTOCK ©

Ta Mok's Lake (p182)

# Khmer Rouge Trails in Anlong Veng

POL POT'S LAST RESTING PLACE

The main sights in Anlong Veng, about 1½ hours' drive or 82km west of Prasat Preah Vihear, are locations once associated with Ta Mok (Uncle Mok, aka Brother Number Five). To his former supporters, many of whom still live in Anlong Veng, he was harsh but fair, a benevolent builder of orphanages and schools, and a leader who kept order, in stark contrast to the anarchic atmosphere that prevailed once government forces took over. But to most Cambodians, Pol Pot's military enforcer – responsible for thousands of deaths in successive purges during the terrible years of Democratic Kampuchea – was best known as 'the Butcher'. Arrested in 1999, he died in 2006 while awaiting trial for genocide and crimes against humanity.

On a peaceful lakeside site, **Ta Mok's House** is a spartan structure with a bunker in the basement and five simple wall murals downstairs (one of Angkor Wat, four of Prasat Preah Vihear). About the only furnishings that weren't looted are the floor tiles. There's now a permanent photographic collection of

## CROSSING TO THAILAND AT CHOAM

The **Choam/Chong Sa-Ngam** border crossing (7am to 8pm) connects Anlong Veng in Oddar Meanchey Province with Thailand's Si Saket Province. A *moto* from Anlong Veng to the border, 16km away, costs about US$5 and the road is in good shape. Formalities are straightforward, but note that if you are coming in from Thailand, e-visas are not accepted here. Cambodia visas on arrival are usually charged at a premium of US$35. If heading to Thailand, it should be possible to find a pick-up truck to Phusing, and from there a bus to Khu Khan or Si Saket.

### GIVE PEACE A CHANCE

The **Documentation Center of Cambodia** (p68) has established the Anlong Veng Peace Center to promote reconciliation in this former conflict zone and has information on the Khmer Rouge leadership's roles in the civil war and genocide.

 **WHERE TO SLEEP & EAT IN ANLONG VENG**

**Bot Uddom Guesthouse**
The new annex is arguably top of the class in Anlong Veng, with massive hardwood beds. **$**

**Heng Hotel**
Live the high life up in the Dangrek Mountains at this smart 36-room hotel with hot-water power showers. **$**

**Monorom Restaurant**
A small but tasty selection of local staples and breakfast noodle soups, plus an English-language menu. **$**

## CROSSING TO THAILAND AT O SMACH

The remote **O Smach/ Chong Chom** border crossing (6am to 10pm) connects Cambodia's Oddar Meanchey Province and Thailand's Surin Province, about 75km west of Anlong Veng. Share taxis link Siem Reap and Sisophon with Samraong via NH68. From Samraong, take a *moto* (US$10) or a charter taxi (US$20) for the smooth drive to O Smach and its frontier casino zone. The crossing itself is easy, but a tourist visa for Cambodia costs US$35 and Cambodia e-visas cannot be used at this border. Most nationalities and travellers are just given a 30-day entry on arrival in Thailand. On the Thai side, walk to the nearby bus stop, where regular buses depart to Surin throughout the day.

Khmer Rouge–related images from the 1960s to 1990s, '100 Photos for Memory and Education', as part of the Anlong Veng Peace Center initiative to heal society. To get here, head north from the bridge on NH67 for 600m, turn right (signposted for the house) and continue 200m past the so-called Tourism Information hut.

Swampy **Ta Mok's Lake** was created on Brother Number Five's orders, but the water killed all the trees; their skeletons are a fitting monument to the devastation he and his movement left behind.

For years the world wondered where Pol Pot and his cronies were hiding out: the answer was right here in the densely forested Dangrek Mountains, close enough to Thailand that they could flee across the border if government forces approached. North of Anlong Veng, hidden in these hills near the Thai frontier, are a number of key Khmer Rouge sites.

About 2km before the border, the road splits to avoid a house-sized boulder. A group of **statues** hewn entirely from the boulder by the Khmer Rouge can be seen, and have been preserved as a shrine. The statues depict a woman carrying bundles of bamboo sticks on her head and two Khmer Rouge soldiers, but the latter were decapitated by government forces.

Just after you arrive in the bustling border village of Choam, look for a sign for the **cremation site of Pol Pot** on the east side of NH67. Pol Pot's ashes lie under a rusted corrugated iron roof surrounded by rows of partly buried glass bottles. The Khmer Rouge leader was hastily burned here in 1998 on a pile of rubbish and old tyres – a fittingly inglorious end, some say, given the suffering he inflicted on millions of Cambodians. Pol Pot's spirit, like that of his deputy Ta Mok, is said to give out winning lottery numbers.

The Choam border crossing is a few hundred metres north of here, near a ramshackle smugglers' market. From behind the smugglers' market, a dirt road heads east, parallel to the Dangrek escarpment, and local tourists head along this road to reach **Peuy Ta Mok**, renowned for spectacular clifftop views of Cambodia's northern plains.

## GETTING THERE & AROUND

Buses, minivans and taxis connect Anlong Veng with Siem Reap (128km) to the south and Sra Em (78km), gateway to the mountain temple of Prasat Preah Vihear, and Preah Vihear City (163km) to the east. Find a motorbike taxi if exploring Khmer Rouge sites in the Dangrek Mountains as the road is too steep for a *tuk-tuk* and taxis can't reach the former houses of Pol Pot and Khieu Samphan.

# KOMPONG THOM PROVINCE

Kompong Thom Province

⭐ Phnom Penh

For those not wanting to rush between Phnom Penh and Siem Reap, Kompong Thom Province makes a rewarding stopover, thanks to several intriguing sights spread across the countryside surrounding the provincial capital.

The friendly, bustling town of Kompong Thom sprawls along the lazy curves of the Stung Sen River, which winds its way through the centre. The town itself may be sparse on attractions, but it's a prime launching pad for exploring nearby sights such as the colourful hilltop stupas of Phnom Santuk, or a possible comfortable base for a long day trip to Preah Khan of Kompong Svay (p175) thanks to its boutique hotels.

The most impressive sight is Sambor Prei Kuk, a collection of ancient tree-entwined temples that were once part of Isanapura, the capital of the Chenla Empire. In 2017, the temples became Cambodia's third Unesco World Heritage Site.

## TOP TIP

Kompong Thom is the eponymous provincial capital and a major transport hub on NH6 between Phnom Penh and Siem Reap. NH6 runs right through the town, crossing the Stung Sen River, and is where most hotels, guesthouses and eateries are clustered. There are some English-speaking *tuktuk* drivers in town.

SAILINGSTONE TRAVEL/SHUTTERSTOCK ©

**Sambor Prei Kuk (p184)**

## AN ISANBOREI IMMERSION

**Isanborei** (samborprei kuk.com) is a community-based tourism organisation that works hard to encourage visitors to Sambor Prei Kuk to stay another day. In addition to running a popular community-based homestay program (dorm/double US$4/6), Isanborei offers cooking courses, rents out bicycles and organises oxcart rides. Guides hang around the old entrance near Prasat Sambor – it's well worth hiring one to show you around Isanborei (half/full day US$6/10).. Isanborei also operates *tuk-tuks* to whisk you safely to/from Kompong Thom (US$15 one way).

# KOMPONG THOM PROVINCE

Phnom Santuk (45km); Santuk Silk Farm (52km); Kakaoh (53km)

Isanborei

Prasat Sambor

Prasat Tao

Prasat Yeay Poeun

N    0          400 m
     0      0.2 miles

## STATUES IN THE NATIONAL MUSEUM

Many of the best statues and sculptures from Sambor Prei Kuk are located in the **National Museum of Cambodia** (p51) in Phnom Penh in the impressive pre-Angkorian gallery.

# The Ancient Capital of Sambor Prei Kuk

BRICKS AND MORTAR BEFORE ANGKOR

Cambodia's most impressive group of pre-Angkorian monuments and its third Unesco World Heritage Site, **Sambor Prei Kuk** encompasses more than 100 mainly brick temples huddled in the forest, among them some of the oldest structures in the country. A 45-minute drive from Kompong Thom, the area has a serene atmosphere, with sandy trails looping through shady forest.

Originally called Isanapura, the site was the capital of Upper Chenla in the early 7th century and an important learning centre during the Angkorian era. In the 1970s, it was bombed by US aircraft in support of the Lon Nol government's doomed fight against the Khmer Rouge. Some of the craters can still be seen close to the temples. The area's last landmines were cleared in 2008.

The main temple area consists of three complexes, each enclosed by the remains of two concentric walls. Their basic layout – a central tower surrounded by shrines, ponds and gates – served as an inspiration for the architects of Angkor centuries later.

**Prasat Yeay Poeun** is arguably the most atmospheric temple group, as it feels lost in the forest. The eastern

 **WHERE TO STAY IN KOMPONG THOM**

**Arunras Hotel & Guesthouse**
Dominating Kompong Thom's accommodation scene, this place has 58 good-value rooms with switched-on staff. **$**

**Sambor Village Hotel**
A boutique resort offering spacious, bungalow-style rooms with four-poster beds and chic bathrooms. **$$**

**Kompong Thom Royal Hotel**
This high-rise hotel has rooms fitted to a four-star standard, plus there's a pool and sky bar. **$$**

gateway is being both held up and torn asunder by an ancient tree, the bricks interwoven with the tree's probing roots. A truly massive tree shades the western gate.

The largest of the temple complexes, **Prasat Tao** has excellent examples of Chenla carving in the form of two elaborately coiffed stone lions. It also has a fine, rectangular pond.

The principal temple group, **Prasat Sambor** (7th and 10th centuries) is dedicated to Gambhireshvara, one of Shiva's many incarnations (the other groups are dedicated to Shiva himself). Several towers retain brick carvings in fairly good condition, and there's a series of large *yoni* (female fertility symbols) around the central tower.

# The Hilltop Temple of Phnom Santuk

WAT A LOT OF STUPAS

Its forest-cloaked summit adorned with Buddha images and pagodas, this holy temple mountain (207m) is a popular site of Buddhist pilgrimage. To reach the top, huff up 809 stairs – with the upper staircase home to troops of animated macaques – or take the paved 2.5km road. **Phnom Santuk** hosts an extraordinary ensemble of colourful wats and stupas, a kaleidoscopic mishmash of old and new Buddhist statuary and monuments.

Near the main white-walled pagoda is pyramid-shaped **Prasat Tuch** featuring an intricately carved sandstone exterior. Just beneath the southern side of the summit, there are a number of **reclining Buddhas**; several are modern incarnations cast in cement, while others were carved into the living rock in centuries past. Phnom Santuk has an active wat and the local monks are always interested in receiving foreign tourists.

Boulders located just below the summit afford panoramic views south towards Tonlé Sap. Travellers spending the night in Kompong Thom can catch a magnificent sunset over the rice fields, though this means descending in the dark – bring a flashlight.

The site is 15km south of Kompong Thom. To get here, turn left (east) off NH6 at the sign at about the 149km marker. It's around 2km from the highway to the base of the temple stairs.

## STONE CARVING & SILK WEAVING

The village of **Kakaoh** straddles the NH6 about 2km north of the Phnom Santuk entrance. It is famous for its stonemasons, who fashion giant Buddha statues, decorative lions and other traditional Khmer figures with hand tools and a practised eye. It's fascinating to watch the figures (from 15cm to over 5m in height) slowly emerge from giant slabs of stone.

Nearby **Santuk Silk Farm** is one of the few places in Cambodia where you can see the entire process of silk production, starting with the seven-week life cycle of the silkworm. The farm employs local women as artisan weavers and you can witness them weaving scarves (US$20 to US$35). The entrance is 200m north of the Phnom Santuk entrance, on the opposite side of NH6.

**GETTING AROUND**

Kompong Thom town is the base for touring the province and is 165km north of Phnom Penh, 147km southeast of Siem Reap and 157km south of Preah Vihear City.

Dozens of buses, minivans and share taxis travelling between Phnom Penh and Siem Reap pass through Kompong Thom. They drop passengers right in front of the Arunras Hotel.

Heading north to Preah Vihear City, share taxis cost US$5 and take two hours.

There are *tuk-tuk*s in Kompong Thom that can take visitors on short hops around town or further afield to Sambor Prei Kuk (US$25 return) and Phnom Santuk (US$15 return). Im Sokhom Travel Agency rents out motorbikes and bicycles.

# PURSAT PROVINCE

Pursat
Province

⊕ Phnom Penh

Pursat Province, Cambodia's fourth-largest, stretches from the remote forests of Phnom Samkos on the Thai border eastwards to the fishing villages and marshes of Tonlé Sap lake. Famed for its oranges, it encompasses the northern reaches of the Cardamom Mountains, linked via a web of roads to the eponymous provincial capital of Pursat. NH55 is a particularly beautiful road that cuts through the Cardamoms, winding its way over 'Phnom 1500' before descending to the Thai border at Thmor Da.

Pursat town is marked by huge marble shops that hug the highway. If you're in the market for a life-size statue of a horse, you're in the right place. This dusty provincial capital, known for its carvers, is hardly a headline attraction, but it makes a good base for the floating village of Kompong Luong or an expedition into the wilds of the Central Cardamoms.

## TOP TIP

NH5 passes through the centre of Pursat, which sprawls along the riverbank. Most of the hotels, local restaurants and market are found near the river. For exploring further afield to places like Kompong Luong and the Northern Cardamoms, rent a motorbike or charter a *tuk-tuk* or taxi.

EITAN SIMANOR/GETTY IMAGES ©

**Kompong Luong (p189)**

**SIGHTS**
1 Central Cardamoms
Protected Forest
(see 3) Koh Sampeau
Meas
2 Kompong Luong

**ACTIVITIES,
COURSES & TOURS**
3 Bunrany Hun Sen
Development Centre
4 Phnom Aural
Wildlife Sanctuary

5 Phnom Samkos
Wildlife Sanctuary

**SLEEPING**
6 Osoam Cardamom
Community Centre

## SMALL-HITTING SIGHTS IN PURSAT

**Bunrany Hun Sen Development Centre** teaches cloth and mat weaving, sewing, marble carving and other artisanal skills to young people. Travellers can visit classes and find some bargains on beautiful *krama* (checked scarves) and baskets at the centre's shop.

A bizarre island-park, built in the shape of a ship, **Koh Sampeau Meas** is Pursat's place to see and be seen around sunset. Young locals drop by for aerobics (classes from 5pm) or a game of badminton, while power-walkers pound the circuit between the manicured lawns and Khmer-style pavilions.

# The Northern Cardamom Mountains

WILDLIFE SANCTUARIES AND REMOTE ADVENTURES

Although the Central Cardamoms National Park (CCNP) and adjacent wildlife sanctuaries are slowly opening to ecotourism, the opportunities to explore these areas are still somewhat limited, as the ranger stations mostly exist to combat illegal logging, poaching and encroaching. Pursat is a possible gateway to the Northern Cardamoms, but most visitors going to the ecotourism centre of Osoam make their way there from the south via Koh Kong (p200).

Rangers in the **Central Cardamoms Protected Forest**, who are supported by Conservation International, operate out of three stations in the north

## TRANS-CARDAMOM HIGHWAY

Heading south from **Osoam** (p188), there are improving roads into Koh Kong Province making a journey through the Cardamom Mountains a realistic possibility in the dry season. In the wet season sections of road become impassable.

## WHERE TO STAY IN PURSAT PROVINCE

**Pursat Riverside Hotel**
This 146-room behemoth brings another level of comfort to Pursat and boasts two swimming pools. $$

**Thansour Thmey Hotel**
The name means 'new paradise'; while it's far from that, it does offer intricately carved beds and air-con. $

**Kompong Luong Homestays**
Three rustic homestays with local families offer a fascinating way to experience life on the water. $

## CROSSING THE CARDAMOMS BY MOTORBIKE

In recent years, a network of roads has been created to link north and south sections of the Cardamoms. The best sections of road are NH55 from Pramoay to the Thai border at Thmor Da, zigzagging its way up a 1500m peak before dropping down a river valley to the border. The dirt road then follows the Thai border all the way to Koh Kong, offering spectacular views of rivers and mountains to the east and, eventually, islands in the Gulf of Thailand to the west. This is arguably the best all-round motorbike ride in Cambodia, but should only be attempted by experienced riders.

that are rarely visited. Even so, the rangers and military police based there play a crucial role in defending the territory, particularly at the Kravanh ranger station deep in the jungle south of Pursat.

The most valuable contraband at the front-line Rovieng ranger station is aromatic *mreahprew* (sassafras, or safrole) oil, which is extracted from the roots of the endangered *Cinnamomum parthenoxylon* tree. One tonne of wood produces just 30L of the oil, which has a delightful, sandalwood-like scent. Local people use it in traditional medicine, but it's safrole oil's use as the precursor in the production of the drug MDMA that has caused the most illegal logging of this tree species.

A few kilometres from Rovieng (and 53km southwest of Pursat) are L'Bak Kamronh Rapids, which attract Khmers on holidays. About 25km west of Rovieng, in Pramoay Commune, the old-growth Chhrok Preal Forest can also be visited (though it rarely is).

To prearrange a guide, homestay or guesthouse near the Kravanh or Rovieng ranger station, try contacting forestry official Peov Somanak (017 464663; peovsomanak@gmail.com) for advice.

The 2538-sq-km **Phnom Aural Wildlife Sanctuary** has the country's highest peak, Phnom Aural (1813m), and is just east of the Central Cardamoms National Park. Unfortunately the area is being destroyed from the south and the east by corrupt land speculation and rampant illegal logging, but the long-standing and reputable Phnom Penh–based **Dutch Co Trekking Cambodia** runs three-day trips to the region with a jumping-off point at Kompong Speu and overnight stays in their own Shangri-la Guesthouse offering dorms and bungalows in the rural village of Voar Sar. Phnom Aural can be visited in a day, but most people do it in two or three.

Sandwiched between the Central Cardamoms National Park and the Thai frontier, the 3338-sq-km **Phnom Samkos Wildlife Sanctuary** is well and truly out in the sticks. It is threatened by timber laundering and agricultural concessions, but wildlife still abounds. The sanctuary has Cambodia's second-highest peak, Phnom Samkos (1717m). Its main town is Pramoay, 125km west of Pursat. This remote little outpost has several hotels and guesthouses. Local *moto* drivers can take visitors to nearby ethnic-minority villages.

In the isolated settlement of Osoam, the excellent **Osoam Cardamom Community Centre** (osoamccc.weebly.com) run by the effusive Mr Lim organises hiking, motorbike

**Leaf-litter frog, Phnom Samkos Wildlife Sanctuary**

---

### 🛏 WHERE TO STAY IN THE NORTHERN CARDAMOMS

**Kravanh**
Small town about 35km south of Pursat and a northeastern gateway to the Cardamoms with several family-run guesthouses.

**Pramoay**
The largest town in the north-central Cardamoms, Pramoay has several hotels and guesthouses on NH55.

**Osoam**
Set on the edge of a scenic reservoir, the Osoam Cardamom Community Centre is the place to stay in this village.

and boat trips in the surrounding countryside, as well as day trips and overnights to Phnom Samkos where elephants can be spotted. The property has well-kept rooms along with connections to simple guesthouses and homestays nearby. Electricity is limited and showers come from buckets, but this is about as close to real Cambodia as you can get.

# The Floating Village of Kompong Luong

EXPERIENCE A CAMBODIAN WATER WORLD

**Kompong Luong** has all the amenities you might expect to find in an oversized fishing village, except that here everything floats on water. The result is a charming if slightly ramshackle Venice without the dry land. The cafes, shops, chicken coops, fish ponds, ice-making factory, petrol station and karaoke bars are kept from sinking by boat hulls, barrels or bunches of bamboo, as are the pagodas, the blue-roofed church and the colourful houses. In the dry season, when water levels drop and the Tonlé Sap lake shrinks, the entire aquapolis is towed, boat by boat, a few kilometres north.

The population of this fascinating and picturesque village is partly Vietnamese, so – reflecting their ambiguous status in Cambodian society – you may find the welcome here slightly more subdued than in most rural Cambodian towns, at least from the adults. Children delight in waving hello.

The only way to explore Kompong Luong is, naturally, by boat. The tours aren't particularly informative for independent travellers without a guide, as few captains speak much English, but gliding through the town and simply observing daily life makes this worthwhile, particularly during the golden hour before sunset each day. For the adventurous, there are homestays for overnight stays and some very basic floating restaurants.

The jumping-off point for Kompong Luong is the town of Krakor, 32km east of Pursat.

**TOUR OPERATORS IN THE NORTHERN CARDAMOMS**

**Solo Landscapes**
Run by intrepid Cambodian explorer Sovanda Horn, this company offers ascents of Phnom Aural and other mountains in the Cardamoms, as well as multiday treks with overnight camping.

**Asia Planet Tour**
Operated by expat adventurer Valentina, who has spent years criss-crossing the Cardamoms in search of remote waterfalls, memorable viewpoints and secret camping spots.

**MORE FLOATING VILLAGES**

There are several floating villages on the Tonlé Sap River near **Kompong Chhnang** (p190) and some very popular floating villages on the Tonlé Sap lake around **Siem Reap** (p88).

**GETTING AROUND**

NH5 runs through the northern fringes of Pursat Province and offers good road connections by bus, minivan and taxi to Phnom Penh or Battambang. Heading south, NH55 climbs into the Cardamom Mountains at Kravanh before heading due west to the Thai border at Thmor Da. There is some local transport available in places like Pursat, Pramoay and Osoam, but it is easier to explore with your own wheels if you have the budget to charter a taxi or rent a motorbike.

# KOMPONG CHHNANG PROVINCE

Kompong
Chhnang
Province

⭐ Phnom Penh

Kompong Chhnang Province is relatively wealthy, thanks to its proximity to the capital, fishing and agricultural industries and abundant water resources. While nothing much may be happening in the sleepy provincial capital of Kompong Chhnang (Clay Pot Port), the bustling dock on the Tonlé Sap River is the jumping-off point for serene boat rides to two floating villages. Skimming through the watery streets in a tiny wooden paddleboat as the late-afternoon sun sends a shimmer over the river is a gorgeous way to end a day. Outside the towns you'll find a lush landscape of yellow-green rice fields. In the tiny hamlets where cows slumber beside hay bales, the area's distinctive pottery is crafted underneath stilted homes, providing another reason to linger.

## TOP TIP

Kompong Chhnang is close enough to Phnom Penh that it can be visited on a day trip by bus, taxi or motorbike from the Cambodian capital.

CAROL MOIR/SHUTTERSTOCK ©

**Floating village, Tonlé Sap**

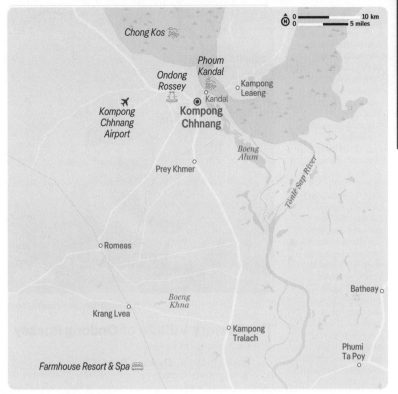

Chong Kos

Phoum Kandal

Ondong Rossey

Kampong Leaeng

Kandal

Kompong Chhnang Airport

**Kompong Chhnang**

Boeng Alum

Prey Khmer

Tonlé Sap River

Romeas

Batheay

Boeng Khna

Krang Lvea

Kampong Tralach

Phumi Ta Poy

Farmhouse Resort & Spa

# Floating Villages on the Tonlé Sap

A RIVER RUNS THROUGH IT

Much less visited than other floating villages near Siem Reap, the Tonlé Sap River hamlets of **Chong Kos** and **Phoum Kandal** are home to colourful wooden houses, with tiny terraces strung with hammocks, all built on rickety DIY pontoons.

Chong Kos is a Cambodian village while Phoum Kandal is a Vietnamese village. To fully explore the villages, hire a wooden boat (with captain) at Kompong Chhnang dock to paddle you through these buoyant settlements, complete with shops, satellite TV and mobile vegetable vendors. A two-hour boat ride will allow you to see both villages. Hiring a paddleboat offers the chance to glide within the maze of watery streets to glimpse how village life functions when everything floats.

**Chong Kos**

## SUGAR PALM TREE

The national tree of Cambodia (known as *dam tnaot* to the Khmers), the ubiquitous sugar palm dots the rural landscapes of Kompong Chhnang. The unripened fruit can be eaten in savoury dishes, while the fleshy ripened fruit is used in Cambodian desserts. Palm juice is harvested from the trees and can be consumed sweet or fermented into palm wine. The leaves are used for everything from roof thatch and mats to boxes and fans. The hard wood is fashioned into everything from canoes to cutlery, making it one of the most versatile trees in Cambodia.

PACK-SHOT/SHUTTERSTOCK ©

**Making pottery, Kompong Chhnang**

# The Pottery Village of Ondong Rossey
A CAMBODIAN CRAFT VILLAGE

The quiet village of **Ondong Rossey**, where the area's famous red pottery is made under every stilted house, is a delightful 7km ride west of town through serene ricefields dotted with sugar palms, many with bamboo ladders running up the trunk. The unpainted pots, decorated with etched or appliqué designs, are either turned with a foot-spun wheel (for small pieces) or banged into shape with a heavy wooden spatula (for large ones).

The golden-hued mud piled up in the yards is quarried at nearby Phnom Krang Dai Meas and pounded into fine clay before being shaped and fired; only at the last stage does it acquire a pinkish hue. Pieces can be purchased at the Pottery Development Centre in the heart of the village, although you'll get better deals buying directly from the potters at their houses.

## DECORATIVE CERAMICS

The pottery of Kompong Chhnang is generally unglazed and in its native clay colour. For more decorative pottery drawing on the ceramics of ancient Angkor, visit the **Khmer Ceramics Centre** (p103) in Siem Reap.

 **WHERE TO SLEEP & EAT IN KOMPONG CHHNANG**

**Sovann Phum Hotel**
The newer wing at the back offers positively boutique-style rooms and a 1st-floor swimming pool. $

**Sok San Restaurant**
There's an English menu at this local restaurant, specialising in fried everything plus soups on the side. $

**Heng Chamreun Bakery**
This glistening bakery sells good sandwiches, rice cakes and other snacks ideal for a road trip. $

# The Khmer Rouge Airport

A LEGACY OF SLAVE LABOUR

The Khmer Rouge were not known as great builders, but in 1977 and 1978, slave labourers built an airfield using cement of such high quality that even today the 2440m runway and access roads look like they were paved just last week.

No one knows for sure, but it seems that **Kompong Chhnang Airport** – never operational under the Khmer Rouge – was intended to serve as a base for launching air attacks against Vietnam. Chinese engineers oversaw the work of tens of thousands of Cambodians suspected of disloyalty to the Khmer Rouge. Anyone unable to work was killed, often with a blow to the head delivered with a bamboo rod. In early 1979, as Vietnamese forces approached, almost the entire workforce was executed. Estimates of the number of victims, buried nearby in mass graves, range from 10,000 to 50,000.

In the late 1990s, a plan to turn the airport into a cargo hub for air-courier companies came to nought. These days, local teenagers tool around on their motorbikes, while cows graze between the taxiway and the runway. On hot days, the sun creates convincing mirages.

On an anonymous slope a few kilometres away, the Khmer Rouge dug a **cave** – said to be 3km deep – apparently for the purpose of storing weapons flown in from China. Now home to swirling bats, it can be explored with a torch (flashlight), but lacking ventilation, it gets very hot and humid. On a hillside near a cluster of bullet-pocked cement barracks, stripped of anything of value, is a massive cement **water tank**. Inside it's a remarkable echo chamber.

The airport is about 12km west of town. Take NH5 towards Battambang for 7km and turn left onto a concrete road.

## THE SMILING GECKO

For an immersive rural experience in comfort and style, consider a stay at the **Farmhouse Resort & Spa**, formerly known as Smiling Gecko Farmhouse. The Smiling Gecko organisation supports disadvantaged youth by offering training and employment in hospitality. The accommodation is in boutique wooden houses, mirroring the style of the traditional Khmer house but with stylish furnishings and bathrooms. The menu is predominantly organic thanks to the on-site farm; chef Mariya has also trained in international cooking techniques in Switzerland. Farmhouse offers a series of countryside experiences in the area, like ricefield visits and temple tours. There's also a spa and yoga sala to unwind.

Use this QR code to book a room at the Farmhouse Resort & Spa.

---

### GETTING AROUND

Kompong Chhnang sits strategically on NH5 with bus, minivan and taxi connections to Phnom Penh (91km) and Pursat (93km). Due to its proximity to the capital, few travellers stay the night here. The Phnom Penh to Battambang railway line also passes through the province via Tuek Phos, 30km to the south. There used to be boat connections to Phnom Penh and Siem Reap, but these no longer operate.

A several-hour *tuk-tuk* tour taking in the pottery villages costs around US$10. A *moto* should be about US$5.

# SOUTH COAST & ISLANDS

## BEACHES, ISLANDS, ECOTOURISM & HISTORY

Cambodia's South Coast tempts visitors with dreamy white-sand beaches, but the region is also home to rainforests, mountains and historic towns.

After all that temple-hopping, the beach is calling. Cambodia's South Coast has strips of sand for every taste. There are the superb beaches on the idyllic islands of Koh Rong and Koh Rong Sanloem, as well as the laid-back resort town of Kep with its delicious crabs, intriguing history and Khmer-style seaside fun. Divers can find underwater paradise at the little-visited Koh Sdach Archipelago, or head to the hidden hippie haven of Nesat Beach if you really want to escape the crowds.

But there's so much more to this region than just sea and sand. The riverine town of Kampot has emerged as one of Cambodia's most popular destinations, thanks to its supremely relaxed vibe, adventure

sports, the dramatic limestone peaks and caves of the surrounding countryside, and remnants of the colonial past such as the spooky Bokor Hill Station.

Head north of the hectic, edgy port of Sihanoukville and there's a whole different landscape to experience. The national parks of the Koh Kong Conservation Corridor with their rainforests and waterfalls stretch east and south from the border with Thailand into the fabled Cardamom Mountains. Excellent ecotourism projects offer the opportunity for treks, boat trips and wildlife encounters. Relatively few travellers visit, too, so you're likely to have all that beauty and biodiversity to yourself. There's really something for everyone here.

## THE MAIN AREAS

**KOH KONG**
Ecotourism and national parks.
**p200**

**SIHANOUKVILLE**
Gateway to the islands. **p209**

**KOH RONG**
Stunning beaches and upscale resorts. **p214**

PAGNARITH SAO/SHUTTERSTOCK ©

**Kampot (p226)**

**KOH RONG SANLOEM**
Hidden bays and backpacker
fun. **p222**

**KAMPOT**
Riverside relaxation, adventure
sports and history. **p226**

**KEP**
Seafood, sunsets and
apocalyptic architecture. **p234**

# Find Your Way

This region sprawls across Cambodia's southwest, including the provinces of Takeo, Kep, Kampot, Preah Sihanouk and Koh Kong. We've picked the best places to experience its beaches, national parks and history.

Osoam

Central Cardamom National Park

Hat Mai Rut

*Phnom Knang Trapeang (1213m)*

Hat Ban Chun

*Cardamom Mountains (Chuŏr Phnom Krâvanh)*

Khlong Yai

Chamna

Thma Bang

Hat Lek

Chumnoab

**Koh Kong**

### Koh Kong, p200
Head east and south of town for the rainforests, waterfalls and mountains of the Koh Kong Conservation Corridor and community-based ecotourism projects.

Tatai

Southern Cardamom National Park

Peam Krasaop Wildlife Sanctuary

Koh Kapi

Trapeang Rung

Ch'Pha

*Koh Kong Island*

Alatang

Praek Khsach

Andoung Tuek

### Koh Rong, p214
Cambodia's original island paradise still has some of the country's finest beaches, but the backpacker huts have mostly given way to more upscale accommodation.

Ta Nhi

Ta Op

Kiri Sakor

Botum Sakor National Park

*Gulf of Kompong Som*

*Koh Totang*

*Koh Sdach*

Ta Nun

Thmor Sor

Stung Ha

### Koh Rong Sanloem, p222
A handful of beautiful beaches surround a mostly untouched jungle wilderness. It's less busy than Koh Rong and now home to the traveller scene on the islands.

*Koh Rong*

Koh Tuch

**Sihanoukville**

*Koh Rong Sanloem*

Rea

### Sihanoukville, p209
Cambodia's major port is frenetic and its casinos and clubs are aimed at Chinese visitors, but it's also the jumping-off point for the islands.

0 — 50 km
0 — 25 miles

## TRAIN

The railway line that runs from Phnom Penh to Sihanoukville, with stops in Takeo, Kep and Kampot, is increasingly popular with travellers. Trains are more comfortable and scenic than going by road, as well as cheaper, but generally slower.

## CAR & MOTORBIKE

Hiring a car and driver to move around the South Coast is a sound decision, as there's very little public transport apart from links between major towns. Renting a motorbike is another option, with most main roads in reasonable condition.

## MINIVAN & BUS

Minivans connect the major towns of the South Coast, with buses currently restricted to routes to/from Phnom Penh and Siem Reap. More bus routes may emerge in the future as public transport reboots postpandemic.

### Kampot, p226

Relaxed riverside location, plus kayaking and rock climbing, caves, temples and colonial-era buildings, as well as the best dining on the South Coast.

*Knong rapeur 1000m)*

Kirirom National Park
Kirovong III Dam

Sre Ambel

Plauv Bombek
Sre Ambel

Veal Renh

Prek Apmpil

Ream National Park
Thmor Thom
*Ko Thmei*
*Koh Seh*

*Koh Tonsay*
*Koh Po*

*Phu Quoc Island*

Bokor National Park

**Kampot**

**Kep**
Prek Chak
Xa Xia
Ha Tien

Chhuk

*Phnom Voa*

Tani

Phnom Tchea Tapech

Tuk Meas

Kompong Trach

**○ PHNOM PENH**

Phnom Tamao Wildlife Rescue Centre

Angk Tasaom

Angkor Borei

**● Takeo**

Kirivong

Phnom Den

### Kep, p234

Atmospheric seaside town famed for its pepper-flavoured crabs and abandoned modernist villas. There are also islands and a national park to explore.

197

# Plan Your Days

Hit the beaches for sure, but also spend a few days exploring Kampot and the surrounding area. Alternatively, head north to the rainforests, hills and wildlife of the Koh Kong Conservation Corridor.

Long Set Beach, Koh Rong (p217)

## If You Only Do One Thing

Choose between the beaches of the bigger, more developed **Koh Rong** (p214) and those of neighbouring **Koh Rong Sanloem** (p222), although they're close enough to commute between the two. Boutique resorts dot the kilometres of gleaming white-sand beaches that line both coasts on Koh Rong, while Koh Rong Sanloem has hostels on the main beach and perfect, palm-fringed bays hidden away on the less visited other side of the island. There's decent diving off both islands, as well as boat and fishing trips. Make sure to take a night tour to snorkel and swim amidst the bioluminescent plankton found off these islands.

SONDIPON/SHUTTERSTOCK ©

## SEASONAL HIGHLIGHTS

Hotel prices drop by up to 50% in the rainy season. Accessing the Koh Kong Conservation Corridor is easiest in the dry season.

### JANUARY

**Chinese New Year** falls in January or February and Sihanoukville's large Chinese community is out celebrating.

### FEBRUARY

The crowds are thinning out on the **islands** but the weather is still superb and the ocean calm.

### MARCH

It's getting hotter, but the **wildlife** in the Koh Kong Conservation Corridor (p204) is out and about.

FROM LEFT: YUG/SHUTTERSTOCK ©, CHAINFOTO24/SHUTTERSTOCK ©, EMMA PETRICHOR/SHUTTERSTOCK ©

## Three Days to Travel Around

Make laid-back **Kampot** (p226) your base and venture out to the limestone peaks of the surrounding countryside, where there are caves, temples and rock-climbing opportunities. Visit eerie **Bokor Hill Station** (p231), a French retreat from the colonial period, and boat, kayak or paddleboard on the river. An easy day trip from Kampot is **Kep** (p234), a locals' favourite for seaside frolics and crab dinners. Tour the ruins of the modernist villas dotted around town, jump a boat for the beaches of **Koh Tonsay** (p236) or hike into **Kep National Park** (p236), which overlooks the ocean. Spend your evenings sampling Kampot's increasingly sophisticated restaurant scene.

## More Than a Week

After a few days on the islands, travel north along the coast from **Sihanoukville** (p209). Some of the best diving in Cambodia can be found in the **Koh Sdach Archipelago** (p220), or kick back at **Nesat Beach** (p212), a newly established community of travellers and expats on a little-seen strip of the coast. Then head further north to the ecotourism hub of **Chi Phat** (p205), where you can trek, mountain bike or boat through the southern Cardamom Mountains in search of wildlife. Close to the border with Thailand is **Koh Kong** (p200), the launchpad for journeys along the **Koh Kong Conservation Corridor** (p204).

**MAY**

Placid seas, optimum visibility and fewer visitors make this a fine month for **diving** in the Koh Sdach Archipelago (p221).

**JULY**

The **durians** grown around Kampot are famed across Cambodia. This is the best month to sample them.

**NOVEMBER**

The rainy season is over and temperatures are comfortable – the perfect time for **trekking** in the Cardamom Mountain (p207).

**DECEMBER**

The annual **Sea Festival** takes place across the South Coast, with concerts, seafood and sports all on the agenda.

# KOH KONG

Koh Kong ● ◆ Phnom Penh

Koh Kong was once regarded as Cambodia's Wild West. Just 8km south of the border with Thailand and located on the Koh Poi River, which empties into the Gulf of Thailand south of town, Koh Kong's isolated and unregulated frontier economy was dominated by smuggling and gambling.

Remnants of that seedy past still cling on in low-rise Koh Kong's dusty sprawl of streets, but these days a steady stream of Khmer migrant workers head to Thailand, while the new port being constructed on the riverfront is expected to boost legal trade.

There are a few meaningful sights in and around town, which is a popular destination for locals. For most visitors, though, Koh Kong is the launchpad for nature-filled adventures in the jungle and mountains of the Koh Kong Conservation Corridor. Tourism infrastructure here was hit hard by the COVID-19 pandemic, but is expected to bounce back in time.

## TOP TIP

Koh Kong spreads away from both banks of the Koh Poi River. Hotels, restaurants and banks can be found on the streets straggling back from the riverfront for a few blocks to the main market, where *moto* (motorcycle taxi) and *remork-moto (tuk-tuk)* drivers await.

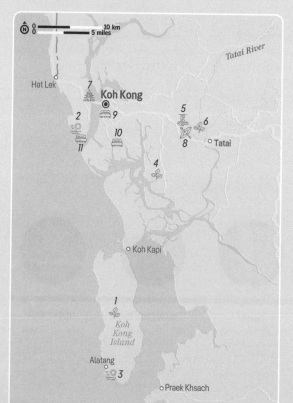

**SIGHTS**
1 Koh Kong Island
2 Koh Yor Beach
3 No.6 Beach
4 Peam Krasaop
Wildlife Sanctuary
5 Tatai Waterfall
6 Tatai
Wildlife Sanctuary
7 Wat Neang Kok

**ACTIVITIES,
COURSES & TOURS**
8 Tatai River

**SLEEPING**
(see 9) 99 Guesthouse
9 Apex Koh
Kong Hotel
10 Mangrove
Sanctuary Resort
(see 9) Nathy
Hotel Koh Kong
11 Young,
Wild & Free

Mangrove forest, Peam Krasaop Wildlife Sanctuary

# Mangrove Islands & Fishing Hamlets

MAGNIFICENT MANGROVES

Anchored to alluvial islands – some no larger than a house – the magnificent mangroves at the 260-sq-km **Peam Krasaop Wildlife Sanctuary** protect the coast from erosion, offer vital breeding grounds for fish, shrimp and shellfish and are home to a lot of birdlife. Much of Peam Krasaop is on the prestigious Ramsar List of Wetlands of International Importance. The sanctuary (located 5.5km east of Koh Kong) is all the more important because similar mangrove forests in Thailand have suffered from short-sighted development, even if parts of Peam Krasaop itself are under threat from increased shrimp farming and sand dredging.

An 800m walkway leads from the sanctuary entrance through the mangrove forest to a rickety wooden bridge and onto a 15m-high observation tower with views over the area. The walkway lacks guard rails and isn't in great condition, so watch your step.

But the best way to tour the sanctuary is by boat, which are available for hire at the entrance. A 2½-hour trip takes visitors deep into the mangroves, stopping at fishing hamlets. Their residents use traps to catch fish, which are kept alive until

## SWIFTLET KNOWLEDGE

Koh Kong has its own soundtrack: a high-pitched chirping that never seems to stop. The deafening cacophony of bird calls is pumped out from rooftop megaphones and is aimed at coaxing Koh Kong's colonies of swiftlets into building nests out of their saliva in the tall, tower-like concrete structures they inhabit all over town.

The nests are the key ingredient in bird's-nest soup, a high-protein delicacy that's supposed to boost the immune system and is popular in China and Southeast Asian countries with large Chinese communities. You'll see and hear swiftlet colonies throughout the South Coast, but only in Koh Kong are they loud enough to drown out the traffic.

## WHERE TO EAT IN KOH KONG

**Crab Chak**
Deservedly popular seafood restaurant on Koh Yor Beach. Crab is a highlight here. **$$**

**Anon Cafe & Restaurant**
Pan-Asian and European dishes in this smart (for Koh Kong) spot. Good coffee and smoothies. **$$**

**I Love Pizza**
Italian-run, with an open kitchen. Homemade pasta as well as pizza and a modest wine list. **$**

**BEST PLACES TO STAY IN KOH KONG**

**Nathy Koh Kong Hotel $**
Best budget option, near the market. Modern, clean and compact rooms with comfy beds.

**Apex Koh Kong Hotel $**
Old-fashioned but sizeable rooms with hot water and air-con set around a small swimming pool.

**99 Guesthouse $**
Low-key, clean, quiet and centrally located guesthouse with anonymous budget rooms.

**Young, Wild & Free $$**
Beachside bamboo bungalows with sea views and shared bathrooms. Good restaurant and bar.

**Mangrove Sanctuary Resort $$**
Big concrete bungalows with balconies surrounded by the mangrove forest of Peam Krasaop.

CAVAN IMAGES/GETTY IMAGES ©

Boat trip, Tatai River

market time in partially submerged nets attached to floating wooden frames. Further out are mangrove islands with isolated little beaches occupied by hermit crabs.

## Tour Cambodia's Biggest Island

GULF OF THAILAND BEACHES

Nestling south of Koh Kong in crystal-clear seas where you can make out individual grains of sand in a couple of metres of water, **Koh Kong Island** is the largest of Cambodia's islands. There are seven palm-fringed beaches here, all located along the west coast and backed by verdant forest. The best is the pragmatically named **No.6 Beach**, where a narrow channel leads to a hidden lagoon. Watch out for sand flies on all the beaches. In contrast, the east coast is lined with mangroves and overlooked by dramatic hills.

There's a big military presence on Koh Kong Island and access is tightly controlled (the jungle interior is completely offlimits). Strong onshore winds mean it's impossible to visit in the rainy season (June to October). **Young, Wild & Free** can arrange trips here.

 **WHERE TO STAY AROUND TATAI**

**Donut Guesthouse**
The budget option. Fan-cooled, cold-water bungalows set on a farm close to the river. **$$**

**Canvas & Orchids Resort**
Luxurious tent-villas on pontoons on the river. Mountain views and a fine restaurant. **$$$**

**Rainbow Lodge**
Sustainable jungle chic. Solar-powered bungalows with all meals included and only accessible by boat. **$$$**

**Koh Yor Beach**, also known as Rakhlong Beach, is around 6km south of Koh Kong on the far western side of the peninsula that forms the west bank of the Koh Poi River. It's a pretty enough strip of sand and is fine for swimming. It gets busy with locals at weekends and holidays, otherwise it's mostly people-free.

On the way to the beach is the intriguing **Wat Neang Kok**, which sits on a rocky promontory on the western bank of the Koh Poi River and has gruesome life-size statues of sinners undergoing violent punishment in the Buddhist hell.

## Cruise the Tatai River

BOAT THROUGH THE JUNGLE

The Tatai River winds through remote jungle that's home to all manner of birds and wildlife. A journey here is a uniquely tranquil experience, with almost all access by boat or kayak and nights spent listening to the sounds of the rainforest. The area is part of the 1442-sq-km **Tatai Wildlife Sanctuary**, which is known especially for its rare butterflies, birds and insects.

There are a number of ecolodges sited along the river and they can organise boat and kayak trips and jungle treks to various sights. **Tatai Waterfall** is a thundering set of rapids in the rainy season (June to October) that cascades over a 4m rock shelf. The water comes from the Cardamom Mountains and is clean, so you can swim here. The falls can be accessed by boat or kayak, or via a diabolical track that shouldn't be driven unless you're a very experienced motorbike rider. Upriver from the waterfall and only accessible by jungle trails is a body of water that becomes a 'lake' in the rainy season and is also good for swimming.

Tatai River is normally accessed via the Phun Daung Bridge, which is located 18km east of Koh Kong. Boats from the various lodges pick up guests there and transport them upriver.

### GETTING TO THAILAND FROM KOH KONG

The **Cham Yeam/Hat Lek** border crossing is one of Cambodia's busiest land frontiers and enables travellers to jump from the South Coast to the beaches of Thailand. The border is 8km north of Koh Kong and crossing to Thailand is normally straightforward. If you're coming from the other direction, though, you may be asked to pay an extra fee for your Cambodia visa, which should cost US$30. Already having a visa before you cross here is a sound idea.

Once in Thailand, minivans (140B) make the 1½-hour run to Trat's bus station, where there are frequent buses to Bangkok or it's an easy hop to the nearby island of Koh Chang.

**GETTING THERE & AROUND**

Daily minivans travel to Phnom Penh, Kampot and Sihanoukville and will pick up from your accommodation. Shared taxis go to the same destinations, as well as Osoam, Andoung Tuek and Kiri Sakor, and depart from the abandoned bus station on the northeastern edge of town.

Motorbikes (US$8 per day) can be rented at Young, Wild & Free. Harry (016 629941) is a reliable, English-speaking *tuk-tuk* driver. A *tuk-tuk* to the Thai border is US$5, while a return trip to Koh Yor Beach is US$10. Count on US$40 for a full-day hire.

Koh Kong

Southern Cardamom
National Park

Chi Phat

Botum Sakor
National Park

# Beyond Koh Kong

A wonderfully diverse, wildlife-rich landscape
of rainforests, rivers, mountains and waterfalls
awaits travellers who venture beyond Koh Kong.

Outside Koh Kong are some of Cambodia's most outstanding
sites of natural beauty. The national parks and wildlife sanctuaries here are part of the Koh Kong Conservation Corridor,
which stretches east and south from Koh Kong to the Gulf of
Kompong Som, the bay northwest of Sihanoukville.

The corridor is part of the 20,746-sq-km Cardamom Rainforest Landscape, the largest mainland forest watershed in
Southeast Asia. Prime places for wildlife-spotting include the
area around Chi Phat, Southern Cardamom National Park and
Botum Sakor National Park.

Some excellent community-based ecotourism projects operate in the corridor, allowing visitors the chance to explore the
region's ecosystems while also contributing to their ongoing
conservation.

**TOP TIP**

Hire a car and driver or
a motorbike, as there's
very little public transport
beyond Koh Kong.

**Andoung Tuek (p207)**

CRISTINA STOIAN/SHUTTERSTOCK ©

Sun bear, Wildlife Alliance Release Station (p206)

# Community-Based Ecotourism in Chi Phat

GATEWAY TO SOUTHERN CARDAMOM MOUNTAINS

The riverside village of Chi Phat, 125km southeast of Koh Kong in the Southern Cardamom Mountains (a 2½-hour drive by car), has emerged as one of the stars of Cambodia's burgeoning roster of ecotourism ventures. Backed by the Wildlife Alliance NGO, Chi Phat's residents now manage and operate a successful community-based ecotourism project (CBET) that takes visitors deep into one of the last true wilderness areas left in Southeast Asia, while also contributing to the conservation and protection of this enormously biodiverse region and providing alternative livelihoods for the locals.

Chi Phat's transformation from an area once notorious for illegal logging, land grabs and poaching into a worthy ecotourism hub has been accompanied by increasing recognition of just how special the Cardamom Mountains are. The remote peaks here – some as high as 1800m – are covered in emerald-hued forest and cut through by 22 major waterways. The rainforest is one of Asia's seven elephant corridors and home to endangered species such as tigers, sun bears, Siamese crocodiles, royal turtles and pangolins. There are

## THE IMPACT OF ECOTOURISM ON CHI PHAT

**Sovann On** manages Chi Phat's CBET (chi-phat.org). He was born and raised in Chi Phat.

**How has CBET impacted Chi Phat?** Ecotourism has brought development and better infrastructure to Chi Phat. We provide proper jobs for local people and protect our natural resources for future generations.

**How has ecotourism changed the lives of local people?** We have 332 families in our community and they all profit directly or indirectly from ecotourism. They provide accommodation for tourists or work as guides, cooks and drivers.

**Are Cambodian people more aware now of the need to protect the environment?** Yes, I think the mindset has changed. We get a lot of domestic tourists now because people want to get back to nature here.

---

### WHERE TO EAT IN THE KOH KONG CONSERVATION CORRIDOR

**Chi Phat Visitors Centre**
The only formal restaurant in Chi Phat does pretrek breakfasts and Khmer dishes; there's also a bar. **$**

**Koh Andaet Cafe & Lodge**
Riverfront eatery in Tatai with great views and a friendly and helpful owner. European and Khmer dishes. **$**

**Chi Phat Food Stalls**
There are noodle and barbecue food stalls in the village for snacking with the locals. **$**

## BACK TO THE WILD

At the **Wildlife Alliance Release Station** near Chi Phat, visitors can see sun bears, pangolins, porcupines, monkeys and hornbills being rehabilitated and readied for release back into the wild after being rescued from animal traffickers. Tours can be arranged by the CBET (p205) in Chi Phat and include the chance to meet the animals at feeding times, as well as opportunities for jungle treks, river swims and checking the camera traps that monitor newly released animals.

The 40-minute motorbike journey from Chi Phat to the release station is an adventure in itself. It's a thrilling ride through forests, over streams and across grasslands. Watch out for the buffaloes!

MICHELLE HOLIHAN/SHUTTERSTOCK ©

**Hornbill, Wildlife Alliance Release Station**

also many primates and rare birds like the great hornbill, flycatchers and ibises.

Protected by the Cambodian government since 2016, the Cardamoms have escaped the worst ravages of land developers and logging companies thanks to their sheer remoteness. Ecologically, much of the region is in pretty good shape and some say that the potential for ecotourism here is on a par with Kenya's game reserves or Costa Rica's national parks.

All tours out of Chi Phat are run by the CBET and need to be booked in advance through the community visitors centre in the village. There are 200km of tracks and trails to hike around Chi Phat, and treks of between one and seven days are possible. Along the way, you'll sleep in hammocks or camp. If you're lucky, you'll hear gibbons and see monkeys, as well as wild pigs and birds and elephant tracks. The guides are mostly former poachers and hunters.

Boat tours travel up the pretty **Preak Piphot River** for sunrise birdwatching trips and sunset stargazing (with a beer or cocktail to hand). You can also kayak and there's good moun-

## WHERE TO STAY IN THE KOH KONG CONSERVATION CORRIDOR

**Cardamom Cottage**
Wooden bungalows set around an attractive garden close to Chi Phat's visitors centre. **$**

**Srey Mom Guesthouse**
Simple, stilted, fan-only wooden bungalows with basic shared bathrooms. In Chi Phat. **$**

**Bearcat**
Friendly family at this homestay in a double-decker house just off Chi Phat's main drag. **$**

tain biking, with one- and two-day tours taking visitors to waterfalls, villages and traditional burial-jar sites.

The CBET operates a number of homestays and bungalows dotted around Chi Phat, all part of the campaign to enable locals to generate some income from tourism. There's a reasonable restaurant and bar at the community visitors centre. Make sure to bring cash, as there's no ATM in Chi Phat or nearby. The CBET is open all year but access to certain areas can be difficult in the rainy season (June to October). November to March is the prime time to visit.

# Explore Botum Sakor National Park

ENDANGERED WILDLIFE, MANGROVES & BEACHES

Spanning a 35km-wide peninsula separated from Sihanoukville by the Gulf of Kompong Som and encircled by mangrove forests and beaches, the Botum Sakor National Park is another superbly biodiverse sanctuary. The 1825-sq-km park is a couple of hours' drive south of Koh Kong (around 120km) and is mostly vivid evergreen rainforest and grassland that's home to elephants, pangolins, slow lorises, sun bears, fishing cats, hog badgers and hog deer, as well as elusive gibbons, otters, civets and many bird species.

Unfortunately, their habitats are under threat as around 75% of Botum Sakor has been sold off to build a Chinese-backed airport, four-lane highway and massive resort complex, although work on that appeared to have slowed when we visited. Such rampant overdevelopment is the reason why the Koh Kong Conservation Corridor was established in the first place. Thankfully, the Wildlife Alliance NGO has stepped in and taken over management of 10% of the park in order to protect it.

Visitors should make tracks for the much less developed eastern side of Botum Sakor. Boats can be hired in **Andoung Tuek**, the closest town, to take you along four mangrove-lined streams that are rich in primate life – pileated gibbons, long-tailed macaques and black-shanked douc langurs. Also on the east coast of the park is the photogenic fishing village of **Thmor Sor**, which is mostly built on stilts and stretches out over the bay for almost 1km.

# Wildlife Encounters in Southern Cardamom National Park

EXPLORE CAMBODIA'S LARGEST NATIONAL PARK

Cambodia's newest national park (established in 2016) and also its largest at 4104 sq km, the Southern Cardamom National Park is home to numerous threatened species, includ-

## PANGOLIN REVIVAL

For proof that the Koh Kong Conservation Corridor is effective at protecting rare species, look no further than the region's rebounding pangolin population.

The nocturnal anteaters are one of the world's most trafficked mammals, prized for their meat (which is considered a delicacy in China and Vietnam) as well as blood and scales (used in traditional Chinese medicine). Until very recently, their numbers were freefalling in the Cardamom Mountains.

But with rescued pangolins being released back into the wild around Chi Phat and much more awareness of their plight, they may be making a modest comeback. Research by the Wild Earth Allies NGO suggests that the poaching of pangolins in the Cardamoms has declined significantly since 2020.

**Stung Areng Homestays**
The CBET in Stung Areng arranges bed and board in basic bungalows with local families. $

**Kim Chhoun Guesthouse**
Fan-only, cold-water rooms are available here if you're stuck in Andoung Tuek for the night. $

**Cardamom Tented Camp**
Safari-like tents and a top eatery at this ecolodge in the Botum Sakor National Park. $$$

## CARDAMOM RAINFOREST LANDSCAPE

Comprising 11 national parks, biodiversity corridors and wildlife sanctuaries, the Cardamom Rainforest Landscape is thought to be the largest contiguous protected area in Southeast Asia. It spreads for 20,746 sq km across seven provinces in southwest Cambodia and is home to an enormous variety of birds and wildlife, much of it under threat from illegal logging and poaching.

It was only in 2016 that the area was afforded official protection by the Cambodian government. Now a number of NGOs, including Wildlife Alliance, Flora & Fauna International and Mother Nature Cambodia, work with the authorities to protect the area's 16 distinct ecosystems so that future generations can enjoy one of Cambodia's national treasures.

ing Asian elephants, Siamese crocodiles, sun bears, gibbons and pangolins. Much of the park is extremely remote and illegal hunting and logging are issues.

A couple of CBETs offer the chance to delve into the park. They operate out of **Stung Areng**, 84km east of Koh Kong and around two hours by car, and the village of **Osoam**, 90km northeast of Koh Kong and a two-hour drive by car, at an altitude of 700m (bring warm clothes). The projects offer treks, boat and mountain-bike trips, and accommodation in very simple homestays. Treks here can be quite rugged. Bring cash as there are no ATMs nearby.

Note that that the Osoam operation is an informal CBET and less well organised than the CBET in Stung Areng. Visitors to Stung Areng have a better chance of spotting rare animals in the surrounding Areng Valley, while there's also the tantalising possibility of treks from Stung Areng to the 1160m-high peak of **Khnong Phsar**, on the border of Koh Kong and Kampong Speu Provinces.

About 13km south of Osoam is the **Crocodile Protection Sanctuary**, home to around 40 endangered Siamese crocodiles. The Cardamom Mountains are now the only place where they live in the wild. The best time for viewing them is December to May.

### KOH SDACH ARCHIPELAGO ACCESS

The southwestern tip of Botum Sakor National Park is where boats depart for the 10-minute journey to Koh Sdach Island, the gateway to the dive sites of the largely tourist-free **Koh Sdach Archipelago** (p220).

---

 **GETTING THERE & AROUND**

Andoung Tuek, 98km south of Koh Kong, is the jumping-off point for Chi Phat and the Botum Sakor National Park. All minivans travelling to/from Sihanoukville and Koh Kong can drop you here. The CBET (p205) in Chi Phat will organise a motorcycle taxi (US$7) or a long-tail boat (US$15 per person) for the last leg of the

journey to Chi Phat. Boats (US$60) can be hired in Andoung Tuek for trips into Botum Sakor National Park.

A sole shared taxi heads to Osoam (US$15) from Koh Kong daily at 2pm. For Stung Areng, you'll need a private taxi (US$80).

# SIHANOUKVILLE

Phnom Penh

Sihanoukville

Sihanoukville, Cambodia's principal port, has been battered in recent years by powerful external forces. First a giant wave of investment swept in from China, resulting in unchecked development and crime washing away much of the city's charm. Then, just as Sihanoukville seemed set to seal its transformation into a gambling and sin destination for Chinese tourists, along came COVID-19 to rob the casinos and clubs of their customers.

The presence of many abandoned or half-built casinos, hotels and shops gives Sihanoukville a vaguely apocalyptic feel. On the upside, the roads are much better and efforts are being made to improve the water quality off the city's still good-looking beaches.

Most travellers pass through on their way to the islands, only overnighting if they have to. Despite Sihanoukville's dubious reputation, almost all illegal activity involves Chinese and/or locals. The vast majority of visitors encounter no problems.

## TOP TIP

Sihanoukville is big and spread out. The little tourist infrastructure remaining for non-Chinese visitors mostly clusters on or around Serendipity Beach Rd, Otres Beach and the far southern end of Ochheuteal Beach. Prices are higher here than elsewhere on the South Coast.

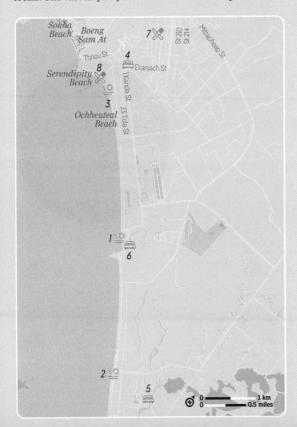

**SIGHTS**
1 Ochheuteal Beach
2 Otres Beach
3 Serendipity Beach

**SLEEPING**
4 Onederz
5 Sok Sabay
6 Sunset Lounge

**EATING**
7 Sandan
8 Yasmine Cafe

# Seaside Fun in Sihanoukville

CITY BEACH BUMMING

Sihanoukville's beaches are still eye-catching, lengthy strips of powdery white sand backed by swaying casuarinas and co-conut palms, despite the opprobrium the redevelopment of the city attracts. Unfortunately, water quality remains an issue, but the local government is working to resolve that by putting in place proper sewage disposal. If you want to swim, check the local conditions before putting your head underwater.

**Otres Beach** is Sihanoukville's standout stunner, a wide and long expanse of blinding-white sand 5km south of the city centre. Until Chinese money moved into town, Otres was a key stop on the travellers' trail in Southeast Asia. Bars, restaurants and guesthouses clustered a couple of blocks back from the beach in Otres Village. Most have now closed or moved elsewhere, but a few places hang on and a small stream of travellers still visit before or after heading to the islands. Otres is also the best beach for swimming.

Just north of Otres is **Ochheuteal Beach**, which runs for 4km to the city centre. It's certainly pretty enough and great for sunbathing and picnics – at weekends it's fun when the locals come to party – but check the water before going in. The far northern end of Ochheuteal is known as **Serendipity Beach**, which is now backed by a line of mostly vacant shops. Don't swim there.

## BEST PLACES TO EAT & STAY IN SIHANOUKVILLE

**Onederz $**
Centrally located budget option. More basic than other Onederz hostels.

**Sunset Lounge $$**
Popular guesthouse and restaurant at the far southern end of Ochheuteal Beach.

**Sok Sabay $$**
Low-key resort with OK bungalows in what's left of Otres Village, near the beach.

**Sandan $$**
Creative Cambodian cuisine. One of the few places with some atmosphere.

**Yasmine Cafe $$**
European, Khmer and Thai dishes by Serendipity Beach. Good for a quiet drink.

### OTRES BEACH EVACUEES

Some of the expats who had businesses in Otres Village have now migrated to unspoilt **Nesat Beach** (p212), a few hours north of Sihanoukville.

## GETTING THERE & AROUND

The train linking Sihanoukville with Phnom Penh via Kampot and Kep is popular with travellers. Minivans go to the same places, plus Koh Kong, Andoung Tuek and Sre Ambel (for Nesat Beach).

All ferries to Koh Rong and Koh Rong Sanloem (both US$25 for an open return, 40 to 60 minutes) now depart from the Sihanoukville Port Ferry Dock, a 15-minute *tuk-tuk* drive (US$3) north of Serendipity Beach. A slower

and cheaper cargo boat (US$5, 1½ to three hours) departs daily at 2pm from Pier 52 at the port for Koh Rong Sanloem and Koh Rong.

At the time of writing, Sihanoukville's airport, 15km east of the city, had direct flights to Siem Reap and Ho Chi Minh City in Vietnam.

*Moto* and *tuk-tuk* drivers are found all over town. Overcharging is common; bargain hard. Ask your accommodation about motorbike hire.

Nesat Beach

Sihanoukville

Koh Ta Kiev  Koh Thmei

# Beyond
# Sihanoukville

Head north and southeast of Sihanoukville for gorgeous beaches, little-seen islands and a unique community of travellers.

Travellers who venture beyond Sihanoukville are rewarded with near-empty mainland beaches, jungle-clad islands which see far fewer visitors than the glamour twins Koh Rong and Koh Rong Sanloem, and the chance to spot endangered wildlife.

North of Sihanoukville are mostly untouched beaches that hug the Gulf of Kompong Som. They include Nesat Beach, which has emerged as a new destination for travellers seeking simplicity and a communal life.

South and east of Sihanoukville are Koh Ta Kiev and Koh Thmei, two off-the-grid islands sitting in the Gulf of Thailand, where rare birds abound and it's sometimes possible to see dolphins. It's all about getting away from the tourist trail here.

## TOP TIP

There's little public transport or visitor infrastructure. Roads are in reasonable condition, so hiring a motorbike makes sense.

**Koh Ta Kiev (p213)**

SONDIPON/SHUTTERSTOCK ©

211

## CASINOS & CRIME

The Nesat Beach scene has emerged in part because so many foreigners have fled Sihanoukville since Chinese money started pouring into the city in 2017. Much of that investment has gone on building casino resorts for punters from China, where gambling is illegal. But underground betting has also proliferated, along with online and phone scam operations controlled by Chinese gangs but staffed by people trafficked from across Asia with false promises of legitimate work. An international outcry over the people-smuggling has prompted some law-enforcement action from both Cambodia and China, but Sihanoukville seems unlikely to lose its notoriety as one of Southeast Asia's crime capitals any time soon.

CANNET/SHUTTERSTOCK ©

**Prek Touek Sap, Ream National Park**

# Escape the Crowds at Nesat Beach

A TRAVELLER PARADISE

The tucked-away traveller community at Nesat Beach, 85km north of Sihanoukville and around 2½ hours by minivan and motorcycle taxi, is building its own Southeast Asian paradise. This hamlet of Western-run guesthouses, restaurants and cafes linked by dirt tracks has been literally carved out of the jungle and comes complete with its own driftwood-decorated night-life spot, the mellow **Klub Haus**, as well as a **night market** with food and handicrafts.

A mix of long-term expats, families and passing travellers stay here, mostly European but all committed to the idea of creating something unique and special. It's a superbly relaxed spot and visitors often end up staying far longer than they anticipated.

Palm-lined Nesat Beach is 5km further down the unsealed road that connects this part of the coast with the nearest town, Sre Ambel. It's one of 11 beaches (mostly white-sand and utterly empty) in the area, and there are also mangrove forests nearby. A few guesthouses and resorts perch right on the coast, but all are aimed at Khmer visitors.

 **WHERE TO STAY IN NESAT BEACH**

**The Cocoon**
Run by friendly Sybil, with six compact but comfy rooms as well as a splash pool. **$**

**Done Right**
Eight-bed dorms with shared bathrooms, great lounge area and a popular restaurant–bar. **$**

**CornerStone**
Sizeable rooms, an apartment, communal meals and a roof terrace draw loyal guests. **$$**

Technically, the Nesat Beach community is part of Chrouy Svay village but the locals, who have welcomed the newcomers and the opportunity to boost their incomes, now refer to the settlement as **Phum Barang**, or 'foreigner village'. More guesthouses and restaurants were readying to open at the time of writing, so get here before everyone else does.

## Switch Off on Little-Visited Islands

GET BACK TO NATURE

Nestling in the Gulf of Thailand south and east of Sihanoukville, **Koh Ta Kiev** and **Koh Thmei** are all about escaping the 21st century, while also spotting dolphins and any number of rare birds. Both islands are accessible only by small boats and are off the grid and reliant on solar power. There are no parties or bars, just a few simple guesthouses and resorts with in-house restaurants. Days are spent on or in the sea and jungle, and nights are about listening to the lapping of the waves and the wildlife in the forests.

Just 1km off the coast, Koh Ta Kiev's jungle interior is ringed by isolated beaches and bays, rocky cliffs and mangroves. Although parts of the island have been leased for development, nothing has really changed and you still have to hike through the forest to get to the different beaches. The best ones are **Long Beach** on the west coast and **Plankton Beach** in the south, where you can snorkel with bioluminescent plankton. Both offer basic accommodation.

Right on the maritime border with Vietnam and only a few hundred metres off the coast, Koh Thmei is much bigger but has so far escaped the developers. The only place to stay is **Koh Thmei Resort**, which has tidy bungalows on a private beach. The island has super birdwatching possibilities and the chance to view dolphins offshore, as well as snorkelling, sea kayaking and hiking.

**DOLPHIN SPOTTING**

**Ream National Park** has been gutted by Chinese-backed development, but it's still possible to see dolphins along the **Prek Touek Sap Estuary**, winding through what's left of the park before emptying into the Gulf of Thailand. Boat trips along the estuary can be arranged via the park's Ranger Station. Both Irrawaddy dolphins and Indo-Pacific humpback dolphins have been spotted here; January to April is the best time to view them. They're most often found at the mouth of the estuary, while visitors to Koh Thmei sometimes find their boats flanked by dolphins and flying fish.

**MEKONG RIVER DOLPHINS**

Apart from the Prek Touek Sap Estuary and nearby Koh Thmei, the only other place in Cambodia to see dolphins is around **Kratie** (p250), where freshwater Irrawaddy dolphins gambol in the Mekong.

**GETTING THERE & AROUND**

For Nesat Beach, minivans heading north of Sihanoukville can drop you in Sre Ambel, from where it's another 18km by motorcycle taxi (US$5) or *tuk-tuk* (US$15). Motorbikes (US$5 per day) can be rented at The Cocoon.

Guesthouses on Koh Ta Kiev have their own boats and pick up guests from Ream Beach, which is around 20km from Sihanoukville (US$15 for a *tuk-tuk*). The sole resort on Koh Thmei picks up guests from the fishing village of Koh Kchhang, about 40km east of Sihanoukville.

# KOH RONG

Phnom Penh

Koh Rong

Cambodia's original tropical paradise, Koh Rong seduces visitors with turquoise waters and kilometres of white-sand beaches backed by palms and jungle. There are 22 beaches scattered around the 61km-long coastline, so there's a strip of sand for everyone, whether you want coupled-up bliss, rustic remoteness or resort life. Boat trips – snorkelling, plankton viewing and fishing – are the main activity and can be arranged everywhere.

Before the pandemic, Koh Rong was a raucous party island for young travellers and the main settlement of Koh Tuch was jammed with bars, restaurants and crashpads. Now boutique resorts line the east and west coasts and the backpacker scene has mostly shifted to neighbouring Koh Rong Sanloem.

With an airport being built, Koh Rong is set for more changes. But for now, it's home to exquisite beaches and a sea that shimmers with phosphorescence at night. Enjoy it while you can.

## TOP TIP

Koh Tuch in the south is Koh Rong's hub. Sok San and Prek Svay, on the west and northeast coast respectively, are the other sizeable settlements. Paved roads now run around most of Koh Rong. You'll need a motorbike or motorbike taxi if you want to explore the island.

SONDIPON/SHUTTERSTOCK ©

**Koh Tuch Beach (p217)**

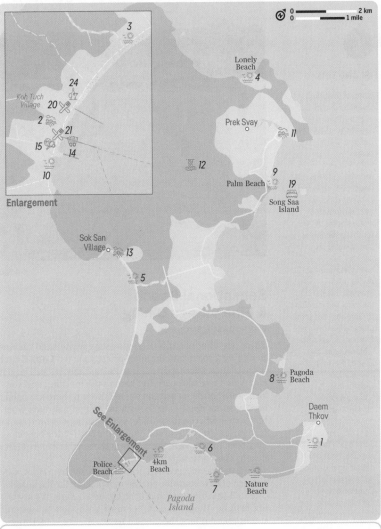

0 ___ 2 km
0 ___ 1 mile

3

Lonely
Beach
4

Prek Svay

11

Koh Tuch
Village

24

20

2

21

15

14

10

Enlargement

12

Palm Beach

9

19
Song Saa
Island

Sok San
Village   13

5

8   Pagoda
Beach

Daem
Thkov

1

See Enlargement

Police
Beach

4km
Beach

6

7   Nature
Beach

Pagoda
Island

**SIGHTS**
1 Coconut Beach
2 Koh Tuch
3 Koh Tuch Beach
4 Lonely Beach
5 Long Beach
6 Long Set Beach
7 Nature Beach
8 Pagoda Beach
9 Palm Beach
10 Police Beach

11 Prek Svay
12 Prek Svay Waterfall
13 Sok San

**ACTIVITIES,
COURSES
& TOURS**
14 Koh Rong
Dive Center
15 Three Brothers

**SLEEPING**
(see 11) Firefly
Guesthouse
(see 4) Lonely
Beach Eco Resort
(see 9) Palm Beach
Bungalow Resort
19 Song Saa
Private Island

**EATING**
20 Bamboo
21 Buffalo
(see 13) Hakobune
(see 13) Moon
Restaurant
(see 13) Seng
Piset Restaurant

**DRINKING**
24 Runaways

DIEGO FIORE/SHUTTERSTOCK ©

Sok San

## ISLAND TIPS

None of the South Coast's 60-odd islands (there's no official number) have banks or ATMs – bring cash.

Pack insect repellent and decent antiseptic. Bites and cuts can quickly become infected in the tropics. A torch (flashlight) or headlamp is also useful.

Accommodation prices drop dramatically during the rainy season (June to October), but some places shut down and there are fewer ferries.

Monkeys on the islands are wild animals. Don't engage with them.

If you have an onward transport connection booked from Sihanoukville, don't catch the last possible boat when departing the islands. Water transport in Cambodia doesn't run to schedule, and changing weather conditions can result in delays and cancellations.

# Sensational Beach & Fine Village Dining

WEST COAST & SOK SAN

There are 7km of drop-dead-gorgeous white sand on Koh Rong's west coast, and the appropriately named **Long Beach** is the island's finest strip of sand. Remarkably, it's still largely empty and undeveloped. Get here in the morning and you'll have much of the beach to yourself. Even if there are people here, visitors don't have to walk far to find a stretch where they can sunbathe in solitude, while gazing out on tranquil turquoise waters disturbed only by the odd fishing boat chugging back to **Sok San**, the village at the northern end of Long Beach. There are superb sunsets, too.

Sok San has emerged as a destination in its own right, with a clutch of new boutique charmers replacing the backpacker-oriented guesthouses that once clustered here. It's a working fishing village made up of mostly wooden houses, and staying here offers the chance to experience something of local life on Koh Rong. In the evenings it's extremely peaceful, with nightlife consisting of grazing on seafood while gazing at the ocean.

 **WHERE TO STAY ON THE WEST COAST**

**White Sand Ark**
Light and minimalist rooms in Sok San with Japanese-style tatami beds raised off the floor. Amenable staff. **$$**

**Sok San Beach Resort**
Longstanding, efficient place with comfortable rooms and bungalows on a magnificent stretch of Long Beach. **$$**

**Golden Beach Resort**
Flash Sok San newcomer with stylish bungalows and a nice pool. Good family option. **$$$**

The village has also emerged as the unlikely star of Koh Rong's dining scene. There are very few restaurants outside the resorts elsewhere on the island, but Sok San has the best Khmer eatery on Koh Rong, as well as places offering sushi and sashimi and Thai and Chinese dishes. You're spoiled for choice here.

# Beach Bliss & Secluded Bays

EAST & SOUTH COASTS

Koh Rong's east and south coasts feature a series of outstanding beaches that wind and curl along the shoreline from Pagoda Beach in the east all the way south to Koh Tuch. They're interspersed with tucked-away bays and coves and backed by thickly forested hills that are home to macaque monkeys. Many of Koh Rong's best beaches can be found along this part of the coast and it's possible to walk between some of them on jungle trails. From Coconut Beach at the far eastern edge of the island, a reasonably fit and intrepid person can make it to Koh Tuch in two sweaty hours.

**Pagoda Beach** is absolutely extraordinary, a wide and expansive stretch of gleaming white sand that your feet sink into up to the ankles. Seven boutique resorts are spaced out along the beach. They attract couples – this is prime honeymoon territory – and families who want a self-contained experience rather than beach-hopping around the island.

Further south past Daem Thkov, the smallest of Koh Rong's settlements, is pretty **Coconut Beach**, set in a secluded cove overseen by steep hills. It's smaller than the other beaches nearby, but you can sometimes see bioluminescent plankton at night. There are just three places to stay and it's popular with budget travellers looking for peace and quiet.

It's a half-hour walk from Coconut Beach to **Nature Beach**, where there are family-oriented resorts, and a short stroll on from there to **Long Set Beach**, another picture-postcard vision of soft and powdery white sand that curves gently around a big bay and is great for swimming. It's mostly mid-range resort territory here, although there are still a couple of budget options.

Beyond Long Set and a small headland lies **Koh Tuch Beach**, which hugs the bay that is home to Koh Rong's main harbour. At its far eastern end, where guesthouses sit in the forest that presses right up to the sand, this is still an attractive beach that's fine for swimming. As you get closer to the piers where ferries arrive and depart, the water quality deteriorates.

**Koh Tuch** itself is much quieter than it once was, with the backpacker scene having mostly decamped to Koh Rong

## BEST PLACES TO EAT ON KOH RONG

**Bamboo $**
The best pizzas in Koh Tuch, with veggie and vegan options available

**Seng Piset Restaurant $$**
Super seafood and tasty Khmer options on a shady deck above the sea in Sok San.

**Hakobune $$**
Sushi, sashimi, Japanese-style BBQ and potent cocktails at this Sok San place.

**Moon Restaurant $$**
A Sok San winner run by a friendly family, with seafood specialities and Thai salads.

**Buffalo $$**
Koh Tuch's smartest restaurant; pan-Asian fusion dishes, succulent meat cuts and a wine list.

 **WHERE TO STAY ON THE EAST & SOUTH COASTS**

**Nest Beach Club**
Koh Rong's only hostel sits at the far western end of Long Set Beach. Hosts 'Nestival' every Saturday. **$**

**Coconutbeach Bungalows**
Simple bungalows, plus rooms and tents, perched above Coconut Beach. Family-run, with a nice communal area. **$**

**White Beach Bungalows**
Attractive wooden bungalows at the eastern end of Koh Tuch Beach. You'll pay more for air-con. **$$**

**BEST PLACES TO STAY ON THE NORTH & NORTHEAST COASTS**

**Palm Beach Bungalow Resort $**
Functional wooden bungalows and dorms right by Palm Beach. Popular with young adventure tour groups.

**Firefly Guesthouse $**
Basic but rather charming digs in an over-the-water stilted wooden house in Prek Svay.

**Lonely Beach Eco Resort $$**
Simple wooden bungalows (solar power, bucket showers, no fans) on Lonely Beach. French and Khmer restaurant.

**Song Saa Private Island $$$**
Exclusive resort with luxurious villas perched over the sea on twin islands 500m off the coast.

Sanloem. The wild, all-night parties that took place on **Police Beach**, on the western side of Koh Tuch, are now just a memory. Many restaurants and bars have also closed, although **Runaways** on the main drag keeps the hippie traveller vibe going with occasional banging nights and seafront barbecue places set up in the evenings.

Based on one of the piers at the port is **Koh Rong Dive Center**, although it does most of its diving off Koh Rong Sanloem. **Three Brothers**, which organises daily boat trips, is nearby.

# Channel Your Inner Robinson Crusoe

NORTH AND NORTHEAST COASTS

Koh Rong's north and northeast coasts are for travellers really looking to get away from it all. This is the least developed part of the island and the roads are still mostly unpaved, although work on them is starting, so the beaches here are accessed by dirt tracks that are difficult to drive and find. The reward is splendid isolation in stunning surroundings.

**Lonely Beach** in the far north more than lives up to its name – it's the perfect place to act out your Robinson Crusoe fantasies. The golden-sand beach, backed by thick jungle, is glorious and curves around a highly photogenic bay. The sole accommodation here is more a way of life than a resort, and some people stay for months.

The closest settlement to Lonely Beach (a 45-minute walk) is the pleasant fishing village of **Prek Svay**, which has stilted wooden houses over and by the water. Prek Svay sees comparatively few foreigners and a stay here is a great chance to tap into the rhythms of local life.

South of the village is isolated **Palm Beach**, where you can unwind on a small but picturesque strip of sand surrounded by forest. Jungle trails from here lead to hidden waterfalls, including **Prek Svay Waterfall**, a triple-drop waterfall with a couple of lovely pools for swimming.

 **GETTING THERE & AROUND**

Fast ferries (US$25 open return, one hour) depart daily for Sihanoukville and Koh Rong Sanloem from Koh Tuch's main pier. In high season (December to February), ferries may pick up passengers at other beaches around the island as well. If you want to stay in Koh Rong Sanloem before returning to Sihanoukville, you don't need to buy another ticket. It's essential to confirm your return date to Sihanoukville a day or two before departure.

A slower and cheaper cargo boat (US$5, three hours) departs daily for Sihanoukville at 7am.

Long-tail boats can be hired in Koh Tuch to shuttle you to other beaches on Koh Rong for US$10 and up per person depending on the destination.

*Motos* can zip you around the island for US$5 to US$20 depending on where you're going. Motorbikes (US$10 per day) can be hired at guesthouses and in Koh Tuch.

# Beyond Koh Rong

Beyond Koh Rong are tourist-free islands, remote reefs and some of the best diving in Cambodia.

Visitors who venture beyond Koh Rong and neighbouring Koh Rong Sanloem get to experience a little-travelled seascape of small, jungle-dominated islands whose reefs teem with life. Some of the best diving in Cambodia can be found here, along with authentic fishing villages. Little English is spoken, but visitors will get a real insight into island life.

North of Koh Rong are the 12 islands of the Koh Sdach Archipelago, home to numerous impressive dive sites and the largest settlement in these parts. Southwest of Koh Rong Sanloem are the exclusive diving spots off barely seen Koh Tang, site of the Vietnam War's last battle, and Koh Prins. For now, both islands are completely untouched by tourism.

## TOP TIP

The best way to see the islands is with a dive operator, whether you want to dive or just snorkel.

**Koh Sdach Archipelago (p220)**

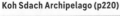

CAMNET/SHUTTERSTOCK ©

## REMOTE ISLANDS

A three-hour boat ride southwest of Koh Rong Sanloem and five hours from the mainland, **Koh Tang** and **Koh Prins** are among the most remote of Cambodia's islands. They're uninhabited bar for a small military presence. Divers come here for vibrant reefs and an array of marine life including stingrays, razorfish, batfish and barracudas.

Koh Tang was also the site of the last battle of the Vietnam War. US marines landed on Koh Tang in May 1975 to free the crew of an American cargo boat hijacked by the Khmer Rouge. They underestimated their enemy and were forced to retreat. It was the only occasion when US soldiers clashed directly with the Khmer Rouge.

CANNET/SHUTTERSTOCK ©

Diving areas, Koh Sdach

# Stay in an Authentic Fishing Village

ISLAND LIFE ON KOH SDACH

The **Koh Sdach Archipelago** is a grouping of 12 modest islands around 16km northwest of Koh Rong, but close to the mainland and accessed via a short boat ride from the southwestern tip of the Botum Sakor National Park (p207). While they're best known for having some of the most impressive dive sites in Cambodia, a trip here is also a chance to experience life in an authentic fishing village that sees very few foreigners.

**Koh Sdach** (King's Island) is the only significant settlement, home to 3000-odd people. The local economy is centred on the fishing boats that jam the harbour, and the village is a jumble of streets lined with wooden houses and backed by macaque-infested jungle. It's dominated by a lively market. From the late afternoon, food stalls appear and it's fun to join the locals as they saunter in their pyjamas, while snacking on skewers of squid.

 **WHERE TO STAY IN KOH SDACH**

**Monorom Guesthouse**
Clean and comfortable rooms at this family-run guesthouse in the middle of Koh Sdach's main drag. **$**

**Mean Chey Guesthouse**
Sprawling complex of anonymous bungalows on the west coast, but close to the harbour. **$$**

**Koh Sdach Resort**
Newcomer on the west coast with posh tented bungalows perched on the island's one sandy beach. **$$$**

There are a couple of guesthouses and a sole resort overlooking the island's one real beach. Boat trips can be arranged and there are some excellent snorkelling opportunities for nondivers.

Change is coming to the archipelago, as it's impacted by the development of Botum Sakor. Some islands have been earmarked for resorts, and artificial beaches are being created at the expense of the coral reefs that surround them – all the more reason to get here soon.

# Underwater Adventures

DIVING THE ISLANDS

The Koh Sdach Archipelago is a wonderful place for underwater adventures. Reefs here are multicoloured and thriving and there's an abundance of out-of-the-ordinary marine life. Koh Sdach Island has two dive shops, **Octopuses Garden Diving Centre** and **Kuda Divers**, both run by welcoming and professional Norwegians. In addition to open-water diving courses for novices, they organise dive and boat trips to the surrounding islands, which are also great for snorkelling. Both shops offer simple accommodation and meals to anyone diving with them.

What makes the archipelago so special for divers is the biodiversity and the fact that the best dive sites can be reached on day trips rather than on pricey liveaboards. And there are never more than a couple of dive boats in the same place.

Prime spots include **Shark Island**, where as well as reef sharks, bull and whale sharks are sometimes seen. There is also a shipwreck here. **Condor Reef**, 30km south of Koh Sdach, is an amazing reef in the middle of the ocean, with supreme visibility and the chance to spot big pelagic fish, sharks and turtles.

Within the archipelago, noteworthy destinations include **Turtle Island**, with many different reef fish, giant barracudas, cobia and batfish, and **Koh Chan**, where stingrays, clownfish and amazing coral await. November to May is the peak diving season.

## DIVING KOH SDACH

**Kristoffer Fjeldså** runs Octopuses Garden Diving Centre (octopuscambodia.com) on Koh Sdach Island.

**Why dive Koh Sdach?** It has better biodiversity than other places. The reefs are healthy and you can expect to see a million fish. Shark Island and Condor Reef are absolutely world-class dive sites with great visibility and fantastic underwater scenery.

**Is it a good place to learn to dive?** Yes. The water is clear and there are no big groups of divers. You also get to see more fish than you imagined possible.

**Have the islands changed since you've been here?** The development on the mainland has had an impact, but this is still a place to experience beautiful nature.

## GETTING THERE & AROUND

From Kiri Sakor at the southwestern tip of the Botum Sakor National Park, motorboats make the 10-minute run to Koh Sdach Island for US$3 to US$5, depending on your bargaining skills.

Shared taxis go to Kiri Sakor from Koh Kong and Sihanoukville, or you can travel to Andoung Tuek by minivan and then hop a motorcycle taxi (US$20) for the 70-minute journey to Kiri Sakor. A private taxi from Sihanoukville costs US$80.

Motorcycle taxis and *tuk-tuks* wait at Koh Sdach's pier, but you can walk to anywhere on the island in 15 minutes or less.

# KOH RONG
# SANLOEM

⊗ Phnom Penh

● Koh Rong San

With a handful of fabulous beaches dotted around a jungle-wrapped coastline, Koh Rong Sanloem is a tropical island fantasy come true. It's smaller than near neighbour Koh Rong and has a thickly forested interior. There are still no real roads connecting the different beaches on the island, so each one retains a distinct personality and attracts a different crowd.

Saracen Bay on the east coast is the busiest beach, its shiny white sand curving around the bay for 2.5km. On the west coast are Lazy Beach and Sunset Beach, where the vibe is so chilled you don't need air-conditioning. Accessible only by boat is M'Pai Bay, the site of the island's sole village.

Koh Rong Sanloem is now home to the backpacker scene on the islands, but it's a mellow one and there are no full-moon parties as yet. Despite evidence of some desultory development, this is still an island paradise.

## TOP TIP

There's no transport on the island, and hardly any real roads, so you're tramping between the different beaches or hiring a long-tail boat. Avoid hiking through the jungle at night.

**Saracen Bay, Koh Rong Sanloem**

MUAZ JAFFAR/SHUTTERSTOCK ©

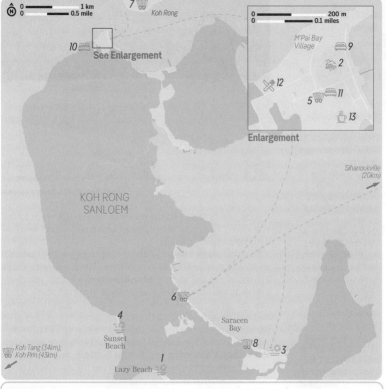

**SIGHTS**
1 Lazy Beach
2 M'Pai Bay
3 Saracen Bay
4 Sunset Beach

**ACTIVITIES,
COURSES & TOURS**
(see 5) Adventure
Travel Co
5 Bubbles
Up Dive Centre
6 Dive Shop Cambodia
7 Koh Koun

8 Scuba Nation
(see 4) Sunset
Adventures

**SLEEPING**
9 Beach House
10 Cliff Hostel
11 Ing Ing Guesthouse

**EATING**
12 Bar Bok Bowie

**DRINKING
& NIGHTLIFE**
13 Seapony Cafe

# Diving & Boat Trips

SARACEN BAY BEACH

The long and graceful crescent of white sand at **Saracen Bay** is
Koh Rong Sanloem's most popular beach. It is home to the vast
majority of accommodation on the island, including upmarket

 **WHERE TO STAY AT SARACEN BAY**

**Sara Resort**
Efficient, welcoming place in
the middle of the beach. Nice
pool and a decent restaurant.
**$$$**

**Eden Beach Resort**
Smart newcomer with
attractive bungalows set
around a leafy garden and
pool. Amiable staff. **$$$**

**La Passion by Achariyak**
Roomy and posh bungalows
set in a huge, jungly garden.
Infinity pool and private beach.
**$$$**

223

## WHY I LOVE KOH RONG SANLOEM

**David Eimer**, writer

I love arriving at the rickety wooden piers at Saracen Bay and jumping with glee onto the flour-like white sand. But it's even better waking up on Koh Rong Sanloem, when the beaches are bathed in soft morning light and the turquoise sea beyond them looks so inviting.

Trekking along the jungle trail to Sunset Beach with monkeys muttering in the light-dappled trees, birds calling to each other and insects chattering, is a different pleasure, a case of beauty and the beasts. When finally I step out of the forest onto the golden sand, it always feels like I've earned the right to my own piece of paradise.

**Lazy Beach, Koh Rong Sanloem**

resorts and hostels, but the beach is big enough never to feel crowded. This is also where ferries arrive and depart for Sihanoukville and Koh Rong.

Boat, kayaking and paddleboarding trips are the main activity and can be booked everywhere. The most worthwhile excursion are the nightly **plankton tours** – they take people out to the shoals of bioluminescent plankton that congregate off various parts of the island depending on the season. Swimming or snorkelling through the plankton as they glow like a starry sky is a memorable experience and kids love it.

Diving is another excellent choice and two dive operators, **Dive Shop Cambodia** and **Scuba Nation**, can be found at opposite ends of the beach. They run the full gamut of Professional Association of Diving Instructors (PADI) courses, as well as fun dives and liveaboards, and offer basic accommodation for people diving with them. Koh Rong Sanloem is blessed with beautiful, healthy coral and lots of reef fish, as is uninhabited **Koh Koun** just to the north of the island. A few hours to the southwest are the remote, barely seen islands of Koh Tang and Koh Prins (p220), where bigger and rarer marine life awaits.

# Hidden Beaches & Jungle Adventures

SUNSET BEACH & LAZY BEACH

In the 1996 novel and subsequent movie *The Beach,* travellers have to swim and surmount forest-covered hills to reach the beach of their dreams. Getting to **Sunset Beach** on Koh Rong Sanloem's west coast isn't quite as dramatic a journey, but it's still a test. The reward is a spectacular beach that's as beautiful as any in Cambodia.

 **WHERE TO STAY AT SUNSET & LAZY BEACH**

**Sunboo Beach Bungalows**
Serene Sunset Beach spot with simple but nice bungalows and a few dorm beds. Daily yoga sessions. **$$**

**Lazy Beach**
The sole resort on Lazy Beach. Fan-only, cold-water wooden bungalows and a solid restaurant; no wi-fi. **$$**

**Robinson's Bungalows**
Sunset Beach veteran with basic bungalows, tents and a cool communal area. Small outdoor gym, too. **$$**

Start by swapping your flip-flops for runners or boots and dumping any heavy luggage at Dive Shop Cambodia in Saracen Bay, who'll store it for a dollar a day. The 45-minute trail to Sunset Beach begins behind the shop and it gets progressively harder the further into the jungle you head. The final stretch is a gruelling scramble over rocks – there's a guide rope to cling onto – until you finally emerge onto a golden-sand beach that curves around a delightful bay.

A handful of resorts nestle here. You probably won't get any wi-fi, so do as everyone else does and just chill out. If you are feeling active, **Sunset Adventures** offers boat trips, kayaking, rock climbing and yoga.

Also on the west coast is **Lazy Beach**, which is accessed by a much easier 20-minute trail that begins just past Sara Resort (p223). It's a decent choice for families, as the tranquil water here is perfect for swimming. There's good snorkelling off either end of the beach.

# Fishing Village Life & Island Bohemia

M'PAI BAY & MONKEY MADNESS

Up on the far northern coast is **M'Pai Bay**, the only settlement on Koh Rong Sanloem. Staying in this working fishing village feels very different to the beaches further south, which can't be accessed from here except by boat. Prior to the pandemic, M'Pai Bay was a favourite with travellers looking for a more organic vibe than a beach resort, and there's a vaguely bohemian feel to some of the guesthouses scattered throughout the village. It's still popular with people staying long-term on the island.

The grainy yellow-sand beach in the village itself is nothing special, but there are nicer alternatives within walking distance, as well as a headland past the pier with great sunset views. M'Pai Bay is also opposite the superb reefs of uninhabited Koh Koun. **Bubbles Up Dive Centre** and **Adventure Travel Co** in the village run diving and snorkelling trips there.

Southeast of M'Pai Bay is Clearwater Bay, which is now in the hands of a Chinese developer. The next bay beyond is home to the infamous **Mad Monkey** hostel, which has its own private beach and sunset bar across from a small navy base. What the sailors think of the antics that go on there is unknown. But if your idea of fun is playing drinking games where you end up naked, this is the place for you.

**BEST PLACES TO STAY & EAT IN M'PAI BAY**

**Cliff Hostel $**
Supreme views from the cliff-side restaurant–bar, poky rooms and a 33-bed dorm.

**Ing Ing Guesthouse $**
Compact and clean rooms with shared balconies at this friendly, family-run place.

**Beach House $$**
Beachfront guesthouse with small rooms, but hot water and air-con – a rarity in M'Pai Bay.

**Bar Bok Bowie $**
Asian-style tapas, cocktails and an upstairs deck for sunset-watching. Closed Mondays and Tuesdays.

**Seapony Cafe $**
Aussie-run bakery-cafe that does great breakfasts and has veggie options. Closed Tuesdays.

**GETTING THERE & AROUND**

Daily fast ferries (US$25 open return, 40 minutes) connect Koh Rong Sanloem with Koh Rong and Sihanoukville. Confirm your return date in advance. Ferries arrive and depart from Saracen Bay but most also stop at M'Pai Bay.

A slower and cheaper daily cargo boat (US$5, three hours) also links Koh Rong Sanloem, Koh Rong and Sihanoukville. It departs Koh Rong Sanloem at 8am.

Long-tail boats can shuttle you between beaches but are pricey. Count on US$25 to travel from Saracen Bay to M'Pai Bay.

# KAMPOT

Kampot has become an essential stop for travellers thanks to its delectable location on the Prek Tek Chhoun River, which serves as the city's playground. Equally enticing is Kampot's old town, which appears to have gone into hibernation in the 1950s and forgotten to wake up. Beyond Kampot are gorgeous limestone formations bursting with caves and hidden temples, as well as the Bokor Hill Station, a striking and spooky former French retreat inside the Bokor National Park.

Just 8km from the Gulf of Thailand, Kampot was Cambodia's major port until Sihanoukville was founded in 1959. The city has long had an influential Chinese population, who built the shop houses that line the streets of the old town along with some choice remnants of colonial-era architecture. These days Kampot is also home to the largest expat community on the South Coast, which has boosted the city's already decent dining scene.

## TOP TIP

Accommodation options spread along both banks of the river, but the majority of Kampot's tourist infrastructure is in and around the old town, which is easy to navigate on foot or by bike. For trips outside town, hire a motorbike or one of the many motorcycle taxis or *tuk-tuks*.

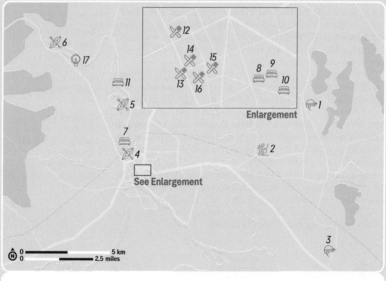

**ACTIVITIES, COURSES & TOURS**
(see 2) Climbodia
1 Phnom Chhnork
2 Phnom Kbal Romeas
3 Phnom Sorsia
4 Prek Tek Chhoun River

5 SUP Asia
6 Tek Chhouu

**SLEEPING**
7 Karma Traders
8 Magic Sponge
9 Monkey Republic

10 Onederz
11 Yellow Sun Hostel

**EATING**
12 Ecran Noodles
13 Fish Market
14 Laundry Cafe Burger Bar

15 Tertulia
16 Twenty Three Bistro

**ENTERTAINMENT**
17 Arcadia Backpackers & Water Park

**Kayaking, 'Green Cathedral'**

# Kayak the Prek Tek Chhoun River

RIVER ROMPS & WATER SPORTS

Rising and falling with the moons, the Prek Tek Chhoun River provides Kampot with a ready-made watersports park. You can swim from almost all the accommodation along the river and most places hire out water transport ranging from kayaks to boats, and even water-skis if you really want to show off.

Head upriver for just a short distance and Kampot's urban sprawl is replaced by dense foliage in different shades of green that lines both banks of the river, along with hidden temples and small fishing villages. Kayakers can head for the so-called 'Green Cathedral', a narrow waterway over which trees and plants have formed a natural arch. The waterway loops off the river around 5km north of Kampot and is a gentle 90-minute paddle. More experienced kayakers can tackle the modest rapids at **Tek Chhouu**, about 10km north of town.

*continued on p229*

## BEST BACKPACKER ACCOMMODATION IN KAMPOT

**Karma Traders $**
The pool and rooftop bar make this a winner. It's a 20-minute walk north of the old town

**Onederz $**
Excellent pool, restaurant, dorms with sizeable lockers, and bright but spartan rooms.

**Monkey Republic $**
Longstanding, efficient and large hostel with spacious dorms and a popular bar.

**Magic Sponge $**
No dorm, but the doubles with shared bathroom are a snip for central Kampot.

**Yellow Sun Hostel $**
Great riverfront location 6km north of Kampot. Dorms and bungalows are basic.

---

 **WHERE TO STAY ON THE RIVER IN KAMPOT**

**Bamboo Bungalows**
Modest and peaceful resort with clean, compact and modern bungalows, rooms and four-bed dorms. $

**Sabay Beach**
Attractive bungalows and rated restaurant on a lovely stretch of the river, 10km north of Kampot. $$

**Amber Kampot**
Luxurious, huge, yet minimalist rooms at this Japanese-owned newcomer. Spa, gym, pool and riverside restaurant. $$$

## KAMPOT OLD TOWN WALKING TOUR

One of the pleasures of a trip to Kampot is idly strolling the streets of the old town, enjoying the vibrant mix of architectural styles: art deco, French colonial and Sino-Portuguese-style shop houses. Kampot's compact centre makes walking easy, but you could also do the following route on a bike.

Start at the **1 Durian Roundabout**, where an oversized durian sculpture overlooks the traffic. Sometimes lit up at night, it's the city's most distinctive landmark and commemorates Kampot's former status as the durian capital of Cambodia. Walk south for 300m to check out the **2 Old Royal Cinema**, an example of modernist Khmer architecture that's now sadly disused, before returning to the roundabout and walking west down St 700 until you reach the riverfront and the 1920s **3 Old French Bridge**, open only to motorcycles and pedestrians. Turn

left at the bridge and head down the riverfront to the 1940s art deco splendour of the **4 Fish Market**, now a popular restaurant.

Opposite the Fish Market is the **5 Old Market**, wrapped in a 1930s concrete art deco facade. This is the heart of the old town and the streets around it are a beguiling mix of Sino-Portuguese-style shop houses and French colonial houses. Some, like the **6 Columns**, have been converted into boutique hotels. Return to the riverfront and walk a few hundred metres south to where a trio of fine French-era buildings await. The **7 Red Cross Building**, **8 National Bank of Cambodia** and **9 Kampot Provincial Museum** (the former governor's mansion) sit close to each other and have all been restored. It's a short walk east from here to the tranquil **10 Lotus Pond**, around which the locals perambulate and where the tour stops.

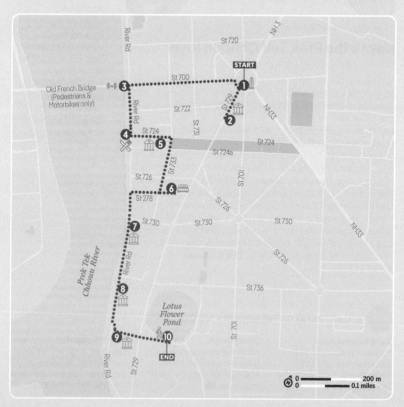

*continued from p227*

Paddleboarding is another popular river activity. **SUP Asia** organises a variety of tours along the river, which include lessons for beginners, as well as venturing to the mangroves on the coast between Kampot and Kep. It also runs customised tours – birdwatching is an option.

If you just want to muck around in the river with a beer close to hand, there's **Arcadia Backpackers & Water Park**. We don't recommend the run-down and basic dorms, but the water slide and zip line are fun. Nonguests can access the water park for US$6.

## Hit the Hills Around Kampot

CAVES & CLIMBING

Just outside Kampot is a breathtaking landscape of foliage-covered limestone formations which glow a dazzling green in the sun and are pockmarked with caves. A trip out to the hills takes visitors along potholed tracks through villages where the durians that Kampot is famous for are grown.

**Phnom Chhnork** rises from rice fields some 12km northeast of Kampot. Guides will be waiting for you, although they're not strictly necessary as you climb the 203-step staircase that leads up the hillside and then down into a cavern that's as graceful as any church. The views from the hill are especially magical in the late afternoon.

Inside the cave are stalactite elephant shapes and tiny chirping bats. The highlight, though, is a remarkable 7th-century brick temple dedicated to the Hindu god Shiva. It's in great condition thanks to the protection afforded by the cave. Also worth a visit is the holy hill of **Phnom Sorsia**, 11km southeast of Phnom Chhnork. It's riddled with caverns, including the White Elephant Cave, where there's a stalagmite resembling a pachyderm's head.

Another great way to experience the hills is to climb them. **Climbodia** runs daily, year-round trips to **Phnom Kbal Romeas**, 7km east of Kampot. Novices are welcome and after climbing and abseiling, you can also do some caving. It can arrange more challenging trips for veteran climbers and spelunkers.

THE GUIDE
SOUTH COAST & ISLANDS

### BEST PLACES TO EAT IN KAMPOT

**Laundry Cafe Burger Bar $**
Kampot's finest burgers – juicy and substantial. Australian, Hawaiian, Khmer and Mexican variations available.

**Ecran Noodles $**
Street-side joint with delicious hand-pulled noodles and dumplings. There are veggie options, too.

**Twenty Three Bistro $$**
Relaxed but sophisticated place with great food and cocktails. Closed Mondays and Tuesdays; book ahead.

**Tertulia $$**
Portuguese fine dining in a colonial-era building. Closed Tuesdays and Wednesdays.

**Fish Market $$**
Tasty dishes, if overpriced. The breezy riverside location in an art deco building is perfect.

### GETTING AROUND

The railway line that connects Kampot with Phnom Penh, Sihanoukville and Kep is slow but scenic and now a popular option with travellers. Daily minivans head to the same destinations. Giant Ibis has two daily buses to Phnom Penh and a night bus to Siem Reap.

*Moto* and *remork-moto* drivers can be found all over town. Most accommodation rents out motorbikes and bicycles, although motorbikes are cheaper at Bison Tours (US$5 per day). Kampot Dirt Bike Shop rents trail bikes for US$25 a day, including helmet and goggles.

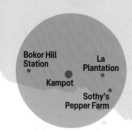

# Beyond Kampot

Venture beyond Kampot for an eerie, desolate French hill station atop a mountain and pepper plantations.

There's far more to the Kampot region than the Prek Tek Chhoun River and limestone karst formations. Travellers can head east or west of Kampot for mountains, relics of the colonial era and pepper plantations.

The Bokor Hill Station sits on a mountain west of Kampot inside the wildlife-rich Bokor National Park, its unsettling buildings acting as derelict reminders of French colonial rule. East of Kampot are the plantations that produce the pepper that Kampot is famous for. Tours of the plantations have become one of the most popular activities for visitors.

Much less seen are the mangrove forests on the coast south of Kampot. The town's tour operators can organise paddleboarding and kayaking trips.

## TOP TIP

Most Kampot accommodation can arrange tours of the surrounding area. They're often the most convenient way to see the sights.

**Bokor Hill Station**

CULTURA RM EXCLUSIVE/GARY LATHAM/GETTY IMAGES ©

Catholic Church, Bokor Hill Station (p232)

# Misty Mountaintop, Spooky Retreat

BOKOR HILL STATION

Sitting atop 1081m-high Phnom Bokor and around 39km west of Kampot (an hour by *tuk-tuk*), **Bokor Hill Station** is a former French retreat constructed so that the colonists could escape the oppressive heat of the lowlands. It's famed for its refreshingly cool climate and creepy derelict buildings that had their heyday before WWII. When mist shrouds the silent structures and the wind keens through them, it can get pretty spooky up here. The dramatic setting attracts filmmakers – Bokor was the location for the climax of the 2002 Cambodia-set movie *City of Ghosts*.

Set in the Damrei Mountains, the hill station was built in the early 1920s, but the French soldiers and settlers didn't get to enjoy it for very long. They abandoned Bokor in the late 1940s, in the face of local insurrections by Khmer groups fighting for independence. Bokor was revived as a resort for rich Cambodians in the early 1960s, but by 1972 it was in the hands of the Khmer Rouge. Bokor was one of the few places the Vietnamese army really had to fight for during their 1979 invasion that toppled Pol Pot's regime, as the Khmer Rouge defended the abandoned buildings for several months. As

## CAMBODIA'S FORMER DURIAN CAPITAL

The giant durian sculpture atop Kampot's main roundabout (p228) isn't just a bizarre example of public architecture, it's a reminder that Kampot was once the durian capital of Cambodia. Durians – a pungent, custard-coloured fruit that's definitely an acquired taste – were the main crop around Kampot, along with pepper, until the civil war of the 1960s and '70s. The durian plantations disappeared with the advent of the Khmer Rouge, who killed their owners and planted rice instead.

But Kampot's durian industry has revived and visitors travelling to the pepper plantations in the area will pass plenty of durian farms. If you want to sample the fruit, there are durian vendors around Kampot's Old Market.

## WHERE TO DRINK IN KAMPOT

**Oh Neil's**
Kampot fixture that winds the clock back to 1990s Southeast Asia. Blues soundtrack, welcoming vibe.

**La Gorda**
Atmospheric bar with artfully distressed walls, decent cocktails, craft beers and a selection of Spanish tapas.

**Rusty Keyhole II**
This British-run place with Sunday roast lunches is where Kampot's expats come to watch sport. Closed Wednesdays.

LENNS/SHUTTERSTOCK ©

**Wat Sampov Pram**

### A WILDLIFE-RICH HERITAGE PARK

Bokor Hill Station is part of the almost 1500-sq-km **Preah Monivong Bokor National Park**, one of only two Association of Southeast Asian Nations (Asean) Heritage Parks in Cambodia. The park gets its name from King Sisowath Monivong, who died at Bokor in 1941.

Most of the park is at an altitude of 1000m. It is home to black and sun bears, gibbons and other primates, clouded leopards, slow lorises, pangolins and over 300 species of bird. Visitors will see plenty of monkeys on the road up to the hill station, but much of the wildlife is nocturnal and stays in the most remote areas to avoid the poachers and illegal loggers who still plague the park.

late as the early 1990s, Bokor was still a stronghold of Khmer Rouge holdouts.

The centrepiece of the hill station is **Le Bokor Palace**, a grand hotel which opened in 1925. It's one of the few buildings still in use, after extensive restoration, but nonguests are currently not allowed inside. It is possible to walk around the hotel, which is a favourite with senior government officials. Nearby is the **Catholic Church**, which still holds its cross aloft, while fragments of glass brick cling to the corners of the nave windows. The subdividing walls inside were added by the Khmer Rouge when they were fighting the Vietnamese.

Also at the summit is **Wat Sampov Pram** where, if the weather is right, there are sensational panoramic views of the coastal plain that surrounds Kampot. Around 4km away are the two-tiered **Popokvil Falls**, which are impressive during the rainy season (June to October).

Bokor was leased to a Cambodian developer in 2008 and visitors will pass numerous half-built hotels and apartment complexes on the access road to the summit. The most glaring sign of development is the vast **Thansur Sokha**

### WHERE TO FIND CAFES IN KAMPOT

**Cafe Espresso**
You can smell the coffee beans roasting as you approach. Quality sandwiches, burgers and wraps, too. **$**

**Epic Arts Cafe**
Affable NGO-backed place with homemade cakes and a shaded terrace. A popular breakfast/brunch stop. **$**

**J-Break**
Join Kampot's hipsters at this big riverside cafe. Western and Khmer dishes and sundowners as well. **$**

**Hotel**, close to Wat Samprov Pram. It looks hideous from the outside, but it has a restaurant – the only other place to eat at Bokor is an overpriced eatery by Popokvil Falls which shuts at 4pm. Rooms are big and well maintained, and much more reasonably priced than the eye-wateringly expensive Le Bokor Palace, should you want to stay overnight and brave Bokor's ghosts.

# Kampot's Pepper Plantations

SPICE UP YOUR LIFE

Before Cambodia's civil war, no Paris restaurant worth its salt would have been without pepper from Kampot Province. Kampot's pepper plantations, though, were all but destroyed by the Khmer Rouge, who believed in growing rice, not spice. But in recent years Kampot pepper – delicate and aromatic but packing a powerful punch – has made a comeback, thanks to a collection of eco-entrepreneurs and foodies who are passionate about pepper.

Most plantations are family farms scattered in the valleys east of Kampot. Some are just across the border in neighbouring Kep Province. Black, red and mild white peppercorns are plucked from the trees from February to May, while the picking season for green pepper is September to February. Tours of the farms, some of which have restaurants, take visitors through the fields and harvesting process, as well as offering the chance to load up with high-grade pepper, a lightweight gift that will stay fresh for years if stored properly.

**La Plantation**, 17km east of Kampot and a 45-minute drive, runs informative daily free tours of its organic farm in English and French, which include spice tasting. Visitors can do a cooking class here. La Plantation also has a shop in Kampot. **Sothy's Pepper Farm**, an hour's drive southeast of Kampot and 15km northeast of Kep, has a worthwhile free tour, a good restaurant and a few rustic bungalows if you want to stay on a working farm.

**BEST PLACES TO STAY IN KAMPOT OLD TOWN**

**Rikitikitavi $$**
Sizeable, stylish rooms with comfy beds. The restaurant–bar is great for a riverside sundowner.

**Hotel Old Cinema $$**
Converted movie palace featuring hip, cosy rooms with cute bathrooms. Small pool and good restaurant.

**Columns $$**
Former shop houses converted into a boutique charmer that blends modern and colonial-period decor.

**Two Moons $$**
Spacious and light rooms and inviting pool just south of the old town. Good family option.

**KAMPOT PEPPER**

Although it's called Kampot pepper, some of the pepper farms are actually around **Kep** (p234) and easy to visit from there. The green peppercorns grown in the area are a great garnish for the crabs that Kep is known for.

**GETTING AROUND**

Motorcyclists will enjoy the switchback ascent, lined with monkeys, to Bokor Hill Station. *Tuk-tuks* do the return trip from Kampot for US$30. Every Kampot hostel runs tours to Bokor, for US$12 to US$15 per person.

A return trip to La Plantation by tuk-tuk will cost US$20. A trip to Sothy's Pepper Farm will cost more; it's easier to access from Kep.

# KEP

Kep is Cambodia's original seaside resort. Founded by French colonists, it became a favoured destination for Khmer high-rollers in the 1960s. The Cambodian royal family holidayed here and the late King Sihanouk's abandoned, unfinished mansion is one of the many derelict modernist villas that are scattered around Kep, contributing to the slightly unreal ambience of the town.

Today, Kep is still popular with locals, who flock to its beach and those of the neighbouring island of Koh Tonsay on weekends and holidays for old-fashioned seaside fun: floating around in inner tubes and feasting on the pepper-flavoured crabs that Kep is famous for.

Many foreigners find it easy to hang out in Kep, too, content to move between their resorts, the beach and crab restaurants, with the option of venturing into Kep National Park for some easy hikes. You're on Kep time here, and the clock runs slow.

## TOP TIP

There's no real centre to Kep, which meanders along the coast for a good 5km. Accommodation is spread out along the shoreline or perched just above the town on the roads that wind towards Kep National Park. Restaurants can be found at the Crab Market or near the beach.

**SIGHTS**
1 Kep National Park
2 Koh Tonsay

**ACTIVITIES,
COURSES & TOURS**
3 Kep Adventures

**SLEEPING**
4 Bird of Paradise
Bungalows
5 Botanica Guesthouse
6 Khmer Hands Resort
7 Knai Bang Chatt
8 Simone Guesthouse
9 Veranda Natural
Resort

**EATING**
10 Holy Crab
(see 10) Kep Su Mer
(see 10) Magic Crab
(see 10) So Kheang

**DRINKING
& NIGHTLIFE**
11 Led Zep Cafe

**Koh Tonsay (p236)**

# Abandoned Villas & Cave Temples

A TOUR OF KEP

Hidden amid overgrown gardens throughout Kep are the husks of once-handsome, now-abandoned **modernist villas**. They are a reminder of Kep's glamorous past as Cambodia's premier seaside destination in the 1950s and '60s. Even now, it's possible to discern the clean lines and lack of adornment that characterised the buildings of the modernist movement. The villas were abandoned when the Khmer Rouge evacuated Kep and killed many of their owners. A few have been renovated, but most have remained empty (bar the ghosts) for over 45 years, quietly decaying even as Kep has rebounded in recent times.

A different sort of journey into darkness are the cave temples hidden in the limestone karst hills east of Kep. **Wat Kiri Sela** is riddled with more than 100 stalactite-laden caverns and passageways that are home to Buddhist shrines. Another 1km on from the temple is a further complex of caves and

**BEST CRAB RESTAURANTS IN KEP**

**Magic Crab $$**
Crabs in coconut sauce or peppered. Generous portions, friendly service and fine sunset views.

**So Kheang $$**
A more local experience than other restaurants at the Crab Market. Peppered crabs are the speciality.

**Kep Su Mer $$**
Solid, reasonably priced crab and seafood dishes, although the atmosphere can be lacking sometimes.

**Holy Crab $$**
Swish design for Kep and it offers both Khmer and European dishes, like crab linguini.

---

🍴 **WHERE TO EAT IN KEP**

**Kep Coffee Cafe**
Substantial breakfasts, salads, burgers and a few Mexican-themed dishes. Shuts at 6pm; closed Mondays. **$**

**Arts Cafe**
NGO-backed place perched over the ocean at the Crab Market. Good Khmer and European food. **$**

**Italian Corner**
Tasty and authentic antipasti, homemade pasta and pizza, plus wine list and tempting desserts. **$**

## BEST PLACES TO STAY IN KEP

**Khmer Hands Resort $**
Basic bungalows and rooms in a lovely garden. Doubles as a hospitality training school.

**Bird of Paradise Bungalows $$**
Cute bungalows set around a jungly garden near the beach and crab market.

**Botanica Guesthouse $$**
French-run, comfortable air-con bungalows with terraces and hammocks. Nice pool.

**Veranda Natural Resort $$$**
Hillside resort with smart wood, bamboo and stone rooms. Great pools and sunset views.

**Knai Bang Chatt $$$**
Seafront resort with good restaurant and service. Rooms are rather simple for the price.

a water hole. Climb the steep and dangerous steps cut into the side of the hill here for great views over the surrounding countryside.

**Kep National Park** snuggles in the hills above Kep and has awesome sea views to the west, south and east. An easily walkable 8km circuit winds through the thickly forested park, which is home to lots of monkeys and birdlife. Check the map at the endearing **Led Zep Cafe** near the park entrance for routes.

# Kicking Back on Koh Tonsay

RUSTIC ISLAND LIFE

Koh Tonsay (Rabbit Island) is the place to come if Kep is just too lively for you. A 20-minute boat ride from Kep, Koh Tonsay is a small, densely forested island that can be circumnavigated in a strenuous two hours and is home to a handful of palm-lined, golden-sand beaches that are a refreshingly rustic alternative to the more glamorous islands off Sihanoukville.

There are no high-end resorts (although one is under construction at the southern tip of Koh Tonsay), just a selection of rudimentary bungalows that look over the main beach (the only one with accommodation). There are a couple of coral reefs on the southern side of the island to explore (bring a mask and snorkel as they can be hard to find on the island), but the main activities are lazing around, beachcombing alongside pecking chickens and friendly dogs, eating seafood and falling asleep to the sound of the waves.

The island gets busy on weekends with local day-trippers, but at other times it's super-relaxed. Some travellers love the vibe here and end up staying for weeks. **Simone Guesthouse** in the middle of the beach has an English-speaking owner and the best restaurant. Beyond Koh Tonsay are tiny **Koh Pos** and **Koh Svay**, which can be visited by long-tail boat. **Kep Adventures** also runs tours to the islands.

### GETTING THERE & AROUND

Kep is a stop on the railway line that links Phnom Penh with Takeo, Kampot and Sihanoukville. A *tuk-tuk* from the station to town is US$5.

Daily minivans run to Phnom Penh, sometimes via Kampot, and Sihanoukville.

Boats to Koh Tonsay (US$25 return for up to six people) leave from Rabbit Island Pier, east of Kep Beach, between 8am and 5pm.

*Tuk-tuks* make the 45-minute run to Kampot for US$10. They can also get you to Wat Kiri Sela. A day hire of a *tuk-tuk* is US$30. Chanthan (096 6520018) is a reliable, English-speaking driver.

Motorbikes (US$5 per day) and bicycles (US$2 per day) can be hired at guesthouses.

# Beyond Kep

Angkor Borei
Phnom Da
Phnom Bayong
Kep    Kirivong
Waterfall

Northeast of Kep are ancient temples, waterfalls and sleepy towns set amid a serene landscape of paddy fields.

Little-visited Takeo Province, to the east of Kep and scrunched up against the border with Vietnam, is predominantly rural and poor, but is also home to some hugely significant pre-Angkorian temples, as well as lakes and waterfalls. Base yourself in the tourist-free provincial capital Takeo. Also called Doun Kaev, this languid lakeside town is known for its freshwater lobster and silk-weaving communities. From Takeo, it's an atmospheric boat ride to the amazing temple-topped hills of Phnom Da and the archaeological museum at Angkor Borei.

South of Takeo is the almost equally ancient clifftop temple of Phnom Bayong and the picturesque Kirivong Waterfall, a top spot for hanging out with the locals.

## TOP TIP

Motorbikes are hard to hire, but motorcycle taxis can get you around. It's wise to book boat transport in advance.

**Temple, Angkor Borei (p238)**

NHUT MINH HO/SHUTTERSTOCK ©

HEMIS / ALAMY STOCK PHOTO ©

Temple, Phnom Da

## TAKEO LOBSTER

**Takeo** is famous for the giant freshwater lobster (otherwise known as crayfish), which is farmed in Roka Khnong Lake. The crustaceans mature between October and December and, at weekends, well-heeled Khmers drive down from Phnom Penh just to sample them. At other times of the year, smaller specimens are available.

Many restaurants in Takeo tempt passers-by with large water tanks of lobsters just waiting to be boiled or grilled alive. Be warned that they don't come cheap: count on US$45 for a kilo of the big boys. Smaller ones go for US$25 a kilo. **Stung Takeo**, a restaurant with an inviting deck over the lake, is a good place to try them.

# Visit a Cradle of Khmer Civilisation

ANGKOR BOREI & PHNOM DA

From the Roka Khnong Lake in Takeo, a 50-minute boat ride along a canal leads to two pre-Angkorian sites that are now regarded as one of the cradles of Khmer civilisation. Archaeologists have discovered items here dating back to 400 BCE, including the earliest-known examples of Khmer inscriptions.

**Angkor Borei** served as an 8th-century capital during the Chenla period. But it was already an important centre during the earlier Funan period between the 1st and 6th centuries CE, when the great maritime trade route between India and China passed the nearby Mekong Delta. A hint of Angkor Borei's former importance can be seen in the moated wall that runs for almost 6km around the village. The small museum at Angkor Borei, which was overhauled in 2019, features exhibits from both the Funan and Chenla periods.

Another 3km on from Angkor Borei is **Phnom Da**, which isn't accessible by boat if water levels are low. The Hindu-influenced temples and grottoes here are where the earliest examples of Khmer sculpture were found. Hike up to the

## WHERE TO SLEEP & EAT IN TAKEO

**Daunkeo Guesthouse**
Big, functional rooms, with communal terraces and a plant-filled garden, by the lake. Slack service. **$**

**Alice Villa**
Takeo's best option: standard rooms are nothing special, but bungalows have comfy beds and decent bathrooms. **$$**

**Le Petit Bistro de Takeo**
It's a pleasure to find this authentic and atmospheric French garden restaurant in sleepy Takeo. **$$**

top of the hill for fantastic views towards Vietnam and the Mekong Delta.

The boat journey to the temples offers great glimpses of rural waterside life, especially in the rainy season (June to October) when the surrounding rice fields are flooded and the landscape is supremely photogenic.

# Clifftop Temple & Mekong Delta Vistas

PHNOM BAYONG & KIRIVONG WATERFALL

Head 43km south of Takeo (an hour by motorbike) through the rice fields and almost to the frontier with Vietnam to reach **Phnom Bayong**, a clifftop temple with stupendous views over the pancake-flat Mekong Delta. During the rainy season (June to October), when the patchwork of rice paddies in the Delta are flooded and glowing a bright lime green, the vista is absolutely magical. Sunset views are jaw-dropping, too.

Phnom Bayong was constructed in the 7th century to celebrate the Chenla Kingdom's vanquishing of Funan, the state which built the temples at Angkor Borei and Phnom Da. The *linga* (phallic symbol) that was originally in the temple's inner circle is now in a Paris museum, but a number of flora- and fauna-themed bas-relief panels can still be seen, for example on the lintels of the three false doorways and carved into the brickwork.

From the parking area it's a 30-minute walk along a twisting, concrete path to the base of the temple (it can also be driven on a motorcycle). From there, it's a 10-minute haul up a crumbling staircase to the temple itself.

The closest town to Phnom Bayong is **Kirivong**, 3km to the east. Around 3.5km west of the town is the gentle and modest **Kirivong Waterfall**, where you can swim. It's fun on weekends when the locals flock here for picnics and bathing.

## GETTING TO VIETNAM FROM KEP & TAKEO

From Kep, the **Prek Chak/Xa Xia border crossing** is popular with travellers heading to Phu Quoc or Ho Chi Minh City. A *tuk-tuk* from Kep to the frontier is US$15. Formalities are normally straightforward, although you may be asked for small additional 'processing' fees. From the border it's 7km by *moto* to Ha Tien (US$5), where there are daily ferries to Phu Quoc and buses to other destinations.

From Takeo, the seldom-used **Phnom Den/Tinh Bien border crossing** connects Cambodia to Chau Doc in Vietnam. The frontier is 47km southeast of Takeo, US$20 to US$25 by *moto*. On the Vietnamese side, bargain hard with waiting *moto* drivers for the 30km ride to Chau Doc (US$15).

## GETTING THERE & AROUND

Takeo is a stop on the train line that runs from Phnom Penh to Sihanoukville via Kep and Kampot. Takeo's station is 4km out of town, a US$2 ride on a moto. Otherwise, any minivan heading north or south to/from Phnom Penh can drop you at Angk Tasaom, 10km northwest of Takeo (US$5 in a *tuk-tuk*).

Book water transport to Angkor Borei and Phnom Da (US$40 return) before you arrive, as there are fewer boats around these days. Kit (092 839654) is a boat driver who has some English. *Moto* and *tuk-tuk* drivers can be found lakeside near the market. A *moto* to Kirivong (for Phnom Bayong) should cost US$20.

Bou Sraa waterfall, Mondulkiri Province (p264)

## THE MAIN AREAS

**KOMPONG CHAM**
Bustling riverside city. p246

**KRATIE**
Dolphins and mellow Mekong
sunsets. p250

**STUNG TRENG**
Mekong Discovery Trail and
gateway to Laos. p254

# EASTERN CAMBODIA

## ECOTOURISM, ELEPHANTS & INDIGENOUS COMMUNITIES

Little-visited eastern Cambodia offers a stunning landscape of forests, hills, rivers and waterfalls and is the best place in the country for wildlife encounters.

In Cambodia's 'Wild East' the paddy fields and sugar palms of the lowlands give way to a majestic panorama of mountains and rainforests cut through by rushing rivers and populated by impressive wildlife. You'll find elephants and singing gibbons in Mondulkiri Province, endangered freshwater Irrawaddy river dolphins around Kratie, as well as an array of rare birds across the region.

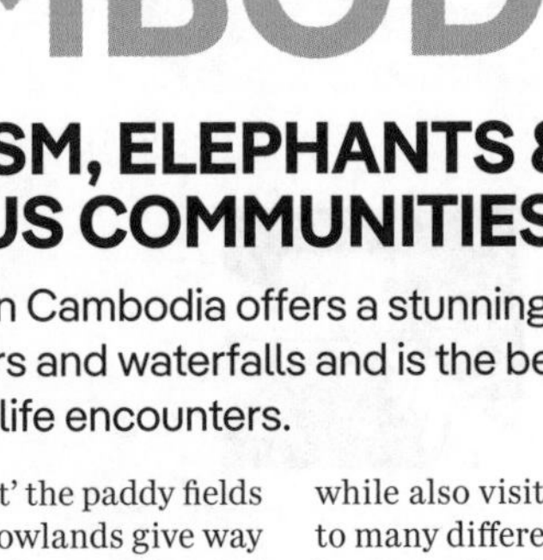

Ecotourism is a big deal here and one of Cambodia's biggest national parks occupies a chunk of the east, where illegal logging and land grabs continue to be a problem in certain areas. Travellers can trek, bike or kayak through the countryside, swim in crater lakes or bathe under waterfalls, while also visiting villages that are home to many different ethnic minority groups, known collectively as Khmer Leu (Upper Khmer) or *chunchiet* (ethnic minorities).

The main towns in Mondulkiri, Ratanakiri and Stung Treng Provinces are little more than overgrown villages, tourist infrastructure is a work in progress and the red-earth roads look like papaya shakes in the rainy season (June to October). But there are plenty of places to stay and the locals are welcoming. In contrast, the riverine towns of Kratie and Kompong Cham are more developed and offer temples and some decent eating options, as well as the chance to kick back and enjoy the fine sight of the sun setting over the Mekong.

©ORAN_SAFAREK/SHUTTERSTOCK ©

---

**RATANAKIRI PROVINCE**
Virachey National Park and ethnic minority villages. p258

**MONDULKIRI PROVINCE**
Elephant and gibbon sanctuaries. p263

241

# Find Your Way

Eastern Cambodia encompasses Kompong Cham
and the four provinces east of the Mekong River:
Kratie, Stung Treng, Ratanakiri and Mondulkiri. Much
of the region is off the tourist map, making it a great
place for adventures.

CAMBODIA

LAOS

Trapeang Kriel○
Preal
Rumke

Thala Boravit
**Stung Treng**

### Stung Treng, p254
Venture north and south of
town for boat, bicycle, kayaking
and trekking trips, as well as
village homestays, along the
worthy Mekong Discovery Trail.

Mekong

Sambor
Sandan
Kampi
Phnom Sombok ○

◉ **Kompong
Thom**

### Kratie, p250
This charmer of a town is the only place
in Cambodia to see Irrawaddy river dolphins and is famed for stunning sunsets
over the Mekong River.

**Kratie**

**Kompong
Chhnang**
◉

Stung
Trang
Spoe
Tbong

Chhlong

Skuon ○  Prey Chor ○

### Kompong Cham, p246
Surrounded by traditional villages and
historic temples, Kompong Cham's
amiable riverside setting offers an
accessible slice of authentic Cambodia.

**Kompong Cham**
Suong
Chup
Prey
Chung
Kran

Krek (Kraek)

Trapeang
Plong

**PHNOM
PENH** ✪

**Prey Veng**
◉
Romeas
Hek

Me Sang

Neak Luong ○  ○ Ba Phnom
Kompong Suong

Banteay
Chakrey
**Svay Rieng** ◉

**Takeo**
◉

Chiph

FROM LEFT: DEMAMIEL62/SHUTTERSTOCK ©, SERGIO CASAL/SHUTTERSTOCK ©

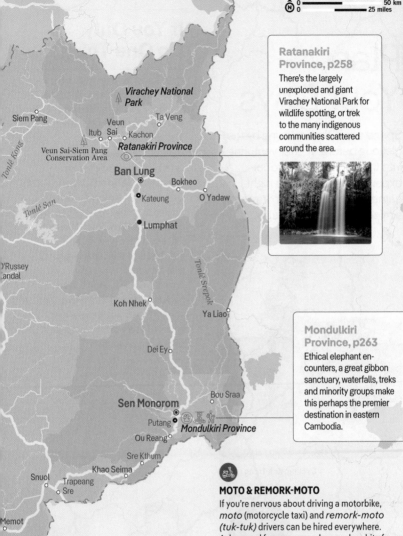

0 — 50 km
0 — 25 miles

Virachey National Park

Siem Pang

Veun Sai

Ta Veng

Itub

Kachon

*Ratanakiri Province*

Veun Sai-Siem Pang
Conservation Area

*Tonlé Kong*

*Tonlé San*

Ban Lung

Bokheo

Kateung

O Yadaw

Lumphat

O'Russey
Landal

*Tonlé Srepok*

Koh Nhek

Ya Liao

Dei Ey

Bou Sraa

Sen Monorom

Putang

*Mondulkiri Province*

Ou Reang

Sre Kthum

Khao Seima

Snuol

Trapeang
Sre

Memot

Bavet

VIETNAM

## Ratanakiri Province, p258

There's the largely unexplored and giant Virachey National Park for wildlife spotting, or trek to the many indigenous communities scattered around the area.

## Mondulkiri Province, p263

Ethical elephant encounters, a great gibbon sanctuary, waterfalls, treks and minority groups make this perhaps the premier destination in eastern Cambodia.

### MOTO & REMORK-MOTO

If you're nervous about driving a motorbike, *moto* (motorcycle taxi) and *remork-moto (tuk-tuk)* drivers can be hired everywhere. Ask around for someone who speaks a bit of English and you'll get an unofficial guide as well.

### CAR & MOTORBIKE

Renting a car and driver to get around eastern Cambodia is a decent choice, as public transport is very limited apart from connections between major towns. Hiring a motorbike is another option, but be aware that the roads are in generally poor condition.

### BUS & MINIVAN

Currently, most public transport in eastern Cambodia is via minivans. They link all the major towns and will pick you up from your accommodation if you book ahead (which is wise). Bus routes are currently limited to services to/from Phnom Penh.

# Plan Your Days

Spend some time relaxing by the Mekong before or after venturing into the uplands for outdoor experiences. Factor in a night camping in the jungle or staying in a minority village homestay.

AFRICA924/SHUTTERSTOCK ©

**Cycling, Koh Trong (p252)**

## If You Only Do One Thing

Make tracks for **Sen Monorom** (p264) in Mondulkiri Province, the base for a visit to the **Elephant Valley Project** (p266) where you can wander the forest alongside rescued pachyderms, or trek into the jungle before dawn at the **Jahoo Gibbon Camp** (p265) to hear the amazing singing of yellow-cheeked crested gibbons. Visiting either of these places will also give you an insight into the life of the Bunong minority, who are deeply involved in both projects. Come nightfall, head back to Sen Monorom, where an impressive dining scene has emerged as a welcome surprise in such a remote spot.

## Seasonal Highlights

Travelling is easiest during the dry season (November to May). June to October is the rainy season, when roads can be difficult.

**JANUARY**

The **Chinese (and Vietnamese) New Year** falls in January or February and the Chinese-Khmer community is out in celebration.

**MARCH**

Low water levels make this a good time for **dolphin watching** and **kayaking** on the Mekong River in Kratie. (p252)

**MAY**

Head for the **mountains** of Ratanakiri and Mondulkiri Provinces to escape the hottest period of the year in the lowlands.

FROM LEFT: HERNAN J. MARTIN/SHUTTERSTOCK ©, NA-ME/SHUTTERSTOCK ©, CAMNET/SHUTTERSTOCK ©

# Three Days to Travel Around

Combine a visit to Mondulkiri Province with kicking back in super-relaxed **Kratie** (p250). Head north of town by kayak or boat to visit the pods of **Irrawaddy river dolphins** (p252) who gamble mid-Mekong here, then spend an afternoon cycling around **Koh Trong** (p252), a small island of farms located just opposite Kratie. Make sure to be back to watch the sun set over the Mekong, one of the pleasures of a visit to Kratie. In the evening, take in some of the fine French colonial architecture before dinner in one of the new Asian fusion restaurants that have opened up.

# More Than a Week

Loop north from Kratie to **Stung Treng** (p254) by mountain bike or long-tail boat, exploring the villages along the **Mekong Discovery Trail** (p256) and sleeping in homestays. From Stung Treng, travel east by minivan to **Ban Lung** (p260), the sleepy capital of Ratanakiri Province. Close to town is emerald-hued **Boeng Yeak Lom** (p260), a candidate for Cambodia's most beautiful lake, as well as several waterfalls. Treks further afield lead to many different indigenous communities, or you can plunge into the 3380 sq km of the **Virachey National Park** (p261), where clouded leopards, elephants, bears, primates and rare birds roam.

**AUGUST**

Eastern Cambodia's **waterfalls** are in full flow thanks to the rainy season; they are less impressive in the dry months.

**SEPTEMBER**

Glorious wildflowers are blooming across Mondulkiri's hills, making it the perfect month to visit the **elephants and gibbons** (p261).

**OCTOBER**

Dragon boats race along the Mekong in Kompong Cham (p246) in honour of **Bon Om Tuk**, Cambodia's annual Water Festival.

**NOVEMBER**

Prime time for **trekking** in Ratanakiri Province (p258). The rains have stopped, but the landscape is still green and inviting.

# KOMPONG CHAM

Kompong Cham

Phnom Penh ✪

Once considered Cambodia's third city, after Phnom Penh and Battambang, Kompong Cham came to prominence as an important trading post in the colonial period thanks to its location on the banks of the Mekong. These days, it's a bustling, low-rise provincial capital that comes alive in the late afternoon and early evening, when the locals promenade along the riverfront in big numbers and the nearby night market gets busy.

The French legacy is visible from the colonial-era buildings, including an old lighthouse, that still dot the city. And all around Kompong Cham are historic temples and traditional farming, fishing and silk-weaving villages, which offer an accessible taste of rural Cambodia.

Fewer foreigners visit than once did, but those who do experience something of Khmer life outside the tourist hubs, making Kompong Cham a worthwhile stop if you're going further north.

## TOP TIP

The majority of Kompong Cham's hotels and restaurants cluster together on or near a stretch of the riverfront that is easy to navigate on foot. You'll also find transport, ATMs and the night market here, while the main shopping market is a couple of blocks back from the river.

FRENTAN/SHUTTERSTOCK ©

**Bamboo bridge, Koh Paen (p249)**

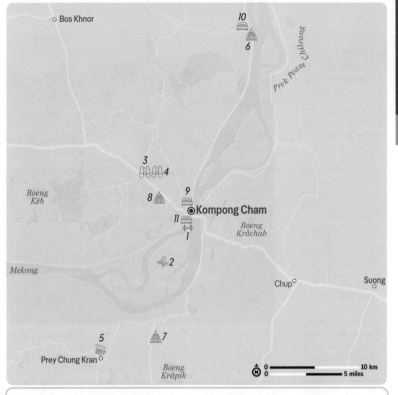

**SIGHTS**
**1** Bamboo Bridge
**2** Koh Paen
**3** Phnom Pros
**4** Phnom Srei
**5** Prey Chung Kran

**6** Wat Hanchey
**7** Wat Maha Leap
**8** Wat Nokor Bachey

**SLEEPING**
**9** Daly Hotel

**10** Hanchey
Bamboo Resort
**11** KC River Hotel
**(see 9)** LBN Asian Hotel
**(see 9)** Tmor Da
Guesthouse

**EATING**
**(see 9)** Lazy
Mekong Daze

# Kompong Cham's Historic Temples

UNIQUE PAGODAS & FINE MEKONG VIEWS

Commanding some of the best Mekong River views in all Cambodia, the hilltop **Wat Hanchey** was an important centre of worship in the pre-Angkorian Chenla period. If you can tear your eyes away from the superb sight of the Mekong winding through the surrounding countryside, you'll find the remains of several 8th-century structures in the large compound. The absolute highlight is a remarkable Chenla-era brick sanctuary with well-preserved inscriptions in ancient Sanskrit on the doorframe. Wat Hanchey is 20km north of Kompong Cham on a not very good road.

Southeast of Kompong Cham is beautiful **Wat Maha Leap**, one of the last wooden pagodas still standing in Cambodia.

## GETTING TO VIETNAM FROM KOMPONG CHAM & KRATIE

From Kompong Cham, the **Trapeang Plong/Xa Mat** border crossing is convenient for Ho Chi Minh City. Hop on any minivan heading to Snuol on NH7 and get off at the roundabout in Krek (Kraek). From there, it's a 20km *moto* ride south to the border. Make sure you already have a visa for Vietnam, if you require one.

From Kratie, the closest border crossing is **Trapeang Sre/Loc Ninh**. Head first to Snuol and then catch a *moto* 18km south to the border. You'll need a Vietnam visa if your nationality requires one. On the Vietnamese side, *moto* drivers and taxis can take you to the nearest town, Binh Long.

PETER STUCKINGS/SHUTTERSTOCK ©

**Wat Hanchey (p247)**

The structure is supported by wide tree trunks painted black and resplendent in gilded patterns, while the central part of the ceiling is covered in intricate panels depicting the life of Buddha. You can travel here by private boat from July to December for great glimpses of riverside life; otherwise it's a 40km trip by road.

Also worth checking out are **Phnom Pros (Man Hill)** and **Phnom Srei (Woman Hill),** which offer fine views from the pagodas that sit atop them. They are around 7km northwest of town. Combine your visit with a stop at **Wat Nokor Bachey**, where the original 12th-century structure has been artfully absorbed into a thoroughly modern temple.

 **WHERE TO EAT IN KOMPONG CHAM**

**Smile Restaurant**
Longstanding, NGO-backed, bright and friendly place with a menu of European, Khmer and Southeast Asian classics. **$$**

**Lazy Mekong Daze**
English-speaking owner serves up the tastiest pizzas in town. It also acts as a mellow riverfront bar. **$$**

**Night Market**
Locals flock here for cheap eats. There are many food stands on the riverfront as well. **$**

# Silk-Weaving Villages & Mekong Islands

A TASTE OF COUNTRY LIFE

Any journey outside Kompong Cham plunges you straight into a landscape of stilted wooden houses in villages linked by rickety bridges over the tributaries of the Mekong, interspersed by corn fields and rubber plantations. Journeys to the surrounding temples will give you a taste of rural Cambodian life, but Kompong Cham is also renowned for its high-quality silk and you'll see many traditional weaving looms in the nearby villages.

The tiny settlement of **Prey Chung Kran** is the centre of the local silk-weaving industry, known for its *krama*, the scarves that are a symbol of Khmer identity. The village is about 4km from Wat Maha Leap (p247) and it's fascinating to watch the weavers at work. The dyeing process is especially interesting, as that's when the typical diamond-and-dot tessellations on a *krama* are created.

You can also experience rural living on **Koh Paen**, a serene island of fruit and vegetable farms that sits in the Mekong just south of Kompong Cham. A splendid **bamboo bridge** links Koh Paen to the mainland during the dry season (November to May). It's built by hand every year and from a distance looks like it's made out of matchsticks. Sandbars appear around the island in the dry season, too, acting as makeshift beaches. There are other little-seen Mekong islands upriver; **Lazy Mekong Daze** can arrange boat trips to them.

## BEST PLACES TO STAY IN KOMPONG CHAM

**Tmor Da Guesthouse $**
Comfortable budget riverfront digs. Some rooms have balconies and river views.

**Daly Hotel $**
Impersonal but efficient hotel with large rooms, one street back from the river.

**Hanchey Bamboo Resort $$**
Spacious bungalows and a simple dorm on a hilltop; great Mekong views.

**LBN Asian Hotel $$**
The town's smartest option: decent beds and bathrooms, restaurant and rooftop bar.

**KC River Hotel $$**
Less swish twin to the LBN at the other end of the riverfront.

## GETTING AROUND

Kompong Cham is 120km northeast of Phnom Penh. Currently, minivans make the three-hour journey. Minivans also connect Kompong Cham with Kratie and Stung Treng. There are no scheduled boat services from Kompong Cham any more, but Lazy Mekong Daze can arrange a private boat to Kratie.

*Moto* and *remork-moto* drivers congregate on the riverfront near the hotels and guesthouses. Expect to pay US$25 to US$30 a day for a *remork-moto*, or US$15 to US$20 for a *moto*, to the surrounding sights. Motorbikes and bicycles (US$7/2 per day) can be hired from Lazy Mekong Daze.

# KRATIE

Kratie (pronounced 'kra-cheh') is a supremely mellow riverside town that often prompts travellers to linger for longer than they expected. Now the only place in mainland Cambodia to see rare freshwater Irrawaddy river dolphins, Kratie also enjoys some of the country's most photogenic Mekong sunsets.

Spared the wartime bombing that destroyed so many other provincial capitals, the town still has some well-preserved colonial-era architecture as well as temples in the surrounding countryside. And just across the Mekong is Koh Trong, a car-free island that offers a slice of rural life.

But Kratie is as much about atmosphere as it is about sights. Watching the red sun sink into the Mekong, cold drink in hand, never gets old. Word about Kratie is spreading and you'll find the beginning of a travellers' scene here. It's also a logical place to break the journey if you're travelling further north or to Laos.

Kratie

Phnom Penh ✪

## TOP TIP

Most of Kratie's tourist infrastructure is on or near the riverfront in the centre of town. *Remork-moto* and *moto* drivers can spin you out to the sights, or you can rent a motorbike or bicycle.

V.OFF/SHUTTERSTOCK ©

**Koh Trong (p252)**

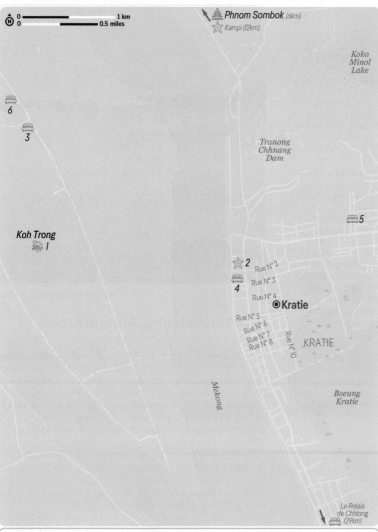

**HIGHLIGHTS**
1 Koh Trong

**ACTIVITIES,
COURSES & TOURS**
2 Cambodian Rural
Discovery Tours

**(see 2)** Sorya
Kayaking Adventures

**SLEEPING**
3 Koh Trong
Community Homestay 1
4 Mekong Dolphin Hotel

5 River Dolphin Hotel
6 Soriyaburi
Villas Resort
**(see 2)** Sorya
Guesthouse

## ISLAND LIFE

**Koh Trong** sits opposite Kratie in the middle of the Mekong and offers the chance to experience a traditional farming community. Pomelos are the big crop; there's also a floating Vietnamese village off the island's southwest coast.

A 13km concrete path loops around car-free Koh Trong, making cycling easy (hire bikes at the ferry dock). You can stay at the **Koh Trong Community Homestay 1** or there's the upmarket Soriyaburi Villas Resort.

The ferry for Koh Trong makes the 10-minute crossing frequently from a dock around 300m north of the Sorya Guesthouse.

CHARLIE WARADEE/SHUTTERSTOCK ©

Dolphin-spotting tour, Kratie

# Dolphin Watching Around Kratie

UP CLOSE WITH IRRAWADDY RIVER DOLPHINS

**Kampi**, about 15km north of Kratie, is the only place in mainland Cambodia where you can get up close with endangered freshwater Irrawaddy river dolphins. Until very recently, dolphins could also be seen further north near the border with Laos, but that community has sadly died out. Now there are just 92 dolphins in Cambodia, inhabiting a 190km stretch of the Mekong running north from Kratie, according to the WWF. They are equally scarce elsewhere in Southeast Asia.

The blue-grey cetaceans can grow up to 2.75m long and are recognisable by their bulging foreheads and small dorsal fins. They can live in fresh or saltwater, although they are seldom spotted in the sea. For more on these rare creatures, check worldwildlife.org/species/irrawaddy-dolphin.

Before the civil war, Cambodia was thought to be home to as many as 1000 river dolphins. But during the Khmer Rouge period, many were hunted for their oils. Their numbers continued to plummet in the decades that followed, even as efforts to protect them were stepped up, including a ban on fishing and commercial motorised boat traffic on parts of the

## WHERE TO EAT IN KRATIE

**Street Three Eatery**
Khmer cuisine with a twist and European breakfasts. Fresh, locally sourced ingredients and a nice vibe. **$**

**Mekong MoJo**
New vegan place with a chilled courtyard setting. Tasty Asian fusion menu and cocktails, too. **$$**

**Jasmine Boat Restaurant**
Overpriced pan-Asian and European dishes on the riverfront, but good for a happy-hour sundowner. **$$**

Mekong between Kratie and Stung Treng. Those measures may finally be paying off, as the dolphin population has seen a small increase since 2015.

From Kampi, motorboats make hour-long trips out onto the Mekong to view the dolphins at close quarters. The pods tend to congregate close to the eastern bank of the river and you can view them from between 10m and 40m away. Often, there's only one or two boats out on the river and it's easy to see the dolphins as they surface and arch out of the water before diving. Boat drivers cut their engines once they get near the dolphins as the sound disturbs them. The dolphins can be seen year-round and are active throughout the day.

A more ecofriendly and energetic way to view the dolphins is by kayak. Kratie-based **Sorya Kayaking Adventures** runs excellent half-day tours that take you past secluded sandbar beaches and through flooded forest, getting you near the dolphins without any engine noise. Its fleet of kayaks includes tandem ones. **Cambodian Rural Discovery Tours** in Kratie also offers a worthwhile one-day dolphin tour, while **SUP Asia**, based in Kampot (p226), has one-day paddleboard tours to see the dolphins.

Combine a journey out to Kampi with a stop at **Phnom Sombok**, where mischievous macaque monkeys line the stairs leading to a small hilltop pagoda with great views of the Mekong. The temple is just off the road between Kratie and Kampi.

## BEST PLACES TO STAY IN KRATIE

**Sorya Guesthouse $**
Genial staff and a top-floor restaurant/bar.

**River Dolphin Hotel $**
Away from the riverfront and looking its age, but an OK budget option.

**Mekong Dolphin Hotel $$**
The big rooms are comfortable and some have river views and balconies.

**Soriyaburi Villas Resort $$$**
Stylish rooms set around a super garden on Koh Trong, with a pool and restaurant.

**Le Relais de Chhlong $$$**
Riverside colonial-era hotel 30km south of Kratie with a garden, pool and restaurant.

### MORE DOLPHIN SPOTTING

Apart from Kratie, the only other places in Cambodia to see dolphins are on the South Coast at the **Prek Touek Sap Estuary** (p213) and nearby **Koh Thmei** (p213), both part of the Ream National Park.

### GETTING AROUND

Daily minivans connect Kratie to Phnom Penh, Siem Reap, Kompong Cham, Sen Monorom, Ban Lung and Stung Treng, where you can catch onward transport to the border with Laos.

Private boat trips can be arranged by guesthouses and Cambodian Rural Discovery Tours. Most guesthouses rent motorbikes and bicycles (US$7/4 per day).

*Moto* and *remork-moto* drivers can get you to the sights. Count on US$12 for a return trip in a *tuk-tuk* to see the dolphins or US$25 for a full-day hire.

# STUNG TRENG

● Stung Treng

Phnom Penh ✪

Just 65km south of the frontier with Laos, scrappy Stung Treng is a starting point for adventures along the worthy Mekong Discovery Trail, which heads north of Stung Treng and south to Kratie, shadowing the Mekong all the way. If you're travelling to or from Laos, you'll also pass through here.

Located on the Tonlé San River, close to its confluence with the Mekong, Stung Treng's unremarkable appearance belies the fact that this region has a long history as part of both the Angkorian Empire and various Lao kingdoms, before being assigned to Cambodia by the French during the colonial period. It's not unusual to hear Lao spoken here.

Beyond Stung Treng town are forests, rivers and waterfalls and many opportunities for trekking, biking and kayaking. You are likely to have them all to yourself, as the area's obvious tourist potential remains largely untapped.

## TOP TIP

Hotels, restaurants, banks, minivans and *motos* congregate around Stung Treng's main market, a block back from the riverfront. There are currently very few motorbikes available for hire, but accommodation can arrange transport. It's not uncommon to hear Lao spoken here.

SOK RATHA/SHUTTERSTOCK ©

**Preh Nimith waterfall (p257)**

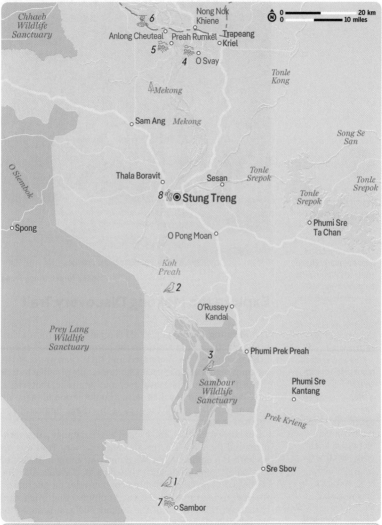

**Flooded forest, Stung Treng**

### BEST PLACES TO STAY IN STUNG TRENG

**Savet Guesthouse $**
These budget digs near the market have spacious rooms with balconies and hot water. Helpful owner.

**Apsara Guesthouse $**
Close to the river and transport, with hot water and clean rooms. No English spoken.

**4 Rivers Hotel $$**
The most appealing option: river views, restaurant and a rooftop bar that's open sometimes.

**Angkor Meas Hotel $$**
Anonymous but modern and well-kept Chinese-style hotel. Also has a restaurant and small pool.

# Explore the Mekong Discovery Trail

TRAVEL THE UNSEEN MEKONG

The **Mekong Discovery Trail** is a network of routes running for 180km from Kratie to the border with Laos, taking in some of the least populated and little-seen areas of the Mekong region in northeast Cambodia. It's possible to trek the different trails or travel by mountain bike, motorbike, long-tail boat and kayak or with a combination of them all. Accommodation along the way is in village homestays or you can camp.

Established in 2006, and backed by the Cambodian government and the UNWTO, the Mekong Discovery Trail was set up with the laudable aim of opening up community-based tourism in some of the least visited parts of Cambodia. One of the goals was to give fishing communities an alternative income, to help protect the river dolphins and other rare species on this stretch of the Mekong. Official funding for the programme has now lapsed, but a number of private tour companies keep the trail alive.

 **WHERE TO EAT IN STUNG TRENG**

**Ponika's Palace**
English-speaking owner serves up a tasty mix of European, Indian and Khmer dishes. Cold beers, too. **$**

**Sidewalk Cafe**
Burgers, sandwiches and good coffee (as well as glacial air-con) in a cheerful, popular setting. **$**

**Blue River**
Floating on the river, this is the most atmospheric Khmer restaurant in Stung Treng. **$$**

North of Stung Treng and close to the frontier with Laos, the trail hugs one of the Mekong's wildest and most beguiling stretches. Destinations include the villages of **Preah Rumkel** and **O'Svay**, which have emerged as modest ecotourism hubs thanks to the chance to boat or kayak through flooded forests and around dozens of small islands. There's also the magnificent sight of the Mekong rapids cascading down from Laos here, as well as the massive **Preh Nimith waterfall**, both especially impressive in the rainy season (June to October). You'll find good trekking here, too. Sadly, the small pod of Irrawaddy river dolphins that once inhabited the Mekong near Preah Rumkel has now died out.

Highlights of the trail south of Stung Treng include the islands of **Koh Preah**, **Koh Pdao**, where you may see river dolphins, and **Koh Samseb**. All three are renowned for birdwatching and visitors can take part in community activities. Also popular is the village of **Sambor** – it's home to historic **Wat Sorsor Moi Roi**, which features a few pillars from the original 19th-century wooden structure.

In Stung Treng, **Cambodia Mekong Trail** (also known as **Xplore-Cambodia**) is your best option for journeys along the trail. They organise tours ranging from one to seven days, including a three-day mountain-bike trip between Stung Treng and Kratie (they will transfer your luggage). They can also arrange long-tail boats from the Lao border to Stung Treng and on to the Mekong islands and Kratie, as well as kayaking, trekking, homestays and camping. In Kratie, **Cambodian Rural Discovery Tours** (p253) offers tours to Koh Pdao and to fishing villages along the trail, while **NTFP-EP Cambodia** arranges trips to Koh Pdao and Koh Samseb and a couple of community-based tourism projects in Stung Treng. Book all of these in advance.

## GETTING TO LAOS FROM STUNG TRENG

The remote **Trapeang Kriel/Nong Nok Khiene** border crossing is 65km north of Stung Treng on a not very good road. It's useful for travellers on the overland route through Southeast Asia. Minivans (US$30) depart daily at 1pm from Stung Treng's market for Pakse and Don Det in Laos. You can also hire a car or *moto* to the border, but little onward transport hangs around the Lao side.

Laos visas are available at the border for US$40 (bring passport photos). You may also be asked for a small 'processing' fee. If you're coming from Laos, Cambodia visas at this border cost US$35.

### GETTING AROUND

Daily minivans connect Stung Treng with Phnom Penh, Siem Reap, Kratie, Ban Lung in Ratanakiri Province and Don Det and Pakse in Laos. All depart from the main market, where *moto* and *remork-moto* drivers can also be found. Ponika's Palace has a sole motorbike for rent (US$8 per day). Cambodia Mekong Trail has mountain bikes for hire (US$5 per day). Hotels and tour operators can arrange a car and driver.

# RATANAKIRI PROVINCE

Ratanakiri
Province

Phnom Penh ✪

Remote Ratanakiri Province is a diverse region of outstanding natural beauty that's home to a mosaic of different peoples: the Jarai, Tompuon, Brau and Kreung, as well as Lao. The vast Virachey National Park with its rare wildlife occupies much of the northeast of the province. Treks to minority villages are popular.

The provincial capital Ban Lung is the base for Ratanakiri romps. Ban Lung's most lively spot is its market, where minority people from the surrounding villages gather daily. Just outside town are waterfalls and one of Cambodia's most beautiful lakes.

Ratanakiri is among Cambodia's poorest and least developed provinces, as indicated by the rough roads. You can tell if it's the dry or rainy season here by whether you're covered in red dust or red mud. The best time to visit is November, when the rains are over but the landscape is still verdant.

## TOP TIP

Most hotels, guesthouses, restaurants and banks are near the market or around Boeng Kansaign, the small lake in the centre of Ban Lung. The town is fairly spread out, but motorbikes and bicycles can be rented from guesthouses. *Moto* and *remork-moto* drivers can get you to the nearby sights.

KARIN DE MAMIEL/GETTY IMAGES ©

**Viewing platform, Boeng Yeak Lom (p260)**

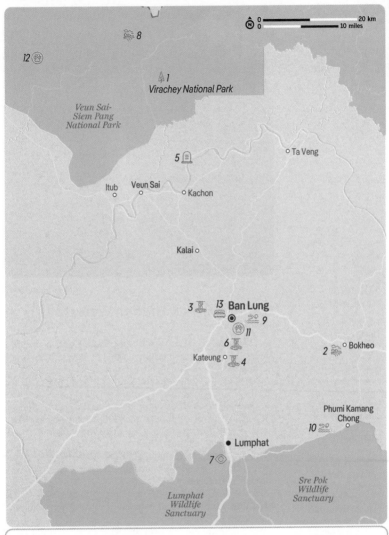

0 ━━━━━━━━━━ 20 km
0 ━━━━━━━━ 10 miles

🗢 8

12 🐾

⛰ 1
**Virachey National Park**

*Veun Sai-
Siem Pang
National Park*

5 🪦

Itub ○   Veun Sai ○   ○ Kachon

○ Ta Veng

Kalai ○

3 ⚱   13 **Ban Lung**
🛏 ⊙
🐾 11   🏊 9
6 ⚱
Kateung ○ ⚱ 4

2 🗢 ○ Bokheo

Phumi Kamang
Chong
10 🏊   ○

● Lumphat

7 ◎

*Sre Pok
Wildlife
Sanctuary*

*Lumphat
Wildlife
Sanctuary*

| | | | |
|---|---|---|---|
| **HIGHLIGHTS**<br>**1** Virachey National Park<br><br>**SIGHTS**<br>**2** Bokheo<br>**3** Chaa Ong Waterfall<br>**4** Ka Tieng Waterfall | **5** Kaoh Paek<br>**6** Kinchaan Waterfall<br>**7** Lumphat<br>**8** Veun Sai<br><br>**ACTIVITIES,**<br>**COURSES & TOURS**<br>**9** Boeng Yeak Lom | **10** Lumkut Lake<br>**11** Parrot Tours<br>**12** Veun Sai-Siem Pang<br>Conservation Area<br><br>**SLEEPING**<br>**13** Family<br>House Homestay | **(see 13)** Ratanakiri<br>Boutique Hotel<br>**(see 13)** Terres<br>Rouges Lodge<br>**(see 13)** Thy Ath Lodge<br>**(see 11)** Tree<br>Top Ecolodge |

VLADIMIR ZHOGA/SHUTTERSTOCK ©

**Chaa Ong waterfall**

**BAN LUNG
TO VIETNAM**

The **O'Yadaw/Le Thanh** border crossing offers quick access to Pleiku in Vietnam. Daily minivans (US$15) connect Ban Lung with Pleiku in five hours. Border formalities are straightforward but make sure you have a Vietnam visa if your nationality requires it.

You can also take a minivan from Ban Lung's market to O'Yadaw and then hop on a *moto* to the border. *Motos* await on the Vietnam side for the 20km journey to Duc Co, where you can catch a bus to Pleiku.

# Crater Lakes & Hidden Waterfalls

SWIMMING IN THE JUNGLE

Just outside Ban Lung is **Boeng Yeak Lom**, a dreamy, emerald-hued crater lake surrounded by jungle. This is one of the most serene and beautiful spots in Cambodia and the water is clear, cool and refreshing. It's a sacred place for the local Tompuon minority, who manage the area. Some of the proceeds from the admission fee go to nearby villages.

There are no trips out onto the 800m-wide lake – the Tompoun people don't do boats – but you can swim from wooden jetties. Keep in mind that there are no lifeguards here, but there are eddies in the middle of the 50m-deep lake. Avoid Boeng Yeak Lom on weekends and holidays, when it's very popular with locals.

If you want a forest-fringed crater lake all to yourself, try **Lumkut Lake**, 48km southeast of Ban Lung. Poor roads mean that access can be difficult in the rainy season (June to October).

Waterfalls are hidden away among the cashew and rubber plantations that surround Ban Lung. Three in particular are worth visiting, especially in the rainy season: **Kinchaan** and **Ka Tieng** are both wide and impressive, while **Chaa Ong** has the highest fall of water.

## WHERE TO EAT IN BAN LUNG

**Green Carrot**
Popular restaurant serving surprisingly sophisticated European and Khmer fare. Veggie and vegan options too. $

**Ta Nam**
Visit this locals' spot for inviting noodle dishes, Vietnamese-style rice porridge and fruit shakes. It closes at 3pm. $

**Coconut Shake Restaurant**
Simple Khmer dishes and coconut shakes at this lakeside hangout for Ban Lung's hipsters. $

You can visit Boeng Yeak Lom and the waterfalls by *tuk-tuk*. Think twice about driving yourself on a motorbike in the rainy season, when the dirt tracks leading to the waterfalls are extremely treacherous.

# Wild Encounters in Virachey National Park

JUNGLE TREKS & WILDLIFE SPOTTING

The massive **Virachey National Park** stretches east to Vietnam, north to Laos and west to Stung Treng Province. Covering 3380 sq km of some of the most isolated jungle, grasslands and mountains in Cambodia, this is the second-largest of the country's national parks and much of it remains unexplored. It's home to elephants, clouded leopards, sun bears, gibbons and other primates, deer, pangolins and the great hornbill, as well as 60 ethnic minority villages scattered around the edges of the park.

So important is Virachey to the Mekong region that it became an Asean Heritage Park in 2003. The park is one of the better-managed ecotourism projects in Cambodia and treks are arranged via private tour companies. Note that many companies are only allowed to lead treks in the park buffer zone, where there's far less wildlife. Contact **Parrot Tours** in Ban Lung to get inside the park proper with minority guides who can speak some English.

The further you venture into the park, the better your chances of seeing rare animals. The signature trek is the **Phnom Veal Thom Wilderness Trek**, a six- to seven-day odyssey which takes visitors deep into the jungle and grasslands where the wildlife is abundant. You'll camp or stay in minority homestays; there's a maximum of six people per trek. January to March is the best time for animal encounters.

# Minority Villages, Cemeteries & Gibbons

TRAVEL UPRIVER TO INDIGENOUS COMMUNITIES

Around 39km northwest of Ban Lung is **Veun Sai**, a sprawling riverside cluster of ethnic minority, Chinese and Lao villages occupying both banks of the Tonlé San. It's known especially for its minority cemeteries. Ratanakiri's *chunchiet* (minorities) bury their dead in the jungle, carving effigies of the deceased to stand guard over the graves. Traditionally, two carved wooden figures (normally male and female) occupy one side of

---

## BEST PLACES TO STAY IN BAN LUNG

**Family House Homestay $**
Friendly place with bungalows, big rooms, a dorm and a cute garden.

**Tree Top Ecolodge $**
Wooden, fan-only bungalows set around a rustic garden. Good views from the restaurant.

**Ratanakiri Boutique Hotel $$**
Comfortable, modern rooms with balconies and fine lake views.

**Thy Ath Lodge $$**
Slightly dated but spacious rooms, some with lake views. There's an attached cafe.

**Terres Rouges Lodge $$$**
Former governor's lakeside mansion, now a stylish hotel with a pool and restaurant.

---

## GIBBON EXPERIENCES

As well as spotting gibbons in Veun Sai, you can also see and hear the world's largest population of rare yellow-cheeked crested gibbons at the excellent **Jahoo Gibbon Camp** (p265) in Mondulkiri Province.

---

 **BAN LUNG TOUR OPERATORS**

**Parrot Tours**
Organises treks inside Virachey National Park, as well as to Veun Sai and minority villages.

**DutchCo Trekking Cambodia**
Specialises in two- to five-day treks in Veun Sai and around Virachey National Park.

**Sona Trekking & Tours**
Sona is half-Kreung, speaks good English and can get you to minority villages; contact him at sonatours168@gmail.com.

## GHOST TOWNS & GEM MINES

Ghost towns stand as testament to Ratanakiri's bitter recent history. Former provincial capital **Lumphat** never recovered from US bombing and is now home to fewer than 800 people, its environs studded with bomb craters. Lumphat is 35km south of Ban Lung on the Tonlé Srepok, the river said to be depicted in the seminal Vietnam War film *Apocalypse Now*.

Ratanakiri means 'gem mountains' in Khmer, and the zircon and amethyst the province is known for has long been exploited. **Bokheo**, close to Lumkut Lake (p260), is a gem mining hotspot. The miners dig large pits and then tunnel horizontally for the precious stones. Ban Lung tour operators can arrange trips to Lumphat and Bokheo.

Tree Top Ecolodge, Ban Lung (p261)

the grave, with two buffalo horns on the other. Newer tombs have figures carved in concrete with modern accessories like mobile phones and sunglasses.

Most cemeteries are strictly off-limits to foreigners. One exception is an ethnic Kachah cemetery in **Kaoh Paek**, a 45-minute boat ride upriver from Veun Sai. **Family House Homestay** (p261) and other tour operators in Ban Lung can arrange visits. If you go, remember the cemeteries are sacred sites, act respectfully, touch nothing and ask permission before taking photos.

Also north of Veun Sai is the memorable **Veun Sai-Siem Pang Conservation Area**, where visitors overnight in the jungle or sleep in a minority homestay before waking early to see and hear northern buffed-cheeked gibbons. The gibbons can only be seen in the dry season (November to June) and visits are limited to six people at a time. **Parrot Tours** (p261) can arrange tours for a group of four to six people.

## GETTING AROUND

Ban Lung is 510km northeast of Phnom Penh. There are daily minivans to Phnom Penh, Siem Reap, Stung Treng, Sen Monorom, Pleiku in Vietnam and Pakse and Don Det in Laos (change vans in Stung Treng). There's also an overnight bus to Phnom Penh.

Guesthouses and Parrot Tours (p261) rent motorbikes and bicycles (US$8/4). *Moto* and *remork-moto* drivers hang out at the market. Mr Happy is a reliable English-speaking *tuk-tuk* driver and guide; contact him through Tree Top Ecolodge (p261). Count on US$35 for a day trip by *tuk-tuk* to sights around Ban Lung.

# MONDULKIRI PROVINCE

Mondulkiri
Province

Phnom Penh ✪

Mondulkiri Province offers a completely different landscape to the lowlands of Cambodia. Instead of rice paddies and palm trees, there's a seductive mix of rolling hills, plains and rainforest in which elephants, primates, bears and very rare Indochinese leopards wander. At an average elevation of 800m, Mondulkiri is windier and cooler than other parts of Cambodia, so bring something warm for the evenings. This is the most sparsely populated region of the country, too, with just six people per square kilometre, so there's no need to worry about crowds.

Sen Monorom, a friendly, overgrown village with a solid dining scene, is the provincial capital and the launching pad for jaunts into the surrounding hills. Ethical elephant and gibbon encounters are the big draw, but the area around Sen Monorom is also dotted with hidden waterfalls and villages that are home to the Bunong minority, making this fine trekking country.

## TOP TIP

Budget hotels, restaurants and banks surround Sen Monorom's market, but smarter accommodation is on the outskirts of town. The major sights are all outside Sen Monorom, but *moto* and *remork-moto* drivers can get you around or cars can be arranged via your hotel.

SNUDUWELA/SHUTTERSTOCK ©

**Trekking, Elephant Valley Project (p266)**

263

**SIGHTS**
1 Bou Sraa Waterfall
2 Keo Seima Wildlife Sanctuary
3 Monorom Falls
4 Romanear Waterfall

**ACTIVITIES, COURSES & TOURS**
5 Elephant Valley Project
6 Jahoo Gibbon Camp
7 Mondulkiri Project

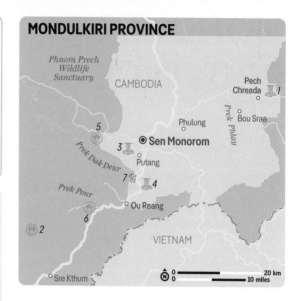

MONDULKIRI PROVINCE

**TREAD LIGHTLY IN THE HILLS**

Tourism brings many benefits to indigenous communities, but there are also negatives: environmental degradation, the domination of the tourism industry by lowland Khmers and the tendency of some visitors to disregard local customs.

The best way to tread lightly in the hills is to hire indigenous guides. The Bunong know the forests better than anyone, and it ensures that some tourist dollars are going directly to Bunong communities. Travelling with a local will enhance your experiences in minority villages, as they will be able to explain the traditions and taboos.

# Bunong Villages & Waterfalls

EXPERIENCE TRADITIONAL BUNONG LIFE

The region around Sen Monorom is the homeland of the Bunong people, the most populous of the ethnic minorities who inhabit the uplands of Cambodia (far more Bunong live across the nearby border with Vietnam, where they are known as the Mnong). Traditionally animist, although many have been converted to Christianity by missionaries, the Bunong are known for their close relationship with the elephants found in Mondulkiri and the efficacy of their traditional herbal medicine.

There are many Bunong villages outside Sen Monorom and day or multiday treks with indigenous Bunong guides can be organised with **Mondulkiri Project**, a local tour company and NGO, or through guesthouses. Many tours offer some form of interaction with elephants, usually walking with them or feeding or washing them. We recommend strongly that you avoid any tour offering elephant rides.

Almost all treks will include stops at some of the waterfalls interspersed among the pepper, coffee, cassava and cashew plantations that are dotted around Sen Monorom. The most impressive is **Bou Sraa**, a double-drop waterfall that plunges into dense jungle and is famous across Cambodia. Others

 **WHERE TO STAY IN SEN MONOROM**

**Avocado Guesthouse**
Compact and clean rooms with hot water. Coffee shop and close to the market and transport. $

**Tree Lodge**
Basic wooden bungalows sprawling down a hillside; it's also the home of Mondulkiri Project. $

**Nature Lodge**
Appealing midranger with a restaurant and comfortable wooden bungalows spread across a large garden. $$

**Bunong village, Sen Monorom**

### WILDLIFE GALORE

The Jahoo Gibbon Camp is part of the almost 3000 sq km of the **Keo Seima Wildlife Sanctuary**, which stretches from Mondulkiri to Kratie Province. The sanctuary is a biodiversity hotspot, with over 950 species including critically endangered Indochinese leopards, elephants, numerous primates, sun bears, wild pigs, deer, lorises and civets. There's also a huge amount of birdlife, such as giant hornbill and peafowl.

Jahoo Gibbon Camp offers day treks and nighttime safaris to various areas in the sanctuary, like a ranger station and a former US army base from the Vietnam War. **Sam Veasna Conservation Tours** in Siem Reap runs birdwatching tours here.

worth checking out are **Romanear** and **Monorom Falls**. You can swim at most of them, but check the state of the water as, unfortunately, it's not always clean.

## Overnight at the Jahoo Gibbon Camp

MEET THE GIBBONS

At the **Jahoo Gibbon Camp**, visitors get to trek into the jungle before dawn to see and hear the amazing singing of yellow-cheeked gibbons. Around 1300 of these rare apes live in the surrounding area – the world's largest population of yellow-cheeked gibbons – alongside equally endangered black-shanked douc langurs, both under threat from habitat loss and human encroachment. Hearing the early morning songs and cries of the gibbons is an unforgettable experience.

Jahoo Gibbon Camp is 30km southwest of Sen Monorom, located near a Bunong village whose population is still animist and who work in partnership with the camp. For every visitor, the camp puts US$30 into a fund managed by the local community, which is used to protect Bunong land and to fund education

### GIBBON ENCOUNTERS

Even rarer than Mondulkiri's yellow-cheeked gibbons are the northern buffed-cheeked gibbons that can be seen and heard at the **Veun Sai-Siem Pang Conservation Area** (p261) in Ratanakiri Province from November to June.

---

**Green House Retreat**
Family-run resort with bungalows linked by wooden walkways in an attractive garden. Helpful staff. **$$**

**Pidoma Resort**
The most luxurious hotel in Mondulkiri: smart bungalows and villas, infinity pool and stunning hilltop views. **$$$**

**Mayura Hill Resort**
Good but overpriced family option in a tranquil setting, with a restaurant, pool and kids' playground. **$$$**

## WHY I LOVE MONDULKIRI

**David Eimer**, writer

Mondulkiri Province encapsulates everything that makes eastern Cambodia such a great place for travellers. It has an eye-catching mix of hills, rainforest, rivers and waterfalls, as well as rare wildlife and a couple of Cambodia's most impressive ecotourism projects. Then there's the chance to interact with some of the ethnic minorities who live in the highlands of Cambodia.

But it's the unique geography of Mondulkiri that makes it so special for me. The rolling grassland plains and the higher elevations give the region a completely different look and feel to the rest of the country. And the welcome from the locals more than makes up for the colder nights here.

SNIJDUWELA/SHUTTERSTOCK ©

**Elephant Valley Project**

scholarships. Bunong guides take small groups into the forest well before first light to be on the spot when the gibbons start vocalising.

As it's an early start, staying overnight is recommended. There are three smart bamboo bungalows, as well as tents, and visitors get the chance to sample Bunong cuisine and to learn something about Bunong culture and life.

High winds in December and January can make it hard to hear the gibbons. September to November is the best time to visit when the landscape is lovely and green. The camp isn't recommended for children under 13 because of their often exuberant reaction to wildlife.

## Spend a Day Walking with Elephants

VISIT THE ELEPHANT VALLEY PROJECT

Legend has it that over one million elephants were employed in the construction of Angkor Wat. In reality, the number was around 6000, but elephants have played an oversized role in Cambodia's history, acting as the transport and tanks that enabled Angkor's god-kings to project their power across Southeast Asia. Traditionally, elephants were trapped in the wild

**WHERE TO EAT IN SEN MONOROM**

**Route 76**
The best European restaurant in eastern Cambodia. Fresh pasta, decent wine list, amiable Italian host. **$$**

**Mondulkiri Pizza**
Fine pizzas with a Khmer twist in a pleasant setting. It also rents a few tidy bungalows. **$$**

**Chom Nor Thmei**
Popular with the locals and especially good for soups. Veggie options and an English menu. **$**

by indigenous peoples like the Bunong, before being put in the service of Angkor's rulers.

Now, though, there are estimated to be just 400 to 600 wild elephants left in Cambodia, with the largest population found in Mondulkiri's forests. Like other Asian elephants, they are under threat from habitat loss – elephants need a lot of room – and ivory poaching. The nonprofit **Elephant Valley Project** (EVP), 10km northwest of Sen Monorom, not only provides sanctuary for 11 former working and tourist elephants, it also protects 3000 sq km of forest and supports local Bunong communities in exchange for the use of their land.

EVP offers visitors the chance to spend half a day to three days hiking out to the forest and spending time with the elephants. There are no rides or feeding the animals here. Instead, you simply walk alongside the pachyderms as they chomp their way through the forest or observe as they wander into the river to bathe. At times, visitors are no more than a metre or two away from the animals, making it a truly immersive experience. English-speaking Bunong guides accompany each group of no more than 12 people to explain elephant behaviour, as well as forest lore and Bunong customs and traditions.

Visitors are also invited to volunteer at the project and there's the opportunity for treks, where in addition to elephants you can spot primates like macaques and langurs and hear gibbons (if you're lucky). You may also see bomb craters – during the Vietnam War, a stretch of the Ho Chi Minh Trail ran through this part of Mondulkiri Province.

There are four big and basic bungalows (fan-only and cold water) for overnight visitors at the base camp, along with shared accommodation for groups. Meals are provided and there's a lounge area for relaxing. You'll be walking 3km to 4km alongside the elephants on forest tracks and up and down some steep inclines, but anyone reasonably fit will manage. Family groups are welcome.

This is the most impressive elephant experience in Cambodia, and one of the most successful of the country's ecotourism endeavors. It's popular, so book in advance. Note that there are no overnight stays on Fridays or Saturdays and no day trips on Saturdays. November to February is the best time to visit, as it's dry but not too hot.

## ELEPHANT ETIQUETTE

Don't approach elephants alone. Only people who work very closely with the animals, like mahouts, can accurately judge their mood.

Elephants don't like being ridden and there is increasing evidence that it is bad for their health.

Keep your distance when taking photos, especially selfies where your back is turned to the animal. Flash photography can spook elephants.

If feeding elephants, have a barrier between you and the animal. Feed them to the trunk, not the mouth. Elephants can lash out if they're not fed correctly or quickly enough.

Only mahouts have the training to be in a river with an elephant. Tourists have been injured while washing them.

## GETTING AROUND

Sen Monorom is 370km northeast of Phnom Penh. Daily minivans travel to Phnom Penh, Siem Reap, Kratie and Ban Lung.

Guesthouses rent motorbikes (US$7 to US$10 per day). *Moto* and *remork-moto* drivers can be found around the market. Count on US$30 to US$35 for a day hire of a *tuk-tuk*. Kim San (088 5623399) is a reliable *tuk-tuk* driver who speaks some English.

# TOOLKIT

The chapters in this section cover the most important topics you'll need to know about in Cambodia. They're full of nuts-and-bolts information and valuable insights to help you understand and navigate Cambodia and get the most out of your trip.

**Arriving**
p270

**Getting Around**
p271

**Money**
p272

**Accommodation**
p273

**Family Travel**
p274

**Health & Safe Travel**
p275

**Food, Drink & Nightlife**
p276

**Responsible Travel**
p278

**LGBTIQ+ Travel**
p281

**Accessible Travel**
p282

**Nuts & Bolts**
p283

**Language**
p284

*Tuk-tuk*, Siem Reap (p88)

ANASTASIA PELIKH/SHUTTERSTOCK ©

# Arriving

Most visitors enter or exit Cambodia by air through the popular international airports of Phnom Penh or Siem Reap; there are limited flights to Sihanoukville for the islands. Lots of independent travellers arrive or depart via the numerous land borders shared with Thailand, Vietnam and Laos. There's also the option to cross via the Mekong River between Vietnam and Cambodia.

### Visas

A one-month tourist visa costs US$30 on arrival at airports and land borders. E-visas can be arranged at evisa.gov.kh for US$37. For longer stays, choose an ordinary business visa for US$35.

### SIM Cards

Cambodian roaming charges are often pretty high, so it pays to arrange a local SIM card as data packages are absurdly cheap. Tourist SIM cards are available free at the airports.

### Border Crossings

Cambodia shares over a dozen land border crossings with neighbours Thailand, Laos and Vietnam. Only a handful accept the e-visa, so plan for a visa on arrival at remote borders.

### Wi-Fi

Free wi-fi is available at all three international airports in Cambodia. There isn't usually free wi-fi at land borders, but you can generally find a cafe or restaurant offering an online fix.

## Public Transport from Airport to City Centre

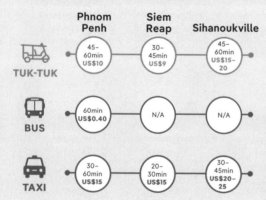

|  | Phnom Penh | Siem Reap | Sihanoukville |
| --- | --- | --- | --- |
| TUK-TUK | 45–60min US$10 | 30–45min US$9 | 45–60min US$15–20 |
| BUS | 60min US$0.40 | N/A | N/A |
| TAXI | 30–60min US$15 | 20–30min US$15 | 30–45min US$20–25 |

## LAND BORDER CROSSINGS 101

Cambodia shares one border crossing with Laos, six crossings with Thailand and seven with Vietnam. Cambodian visas are now available at all the land crossings with Laos, Thailand and Vietnam.

Visas on arrival are available in Laos, while most nationalities enjoy 15 to 30 days visa-free access to Thailand. Vietnam grants visas on arrival only to limited nationalities, so check your passport status before heading to the border. Most borders are open during the core hours of 7am to 5pm. However, some of the most popular crossings are open later in the evening and other more remote crossings close for lunch.

# Getting Around

In addition to planes, trains and cars, motorbikes are a popular form of rental transport, and buses, scenic boats and *remork-motos* (*tuk-tuks*) are ubiquitous.

## TRAVEL COSTS

Car hire with driver
**US$25–75/day**

Motorcycle rental
**US$5–15/day**

Long-distance bus
**US$3/100km**

*Tuk-tuk* ride
around town
**US$2–5**

### Air

Domestic flights can be a time-saving way to avoid Cambodia's unpredictable roads, as the three main airports are well connected to each other. Routes are still recovering from the collapse of tourism during the pandemic and fares are relatively high until more competition is reestablished.

### Bus & Minivan

The most popular form of transport, as all major cities are now well linked by bus to Phnom Penh, but if you're travelling from one end of the country to the other you may have to change buses in a regional hub. **BookMeBus** (bookmebus.com) is a reliable ticket-booking site.

### TIP

*Tuk-tuks* and taxis can be ordered via ride-hailing apps **Grab** (grab. com) and **PassApp** (passapptaxis.com) at prices much lower than on the street.

Scan this QR code to book your tickets.

## KNOW YOUR TUK-TUKS

There are two distinct types of tuk-tuks in Cambodia. The *remork-moto* (or just *remork*) is a canopied trailer hitched to the back of a motorbike for two people in comfort or several more at night. These are a great way to explore temples, as you get the breeze of the motorbike but some protection from the elements. There are also Indian-style auto-rickshaws which are a bit zippier than their Cambodian cousins, but smaller and with less airflow.

## DRIVING ESSENTIALS

Drive on the right.

Speed limit is 40km/h in urban centres, around 80km/h on regional highways and up to 120km/h on new expressways.

An international driving license is required for car rental in Cambodia.

**Car & Motorcycle**

Car and motorcycle rental is comparatively cheap in Cambodia and many visitors rent a car or motorbike for greater flexibility to visit out-of-the-way places and to stop when they choose. Almost all car rental in Cambodia includes a driver, although self-drive rentals are also available in Phnom Penh.

**Train**

Currently there are two lines with daily services. The southern line links Phnom Penh with Sihanoukville via Kampot and Takeo, while the northern line runs from Phnom Penh to Poipet via Pursat and Battambang. There are plans to start services to Thailand and to connect the rail network with Vietnam.

**Boat**

There are scenic boat services between Siem Reap and Battambang, and the Tonlé Sap lake is also navigable year-round, although only by smaller boats between March and July. Fast boats from Phnom Penh to Siem Reap have been put out of business by cheaper buses and minivans.

271

# Money

CURRENCY: **RIEL (R)**

## Credit Cards

Top-end hotels, airline offices and upmarket boutiques and restaurants generally accept most major credit cards, but may charge the customer a percentage fee.

## Digital Payments

Local banks in Cambodia have embraced digital payments, but international services like Apple Wallet or Google Pay are not currently approved in Cambodia.

## ATMs

ATMs are widely available, including in all major tourist centres and provincial capitals. Machines usually give you the option of withdrawing in US dollars or riel. Single withdrawals of up to US$500 are usually possible, providing your account can handle it. Stay alert when using ATMs late at night.

## Tipping

Tips can go a long way in Cambodia.

**Hotels** US$1 per bag plus a small tip for the cleaner at smart hotels.

**Restaurants** A few thousand riel, up to 5% or 10% at fancier restaurants.

**Tuk-tuks** Not expected for short trips.

**Temples** Drop a few thousand riel in the contribution box.

### HOW MUCH FOR A...

National park entry
**US$5**

Museum admission
**US$10**

Local lunch
**US$10**

Train ride
**US$7**

## HOW TO... Save Some US Dollars

Travelling in low season (often referred to as 'green season' in Cambodia) can save quite a lot of money on the cost of boutique hotels and luxury hotels. Another simple saving for travellers is to target the generous happy hours on offer in many bars and restaurants in Cambodia, including everywhere from backpacker bars to luxury hotels; 50% off or 2-for-1 offers are popular.

## KEEPING IT RIEL

The Cambodian government has made a concerted push to promote the Cambodian riel and move away from dollar dependency. Many ATMs now stock both currencies, but will only issue US$100 bills. Despite these moves, the US dollar remains a constant presence. Armed with enough cash, you won't need to visit a bank as it's easy to change dollars for riel at hotels, restaurants and markets. Pay for something cheap in US dollars and the change comes in riel. The Thai baht is also used in the west of the country in towns like Koh Kong, Poipet and Sisophon.

### LOCAL TIP

When travelling overland, organise a supply of US dollars before arriving in Cambodia. Cash in other major currencies can be changed in big cities, but rates are lower for nondollar transactions.

# Accommodation

## Living It Up

In Phnom Penh, Siem Reap and on the South Coast, hotels improve significantly once you start spending more than US$20 a night. Spend between US$30 and US$50 and it's possible to arrange something comfortable with the bonus of a swimming pool. There's been an explosion of boutique hotels; these atmospheric places are usually in the US$50 to US$100 range.

## Experience a Homestay

There are several organised homestays around the country in provinces including Kompong Cham and Kompong Thom, as well as some NGO-established homestays in out-of-the-way places such as Chi Phat and Stung Areng in the Cardamom Mountains. The Mekong Discovery Trail has a slew of homestays between Kratie and the Lao border. There are also plenty of easily accessible homestays in Siem Reap Province.

## Stay in a Guesthouse

Budget guesthouses can be found in nearly all provincial capitals. Costs average US$5 to US$15 for a bed, usually with fan, bathroom and satellite TV. Most guesthouses in this range don't have hot water, but may offer a few pricier rooms where it's available. Basic thatched bungalows with a mattress and fan are found in some coastal destinations and the hills of Mondulkiri and Ratanakiri.

### HOW MUCH FOR A NIGHT IN A...

Boutique hotel
US$50-100

Hostel dorm
US$5-15

Guesthouse
US$5-10

### Camping Out

Camping used to be virtually unheard of in Cambodia until a few years ago, but during the pandemic younger Khmers have really embraced back-to-nature escapes in the countryside. It's still quite unusual to see foreign travellers camping due to the hot climate and the prevalence of cheap accommodation, but community campsites are available in places like Phnom Kulen and Khnong Phsar.

## Crash in a Hostel

Backpacker hostels abound in Cambodia, particularly in popular destinations like Phnom Penh, Siem Reap and Kampot. These are lively and well run, but the dorms are not always great value and often the same price as a private room in a guesthouse. However, most hostels also offer private rooms and some have bonus draws like a swimming pool.

## SOLO TRAVELLERS

Hotels in Cambodia rarely offer a single rate, though there are a few notable exceptions in Siem Reap and Phnom Penh. Local guesthouses offer a more affordable way to sleep comfortably without breaking the bank, particularly in the provinces less travelled. Solo travellers looking to make new friends should consider sleeping in Cambodia's excellent hostels, which range from social party pads to serene and ecofriendly flashpackers. Most include private rooms alongside the dorms for those who prefer privacy, but are a guaranteed way to hook up with fellow backpackers.

# Family Travel

Like in many places in Southeast Asia, travelling with children in Cambodia can be a lot of fun as long as you have the right attitude. The Khmer people adore children and will shower attention on your offspring, who will find playmates and a temporary babysitter at practically every stop.

### Sights & Activities

There are plenty of discounts available for children in Cambodia, ranging from free entry to the temples of Angkor for kids under 12 to half-price access to popular attractions such as waterparks and animal encounters. It pays to have handy ID for tall children under 12, as the Cambodians will assume they are older. Discounts on public transport are rarely available in Cambodia.

### Travelling with Infants

Baby changing facilities in public restrooms are rare in Cambodia and limited to a few tourist-friendly establishments in the big cities. There are now lots of international baby products available in supermarkets and pharmacies in the main towns and cities, but you should bring along a sufficient supply of personalised products if travelling in rural areas.

### Safety First

Most vehicles have seatbelts, but child seats are not common. Request one in advance via a tour operator if booking private transport. Do not let children stray from the path in remote areas, as Cambodia remains blighted by landmines.

### Navigating Pushchairs

City footpaths can be overcrowded, making it tricky to navigate a large pushchair (pram). In rural areas, there won't be a pavement (sidewalk), so prepare to walk along the roadside and consider a durable pushchair with sturdy wheels.

---

### CHILD-FRIENDLY PICKS

**Phnom Tamao Wildlife Rescue Centre (p81)**
Learn how to be a 'bear keeper' or 'elephant keeper' for a day near Phnom Penh.

**Ta Prohm (p80)**
The original jungle temple was used as a backdrop for *Lara Croft: Tomb Raider*.

**Angkor Zipline (p138)**
Fly through ancient jungle around the temples on the Angkor Zipline near Siem Reap.

**Lazy Beach (p235)**
Long home to just one resort, Lazy Beach on Koh Rong Sanloem is a beautiful spot for families.

---

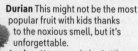

## TROPICAL FRUITS FOR BEGINNERS

**Durian** This might not be the most popular fruit with kids thanks to the noxious smell, but it's unforgettable.

**Lychee** Known as *kulen* in Khmer; lychee season falls around May to July.

**Mango** Mangoes are available year-round in Cambodia, but it's the Khmer New Year fruits that are deliciously turbocharged by the April heatwave.

**Mangosteen** It's said that Queen Victoria offered £100 to anyone who could deliver her a ripe mangosteen, so it's known as the queen of fruit.

**Rambutan** It may be hard to persuade the children to eat this fruit due to its curious appearance, but it's available year-round.

# Health & Safe Travel

## INSURANCE

Visiting Cambodia without medical insurance is incredibly unwise. Hospitals are extremely basic in the provinces, and even major hospitals struggle to cope with serious injuries and illnesses. If you succumb to either in Cambodia, you may require emergency

evacuation to Bangkok. Without an insurance policy, it will cost around US$20,000.

### Drinking Water

The number-one rule is to avoid drinking tap water. Also be careful of ice, although the latter is usually factory-produced, a legacy of the French. Pack a water-purification device or tablets, and if purchasing bottled water, aim for larger bottles that can be decanted into a reusable drink bottle to minimise plastic.

### Mosquito-Borne Diseases

The miniscule mosquito carries many potentially fatal diseases such as malaria, dengue fever and more. For most travellers, the worst impact is some itchy bites that can be avoided with the use of repellent and wearing long, light-coloured clothing at night. However, malaria is present on the Thai border and the southern islands and dengue fever is common in the wet season.

### FAKE MEDS

Only buy prescription drugs from reliable pharmacies or clinics to ensure you don't end up with fake meds.

---

## GETTING TREATMENT IN CAMBODIA

| Calmette Hospital | Royal Angkor Hospital | U-Care Pharmacy | Eurodental Clinic | Tropical & Travellers Medical Clinic |
|---|---|---|---|---|
| Best government hospital in the country. | Best private hospital in Siem Reap. | Reliable chain of pharmacies in Cambodia. | International-standard dental services. | Traveller-friendly clinic in Phnom Penh. |

### Yaba Daba Don't

Watch out for *yaba*, the 'crazy' drug from Thailand, known rather ominously in Cambodia as *yama* (the Hindu god of death). Known as ice or crystal meth elsewhere, this is a homemade methamphetamine produced in labs in Cambodia and the region beyond. The pills are often laced with toxic substances, such as mercury, lithium or whatever else the maker can find.

### MINES & UNEXPLODED ORDNANCE

Never touch any rockets, artillery shells, mortars, mines, bombs or other unexploded ordnance (UXO) you may come across. The most heavily mined part of the country is along the Thai border area, but mines are a problem in much of Cambodia. In short: do not stray from well-marked paths under any circumstances.

# Food, Drink & Nightlife

## A Culinary Enigma

Unlike the culinary giants that are its neighbours Thailand and Vietnam, Cambodia is not that well known in international food circles. However, Cambodian cuisine is also quite special, with a great variety of national dishes – some draw on the cuisine of its neighbours, but all have a unique Cambodian twist, whether your tastes run to spring rolls or curry.

## Where to Eat

Cambodia has great dining options in the cities, but the choice dries up in remote areas.

**Restaurants** These range from local hole-in-the-wall spots to sophisticated bistros. Most cuisines are covered in the cities, but it's mainly Cambodian, Chinese and Vietnamese elsewhere.

**Cafes** Cambodia has a healthy coffee culture, a legacy of the French. The best cafes are found in Phnom Penh and Siem Reap.

**Markets** Most major markets have food stalls, which are an inexpensive place to sample the local cuisine.

### MENU DECODER

**bai** rice
**bobor** rice porridge
**nohm paang** bread
**kyteow** noodle soup
**samlor** traditional soup
**soup chhnang dei** cook-your-own soup in a pot
**sait ch'ruuk** pork
**sait kow** beef
**sait moan** chicken
**trey** fish
**ahntohng** eel
**bawng kawng** lobster
**bawng kia** shrimp
**k'daam** crab
**meuk** squid
**buhnlai** vegetables
**chek** banana
**duong** coconut
**khnau** jackfruit
**menoa** pineapple

**mongkut** mangosteen
**sao mao** rambutan
**svay** mango
**tourain** durian
**kynay** ginger
**m'teh** chilli
**prahoc** fermented fish paste
**teuk sii iw** soy sauce
**teuk trey** fish sauce
**tuek kmom** honey
**ang** grilled
**chien** fried
**chimhoy** steamed
**khor** stewed
**kaa fey** coffee
**tai** tea
**teuk** water
**teuk kalohk** drink similar to fruit smoothie
**teuk koh** ice
**tukalok** fruit shake

### HOW TO... Toast in Cambodia

Cambodians love to toast each other when drinking at restaurants, bars and on special occasions. When Cambodians propose a toast, they usually stipulate what percentage must be downed. If they're feeling generous, it might be just *ha-sip peah-roi* (50%), but more often than not it is *moi roi peah-roi* (100%). This is why they love ice (*tuk-koh* or 'hard water') in their beer, as they can pace themselves over the course of the night. Many a *barang* (foreigner) has ended up face down on the table at a Cambodian wedding when trying to outdrink the Khmers without the aid of ice.

Learn Khmer phrases for 'cheers' to make some new friends. *Chaul mouy* is the most common, literally meaning 'bump one' or 'cheers'. *Sokha pheap lahore* is more like 'to good health' – though a heavy session rarely leads to this outcome.

## HOW MUCH FOR A...

*Kyteow*
(noodle soup)
US$1.50-3

*Bobor* (rice
porridge)
US$1-2

Espresso
US$1-2

Cocktail
US$4-10

Gourmet dinner
US$25-50

Ice cream scoop
US$1.50

Draft beer
US$0.50-2

Glass of wine
US$4-7

### HOW TO...

### Plan a Night Out in Cambodia

A night out in Cambodia usually begins with a sundowner drink on a riverfront, a lakeside or a beach. If those aren't available, anywhere with an outdoor terrace or a rooftop will do, as locals are in search of an elusive breeze.

If it's something more sophisticated you're seeking, you'll need to head to a gourmet Cambodian restaurant or an international eatery, as these places offer a good selection of cocktails and wine by the glass. After dinner, the best options for a pub crawl are Phnom Penh or Siem Reap. Head to **Bassac Lane** (p71) in the Cambodian capital, where there are more than 20 bars crammed into a small network of streets and alleys, plus a whole lot of interesting eateries. In Siem Reap, most visitors head to the infamous **Pub St** (p99) where the volume is permanently turned up to 11, but the up-and-coming **St 26** (p100) or 'Boho' offers a cooler vibe.

For clubbing, Phnom Penh is the only real choice for a big night out. Most clubs don't really get going until about 11pm and roll on to the wee hours. Most don't have cover charges unless there are well-known DJs playing. However, the drinks are a big step up in price from the bars and local restaurants. There are no formal dress codes, but you may get turned away if you're sporting flip-flops or a singlet.

### Cambodian BBQ

A Cambodian BBQ is a popular way to drink with dinner, as these outdoor restaurants serve cheap local beers to accompany the *phnom pleung* (hill of fire). Also popular is *soup chhang dai*, a liquid variation on the tabletop BBQ.

### TIPPLES IN CAMBODIA

Cambodia has a lively local drinking culture, and the heat and humidity will ensure that you hunt out anything on offer to quench your thirst. Coffee, tea, beer, wine, soft drinks, fresh fruit juices and some of the more exotic 'firewaters' are all widely available. Tea is the national drink, but these days it's just as likely to be beer in the glass.

It's never a challenge to find a beer in Cambodia and even the most remote village usually has a stall selling a few cans. Draught beers are available for around US$0.50 to US$2 in the main tourist centres. Popular local brands include old-timers Angkor Beer and Cambodia Beer plus newcomers like Hanuman Beer. There are also lots of imported beers from all over the world, including the excellent Beerlao from across the border.

Local wine in Cambodia generally means rice wine, which is popular with the minority peoples of the northeast. Some rice wines are fermented for months and are superstrong, while other brews are fresher and taste more like a cocktail. Either way, if you're invited to join a session in an ethnic minority village, it's rude to decline. In tourist centres, foreign wines and spirits are sold in supermarkets at bargain prices, given how far they have to travel. International wines start at about US$5 for a bottle, while the famous names of the spirit world cost between US$7 and US$15 for a bottle. That explains the cheap cocktails...

# Responsible Travel

## Climate Change & Travel

It's impossible to ignore the impact we have when travelling, and the importance of making changes where we can. Lonely Planet urges all travellers to engage with their travel carbon footprint. There are many carbon calculators online that allow travellers to estimate the carbon emissions generated by their journey; try resurgence.org/resources/carbon-calculator. html. Many airlines and booking sites offer travellers the option of offsetting the impact of greenhouse gas emissions by contributing to climate-friendly initiatives around the world. We continue to offset the carbon footprint of all Lonely Planet staff travel, while recognising this is a mitigation more than a solution.

## Shop to Support Cambodia

There are lots of good-cause shopping opportunities in Cambodia to help disabled people, vulnerable women and disadvantaged youth. Try **Daughters of Cambodia** (p65) or **Artisans Angkor** (p79) in Phnom Penh.

## Roll Up for a Good Cause

Officially recognised by the Guinness World Records for the 'world's longest circus performance' after performing a marathon 24-hour show to raise funds, **Phare Ponleu Selpak** (p164) is an innovative social enterprise founded in Battambang.

## Dine for a Cause

There are lots of great training restaurants in Cambodia, helping to provide hospitality skills for underprivileged youngsters. Standout places include Phnom Penh's **F3 Friends Futures Factory** (p56) and Siem Reap's **Spoons Cafe** (p106).

## Support Endangered Wildlife

Escape to **Cardamom Tented Camp** (p207), an award-winning ecolodge in the jungle of Botum Sakor National Park on the edge of the Cardamom Mountains, where your stay supports conservation efforts like ranger patrols and wildlife releases.

## A Sanctuary for Elephants

Walk with the herd in the pioneering **Elephant Valley Project** (p266) in Mondulkiri Province; they recently welcomed a baby calf born to a rescued elephant called Gee Pael.

Stay at the **Jahoo Gibbon Camp** (p265) in the remote Keo Seima Wildlife Sanctuary where it's possible to spot the southern yellow-cheeked gibbon on community-based tourism treks that support wildlife conservation.

**Jaan Bai** (p163) in Battambang is an impressive Cambodian restaurant that supports the Cambodian Children's Trust whihch assists disadvantaged young Khmers enter the tourism and hospitality industry.

## De-Mining Cambodia

Meet the 'hero rats' at **Apopo Visitor Centre** (p98) in Siem Reap – they use their incredible sense of smell to sniff out landmines in remote communities in Cambodia, speeding up the critical de-mining of the country.

Scan this QR code to search for birding and eco tours

## Birdlife Conservation

The excellent **Sam Veasna Conservation Tours** (samveasna.com) runs birdwatching experiences supporting conservation efforts across Cambodia. Spot large rare waterbirds at **Prek Toal Bird Sanctuary** (p110) and the elusive giant ibis at **Tmat Boey** (p178).

## Behind-the-Scenes Nature Conservation

**Wildlife Alliance** (wildlifealliance.org) offers responsible tourism initiatives to observe wildlife, including a behind-the-scenes tour at the **Phnom Tamao Wildlife Rescue Centre** (p81) and a visit to the **Wildlife Alliance Release Station** (p206) near Chi Phat.

Head to **Kampi** (p252) near Kratie to spot the rare Irrawaddy dolphin in the Mekong River by kayak.

Experience a homestay in the riverside communities of **Chi Phat** (p205) or **Areng Valley** (p87) in the Cardamom Mountains.

## 50

Cambodia currently produces around 50% of its power from renewable energy sources, including hydropower, solar power, wind power and biomass. Plans for coal-fired power stations were recently halted as China reversed its overseas support for carbon.

## Refill Not Landfill

Refill Not Landfill (refilltheworld.com) is a homegrown Cambodian campaign working with hotels, restaurants and shops to provide refillable water bottles and drinking-water refill stations to help battle the ever-present plastic water bottles.

## RESOURCES

**ecocambodia.org**
Gateway to all things ecotourism-related in Cambodia.

**concertcambodia.org**
An online resource for responsible-tourism initiatives in Siem Reap.

**wildlifealliance.org**
Supporting wildlife protection including immersive visitor activities and a wildlife crimes hotline.

Scan this QR code to find drinking-water refill stations near you

# THE PERILS OF ORPHANAGE TOURISM

Orphanage tourism has brought unscrupulous elements into the world for Cambodian children.

Save the Children says it's often a myth that children in orphanages have no parents. Many are there because their parents simply can't afford to feed, clothe and educate them. Only about one-quarter of Cambodian children in institutions are thought to be genuine orphans.

Many orphanages in Cambodia are scams where children are at risk of abuse and neglect. To be sure, there are legitimate, well-meaning orphanages in Cambodia. But a growing body of evidence, backed by Unicef, Save the Children and Friends International, suggests that even well-run orphanages do more harm than good. Genuine orphans are better off remaining in their home towns with community- or family-based networks.

Travellers should avoid visiting, donating to, or volunteering in Cambodian orphanages. Learn more at thinkchildsafe.org/thinkbefore visiting before you inadvertently contribute to the problem. ChildSafe is a global movement to protect children and certifies hotels, restaurants and other businesses as child-safe, in the fight against human trafficking and sex tourism.

In a similar vein, think carefully before visiting a Cambodian school. You probably wouldn't think of visiting a school in your home country (nor would you likely be allowed to), so why disrupt the daily routine in a Cambodian school?

Visit the website of **Plastic Free Southeast Asia** (plasticfree cambodia.com) for tips on reducing plastic waste locally.

The **Cooperation Committee for Cambodia** (ccc-cambodia.org) lists reputable NGOs, some of which require volunteers from time to time.

Scan this QR code for a list of reputable NGOs.

## A Fair Bargain

The Khmers are not ruthless hagglers, so a persuasive smile and a little friendly quibbling is usually enough to get a price that's acceptable to both you and the seller.

## Photographing Children

There are lots of incredibly photogenic Cambodian children that are happy to have their photograph taken, but always ask for parental permission, and don't encourage child labour by paying children for pictures.

## Dress the Part

It's respectful to keep your shoulders and knees covered in Cambodia, especially when visiting remote villages or religious sites (including Angkor Wat).

# LGBTIQ+ Travellers

The LGBTIQ+ scene in Cambodia is certainly not as wild as that in Thailand, but both Phnom Penh and Siem Reap have plenty of gay-friendly establishments. Siem Reap in particular has a well-developed, if low-key, gay scene centred around its guesthouses.

## Gay-Friendly Destinations

As a diverse and dynamic capital, Phnom Penh is undoubtedly the most gay-friendly destination in Cambodia, with a number of leading gay bars and gay-friendly clubs, as well as one of the only gay dance companies in the country, **Prumsodun Ok & Natyarasa** (p62). Siem Reap is also a gay-friendly international destination with some popular gay bars and a popular drag show at **Barcode** (p111). Other destinations, including Battambang, Kampot and the southern islands, are also gay friendly but don't necessarily have many (or any) gay venues.

### ACCORDING TO THE LAW

While same-sex relations are not illegal, they're also not officially recognised by Cambodian law. According to the Office of the United Nations High Commissioner for Human Rights (OHCHR), LGBTIQ+ Cambodian nationals often face discrimination in their everyday life, which happens both in domestic circles and in public spheres including schools, the workplace or even health facilities.

### LOCAL PRIDE

The gay community in Cambodia comes out for Pride every year with a United Nations Development Programme–supported 'I am what I am' campaign and lots of small-scale events around the capital including concerts, beauty contests and more at **F3 Friends Futures Factory** (p56) in Phnom Penh.

## Attitudes Towards Homosexuality

Generally speaking, Cambodians are tolerant of allcomers, no matter their nationality, religion or sexuality. However, for the older generation of Theravada Buddhists, this tolerance applies more to foreigners than to Cambodians, and some younger Khmers may be reluctant to come out of the closet, particularly in rural communities. As with heterosexual couples, passionate public displays of affection are considered inappropriate.

### Drag Shows

Drag performers take to the stage regularly in Phnom Penh and Siem Reap. In the capital, both **Blue Chilli** (p62) and **Heart of Darkness** (p56) have drag shows from Wednesdays to Saturdays. In Siem Reap, **Barcode** (p111) has regular weekend drag shows.

## GAY TRAVEL WEBSITES

Recommended gay travel websites for planning a trip to Cambodia include the following:

**Cambodia Gay** (cambodia-gay.com) Promoting the LGBTIQ+ community in Cambodia.

**Utopia** (utopia-asia.com/tipscam.htm) Gay travel information and contacts, including some local gay terminology.

# Accessible Travel

Broken pavements, potholed roads and stairs as steep as ladders at Angkor ensure that for most people with restricted mobility, Cambodia is not an easy country in which to travel.

## Accessible Transport

**Mobilituk** (facebook.com/mobilituk) is a homegrown initiative to provide disability-friendly *tuk-tuks* to the local population, with a fold-down steel ramp for wheelchair access.

### Airport

Airports in Cambodia are well equipped for accessible travel, including lifts between levels and entry and exit ramps. Wheelchairs are available for mobility-impaired travellers and there are disabled toilet facilities in the three main airports.

### Accommodation

Most guesthouses and small hotels have ground-floor rooms that are reasonably easy to access, but there are not that many properties that have been purpose-built with disabled access in mind.

## THE SOUTHERN ISLANDS

The main challenge with the islands is getting safely on and off the fast ferries that dock at rickety piers, and reaching beach resorts that are only accessible via the sand.

## Para Champs

Cambodia is fast improving in the regional Association of Southeast Asian Nations (Asean) Para Games, winning a total of 28 medals with seven golds in 2022. The country is particularly strong at team events like basketball and volleyball.

## Seeing Hands Massage

There are several initiatives to support visually impaired people in Cambodia, including the renowned **Seeing Hands Massage** in Phnom Penh and Siem Reap that trains blind masseurs in the art of massage.

## THE TEMPLES OF ANGKOR

The biggest headache also happens to be the main attraction: the temples of Angkor. Causeways are uneven, obstacles common and staircases daunting, even for able-bodied people. Some ramping has been introduced at major temples.

### AMPUTEES IN CAMBODIA

Cambodia has one of the highest numbers of amputees per capita of any country: landmine and UXO explosions killed 19,806 people and injured or amputated more than 45,000 from 1979 to 2021. As many as five to 10 Cambodians are still injured or killed every month.

# 📖 Nuts & Bolts

## OPENING HOURS

Everything shuts down during the major holidays of Chaul Chnam Khmer (Khmer New Year), P'chum Ben (Festival of the Dead) and Chaul Chnam Chen (Chinese New Year).

**Banks** 8am–3.30pm Monday to Friday, Saturday mornings

**Bars** 5pm–late

**Government offices** 7.30am–11.30am and 2pm–5pm Monday to Friday

**Local markets** 6.30am–5.30pm

**Museums** Hours vary, but usually open seven days a week

**Restaurants** International restaurants 7am–10pm or meal times; local restaurants 6.30am–9pm

**Shops** 8am–6pm, later in tourist centres

### Smoking

All hotels and most guesthouses offer nonsmoking rooms. Smoking was officially banned in some public places like cafes, restaurants and bars in 2016, but in practice its enforcement seems down to the individual businesses.

---

---

### Weights & Measures

Cambodians use the metric system for everything but precious metals and gems, where they prefer Chinese units of measurement.

### Discount Cards

Senior travellers and students are not eligible for discounts in Cambodia.

---

## Electricity
### 120V/60Hz (type A)
### 220V/50Hz (type C)

Type A
120V/60Hz

Type C
220V/50Hz

---

## PUBLIC HOLIDAYS

Banks, ministries and embassies close down during public holidays and festivals, so plan ahead. Cambodians also roll over holidays if they fall on a weekend and take a day or two extra during major festivals.

**International New Year's Day** 1 January

**Victory over the Genocide** 7 January

**International Women's Day** 8 March

**Khmer New Year** 14–16 April

**International Workers' Day** 1 May

**King's Birthday** 13–15 May

**Royal Ploughing Ceremony** May (lunar)

**King's Mother's Birthday** 18 June

**Constitution Day** 24 September

**Festival of the Dead** September/October (lunar)

**Commemoration Day** 15 October

**Coronation Day** 29 October

**Water Festival** October/November (lunar)

**Independence Day** 9 November

# Language

Written Khmer is based on the ancient Brahmi script of southern India. The haphazard transliteration system left over from the days of French rule has been simplified in this chapter for the purpose of basic communication.

## Basics

**Hello.** ជំរាបសួរ *johm ree·uhp soo·uh*

**Goodbye.** លាសិនហើយ *lee·aa suhn hao·y*

**Yes.** បាទ/ចាស *baat/jaa (m/f)*

**No.** ទេ *day*

**Please.** សូម *sohm*

**Thank you.** អរគុណ *aw gohn*

**Excuse me/Sorry.** សុំទោស *sohm đoh*

**What's your name?** អ្នកឈ្មោះអ្វី? *nay·uhk chuh·mu·ah ei*

**My name is ...** ខ្ញុំឈ្មោះ ... *kuh·nyohm chuh·mu·ah ...*

**Do you speak English?** អ្នកចេះភាសាអង់គ្លេសទេ? *nay·uhk jes phi·a·saa awn·glay đay*

**I don't understand.** ខ្ញុំមិនយល់ទេ *kuh·nyohm muhn yuhl đay*

## Directions

**Where's (the city centre)?** (មជ្ឈមណ្ឌលក្រុង) នៅឯណា? *(mah·chay·uh mahn·đahl grohng) neuw ei naa*

**What's the address?** សុំអាស័យដ្ឋាន? *sohm aa·say·yah·taan*

**Could you please write it down?** សូមសរសេរឲ្យខ្ញុំ? *sohm saw·say ao·y kuh·nyohm*

**Can you show me (on the map)?** សុំបង្ហាញខ្ញុំ (លើផែនទី) *sohm bawng·hain kuh·nyohm (ler pain·đee)*

## Signs

**Entrance/Exit** ផ្លូវចូល/ផ្លូវចេញ

**Open/Closed** បើក/បិត

**Information** កន្លែងពត៌មាន

**Toilets** បង្គន់

**Police Station** ប៉ុស្ដិ៍ប៉ូលិស

## Time

**What time is it?** ពេលវេនេះម៉ោងប៉ុន្មាន? *ei·leuw nih maong bohn·maan*

**It's (one) o'clock.** ម៉ោង (មួយ) *maong (muy)*

**Half past (one).** ម៉ោង (មួយ) សាមសិប *maong (muy) saam suhp*

**morning** ពេលព្រឹក *behl bruhk*

**evening** ពេលល្ងាច *behl luh·ngee·ihk*

**yesterday** ម្សិលមិញ *muh·suhl mein*

**today** ថ្ងៃនេះ *tuh·ngai nih*

**tomorrow** ថ្ងៃស្អែក *tuh·ngai sah·aik*

## Emergencies

**Help!** ជួយផង! *joo·y pawng*

**Go away!** ទៅអោយឆ្ងាយ! *đeuw ao·y chuh·ngaay*

**I'm lost.** ខ្ញុំវង្វេងផ្លូវ *kuh·nyohm wohng·weng pleuw*

**Call ...!** ជួយហៅ ... មក *joo·y haa·ew ... mao*

**a doctor** គ្រូពេទ្យ *kru baet*

**an ambulance** ឡានពេទ្យ *laan baet*

**the police** ប៉ូលិស *bow·lih*

## Eating & Drinking

**What would you recommend?** មានមុខអ្វីឆ្ងាញ់ពិសេសទេ? *mee·uhn mohk muh·howp ah·wei chuh·ngain bi·seh đay*

**Cheers!** ជយោ! *chuh·yow*

**The bill, please.** សុំគិតលុយ *sohm kuht luy*

## NUMBERS

| | | |
|---|---|---|
| **1** | មួយ *muy* | |
| **2** | ពីរ *bee* | |
| **3** | បី *bei* | |
| **4** | បួន *boo·uhn* | |
| **5** | ប្រាំ *bruhm* | |
| **6** | ប្រាំមួយ *bruhm muy* | |
| **7** | ប្រាំពីរ *bruhm bee* | |
| **8** | ប្រាំបី *bruhm bei* | |
| **9** | ប្រាំបួន *bruhm boo·uhn* | |
| **10** | ដប់ *dawp* | |

## REGIONAL DIALECTS

The Khmer language as spoken in Phnom Penh is generally intelligible to Khmers nationwide. There are, however, several distinct dialects in other areas of the country. Most notably, the Khmers of Takeo province (south of Phnom Penh) tend to modify or slur hard consonant combinations, especially those that contain the sound r, eg *bruhm* (five) becomes *pay·uhm*, and *sraa* (alcohol) becomes *say·aa*. In Siem Reap, sharp-eared travellers will notice a Lao-sounding lilt to the local speech.

### Distinctive Sounds

Some consonant combinations in Khmer can be a bit difficult for English speakers to produce, such as j·r in *j·rook* (pig) or ch·ng in *ch·ngain* (delicious). Happily, unlike Thai and Vietnamese, Khmer doesn't have tones.

### Must-Know Grammar

Khmer grammar is relatively simple – there are no endings for singular or plural, masculine or feminine. Verbs don't change according to tense; often the context will indicate when an action occurred.

### Questions & Requests

To form a yes/no question, place *day* ទេ (no) at the end of a statement. For 'yes', men say *baat* បាទ and women say *jaa* ចាស. For 'no' they both say *day* ទេ.

**Is this seat free?**
កៅអីនេះទំនេរទេ? *gao ei nih dohm-nay day*
(literally: seat this free no)

To make a polite request, use *sohm* សូម (please) before the verb.

**Take me to this address, please.**
សូមជូនខ្ញុំទៅអាសយដ្ឋាននេះ *sohm joon kuh-nyohm deuw aa-sai-yah-tahn nih*
(literally: please take me go address this)

### FRENCH LOAN WORDS

Many household items, medical and technical terms retain their French names in Khmer, especially those which were introduced to Cambodia by the French during the colonial period, such as *robinet* (tap/faucet) and *ampoule* (light bulb).

## WHO SPEAKS KHMER?

Khmer is spoken by approximately 9 million people in Cambodia and is understood by many in neighbouring countries.

Khmer is the only official language of Cambodia.

There are sizeable Khmer-speaking communities in Thailand and Vietnam.

● Cambodia

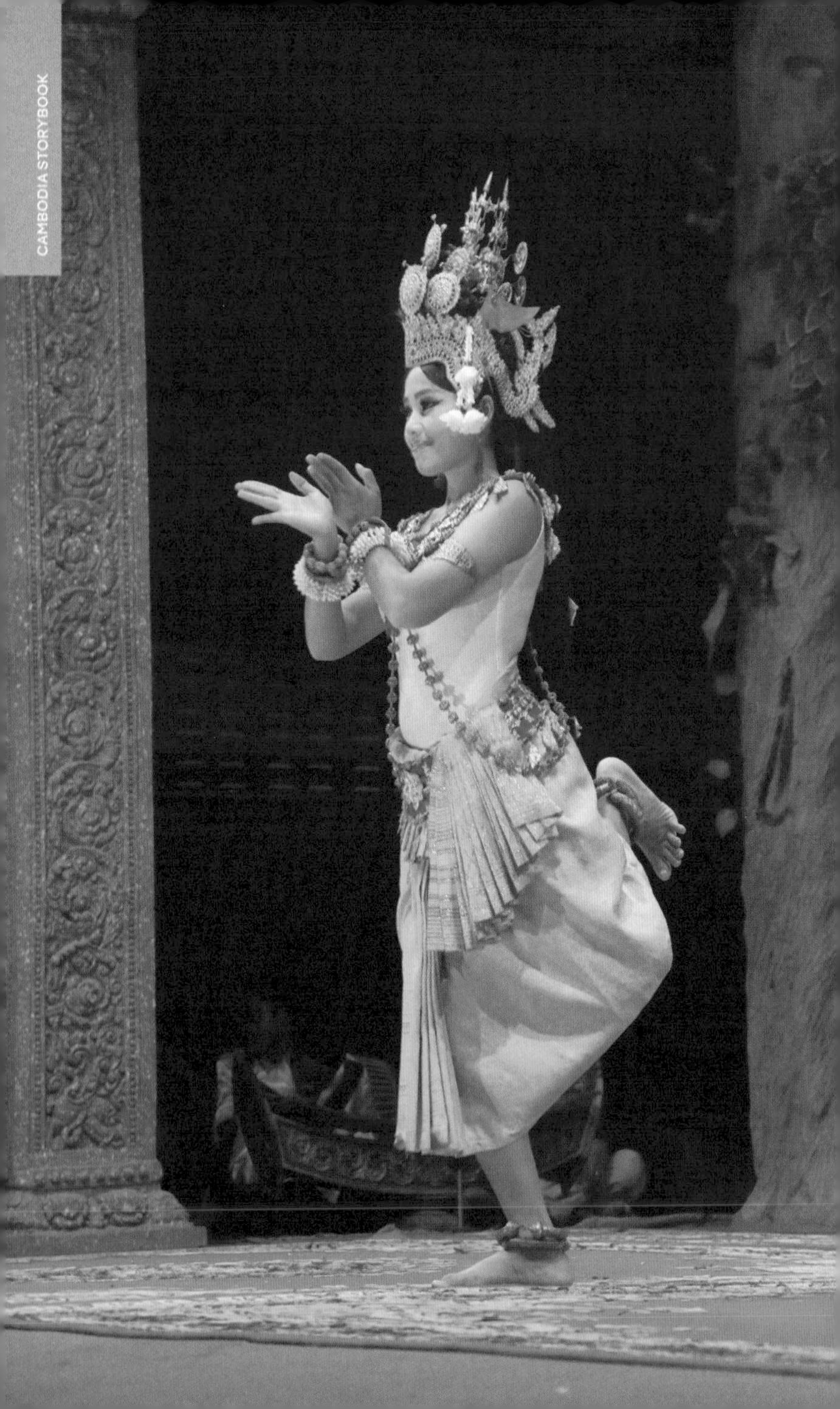

# STORYBOOK

Our writers delve deep into different aspects of Cambodian life

### A History of Cambodia in 15 Places

'The good, the bad and the ugly' sums it up.

**p288**

### Meet the Cambodians

Cambodian society is moving with the times, but don't ignore tradition and a still painful past.

**p292**

### Trials of the Khmer Rouge

The UN-backed war crimes tribunal may have ended, but the scars remain.

**p294**

### The Revival of Cambodian Arts

Crushed by the Khmer Rouge, traditional Cambodian arts are experiencing a modern-day renaissance.

**p297**

### Fresh, Dried, Smoked & Salted

Cornerstones of Cambodian cuisine for centuries, pickling and fermenting are now trending on the global culinary stage.

**p300**

### The French Legacy in Cambodia

Colonial-era architecture abounds and baguettes are everywhere, but vestiges of French rule continue to fade.

**p302**

### Women in Modern Cambodia

Traditional values may run deep in Cambodia, but a new generation of women are finding their voice.

**p304**

### Cambodia's Natural Environment

Homegrown eco-activism is on the rise, but Cambodia faces major environmental challenges.

**p307**

*Apsara* dancer, Siem Reap (p88)
STEVE ESTVANIK/SHUTTERSTOCK ©

# A HISTORY OF CAMBODIA IN
# 15 PLACES

'The good, the bad and the ugly' sums it up. Things were good in the early years, culminating in the vast Angkorian empire. Then came the bad, as ascendant neighbours chipped away at the kingdom. The 20th century turned downright ugly, as a brutal civil war led to the Khmer Rouge genocide, from which Cambodia is rapidly recovering.

**CAMBODIA WAS A** key stop on the Silk Road that linked the regional powerhouses India and China. India had a huge influence on Cambodia by introducing its religious and written traditions from the 1st century CE. The Khmer empire ruled the region for six centuries, distilling Hindu and Buddhist culture into much of modern-day Thailand and Laos. After its collapse, Cambodia was eventually colonised by the French, who left a rich architectural legacy but little else.

The post-independence period was Cambodia's golden era. Phnom Penh grew in size and stature and the temples of Angkor were Southeast Asia's leading tourist destination. But the country was soon sucked into the vortex of the American war in Vietnam. The Khmer Rouge seized power in 1975 and Pol Pot implemented a radical Maoist revolution that killed two million people, a trauma that still haunts Cambodia today.

The Khmer Rouge was overthrown by the Vietnamese in 1979, turning to a decade-long occupation and shaping Cambodian attitudes towards its neighbour. The UN's supervision of the 1993 elections left a legacy of NGOs across the country and a good level of English among the population. With the economy liberalised, international investors have been pouring in money in recent decades, but development has come at a cost for Cambodia's once-pristine environment.

## 1. Phnom Da
### THE KINGDOM OF FUNAN

This hilltop temple near the early capital of Angkor Borei in Takeo Province was a key religious centre of the Funan kingdom. From the 1st century CE, the Indianisation of Cambodia occurred through trading settlements that sprang up on the coast, functioning as important ports of call for boats on the trading route from the Bay of Bengal to the southern provinces of China. The largest kingdom, known as Funan by the Chinese, encompassed an area between Phnom Penh and Oc-Eo in southern Vietnam. Although very little is known about Funan, much has been made of its importance as an early Southeast Asian centre of power.

*For more on Phnom Da, see page 238.*

## 2. Sambor Prei Kuk
### THE CAPITAL OF CHENLA

Cambodia's third Unesco World Heritage Site, Sambor Prei Kuk (pictured) is the most important group of pre-Angkorian temples in the country. It was originally known as Isanapura, the 7th-century capital of the Chenla kingdom. There is little evidence to support the idea that Chenla was a unified kingdom that held sway over all of Cambodia like latter-day Angkor. From the 6th to the 8th century, Cambodia was a collection of competing kingdoms, ruled by autocratic kings who legitimised their rule through hierarchical caste concepts borrowed from India. Look out for an impressive brick temple that is suffocating under the roots of a strangler fig.

*For more on Sambor Prei Kuk, see page 184.*

## 3. Phnom Kulen
### MOUNTAIN OF THE GOD-KING

A popular place of pilgrimage for Khmers today, the sacred mountain of Phnom Kulen, northeast of Angkor, is home to an inscription that tells of Jayavarman II (r 802–50) proclaiming himself a 'universal monarch', or *devaraja* (god-king), in 802 in the city of Mahendraparvata. It is believed that he may have resided in the Buddhist Shailendras' court in Java as a young man and was inspired by the great Javanese temples of Borobudur and Prambanan. Upon his return to Cambodia, he instigated an uprising against Javanese control of coastal Cambodia. Jayavarman II was the first monarch to rule most of what we call Cambodia today.

*For more on Phnom Kulen, see page 146.*

BEIBAOKE/SHUTTERSTOCK ©

## 4. Koh Ker
### THE USURPER CAPITAL

A usurper capital established under Jayavarman IV around 928, Koh Ker is one of the least-studied temples from the Angkorian period, despite the fact it has one of the most iconic structures at its heart, the great pyramid of Prasat Thom (Prasat Prang). Archaeological surveys were carried out in the 1950s and 1960s, but all records were lost during the destruction of the 1970s, helping to preserve the enigmatic status of this complex. Koh Ker was heavily looted during the long civil war and many of the best pieces of sculpture ended up in overseas museums, but are steadily being reclaimed by the Cambodian government.

*For more on Koh Ker, see page 150.*

## 5. Angkor Wat
### SYMBOL OF A NATION

One of the most inspirational monuments conceived in human history, Angkor Wat is widely regarded as the world's largest religious building. The reign of Suryavarman II (r 1112–52) and the construction of his imposing state temple signifies one of the high-water marks of Khmer civilisation. Under the leadership of Suryavarman II, Cambodia was unified once more after years of civil war and Khmer influence was extended to the borders of modern-day Malaysia and Myanmar. He also set himself apart religiously from earlier kings through his devotion to the Hindu deity Vishnu, and Angkor Wat was dedicated to this patron god of preservation.

*For more on Angkor Wat, see page 114.*

## 6. Bayon
### THE FACE TEMPLE

In 1177 the Chams of southern Vietnam, then the kingdom of Champa, sacked Angkor. This attack caught the Khmers unawares, as it came via sea, river and lake rather than the traditional land routes. The Chams burnt the wooden city and plundered its wealth. Four years later, Jayavarman VII (r 1181–1219) struck back, emphatically driving the Chams out of Cambodia and reclaiming Angkor. During his reign, Jayavarman VII embarked on a dizzying array of temple-building that culminated in Angkor Thom. The centrepiece of the great walled city was

Bayon, the temple-mountain emblazoned with signature faces that is one of the most iconic of Cambodia's temples.

*For more on Bayon, see page 126.*

## 7. Siem Reap
DEFEAT BY THAILAND

After the death of Jayavarman VII around 1219, the Khmer empire went into decline. The state religion reverted to Hinduism and outbreaks of iconoclasm saw Buddhist sculpture desecrated. The Thais sacked Angkor in 1351, and again to devastating effect in 1431. The capital was decisively shifted to Phnom Penh and much of Angkor abandoned to the elements, save for the nearby community of Siem Reap, somewhat optimistically translating as 'Siam defeated'. The Siamese capital of Ayuthaya, which enjoyed a golden age from the 14th to the 18th centuries, was in many ways a recreation of the glories of Angkor from which the Thai conquerors drew inspiration.

*For more on Siem Reap, see page 88.*

## 8. Phnom Penh
THE HISTORIC POWERHOUSE

Following the sacking of Angkor by the Thais, the Khmer court moved to Phnom Penh, a strategic location on the confluence of the Mekong and Tonlé Sap rivers. Phnom Penh commanded a more central position in the Khmer territories and was perfectly located for riverine trade with Laos and China via the Mekong Delta. Legend has it that the city of Phnom Penh was founded when an old woman named Penh found four Buddha statues resting on the banks of the Mekong River. She housed them on a nearby hill, and the town that grew up here came to be known as Phnom Penh (Hill of Penh).

*For more on Phnom Penh, see page 43.*

## 9. Udong
STUPA-STUDDED FORMER CAPITAL

Udong served as the capital of Cambodia under several kings between the 17th and 19th centuries, a period during which Cambodia was in terminal decline (ironically, Udon translates as 'victorious'). A number of kings, including King Norodom, were crowned here. The main attractions today are the twin humps of Phnom Udong, which have several stupas on them housing the

remains of important Cambodian monarchs including King Soriyopor (whose final resting place is the Damrei Sam Poan stupa), King Ang Doung and King Monivong, whose ashes are interned in the Mak Proum stupa. Both ends of the hilltop offer great views of the Cambodian countryside.

*For more on Udong, see page 78.*

## 10. Battambang
FRENCH ARCHITECTURAL LEGACY

A painful era of yo-yoing between Thai and Vietnamese masters came to a close in 1863, when French gunboats intimidated King Norodom I (r 1860–1904) into signing a treaty of protectorate. Ironically, it was a genuine protectorate, as Cambodia was in danger of going the way of Champa and vanishing from the map. French control of Cambodia developed as a sideshow to its interests in Vietnam and initially involved little direct interference in Cambodia's affairs. The French left an impressive architectural legacy in towns and cities across Cambodia, and Battambang remains one of the best-preserved French-era centres, with lots of old shophouses.

*For more on Battambang, see page 158.*

## 11. Kampot
THE SPICE TRADE

Cambodia's original coastal port, long before Sihanoukville was established in 1959, Kampot was a gateway to outbound trade and inbound migration of Chinese settlers fleeing the turbulence of the late 19th and early 20th centuries. It was also a province rich in precious spices such as pepper, turmeric, galangal and ginger, all of which were desirable commodities for its giant northern neighbour. Even today, Kampot pepper is considered some of the best in the world with a Unesco Geographical Indication, and it is possible to visit pepper plantations in both Kampot and Kep provinces.

*For more on Kampot, see page 228.*

## 12. S-21 Prison & the Killing Fields of Choeung Ek
HORRORS OF THE KHMER ROUGE

In 1975 Pol Pot's security forces took over Tuol Svay Prey High School in Phnom Penh and turned it into the notorious Security Prison 21 (S-21), which became the largest

centre of detention and torture in Cambodia. Over the next three years, about 20,000 men, women and children who had been detained and tortured there were transported to the extermination camp of Choeung Ek, known today as the Killing Fields. The S-21 prison is now the Tuol Sleng Genocide Museum, a testament to the crimes of the Khmer Rouge during the time of Democratic Kampuchea.

*For more on S-21 and the Killing Fields of Choeung Ek, see pages 68 and 69.*

### 13. Royal Palace
HOME TO CAMBODIAN MONARCHS

King Norodom Sihanouk was a towering presence in the topsy-turvy world of Cambodian politics – a larger-than-life character of many enthusiasms and shifting political positions, whose amatory exploits dominated his early life. Later he became the prince who stage-managed the close of French colonialism, led Cambodia during its golden years, was imprisoned by the Khmer Rouge and, from privileged exile, finally returned triumphant as king. Sihanouk died on 15 October 2012 and more than one million Cambodians lined the streets to welcome his body home to the Royal Palace (pictured) for an elaborate state funeral. His place in history is assured, the last in a long line of Angkor's god-kings.

*For more on the Royal Palace, see page 49.*

### 14. Prasat Preah Vihear
A DISPUTE WITH THAILAND

For generations, Prasat Preah Vihear (called Khao Phra Wiharn by the Thais) has been a source of tension between Cambodia and Thailand. This area was ruled by Thailand for almost two centuries, but returned to Cambodia during the French protectorate. In 1959 the Thai military seized the temple, and Cambodia's government took the dispute to the International Court of Justice (ICJ), gaining worldwide recognition of Cambodian sovereignty in a 1962 ruling. The dispute flared up again in 2008, when Unesco recognised Preah Vihear as a World Heritage Site, but it died down after 2013 when the ICJ confirmed its original ruling that the temple belongs to Cambodia.

*For more on Prasat Preah Vihear, see page 172.*

### 15. Anlong Veng
LAST STAND OF THE KHMER ROUGE

By 1998, the Khmer Rouge was close to defeat in its final major stronghold of Anlong Veng near the Thai border in the far north of the country. The CPP (Cambodian People's Party) announced an all-out offensive against its enemies and by April it was closing in on the kill. Amid the heavy fighting, Pol Pot evaded justice by dying a natural death on 15 April in the captivity of his former Khmer Rouge comrades. Anlong Veng is a peaceful place these days, and it is possible to visit many former sites associated with the Khmer Rouge, including the house of former military commander Ta Mok, known as 'the Butcher'.

*For more on Anlong Veng, see page 181.*

# MEET THE CAMBODIANS

Cambodian society is moving with the times, but don't ignore tradition and a still painful past. MADÉVI DAILLY introduces her people.

**MUCH HAS BEEN** written about the warmth of the Cambodian smile, but our famous grins and welcoming nature often act as a well-meaning smokescreen to a complex national character. If a Khmer Emily Post were to write a manual on local etiquette, it would span several volumes, so dense and tangled the web of social rules that bind some 17 million of us.

Take what we call each other as an amuse-bouche: we may carry the Sanskrit names of stars (Dara), flowers (Bopha) and deities (Devi), but you'll rarely hear these spoken between us. Instead, we love a good nickname: chubby cheeks or lanky arms might turn into a lifelong moniker. You'll be expected to guess a new acquaintance's age and social status within seconds of meeting them, and this will determine which informal or honorific title you use. Tread carefully: calling someone *ming* (auntie) when they deserve the respect of a *yeay* (grandmother) may land you in scalding hot water.

Life in Cambodia flows to the rhythm of Buddhist prayers, a religion practised by some 93% of Cambodians – a startling number given the systematic persecution of Buddhist monks under the Khmer Rouge. It isn't rare for Cambodian boys to go through a few years of monastic life to further their education, with some taking their religious calling more seriously than others. Minorities, meanwhile, are free to worship as they see fit: many Vietnamese are Roman Catholic, Chams are often Sunni Muslims, and Bunongs still cling to animist traditions in the depths of Mondulkiri Province.

The colonial French may have dismissed Khmer entrepreneurship with the saying 'The Vietnamese plant the rice, the Cambodians watch the rice grow', but life in Phnom Penh moves at breakneck speed, in stark contrast to the water-snail's pace of rural areas. A youthful, increasingly connected population (roughly 60% of Cambodians are under 25) means society has no choice but to modernise. Some things never change, though: haggling and hustling are a national pastime, second only to snacking and napping. Generosity is a way of life, too: linger anywhere long enough and you're sure to be offered a slice of fruit or a spot in a hammock.

Most importantly, we like to party. Weddings typically last three gluttonous days and cities empty during Khmer New Year, with villagers clinging comically to overloaded vans for a chance to get home in time for the celebrations. K-pop, predictably, is hugely popular, as is the older, more established hip-hop and R&B scene imported with returning refugees. Busting out your best dance moves is the easiest way to make new friends. Join a *romvong* – a circular dance with perennial appeal – and you may even gain *yeay*'s grudging approval.

## What's in a Name?

'Khmer' and 'Cambodian' are often used interchangeably, though erroneously. The former, one of the oldest ethnic groups in the region, make up 90% of Cambodians, but can also be found in parts of neighbouring Thailand and Vietnam.

## I'M CAMBODIAN...KIND OF

Dakar is where I came wailing into the world at the tail end of 1979, as the Khmer Rouge beat their last retreat towards the hills of Pailin. My mother had moved to France in the early 1970s with a university scholarship, and lost all contact with her family after the fall of Phnom Penh in 1975. She followed my French father to Japan, then Qatar and Senegal; my childhood spanned six other countries.

My story isn't unique: 260,000 Cambodian refugees were resettled abroad after 1975, mostly in the US and France. Mine, by accident of birth, was a life of safety and privilege; we made the inverse journey in 1982, flying in on a Red Cross plane to reunite with my long-lost grandparents. Having lived in the UK most of my adult life, I've had little contact with the Cambodian diaspora, and speak embarrassingly poor Khmer. But I cherish the permanent 'K' visa in my French passport: proof, if required, that I'm still Cambodian.

293

# TRIALS OF THE KHMER ROUGE

The UN-backed war crimes tribunal may have ended, but the scars remain.

**THE KHMER ROUGE** controlled Cambodia for three years, eight months and 20 days, a timespan etched into the consciousness of the older Khmer generation. The Vietnamese ousted the Khmer Rouge on 7 January 1979, but Cambodia's civil war continued for another two decades until 1999. More than 20 years after the Khmer Rouge regime's collapse, the Extraordinary Chambers in the Courts of Cambodia (ECCC) commenced trials to bring those responsible for the deaths of about two million Cambodians to justice.

Case 001, the trial of Kaing Guek Eav, aka Comrade Duch, began in 2009. A key figure, he provided the link between the regime and its crimes in his role as head of S-21 prison. Duch was sentenced to 35 years in 2010, but this was reduced to 19 years in lieu of time already served and his cooperation with the investigating team. For many Cambodians this was a slap in the face, as Duch had already admitted overall responsibility for the deaths of about 17,000 people. Converted into simple numbers, it equates to about 10 hours of prison time per victim. However, a later appeal verdict extended the sentence to life imprisonment; he died serving time in 2020.

Case 002 began in 2011, involving the most senior surviving leaders of the Democratic Kampuchea (DK) era: Brother Number Two Nuon Chea, former DK head of state Khieu Samphan, and former DK Foreign Minister Ieng Sary and his wife, former DK Minister of Social Affairs Ieng Thirith. Ieng Sary died in 2013 and Ieng Thirith was ruled unfit to stand trial due to the onset of dementia. Both Nuon Chea and Khieu Samphan received two separate life sentences – the first for crimes against humanity in 2014, and a second for genocide in 2018. Both parties appealed the latter conviction. Nuon Chea died in 2019 before the ECCC delivered its final ruling in 2022, upholding Khieu Samphan's sentence. He remains the last top-level Khmer Rouge leader alive.

Case 003 was lodged in 2009 against head of the DK navy, Meas Muth, and head of the DK air force, Sou Met. In 2015 the ECCC named additional suspects under Case 004: Im Chaem, a regional commander accused of murder, extermination and

enslavement in the DK's Northwestern Zone; her co-commander, Yim Tith; and top DK Central Zone official Ao An, accused of genocide against the Cham minority. The cases took years to develop amid fierce opposition from the Cambodian government, which wanted to draw a line under proceedings with the completion of Case 002. In 2015 the accused were finally charged, but the indictments collapsed as the Cambodian co-investigating judge on the ECCC panel refused to bring charges.

More than US$330 million was reportedly spent on the trial, against a backdrop of allegations of corruption and mismanagement on the Cambodian side. Some Cambodians feel the trial sends an important political message about accountability that may resonate with the Cambodian leadership today. However, others argue that the trial is a major waste of money, given the overwhelming evidence against the senior leadership, and that a truth and reconciliation commission may have provided more compelling answers to understand what motivated the average Khmer Rouge cadre to kill.

When the ECCC Court upheld the verdict of Khieu Samphan on 21 September 2022, a process that had taken more than 15 years from the formation of the court in 2006 came to a close. The tribunal allowed victims' voices to be heard in an international court of law and has brought some closure to the Cambodians impacted by the death and violence of the Khmer Rouge regime. However, whether or not these verdicts will have an impact on the respect for international law and human rights in the domestic courts of Cambodia remains to be seen.

## Brother Number One: Pol Pot

For the notorious Pol Pot, whose policies heaped misery, suffering and death on millions of Cambodians, the trial began almost a decade too late. Many Cambodians were sceptical about the circumstances of his death on 15 April 1998. Officially, he was said to have died from a heart attack, but a full autopsy was not carried out before he was cremated on a pyre of burning tyres.

Pol Pot was born Saloth Sar in a small village near Kompong Thom in 1925. As a young man he won a scholarship to study in Paris, where he came into contact with the Cercle Marxiste and communist thought, which he later transformed into the politics of extreme Maoism.

In 1963, Sihanouk's repressive policies sent Saloth Sar and his comrades fleeing to the jungles of Ratanakiri Province and around this time he began to call himself Pol Pot. When the Khmer Rouge marched into Phnom Penh on 17 April 1975, few people could have anticipated the hell that was to follow. Pol Pot and his clique were the architects of one of the most radical and brutal revolutions in the history of humankind. It was Year Zero and Cambodia was on a self-destructive course to sever all ties with the past.

After being ousted by the Vietnamese, Pol Pot spent much of the 1980s living in Thailand and was able to rebuild his shattered forces and once again threaten Cambodia until his death in 1998.

For more on the life and times of Pol Pot, pick up one of the excellent biographies written about him: *Brother Number One* by David Chandler or *Pol Pot: The History of a Nightmare* by Phillip Short.

# THE REVIVAL OF CAMBODIAN ARTS

Crushed by the Khmer Rouge, traditional Cambodian arts are experiencing a modern-day renaissance.

**AN INCREDIBLE HERITAGE** of architecture, sculpture, music, performing arts and cinema contributes to Cambodia's rich national character. Visitors have ample opportunity to drink it all in, from the Temples of Angkor, the ultimate embodiment of Khmer artistic prowess, to cultural revival initiatives like the hugely popular circus of Phare Ponleu Selpak in Battambang and Siem Reap.

Khmer architecture and sculpture reached its peak during the Angkorian era (9th to 14th centuries), with some of the finest examples of architecture from this period including Angkor Wat and the temples of Angkor Thom. The Khmer empire produced some of the most exquisite carved sculptures found anywhere on the planet. Even in the pre-Angkorian era, the periods generally referred to as Funan and Chenla, the people of Cambodia were producing masterfully sensuous sculpture. Cambodian sculptors have rediscovered their skills now that there is a ready market among visitors for reproduction stone carvings of famous statues and busts from the time of Angkor.

During the 1950s and 1960s, Cambodia's golden era, a group of young Khmer architects shaped the capital of Cambodia in their own image, experimenting with what is now known as New Khmer Architecture. Vann Molyvann (1926–2017) was the most famous proponent of this school of architecture, designing a number of Phnom Penh landmarks such as the Olympic Stadium, Chaktomuk Theatre and Independence Monument.

The Khmer Rouge's assault on the arts was a terrible blow to Cambodian culture. Indeed, for a number of years the consensus among Khmers was that their culture had been irrevocably lost. The Khmer Rouge not only did away with living bearers of Khmer culture – including golden-era singers like Sinn Sisamouth, Ros Sereysothea and Pen Ran, all of whom disappeared in the early days of the regime – but also destroyed cultural artefacts, statues, books and anything else that served as a reminder of a past it was trying to efface. The temples of Angkor were spared as a symbol of Khmer glory and empire – today they remain a fierce source of national pride – but little else survived.

Despite this, Cambodia is witnessing a resurgence of traditional arts and a growing interest in experimentation in modern

297

arts and cross-cultural fusion. At the forefront of reviving endangered traditional performing arts is the nonprofit Cambodian Living Arts, which helps locals to develop and sustain their careers in the arts through scholarships, fellowships and other support.

While much of Cambodia's golden-era music was lost in the Pol Pot era, musical traditions are literally etched into its history, with bas-reliefs found on monuments in the Angkor region depicting musicians with instruments similar to contemporary Khmer instruments. One form of music unique to Cambodia is *chapaye*, a sort of Cambodian blues sung to the accompaniment of a two-stringed wooden instrument, similar in sound to a bass guitar without an amplifier.

After the war, many Khmers settled in the US, where a lively Khmer pop industry evolved. Cambodians are now returning to their homeland raised on a diet of rap and lots of artists are breaking through, including the hugely popular VannDa. Dengue Fever is the ultimate fusion band, rapidly gaining a name for itself beyond the US and Cambodia; Cambodian singer Chhom Nimol fronts five American prog rockers who dabble in psychedelic sounds.

More than any of the other traditional arts, Cambodia's Unesco-listed Royal Ballet (also known as Khmer Classical Dance) is a tangible link with the glory of Angkor. Its traditions stretch long into the past, when the dance of the *apsara* (heavenly nymph) was performed for the divine king. Early in his reign, King Sihanouk released the traditional harem of royal *apsaras* that came with the crown. Dance fared particularly badly during the Pol Pot years and very few dancers and teachers survived. In 1981, with a handful of teachers, the Roy-

al University of Fine Arts reopened and the training of dance students resumed.

Contemporary dances include the popular *romvong* or circle dance, which is likely to have originated in neighbouring Laos. Dancers move around in a circle taking three steps forward and two steps back. Hip-hop and breakdancing is fast gaining popularity among the urban youth who are in tune with global music trends like K-Pop.

Between 1960 and 1975, more than 300 films were made in Cambodia, including numerous movies by then head of state Norodom Sihanouk. However, the advent of Khmer Rouge rule saw the film industry disappear overnight and it didn't recover for more than a quarter of a century.

At least one overseas Cambodian director has enjoyed major success in recent years: Rithy Panh. His film *The Missing Picture*, which used clay figurines to tell his personal story of survival under the Khmer Rouge, was nominated for an Academy Award for Best Foreign Language Film in 2014. His success goes back to 1994, when *The Rice People* was nominated for the Palme d'Or at the Cannes Film Festival. *The Last Reel* (2014), directed by Kulikar Sotho, is another film that explores the impact of Cambodia's dark past on the next generation and it won the Spirit of Asia Award at the Tokyo International Film Festival.

A number of international films have been shot in Cambodia since the turn of the millennium, including *Lara Croft: Tomb Raider* (2001), *City of Ghosts* (2002) and *Two Brothers* (2004), all worth seeking out for their beautiful Cambodian backdrops. Angelina Jolie returned to Cambodia to film *First They Killed My Father*, based on the book by Luong Ung and available on Netflix.

# FRESH, DRIED, SMOKED & SALTED

Pickling and fermenting are trending on the global culinary stage. Such techniques have been a cornerstone of Cambodian cuisine for centuries. By Madévi Dailly

**BATHED BY THE** nutrient-rich waters of the Mekong and the Tonlé Sap rivers, Cambodian soil is as fertile as it comes: plant a seed here and within weeks a sapling will be reaching up towards the scorching sun. That's not to say, however, that keeping well fed is a breeze for the country's many subsistence farmers. Temperamental monsoons, a painfully dry spring season and unreliable irrigation systems mean that rice, the main crop, can easily fail. All the more reason to preserve the seasonal bounty of the land, rivers and sea – something Cambodians have excelled at for centuries.

Cambodian cuisine sits somewhere at the crossroads of Thai and Vietnamese fare: less fiery than the former, richer than the latter, and with a taste for robust flavours all its own. You'll find its core components at the local wet market; fish, naturally, is the key ingredient. Ignore anyone waxing lyrical about *amok*: quite how (or why) the delicate fish curry achieved 'national dish' status is probably best left to the swamps of time. *Teuk trey* (literally 'fish water'), fish sauce made from salted oily fish left to ferment in clay pots, is used to season marinades, stir fries and punchy dipping sauces. Gluts of snakehead and

**Fermented crab, Psar Thmei, Phnom Penh (p60)**

catfish are smoked, or carefully left to dry in the sun; for a wholesome start to the day, try chunks of the fish fried with garlic alongside a steaming bowl of *bobor* (rice porridge), or pounded and grilled with a watermelon salad. Powerfully pongy *prahoc* – the cheese of the fish world – is made from crushed mudfish left to rot for a day in the sun, then fermented in salt for up to three years. Grilled in banana leaves, it adds a welcome salty kick to plain jasmine rice. It's an acquired taste, with umami depths so addictive that Khmer Americans have started referring to *prahoc* dips as 'crack sauce' – a worthy accompaniment to a char-grilled steak.

Served family-style, Cambodian meals are built around a balance of flavours and textures: light and rich, crispy and tender, sour and sweet. A spoonful of caramel pork, say, might be followed by a sip of sour soup; tender,

> SERVED FAMILY-STYLE, CAMBODIAN MEALS ARE BUILT AROUND A BALANCE OF FLAVOURS AND TEXTURES: LIGHT AND RICH, CRISPY AND TENDER, SOUR AND SWEET.

smoky beef skewers need the crunch and tang of a green mango salad. Khmer cookery queens say a good meal needs a taste of something that's just a little too much: an extra spoonful of palm sugar, perhaps, or the acidic fizz of a good pickle. Fresh ones are made by giving sliced daikon, carrots and cucumber a quick bath in a sugary vinegar solution; they're just the thing with *bei sait chrouk* (a breakfast dish of grilled pork and rice). *Jrouk spey* (pickled mustard greens) are preserved in a boiling brine, a method yielding crisp, peppery leaves that work well with grilled fish or chicken. Pickled lime, like its Middle Eastern cousin the pickled lemon, adds both citrusy zest and depth of flavour to duck or chicken soup. Foraged from rice paddies, small freshwater crabs are given the aromatic treatment with galangal, holy basil, chilli, garlic, kaffir lime leaves, lime juice and plenty of salt. These prosaically named *kdam prai* (salty crabs) can zhuzh up mango or papaya salads, but they're not for meek taste buds. If your gut flora is up to the challenge, look out for vendors peddling sun-dried clams on large, flat carts as an afternoon snack.

You're unlikely to find these delicacies in restaurants catering to westerners, so it's worth keeping curious when sampling street food or exploring the countryside. If the world can fall in love with Korean kimchi, surely *prahoc* is just waiting for its day in the sun?

**Fishmonger, Phnom Penh (p43)**

LEFT: KONNGUI/SHUTTERSTOCK ©. RIGHT: NATALIA DAVIDOVICH/SHUTTERSTOCK ©

# THE FRENCH LEGACY
## IN CAMBODIA

Colonial-era architecture abounds and baguettes are everywhere, but vestiges of French rule continue to fade.

**IT SEEMS HARD** to escape Cambodia's colonial past at first glance. Despite the fact that the country was only ruled by Paris from 1863 to 1953, Cambodia gets its name from France – Cambodia is the English translation of the French *Cambodge* – while the nation's frontiers were also fixed during the period of French rule. Then there's the colonial-era architecture found across the country, the baguettes sold on every street corner and the coffee sipped in cafes everywhere, all of which gives the impression that France left a lasting legacy in Cambodia.

Look a little more closely, though, and a different story emerges. Foreigners may re-

fer to the country as Cambodia, but many locals use Kampuchea, a Sanskrit-inspired name that goes back 2000-odd years to the Funan era. Others call their country *srok Khmer*, or Khmer Land. Nor should too much be read into the appetite for bread and coffee; pizza and burgers are now also very popular with those who can afford them.

French rule lasted for less than 100 years and, generally, had a lighter impact on Cambodia than it did on neighbouring Vietnam, which France regarded as the more important colony. Cambodians, though, paid higher taxes to the colonists than the Vietnamese did and, by

**French-era post office, Phnom Penh (p61)**

the time the French departed, had comparatively little to show for that in terms of working infrastructure. The railway line from Phnom Penh to Sihanoukville that is popular with travellers today was built after independence, as was Sihanoukville itself, now Cambodia's major port. French archaeologists did reclaim Angkor Wat from the jungle in the early 20th century but, in recent years, both the quality of their restoration work and the dubious narrative that France 'gave' Cambodia back its history has come under fire from academics.

Today, colonial-period architecture is the most obvious and resonant reminder of the French era. Phnom Penh and Battambang, and to a lesser extent Kampot, Kep and Kratie, are home to red-roofed mansions with louver windows and doors, high-ceilinged rooms and balconies, as well as a number of art-deco-inspired buildings such as Phnom Penh's main market or the Old Market in Kampot.

**TODAY, COLONIAL-PERIOD ARCHITECTURE IS THE MOST OBVIOUS AND RESONANT REMINDER OF THE FRENCH ERA.**

**National Bank of Cambodia, Battambang (p228)**

Some of the mansions have been elegantly restored and are in use as hotels, banks or company headquarters. Others are crumbling away, their cream or yellow facades streaked with mould and dirt. But few Khmers willingly choose to live in them, and not just because of the high prices such structures now command. Like most people across Southeast Asia, the locals regard a modern apartment or house as far more preferable than a run-down relic of the past, not least because an old property means the presence of ghosts.

While some French buildings have survived, little of the French language has. It's still possible to see fading official signs written in Khmer and French on government buildings, but few Cambodians speak or learn French now. In the 1970s, the Khmer Rouge killed off as many French speakers as they could find, even though many senior Khmer Rouge leaders attended universities in Paris, and use of the language has continued to decline since then. A 2022 report by the Organisation Internationale de la Francophonie revealed that only around 2.7% of the population speaks French. Studying English or Mandarin is now considered to be far more important.

The colonial period is rarely a subject of public discussion either. History studies are not a priority in schools or universities – many private colleges don't offer history degrees as they are not seen as useful for finding a job – so there is scant awareness of those times. And while there are around half a million French Cambodians, mostly living in Paris and Lyon, Cambodia's relationship with France has become more tenuous in recent years, as Prime Minister Hun Sen has established much closer ties with China. Travellers will still see people playing *pétanque* (a French version of bowls) around the country, but the overwhelming attitude towards the colonial era is one of indifference.

# WOMEN IN MODERN CAMBODIA

Traditional values may run deep in Cambodia, but a new generation of women is finding its voice. By Madévi Dailly

**THERE'S NO DENYING** traditional values are still upheld in Cambodian society – an ancestral framework where the place of mothers, daughters and wives is firmly in the home. The perfect Cambodian woman bears heavy societal expectations on her shoulders: she is humble, modest, chaste, sweet and smiling – a living, breathing embodiment of *apsaras*, the angelic figures depicted in Angkor carvings. For centuries this vision of femininity was enshrined in the Chbab Srey, a now controversial 'code of conduct' for Cambodian girls (there's also a boy's version – the Chbab Pros, which, as you might expect, has a wildly different message). Passed down through oral tradition, this mother's advice to a new bride advocated submissiveness, respecting her husband, walking without rustling her skirt and generally maintaining peace in the home. Arranged into a poem by 19th-century King Ang Duong, the Chbab Srey had traditionally been taught in schools, but was removed from public curriculums in 2007 – a sign of shifting expectations.

Scratch beneath Cambodia's patriarchal surface, in fact, and a more nuanced reality emerges. Women were granted the right to vote in 1955, shortly after independence from France. In the 15 or so years that followed, Sihanouk's Sangkum Reastr Niyum movement (a form of royal-Buddhist socialism, championing both social equality and traditional values) improved opportunities for women.

The number of girls in primary and secondary education grew during the 1960s in response to Sihanouk's vision for a modern Cambodia shining bright as the 'Pearl of Asia'. The movement proved popular, especially in cities, where work in modern offices and exposure to western media led to changes in fashion, including bouffant hair and scandalous hemlines. Influenced by western rock and soul, a distinctive Cambodian style of pop music emerged in the '60s and '70s, giving voice to a generation of young women. Wise-cracking singer Pen Ran, among others, challenged conventions of the time with her risqué dancing and rebellious lyrics, with songs like 'There's Nothing To Be Ashamed Of' or 'It's Too Late Old Man' lambasting Cambodia's old-fashioned views on courtship and female sexuality.

Tragically, the Khmer Rouge era swiftly ended women's growing sense of empowerment. While the regime professed to treat both genders equally, its efforts to wipe out western influences resulted in the execution of prominent cultural figures, among them Pen Ran, her fellow rock stars, Cambodian ballet dancers and other icons. Forced marriages were systematically instituted in a brutal drive to increase the population and control every aspect of people's lives. Domestic and sexual violence were used as the regime's tools. This resulted in widespread, unspoken and untreated trauma, the effects of which still ripple through the generations, amplifying mental health issues, addiction, marginalisation and poverty.

Gender inequalities persist in modern Cambodia. Women re-entered the workforce in droves in the postwar era (roughly 85% or Cambodia's 800,000 garment workers are women), though few have secured line-managing or office roles. But much as in many Southeast Asian countries, women are towering figures in the family home – a far cry from the meek ideal depicted in the Chbab Srey. They inherit wealth and property, and are expected to run the household – including keeping a tight grip on the purse strings. Spending, investing and debt are the domain of savvy, hard-headed women, who gain in experience and respectability with age – a matriarchy in sheep's clothing. Though equal rights, access to education and paid maternity leave are enshrined in the 1993 constitution, there's still a long road ahead to improve quality of life for women, particularly in rural areas, and change the enduring cultural norms preventing true progress.

Introduced in the 1990s, the Ministry of Women's Affairs has made progress with a series of five-year plans spanning economic opportunities, education, healthcare and more. Named Neary Rattanak ('women are precious gems', a retort to the Khmer proverb stating that 'men are gold, women are just a white piece of cloth'), these plans continue to battle entrenched chauvinism. The 2019 census showed a significant increase in literacy levels, in spite of a widening gap between men (91.1%) and women (86.2%), though enrollment rates were the same for young boys and girls, with better retention rates for the latter. Prioritising better care for mothers and babies has resulted in falling maternal and infant mortality rates – a great success story for Cambodia. Government schemes such as the National Social Security Fund have been launched to provide particularly vulnerable women in the garment industry with maternity allowances and pensions, while Unesco's Factory Literacy Programme hopes to encourage greater access to basic worker rights.

Domestic violence, underage sex work and human trafficking are still huge problems, with victims struggling to re-enter society due to the deep-rooted belief that survivors of sexual abuse are impure. Change has been slow. There's no shortage of women active at the grassroots level, such as LGBTIQ+ activist Chhoeurng Rachana, land rights activist Tep Vanny or outspoken relationship guru DJ Nana. But Cambodian women have struggled to gain a foothold on the political stage, taking up only 21% of parliamentary seats against a backdrop of corruption, opposition crackdowns and cultural bias. Mu Sochua, a former minister nominated for a Nobel prize for her work against sex trafficking, fled the country in 2017 for fear of political reprisals. Still, a new generation of Cambodian women continues to find its voice, buoyed by better education, shifting societal expectations and the power of social media. Long may they sing.

# CAMBODIA'S
# NATURAL
# ENVIRONMENT

Homegrown eco-activism is on the rise, but Cambodia faces major environmental challenges.

**CAMBODIA COVERS AN** area of 181,035 sq km, making it a bit more than half the size of Vietnam or about the same area as England and Wales combined. The country's two dominant geographical features are the Mekong River, which slices through Cambodia from the border with Laos in the north to the frontier with Vietnam in the south, and the Tonlé Sap, the largest freshwater lake in Southeast Asia.

Rich sediment deposited by the Mekong during the June-to-October rainy season makes central Cambodia incredibly fertile, which is why the region is home to the majority of the country's population. The Tonlé Sap in the northwest is one of the world's richest sources of freshwater fish, and half of Cambodia's people rely on the lake for fish and for irrigation.

Around 45% of Cambodia is still covered in forest, mainly in the mountainous southwest and east of the country. Those regions are also home to the majority of Cambodia's rare and endangered wildlife, which includes Asian elephants, clouded leopards, freshwater Irrawaddy dolphins, Siamese crocodiles, sun bears and pangolins.

Some animals, like tigers and the kouprey, the wild cattle that were declared to be Cambodia's national animal in the 1960s, are now thought to be essentially extinct as none have been spotted for decades.

With significant chunks of the country still relatively unexplored, such as the Southern Cardamom Mountains and the forests and grasslands of the far northeast, Cambodia is thought to be one of the most biodiverse countries in Southeast Asia. Some 666 bird species are found here including rare giant ibises and masked finfoots. There's also a great variety of butterflies, insects and reptiles, while Flora & Fauna International estimates that there are at least 8260 different plant species.

Marine life is abundant, too. Cambodia has 435km of coastline, some of which is home to mangrove forests, and 60-odd islands, most of which are surrounded by coral reefs. Cambodia's coral is an environmental success story, with 70 different coral species and divers reporting that much of it is healthy and vibrant, in contrast to some of the reefs in neighbouring Thailand.

Unfortunately, that conservation success isn't being replicated on the mainland. Cambodia faces the twin threats of deforestation and an ever-increasing number of dams on the Mekong. With the government striving to grow the economy and signs of unchecked development everywhere, most officials at both local and central government level appear to be ignoring the rising number of homegrown eco-activists out to protect and preserve Cambodia's natural splendours.

Deforestation driven by illegal logging and the clearing of land for industrial agriculture such as rubber plantations is the most pressing concern. Despite the fact that numerous areas are now officially protected, either as national parks, wildlife sanctuaries or protected landscapes, Cambodia continues to lose a frightening amount of forest each year. Global Forest Watch estimates that 26% of the country's tree cover, or 26,400 sq km, disappeared between 2000 and 2020. A May 2022 report by the University of Maryland in the US stated that Cambodia lost 1.5% of its tree cover in 2021 alone, a higher annual loss percentage than any other country in the world.

Clearing forests has a huge impact on wildlife: habitat loss is the biggest single threat to species anywhere. But it's just as detrimental to humans living in the affected areas. Increased flooding and soil erosion are unwelcome by-products of deforestation, while many of the almost 80% of Cambodians living in rural areas depend on forests for food and fuel. For Cambodia's ethnic minorities, who live in the regions most affected by deforestation, forests are also hugely significant culturally and spiritually.

Dams along the Mekong are the other significant menace to the environment. In recent years, China has built eight dams upriver, with more planned, while Laos is constructing two controversial dams. Cambodia has also built dams and the combined impact is now 'stressing' the lower Mekong in Cambodia, according to a 2021 report from the Mekong River Commission. The dams have significantly affected both the amount of sediment deposited by the Mekong to fertilise land and the water flow to Tonlé Sap, the lake whose fish are the source of 70% of Cambodia's protein.

Fisherfolk along the Mekong in northern Cambodia are now reporting catching almost 50% fewer fish than they did five years ago. In 2020, the government announced a 10-year ban on damming the Mekong. But in 2022, a Cambodian conglomerate was given the go-ahead for feasibility studies on building a 1400MW mega-dam north of Stung Treng on one of the wildest and most remote stretches of the Mekong.

Lack of enforcement of environmental laws, as well as official indifference, is the biggest hurdle faced by Cambodia's environmentalists. In 2021, Prime Minister Hun Sen said that deforestation was being caused by poor people chopping down trees for homes and firewood, which is one way of explaining the loss of over 25,000 sq km of forest in two decades.

At the same time, the government has stepped up its harassment of eco-activists. Three young activists from local NGO Mother Nature Cambodia were charged with terrorism in 2021 for revealing that raw sewage was being pumped into the Tonlé Sap River near the Royal Palace in Phnom Penh. Environmentalists across the country routinely face threats, and sometimes worse, for exposing illicit logging operations.

A growing awareness among Cambodians of the environmental challenges their country faces does offer some hope for a different future. Ecotourism projects in the Southern Cardamom Mountains report a big uptick in the number of domestic visitors, while communities in the most affected areas are increasingly monitoring illegal logging themselves. But until the government truly commits to conserving and protecting the country's natural resources, Cambodia will continue to suffer serious environmental damage.

# INDEX

## A

accessible travel 282
accommodation 28, 273, 282, *see also individual accommodation options, locations*
activities 28-9, 36-9
air travel 18, 271, 282
*amok* 32, 72, 300
anastylosis 143
Andoung Tuek 207
Angkor Borei 238
Angkor Centre for Conservation of Biodiversity 92, 107
Angkor Conservation 15
Angkor National Museum 92, 96
Angkor Silk Farm 108
Angkor temples & structures 8-9, 113-51, **90-1, 113**
Angkor Thom 93, 125-41, **125, 132**
Angkor Wat 23, 93, 113-24, 289, **113**
Bakong 123
Banteay Chhmar 157, 169-70
Banteay Kdei 135
Banteay Samré 145
Banteay Srei 92, 142-9, **143**
Banteay Top 170
Baphuon 130, 132
Bayon 23, 126, 127-30, 132, 289-90
Beng Mealea 23, 93, 109, 127, 149
Chau Say Tevoda 139
Chau Srei Vibol 145
Eastern Mebon 140
Kbal Spean 92
Kleangs 133-4

Koh Ker 150-1, **151**
Lolei 123
Phimeanakas 132, 133
Phnom Bakheng 137
Phnom Bok 143
Phnom Chisor 83-4
Phnom Krom 124
Phnom Santuk 185
Prasat Banan 156, 165
Prasat Bram 151
Prasat Chen Chiem Trey 170
Prasat Damrei 176
Prasat Damrei Krap 147
Prasat Krahom 151
Prasat Krau Romeas 146
Prasat Kravan 137
Prasat Leung 151
Prasat Neak Buos 157
Prasat Preah Stung 176
Prasat Preah Thkol 176
Prasat Preah Vihear 157, 172-5, 291
Prasat Rong Chen 146-7
Prasat Thneng 151
Prasat Thom 151
Prasat Tuch 185
Pre Rup 141
Preah Khan 137-8
Preah Khan of Kompong Svay 157, 175-6
Preah Neak Poan 138-40
Preah Palilay 130, 132
Preah Pithu 130
Roluos temples 93, 109, 122-3
Spean Thmor 141
Ta Keo 140-1
Ta Nei 141
Ta Prohm 23, 80, 93, 127, 134-6
Ta Som 140
Thommanon 139
Tonlé Bati 80-1
Western Baray 134, 137
Western Mebon 134
Yeay Peau 80-1
Angkor Thom 93, 125-41, **125, 132**
Angkor Wat 23, 93, 113-24, 289, **113**
Angkor Zipline 37, 93, 138
animals 16-17, 37, 98, 107, 205-8, 232, 261, 278,

307, *see also individual species,* wildlife sanctuaries & zoos
Anlong Svay Waterfall 87
Anlong Veng 181-2, 291
Apopo Visitor Centre 98, 278
*apsaras* 121, 304
Arcadia Backpackers & Water Park 229
architecture 61-2, 63, 160-1, 228, 297, 303
arts 57, 71, 96, 161, 296-7, *see also* architecture, books, craft, dance, film, music, sculpture
ATMs 272

## B

bamboo train 162-3
Ban Lung 245, 260, 261, 262
Banteay Chhmar 157, 169-70
Banteay Kdei 135
Banteay Samré 145
Banteay Srei 92, 142-9, **143**
Baphuon 130, 132
bargaining 28, 280
bas-reliefs 115, 127-30
Bassac Lane 71-2, 74, 277
bats 62, 99, 146, 165, 193
Battambang 156, 157, 158-70, 290, **159**
accommodation 161, 162
activities 35, 160, 162-3, 164
beyond Battambang 167-70, *see also individual locations*
drinking & nightlife 162, 165, 166
entertainment 164
food 34, 161, 163, 164
itineraries 22
shopping 160
tours 160-1
travel within 166
Bayon 23, 126, 127-30, 132, 289-90
BBQ 277
beaches 12-13
Coconut Beach 217
Koh Tuch Beach 217

Koh Yor Beach 202-3
Lazy Beach 224, 225
Lonely Beach 218
Long Beach (Koh Rong) 216
Long Beach (Koh Ta Kiev) 213
Long Set Beach 217
Nature Beach 217
Nesat Beach 199, 212-13
No. 6 Beach 202
Ochheuteal Beach 210
Otres Beach 210
Pagoda Beach 217
Palm Beach 218
Plankton Beach 213
Police Beach 218
Saracen Bay 223-4
Serendipity Beach 210
Sunset Beach 224-5
bears 81, 83, 107, 205, 206, 207-8, 232, 261, 307
beer 14, 86, 100, 277
Beng Mealea 23, 93, 109, 127, 149
bike travel, *see* cycling
birds 16, 81, 177, 201, 232, 307
birdwatching 37, 93, 110-12, 128, 177-8, 213, 279
boat travel 271
boat trips 37
Botum Sakor National Park 207
Chong Kneas 106-7
Chong Kos 191
Koh Dach 77
Koh Kong 201-2, 203
Koh Kong Conservation Corridor 206
Koh Rong 218
Koh Rong Sanloem 224, 225
Koh Sdach 220
Kompong Khleang 109-8
Kompong Pluk 93
Phnom Penh 56
Pursat Province 188
Sangker River 10
Stung Treng 257
Takeo 239
Boeng Toal 177
Boeng Yeak Lom 245, 260-1

Map Pages **000**

Bokheo 262
Bokor Hill Station 199, 231
Bon Om Tuk (Water
    Festival) 29, 85, 157, 245
booking
    accommodation 29
    dining 18
books 8, 31, 296
border crossings 270
    Laos 257
    Thailand 111, 168, 169, 181,
        182, 203
    Vietnam 80, 84, 239,
        248, 260
Bou Sraa 264
breweries 47
Buddhism 55, 130, 185,
    290, 292
Bunong people 264-5,
    267, 292
bus travel 271
business hours 14, 283
butterflies 144

Cambodia Vipassana
    Dhura Buddhist
    Meditation Center 80
camping 87, 257, 273
Cardamom Mountains 47,
    86-7, 156, 187-9, 205-7
Cardamom Rainforest
    Landscape 208
car travel 271
casinos 212
caves 146, 165, 193,
    229, 235
cemeteries 262
Chaa Ong 260
Cham people 292
Cham Yeam 203
Chau Say Tevoda 139
Chau Srei Vibol 145
Chbab Srey 304
Chi Phat 25, 199, 205-7, 279
children, travel with 37, 82,
    108, 274
Chinese New Year 29,
    156, 198
Choam 181
Chong Kneas 106-7
Chong Kos 191
Chreav Waterfall 86
circuses 93, 102-3, 156, 162,
    164, 278
climate 12, 28-9, 54, 156-7,
    198-9, 244-5
climate change 178, 278
clothes 30
coffee 61, 72, 165, 276
Condor Reef 221
conservation 16, 279, 307-9
    Angkor 100, 121

Chi Phat 205
Preah Vihear 178
cooking classes 18, 35
    Battambang 161
    Kampot 233
    Kirirom 84
    Phnom Penh 56
    Siem Reap 102
crab 235
craft 11
    marble 187
    pottery 192
    silk 124, 130, 170, 184
    stone 185
credit cards 272
crocodiles 82, 107, 205,
    207-8, 307
culture 292-3
currency 272
cycling 37, 39, see also
    mountain biking, quad
    biking
    Angkor Wat 119, 121
    Battambang 160
    Chong Kneas 107
    Isanborei 184
    Kampot 228
    Koh Trong 252
    Phnom Penh 71
cyclo travel 47, 64, 160

Damrei Mountains 231-3
dance 292, 299
demographics 292-3, 306
dengue fever 275
dialects 285
digital payments 272
disabilities, travellers
    with 282
discounts 14, 274, 283
diseases 275
distilleries 47, 71
diving & snorkelling 12,
    37, 39
    Koh Rong 218
    Koh Rong Sanloem
        224, 225
    Koh Sdach Archipelago
        199, 221
    Koh Thmei 213
dolphins 37, 213, 244, 245,
    252-3, 279, 307
Dong Plet 178
drag shows 56, 62, 111, 281
dress codes 12, 15, 30,
    49, 280
drinking & nightlife 14,
    35, 276-7, 281, see also
    individual locations
driving 271
drugs 275

eastern Cambodia 241-67,
    242-3, 247, 251, 255,
    259, 264
    accommodation 249,
        252, 253, 256, 261, 262,
        264-5, 267
    activities 244-5, 256-7,
        264-5
    food 248, 252, 256,
        260, 266
    itineraries 244-5
    Kompong Cham,
        see individual location
    Kratie, see individual
        location
    Mondulkiri Province, see
        individual location
    Ratanakiri Province, see
        individual location
    Stung Treng, see
        individual location
    tours 261, 265
    travel within 242-3
Eastern Mebon 140
ecotourism sites 87, 178,
    179, 205, 208
electricity 283
elephants 278, 307
    eastern Cambodia 261,
        264, 266-7
    Kulen Elephant Forest
        93, 107
    Phnom Penh 81-2
    south coast 205, 206-7
entertainment, see
    individual locations
environmental issues 205
    climate change 178, 278
    endangered species
        278, 307
    habitat loss 178, 207, 208,
        232, 309
etiquette 12, 15, 30, 49, 120,
    276, 280
events, see festivals &
    events
exercise 46, 83, 163

F3 Friends Futures Factory
    29, 46, 56-7, 278
Factory Phnom Penh 71
family travel 37, 82, 108, 274
festivals & events 29, 46-7,
    85, 92-3, 156-7, 198-9,
    244-5
    Angkor Photography
        Festival 29
    Bon Om Tuk (Water
        Festival) 29, 85, 157, 245

Chamnor Arts Festival 157
Chinese New Year 29, 156,
    198, 244
Khmer New Year 29,
    85, 292
P'chum Ben 29, 85, 157
Pride Cambodia 29, 281
Royal Ploughing
    Ceremony 29
Sea Festival 29, 199
Tini Tinou International
    Circus Festival 156
film 31, 68, 299
food 18-19, 32-5, 276-7,
    300-1, see also individual
    dishes, individual
    locations
    courses 18, 35, 56, 84,
        102, 161, 233
    etiquette 35
    international cuisine 55,
        60, 61, 65, 71, 80, 82, 85,
        86, 110, 138-9, 164
    Khmer cuisine 50, 51, 72,
        98, 99, 276, 300-1
    language 284
    markets 11
    street food 34
    tours 78, 102
    vegan & vegetarian food
        33, 81, 103

galleries, see museums &
    galleries
gardens, see parks &
    gardens
gay travellers 29, 62, 281
genocide 68, 69, 79, 290-1,
    294-5
gibbons
    Angkor Thom 138
    Angkor Centre for
        Conservation of
        Biodiversity 107
    eastern Cambodia 245,
        261, 262, 265-6
    Phnom Penh 81-2
    south coast 207-8, 232
golf 112
guesthouses 70, 273
guides 68, 119, 146, 264, 267

health 275
highlights 8-19
hiking 36, 39
    Cardamom Mountains
        87, 199
    Central Cardamoms
        National Park 188

hiking, *continued*
Kampot 229
Kirirom National Park
84-5
Koh Rong Sanloem 224
Koh Thmei 213
Mondulkiri Province
264-5, 266-7
Phnom Tbeng 178-9
Prey Veng 178
Pursat Province 188
Ratanakiri Province 245
Stung Treng 257
Virachey National Park 261
Hinduism 118-22, 290
historic buildings & sites
15, 291, *see also* Angkor
temples & structures,
museums & galleries,
temples
Catholic Church (Bokor
Hill Station) 232
Central Post Office 61
Council for the
Development of
Cambodia 62
cremation site of Pol
Pot 182
French Embassy 62
Governor's Residence
160-1
Kamping Puoy 164
Kbal Spean 147-9
Khor Sang House 162
Killing Caves of Phnom
Sampeau 165
Killing Fields of Choeung
Ek 47, 69, 290-1
Kompong Chhnang
Airport 193
Mrs Bun Roeung's
Ancient House 162
National Bank of
Cambodia 228
National Library of
Cambodia 61
Old French Bridge 228
Old Royal Cinema 228
Poeung Tbal 147
Red Cross Building 228
Royal Palace 46, 49, 52
S-21 Prison 68, 290-1
Sra Damrei 146
Sra Srang 93, 135
Ta Mok's House 181-2

Map Pages **000**

history 15, 288-91
Angkor empire 8, 118-22,
126, 127, 131, 133, 149,
169-70, 176, 289-90
Cambodian–Thai border
dispute 173-4, 291
civil war 231, 294
French colonial era 31,
61-2, 160-1, 290, 302-3
Khmer Rouge 31, 62,
68, 69, 79, 83, 164, 165,
181-2, 193, 231-2, 252-3,
290-1, 294-5, 297,
303, 306
homestays 16, 144, 147, 184,
257, 273, 279
horse riding 108
hospitals 275
hostels 63, 98, 273
hot springs 87
hotels 50, 60, 100, 131, 273

ice cream 118
insects 216, 275
insurance 275
internet 270, *see also*
websites
islands 12-13, 25, *see also*
Koh *entries*
itineraries 22-7, 46-7, 92-3,
156-7, 198-9, 244-5, **23**,
**25**, **27** *see also individual*
*locations*

Jayavarman VII 126, 131, 140,
289-90
jungle trips 16-17

K

Ka Tieng 260
Kakaoh 185
Kampi 252-3
Kamping Puoy 164
Kampot 199, 226-33, 290,
**226, 228**
accommodation 227, 233
activities 10, 35, 227-9
beyond Kampot 230-3,
*see also individual*
*locations*
drinking & nightlife
231, 232
food 34, 229
itineraries 24
tours 228
travel within 229
Kaoh Paek 262

kayaking 10, 37, 39, 244
eastern Cambodia 257
northwestern
Cambodia 160
Phnom Penh 84
south coast 203, 213,
225, 227
Kbal Spean 23, 92, 147-9
Kep 199, 234-9, **234**
accommodation 236
activities 236
beyond Kep 237-9,
*see also individual*
*locations*
drinking & nightlife 236
food 235
itineraries 24
travel within 236
Khmer language 31, 34,
276, 284-5
Khmer New Year 29,
85, 292
Khmer people 292
Khmer Rouge 31, 62, 68, 69,
79, 83, 164, 165, 181-2, 193,
231-2, 252-3, 290-1, 294-5,
297, 301, 304
Khnong Phsar 208
Killing Fields of Choeung
Ek 47, 69, 290-1
Kinchaan 260
Kirivong 239
Kirivong Waterfall 239
Kleangs 133-4
Koh Chan 221
Koh Dach 47, 77
Koh Ker 8, 150-1, 289, **151**
Koh Kong 199, 200-8, **200**
accommodation 202
activities 201-2, 203
beyond Koh Kong 204-8,
*see also individual*
*locations*
food 201
itineraries 25
travel within 203
Koh Kong Conservation
Corridor 199, 204-8
Koh Koun 224
Koh Paen 249
Koh Pdao 257
Koh Pos 236
Koh Preah 257
Koh Prins 220
Koh Rong 198, 214-21, **215**
accommodation 216-17,
218
beyond Koh Rong 219-21,
*see also individual*
*locations*
drinking & nightlife 218
food 217
itineraries 25
travel within 218

Koh Rong Sanloem 198,
222-5, **223**
accommodation 223,
224, 225
activities 224, 225
food 225
tours 224
travel within 225
Koh Samseb 257
Koh Sdach Archipelago
199, 220-1
Koh Svay 236
Koh Ta Kiev 213
Koh Tang 220
Koh Thmei 213
Koh Tonsay 199, 236
Koh Trong 245, 252
Koh Tuch 217-18
Kompong Cham 26, 246-9,
**247**
accommodation 249
food 248
travel within 249
Kompong Chhnang
Province 190-3, **191**
accommodation 192, 193
food 192, 193
travel within 193
Kompong Khleang 93,
108-9
Kompong Luong 22, 189
Kompong Phhluk 93, 105
Kompong Thom Province
183-5, **184**
accommodation 184
travel within 185
*krama* 11, 77, 97, 187, 249
Kratie 245, 250-3, **251**
accommodation 252, 253
food 252
itineraries 26
travel within 253
Kuy people 175

landmines 98, 124, 144, 176,
275, 278
language 31, 34, 276,
284-5, 303
*Lara Croft: Tomb Raider* 115,
128, 136, 146, 299
L'Bak Kamronh Rapids 188
lesbian travellers 29,
62, 281
LGBTIQ+ travellers 29,
62, 281
*lingas* 133, 143, 147-9,
151, 239
live music 57
lobster 238
Lumkut Lake 260
Lumphat 262

**M**

macaques 82, 128, 207, 253
Mahendraparvata 147
malaria 275
markets 11, 276
  Crab Market (Kep) 34, 235
  Koh Sdach market 220
  Nesat Beach night
    market 212
  Old Market (Kampot)
    228, 231
  Psar Chaa 93, 97, 99
  Psar Nath 160
  Psar O Russei 53
  Psar Olympic 53
  Psar Reatrey 53
  Psar Thmei 46, 52, 60-1
  Russian Market 46,
    55, 70-1
massages 103, 163, 282
Me Chrey 108
measurements 283
medication 275
meditation 80
Mekong Discovery Trail
  245, 256-7
Mekong River 37, 56, 249,
  252-3
minivan travel 271
Mondulkiri Province
  263-7, **264**
  accommodation
    264-5, 267
  activities 264-5
  food 266
  itineraries 26
  tours 264-5
  travel within 267
money 272
Monorom Falls 265
monsoons 28
monuments, see statues &
  monuments
mosquitoes 275
motorcycle travel 106, 122,
  188, 271
mountain biking 37, 84, 257
mountains
  Cardamom Mountains 47,
    86-7, 156, 187-9, 205-7
  Damrei Mountains 231-3
  Khnong Phsar 208
  Phnom Dat Chivit 84
  Phnom Kulen 37, 92,
    146-7, 289
  Phnom Sampeau 156
  Phnom Tbeng 178-9
M'Pai Bay 225
museums & galleries 15
  Angkor Conservation
    15, 100
  Angkor National Museum
    92, 96
Battambang Museum 161
Bayon Information
  Centre 100
Cambodia Landmine
  Museum 92, 144
Cambodia Peace
  Gallery 161
Develter Gallery 96
Eco Global Museum
  Samdech Techo Hun
  Sen Preah Vihear 173
Gallerists, The 57
Gallery of a Thousand
  Buddhas (Preah
  Poan) 115
Java Creative Cafe 57
Kampot Provincial
  Museum 228
Kbach Arts 71
Khmer Ceramics
  Centre 103
Meta House 57
MGC Asian Traditional
  Textiles Museum 129
Miniature Replicas of
  Angkor's Temples 102
National Museum of
  Cambodia 46, 51-5
Peace Museum of Mine
  Action 124
Preah Norodom Sihanouk
  Angkor Museum 129
Romchiek 5 Artspace
  161, 162
Sosoro Museum 62
Tani Museum
  of Ceramics 103
Tep Kao Sol 161, 162
Theam's House 96
Tuol Sleng Genocide
  Museum 47, 68, 291
Wat Bo Museum 129
music 31, 57, 297, 304

**N**

National Museum of
  Cambodia 46, 51-5
national parks & nature
  reserves 16, 39, see also
  parks & gardens, wildlife
  sanctuaries & zoos
  Botum Sakor National
    Park 207, 268
  Central Cardamoms
    National Park 187
  Central Cardamoms
    Protected Forest 187-8
  Kep National Park
    199, 236
  Kirirom National Park
    84-5
  Phnom Tbeng Natural
    Heritage Park 178-9
Preah Monivong Bokor
  National Park 232
Ream National Park 213
Southern Cardamom
  National Park 207-8
Veun Sai-Siem Pang
  Conservation Area 262
Virachey National Park
  245, 261
nightlife, see drinking &
  nightlife
northwestern Cambodia
  153-93, **154-5, 159, 172,
  184, 187, 191**
  accommodation 161, 162,
    168, 169, 172, 173, 175, 177,
    181, 184, 187, 188, 192, 193
  activities 156-7, 160-1,
    162-3, 164, 177-8, 188-9
  Battambang, see
    individual location
  drinking & nightlife 162,
    165, 166
  entertainment 164
  food 161, 163, 164, 168, 174,
    178, 181, 192, 193
  itineraries 156-7
  Kompong Chhnang
    Province, see individual
    location
  Kompong Thom
    Province, see individual
    location
  Pursat Province, see
    individual location
  shopping 160
  tours 160-1, 178, 189
  travel within 154-5,
    166, 170, 179, 182, 185,
    189, 193

**O**

Ondong Rossey 192
opening hours 14, 283
orphanages 280
O Smach 182
Osoam 208
O'Svay 256
O'Yadaw 260

**P**

Pailin 168-9
pangolins 205, 206, 207,
  208, 232, 261, 307
parks & gardens, see also
  national parks & nature
  reserves
  Coconut Park 82
  Koh Sampeau Meas 187
Royal Gardens
  (Siem Reap) 99
Senteurs d'Angkor
  Botanic Garden 102
Wat Botum Park 52
P'chum Ben 29, 85, 157
Pen Ran 297, 304-6
pepper 233
petanque 71
Peung Ta Kho 146
Peuy Ta Mok 182
Phare Ponleu Selpak 156,
  162, 164, 278
Phare the Cambodian
  Circus 93, 102-3
Phimeanakas 132, 133
Phnom Bakheng 137
Phnom Bok 143
Phnom Chhnork 229
Phnom Da 238, 288
Phnom Den 239
Phnom Kbal Romeas 229
Phnom Khieu 169
Phnom Krom 124
Phnom Kulen 37, 92,
  146-7, 289
Phnom Penh 42-87, 290,
  **44-5, 48, 52, 59, 67, 76**
  accommodation 50, 60,
    63, 70, 78, 79, 84, 85
  activities 46-7, 56, 63-4,
    78, 80, 82, 83, 84-5, 86-7
  drinking & nightlife 53,
    56, 61, 62, 64, 65, 71-2,
    73, 86, 87
  entertainment 56, 57, 62
  food 34, 46, 47, 50, 51, 54,
    55, 56, 61, 64, 65, 70, 71,
    72, 73, 80, 82, 85, 86
  itineraries 22, 46-7
  shopping 53, 60-1, 63, 65,
    70-1, 74, 79, 81
  tours 52, 63-4, 78, 87
  travel within 44-5
Phnom Pros 248
Phnom Sampeau 165-6
Phnom Sombok 253
Phnom Sorsia 229
Phnom Srei 248
photography 29, 280
Phoum Kandal 191
Phum Barang 213
planning 30-1, 283
  budgeting 14, 55, 101,
    161, 272
  clothes 12, 15, 30, 49
  etiquette 12, 15, 30, 120,
    276, 280
podcasts 31
Poipet 169
Pol Pot 182, 296
politics 31, 306, 309
Popokvil Falls 232
pottery 103, 124, 192

*prahoc* 33, 34, 301
prams 274
Prasat Banan 156, 161,
  163, 165
Prasat Bram 151
Prasat Damrei Krap 147
Prasat Krahom 151
Prasat Krau Romeas 146
Prasat Kravan 137
Prasat Leung 151
Prasat Neak Buos 157, 179
Prasat Preah Vihear 27,
  157, 291
Prasat Rong Chen 146
Prasat Thneng 151
Prasat Thom 151
Pre Rup 141
Preah Khan of Kompong
  Svay 157, 175-6
Preah Ko 123
Preah Neak Poan 138-40
Preah Palilay 132
Preah Rumkel 256
Preah Vihear City 173, 174
Preah Vihear Province
  171-82, **172**
  accommodation 172, 173,
    175, 177
  activities 177-8
  beyond Preah Vihear
    Province 180-2, *see also
    individual locations*
  food 174, 178
  tours 178
  travel within 179
Preak Piphot River 206
Preh Nimith Waterfall 257
Prek Chak 239
Prek Svay 218
Prek Svay Waterfall 218
Prek Tek Chhoun River 227-9
Prek Toal 93, 110-11
Prek Touek Sap Estuary 213
Prey Chung Kran 249
Prey Veng 177, 178
Psar Pruhm 168
Pub St 92, 99, 277
public holidays 283
Pursat 187
Pursat Province 186-9, **187**
  accommodation 187, 188
  activities 188-9
  tours 189
  travel within 189
pushchairs 274

quad biking 36, 64, 106

Ratanakiri Province
  258-62, **259**
  accommodation 261, 262
  activities 260-1
  food 260
  itineraries 27
  tours 261, 262
  travel within 262
*remork-moto* travel 271
responsible travel 65, 106-7,
  120, 205, 264, 267, 278-80
rock climbing 36, 225, 229
Roluos temples 93, 109,
  122-3
Romanear 265
Royal Palace 46, 49,
  52, 291
Rumchek 175

S-21 Prison 68, 290-1
safe travel 51, 274, 275, 281
Sambor 257
Sambor Prei Kuk 23, 184-5,
  288-9
sculpture 15, 124
Sen Monorom 244,
  264-5, 266
Shark Island 221
shopping 11, 278, 280, *see
  also individual locations*,
  markets
Siem Reap 88-151, 290,
  **90-1, 95, 97, 132**
  accommodation 98, 99,
    100, 119, 123, 131, 144, 147,
    148, 149
  activities 35, 92-3, 96, 102,
    106, 108, 111, 112, 136, 138
  drinking & nightlife 92, 99,
    100, 109, 140
  entertainment 100,
    102-3, 111
  food 34, 92, 93, 98, 99, 101,
    102, 103, 106-7, 108, 110,
    118, 120, 123, 128, 138-9,
    141, 145, 147, 149
  itineraries 23, 92-3
  shopping 93, 97, 109, 110,
    112, 124
  tours 97, 111, 119, 136
  travel within 91
Sihanoukville 199, 209-13,
  **209**
  accommodation 210
  activities 210

beyond Sihanoukville
    211-13, *see also
    individual locations*
  food 210
  travel within 210
silk 65, 77, 108, 110, 124, 130,
  157, 170, 185, 249
Silver Pagoda 46, 50-1
SIM cards 270
sky bars 53
smoking 283
snorkelling, *see* diving &
  snorkelling
Sok San 216-17
solo travellers 273
south coast & islands
  194-239, 282, **196-7,
  200, 209, 215, 223, 226,
  228, 234**
  accommodation 202,
    206-7, 210, 212, 213,
    216-17, 218, 220, 223,
    224, 225, 227, 232-3,
    236, 238
  activities 198-9, 201-2,
    203, 206, 210, 221, 224,
    225, 227-9, 236
  drinking & nightlife 212-13,
    218, 231, 232, 236
  food 201, 205, 210, 217, 225,
    229, 232-3, 235, 238
  itineraries 24-5, 198-9
  Kampot, *see individual
    location*
  Kep, *see individual
    location*
  Koh Kong, *see individual
    location*
  Koh Rong, *see individual
    location*
  Koh Rong Sanloem, *see
    individual location*
  Sihanoukville, *see
    individual location*
  tours 206, 224, 228, 233
  travel within 196-7, 203,
    208, 213, 218, 221, 225,
    229, 233, 239
spas 103, 163, 193
Spean Thmor 141
Sra Em 172
Sra Srang 93, 135
St 26 92, 100, 277
stand-up paddleboarding
  37, 39, 229, 253
statues & monuments
  Durian Roundabout
    228, 231
  Independence
    Monument 52
  Khmer Rouge memorial
    (Udong) 79
  statue of King Father
    Norodom Sihanouk 52

Statue of the Leper King
    130-1
  Statue of Vishnu (Angkor
    Wat) 114-15
stonemasonry 185
Stung Areng 208
Stung Treng 245, 254-7, **255**
  accommodation 256
  activities 256-7
  food 256
  itineraries 27
  travel within 257
sugar palm 192
swimming 203, 260, 265

Ta Mok 181
Ta Mok's Lake 182
Ta Nei 141
Ta Prohm 23, 93, 127, 134-6
Ta San Mosque 79
Ta Som 140
Takeo 24, 140-1, 238-9
Tatai River 203
taxis 271
Te Tuk Pus Hot Springs 87
Tek Chhouu 227
temples 8-9, *see also*
  Angkor temples &
    structures
  Ang Doung 79
  Arey Ka Sap 79
  Damrei Sam Poan 79
  Mak Proum 79
  Phnom Bayong 239
  Phnom Chhnork 229
  Phnom Da 238-9, 288
  Phnom Vihear Leu 79
  Prasat Neak Buos 179
  Prasat Sambor 185
  Prasat Tao 185
  Prasat Yeay Poeun 185
  Preah Ang Chek Preah
    Ang Chorm Shrine 99
  Sambor Prei Kuk 23,
    184-5, 288-9
  Silver Pagoda 46, 50-1
  Tang You Pagoda 179
  Vihear Prak Neak 79
  Vihear Preah
    Ath Roes 79
  Vihear Preah Keo 79
  Wat Athvear 101
  Wat Bo 100
  Wat Botum 73-4
  Wat Dam Nak 101
  Wat Ek Phnom 165
  Wat Hanchey 247
  Wat Khaong Kang 169
  Wat Kiri Sela 235
  Wat Kor 165
  Wat Langka 73
  Wat Maha Leap 247-8

Map Pages **000**

Wat Moha Montrei 72-3
Wat Nokor Bachey 248
Wat Ounalom 55
Wat Phnom 47, 52, 59
Wat Phnom Yat 168
Wat P'Nouv 162
Wat Preah Ang Thom 146-7
Wat Preah Inkosei 101
Wat Sampov Pram 232
Wat Somrong Knong 162, 165
Wat Sorsor Moi Roi 257
Wat Thmei 101
Terrace of Elephants 129
Terrace of the Leper King 130-3, 132
*teuk trey* 18, 33, 300
theft 51
Thmor Sor 207
Thommanon 139
tipping 35, 272
Tmat Boey 157, 177, 178
toasting 276
Tonlé Sap 22-3, 56, 85, 191
tours, *see also* itineraries
  Angkor Thom 132, 136
  Angkor Wat 119
  Battambang 160
  Chi Phat 206
  Kep 236
  Koh Rong Sanloem 224
  Phnom Penh 52, 56, 61, 63-4, 87
  Prek Toal 111
  Siem Reap 96, 97
train travel 162-3, 271
Trapeang Kriel 257
Trapeang Plong 248
Trapeang Sre 248

travel seasons 12, 28-9, 34, 54, 156-7, 198-9, 244-5
travel to/from Cambodia 270
travel within Cambodia 270, 271
trekking, *see* hiking
tropical fruits 33, 34, 199, 231, 274
*tuk-tuk* travel 271
Tuol Sleng Genocide Museum 47, 68, 290-1
Turtle Island 221

Udong 47, 78-80, 290
Unesco World Heritage sites 8
  Prasat Preah Vihear 172-5
  Sambor Prei Kuk 23, 184-5, 288-9
  temples of Angkor 113-51, 289

vegan travellers 33, 81
vegetarian travellers 33, 103
Vietnamese people 189, 292
visas 270
  Laos 257
  Thailand 111, 168, 169, 181, 182, 203
  Vietnam 80, 84, 248, 260
volunteering 267, 280

wakeboarding 37, 39, 108
walking tours
  Angkor Thom 132
  Kampot 228
  Phnom Penh 52
  Siem Reap 97
water 275
waterfalls 84-5, 86-7, 146, 169, 203, 218, 232, 239, 245, 257, 260, 264-5
water sports 10, 37, 39, 108, 203, *see also individual activities*
weather 12, 28-9, 54, 156-7, 198-9, 244-5
websites 122, 279, 281, 282
weights 283
Western Baray 134, 137
Western Mebon 134
wi-fi 270
wildlife sanctuaries & zoos 16, 37, 93
  Ang Trapeang Thmor Reserve 93, 111-12
  Angkor Centre for Conservation of Biodiversity 92, 107
  Angkor Wildlife & Aquarium 107, 109
  Apopo Visitor Centre 98
  Banteay Srei Butterfly Centre 144
  Crocodile Protection Sanctuary 208
  Elephant Valley Project 37, 244, 266-7, 278
  Jahoo Gibbon Camp 244, 265-6, 278

Keo Seima Wildlife Sanctuary 265
Kulen Elephant Forest 93, 107
Kulen Promtep Wildlife Sanctuary 178
Peam Krasaop Wildlife Sanctuary 201-2
Phnom Aural Wildlife Sanctuary 188
Phnom Samkos Wildlife Sanctuary 188
Phnom Tamao Wildlife Rescue Centre 37, 81-3, 279
Prek Toal Bird Sanctuary 110-11, 279
Tatai Wildlife Sanctuary 203
Tmat Boey 279
Wildlife Alliance Release Station 206, 279
wine 87, 277
women 304-6

*yaba* 275
yoga 83, 225

ziplining 36, 37, 84, 93, 138
zoos, *see* wildlife sanctuaries & zoos